Praise for *Nelson's Trafalgar*

"Captures the din, confusion, and sheer carnage of the battle. Mr. Adkins reminds us that 'in the cramped gun decks the noise of the battle could be felt as much as heard: a maddening sensation of pressure on the skull.'"

—*The Wall Street Journal*

"This illustrious introduction to the Battle of Trafalgar from an archaeologist and historian is one of the best in generations for the nonseafaring reader curious about the nautical epic, and it also handsomely rewards those whose study of the battle goes back a generation or two."

—*Publishers Weekly* (starred review)

"Masterful"

—Bernard Cornwell, *Mail on Sunday* (London)

"Vivid, scrupulous, immensely moving, this is a terrific yarn."

—Christopher Hirst, *The Independent* (London)

ABOUT THE AUTHOR

Roy Adkins is a historian and archaeologist. He is also a Fellow of the Society of Antiquaries of London. His previous books include *The Keys of Egypt: The Race to Crack the Hieroglyphic Code*, *Dictionary of Roman Religion*, and *Handbook to Life in Ancient Rome*.

Nelson's Trafalgar

The Battle That Changed the World

ROY ADKINS

PENGUIN BOOKS

PENGUIN BOOKS

Published by the Penguin Group
Penguin Group (USA) Inc., 375 Hudson Street, New York, New York 10014, U.S.A.
Penguin Group (Canada), 90 Eglinton Avenue East, Suite 700, Toronto,
Ontario, Canada M4P 2Y3 (a division of Pearson Penguin Canada Inc.)
Penguin Books Ltd, 80 Strand, London WC2R 0RL, England
Penguin Ireland, 25 St Stephen's Green, Dublin 2, Ireland (a division of Penguin Books Ltd)
Penguin Group (Australia), 250 Camberwell Road, Camberwell,
Victoria 3124, Australia (a division of Pearson Australia Group Pty Ltd)
Penguin Books India Pvt Ltd, 11 Community Centre, Panchsheel Park,
New Delhi - 110 017, India
Penguin Group (NZ), cnr Airborne and Rosedale Roads, Albany,
Auckland 1310, New Zealand (a division of Pearson New Zealand Ltd)
Penguin Books (South Africa) (Pty) Ltd, 24 Sturdee Avenue,
Rosebank, Johannesburg 2196, South Africa

Penguin Books Ltd, Registered Offices:
80 Strand, London WC2R 0RL, England

First published in the United States of America by Viking Penguin,
a member of Penguin Group (USA) Inc. 2005
Published in Penguin Books 2006

10 9 8 7 6 5 4 3 2 1

Originally published in Great Britain by Little Brown under
the title *Trafalgar: The Biography of a Battle*

Map on page xviii by John Gilkes

THE LIBRARY OF CONGRESS HAS CATALOGED THE HARDCOVER EDITION AS FOLLOWS:
Adkins, Roy (Roy A.)
[Trafalgar]
Nelson's Trafalgar : the battle that changed the world / Roy Adkins.
p. cm.
First published under the title: Trafalgar: the biography of a battle.
London : Little, Brown, 2004.
Includes bibliographical references and index.
ISBN 0-670-03448-7 (hc.)
ISBN 0 14 30.3795 1 (pbk.)
1. Trafalgar, Battle of, 1805. 2. Nelson, Horatio Nelson, Viscount, 1758–1805—Military leadership.
3. Great Britain—History, Naval—19th century. 4. France—History, Naval—19th century.
5. Napoleonic Wars, 1800–1815. I. Title.
DA88.51805 .A35 2005
940.2'745—c22 2005042264

Printed in the United States of America

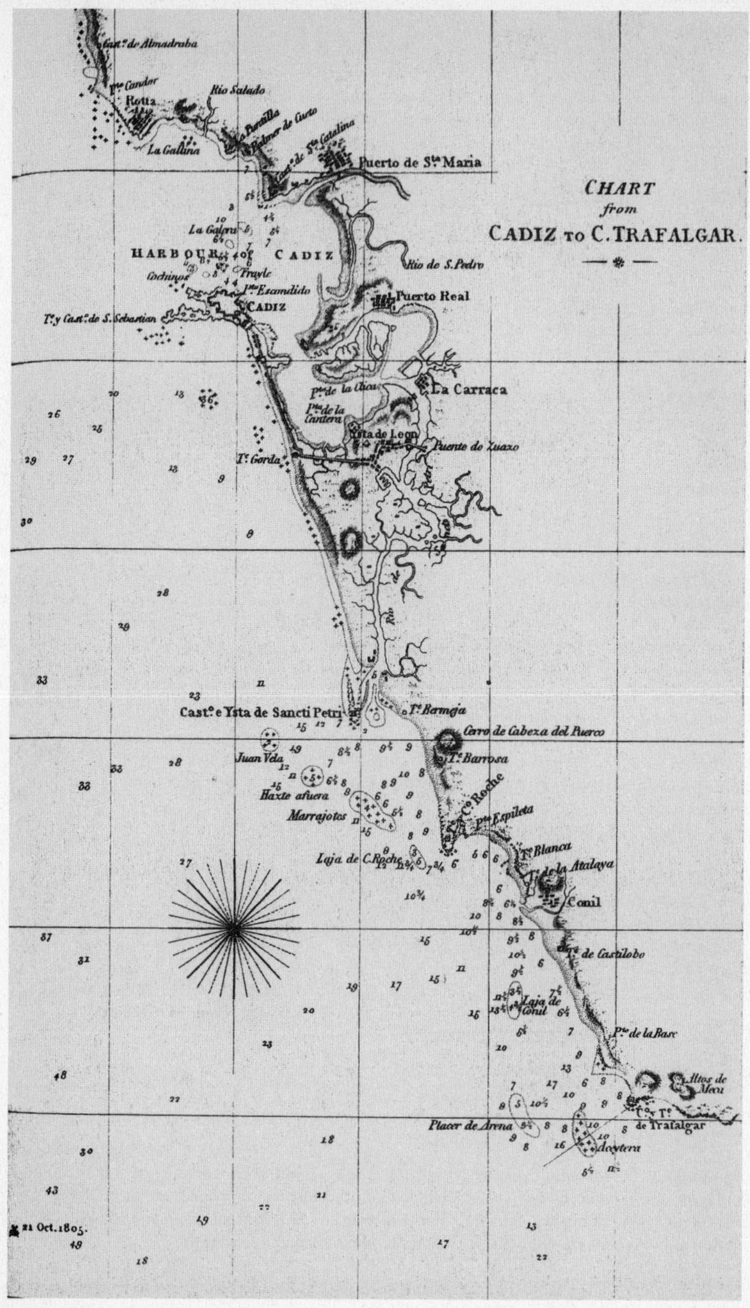

An 1805 chart, showing the treacherous shoals along the dangerous Spanish coastline between Cadiz and Cape Trafalgar

To Lesley, for everything

CONTENTS

List of Maps and Plans xi
List of Illustrations xiii
Introduction: Learning the Ropes xv
Prologue: Opening Fire xix

1 Invasion 1
2 Before the Battle 13
3 The Stage Is Set 29
4 Into Action 67
5 First Shot 93
6 Second Strike 109
7 Slaughter 138
8 Visions of Hell 156
9 Surrender 180
10 Lost and Won 196
11 Hurricane 217
12 The Messengers 256
13 Aftermath 282

14 Fruits of Victory 308

15 Heroes and Villains 326

Ships and Their Captains 351

Notes 357

Acknowledgements 367

Selected Reading 369

Bibliography 375

Index 381

MAPS AND PLANS

Frontispiece: An 1805 chart, showing the treacherous shoals along the dangerous Spanish coastline between Cadiz and Cape Trafalgar (*The Naval Chronicle* 14, 1805, opp. p. 416) v

Map of south-western coast of Spain xviii

Basic plan of a ship 55

Diagram of comparison of ship sizes 56

Diagram of aspects of sailing vessels 70

Plan of the opposing fleets at noon on 21 October 1805 102–3

Plan of the opening phase of the battle at 12.45 p.m. 118–19

Plan of the battle at 1.15 p.m. 148–9

Plan of the battle at 2 p.m. 174–5

Plan of the battle at 2.45 p.m. 182–3

Plan of the battle at 4.30 p.m. 208–9

1809 chart of Cadiz (*The Naval Chronicle* 21, 1809, opp. p. 476) 237

LIST OF ILLUSTRATIONS

FIRST INSERT

Page 1
Top: Rear Admiral Lord Nelson wearing all his decorations. (*Naval Chronicle* 3, 1800, opp. p. 167)
Bottom: Napoleon Bonaparte from a painting by Tallandier. (Giraudon/Bridgeman Art Library)

Page 2
Top: Sailors drinking grog. (*The Log Book or Nautical Miscellany*, p. 17)
Bottom: Ann Hopping. (*Illustrated London News*, 9 May 1863, p. 512)

Page 3
Top: Vice-Admiral Villeneuve. (Giraudon/Bridgeman Art Library)
Bottom: Vice-Admiral Lord Collingwood. (*Naval Chronicle* 15, 1806, opp. p. 353.)

Page 4
Top: Spanish Admiral Frederico Carlos Gravina. (Museo Naval de Madrid)
Bottom: Captain Don Cosmé Churruca. (Museo Naval de Madrid)

Page 5
Top: Nelson and his officers aboard *Victory*. (National Maritime Museum)
Bottom: Nelson giving instructions before the battle. (National Maritime Museum)

Page 6
Top: The Combined French and Spanish Fleet in Cadiz harbour. (National Maritime Museum)
Bottom: A plan of the approach. (National Maritime Museum)

Page 7
Top: A cartoon of a British seaman. (National Maritime Museum)
Bottom, left: Captain Jean-Jacques-Etienne Lucas. (Getty Images)
Bottom, right: Dr. William Beatty. (National Maritime Museum)

Page 8
Top: Nelson's and Collingwood's columns. (National Maritime Museum)
Bottom: A view from the French and Spanish side. (National Maritime Museum)

SECOND INSERT

Page 1
Top: The battle at an early stage. (Allen, 1841, opp. p. 122)
Bottom, left: Captain Thomas Masterman Hardy. (National Maritime Museum)
Bottom, right: Captain Henry Blackwood. (National Maritime Museum)

Page 2
Top: George Duff. (*Naval Chronicle* 15, 1806, opp. p. 265)
Bottom: The shooting of Nelson. (Craik & Macfarlane, 1844, p. 192)

Page 3
Top: The battle at about two o'clock. (Christie's Images, London, UK: www.bridgeman.co.uk/)
Bottom: The battle late in the afternoon. (Allen, 1841, opp. p. 146)

Page 4
Top: The *Achille* on fire. (National Maritime Museum)
Bottom: The scene towards the end of the battle. (National Maritime Museum)

Page 5
Top: Jeanette being rescued. (Bridgeman Art Library)
Bottom: A print of a woman with her child tending the wounded. (*The Log Book or Nautical Miscellany*, 1830, p. 33)

Page 6
Top: A print of a woman searching for her husband. (Glascock, 1835, frontispiece)
Bottom: The morning after the battle. (*Naval Chronicle* 15, 1806, opp. p. 36)

Page 7
Top: Captain John Richard Lapenotiere. (National Maritime Museum)
Bottom: Spanish sailors on the shore. (Palacio del Senado, Madrid)

Page 8
Top: Captain Thomas Norman's gravestone. (Author's photo)
Bottom: The scene on 28 October. (National Maritime Museum)

INTRODUCTION

Learning the Ropes

Britain is an island, with no place more than 70 miles from the coast. Its great seafaring tradition, based on fishing and trade, both coastal and international, mainly had an impact on seaside communities, yet during the wars with France in the eighteenth and nineteenth centuries, seamen were taken as volunteers or by the press-gangs from almost every part of the country. Those who returned after years at sea brought with them a rich vocabulary of nautical words and phrases, drawn not from the merchant marine, but from the Royal Navy. Many of these words and phrases, such as 'swinging the lead' and 'groggy', still retain the meanings they had in Nelson's day, while others such as 'junk' and 'nipper' have subtly changed over the centuries. In this book, any nautical terms that are essential for understanding the story are explained at the point where they first occur. For anyone who wants to find out the precise meanings of the nautical terms of the period, the first port of call is *A Sea of Words* by Dean King, which covers all the most common words and expressions.

As in all battles, the eyewitnesses at Trafalgar did not record minute-by-minute details during the fighting, but set down what they remembered afterwards. Together with the confusion of the battle and the fact that no one could see more than a small part of the action, this led to large differences between individual accounts. The greatest discrepancies are in the precise times of the various incidents, where records may differ not just by minutes but by hours. In this book the sequence and timing of events have been based on the exhaustive analysis of Rear-Admiral A. H. Taylor in his 1950 article in the *Mariner's Mirror*.

Another potential source of confusion is the fact that some British ships had French-sounding names (such as the *Entreprenante*), and some French ships had British-sounding names (such as the *Berwick*). This came about whenever ships retained their original names after being incorporated into the navy that had captured them. Because, up to Trafalgar, more French ships had been taken by the British than vice versa, there tended to be a preponderance of French ship names. The situation was exacerbated by the practice of using old names for new ships, so that a freshly launched British ship might be given the name of a French ship that had been taken by the British, had served in the British Navy and had then been scrapped. Even when the French name of a captured ship was deemed unsuitable, it was often replaced by another French name rather than a British one. Many of the Spanish ships were named after saints, such as the *San Agustín* and the *San Francisco de Asís*, but sometimes a Spanish ship had a name similar to a French one, such as the Spanish *Argonauta* corresponding to the French *Argonaute*. For the commonest nautical names, each nation had its own version: *Neptune* for both a French and British ship and *Neptuno* for a Spanish one. A list of all the ships with their nationalities is given on pages 351–5. Similarly, some men on the British side had surnames of French origin, some were of other nationalities, and some Frenchmen actually fought on the British side. Like the ship name *Neptune*, a few surnames add to the confusion; one such is Lucas, which is French in origin but was imported to England at the Norman invasion and anglicised by the time of Trafalgar.

In some cases the spelling and punctuation in quotations from eyewitnesses have been modernised, and occasionally abbreviations in the original are given in full, but the words themselves have not been changed. When monetary values have been mentioned, the modern equivalent (using a rule of thumb of multiplying the value by fifty) has sometimes also been provided, but this can be no more than a very rough guide.

At the time, sailors had various approximate measurements for distances that are no longer widely used: a pistol shot was about 25 yards, a musket shot approximately 200 yards and a gun shot about 1000 yards. A cable was 200 yards, a fathom 6 feet and a league 6116 yards – equivalent to 3 nautical miles. The nautical mile was then equivalent to 6116 feet, but is now a distance of 6080 feet. A knot was regarded as the speed of 1 nautical mile per hour, or sometimes as just the distance of 1 nautical mile – speeds at that time were still recorded as knots per hour and not simply in knots as used today. For those better acquainted with metric measurements, the following should be noted:

1 foot = 0.30 metres
1 yard = 0.91 metres
1 mile = 1.61 kilometres

The Battle of Trafalgar is one of those rare events in history about which everyone knows something, because – almost instantly – it became part of British heritage and assumed almost mythical status. Here, in the words of people who were present, is the true story of that battle.

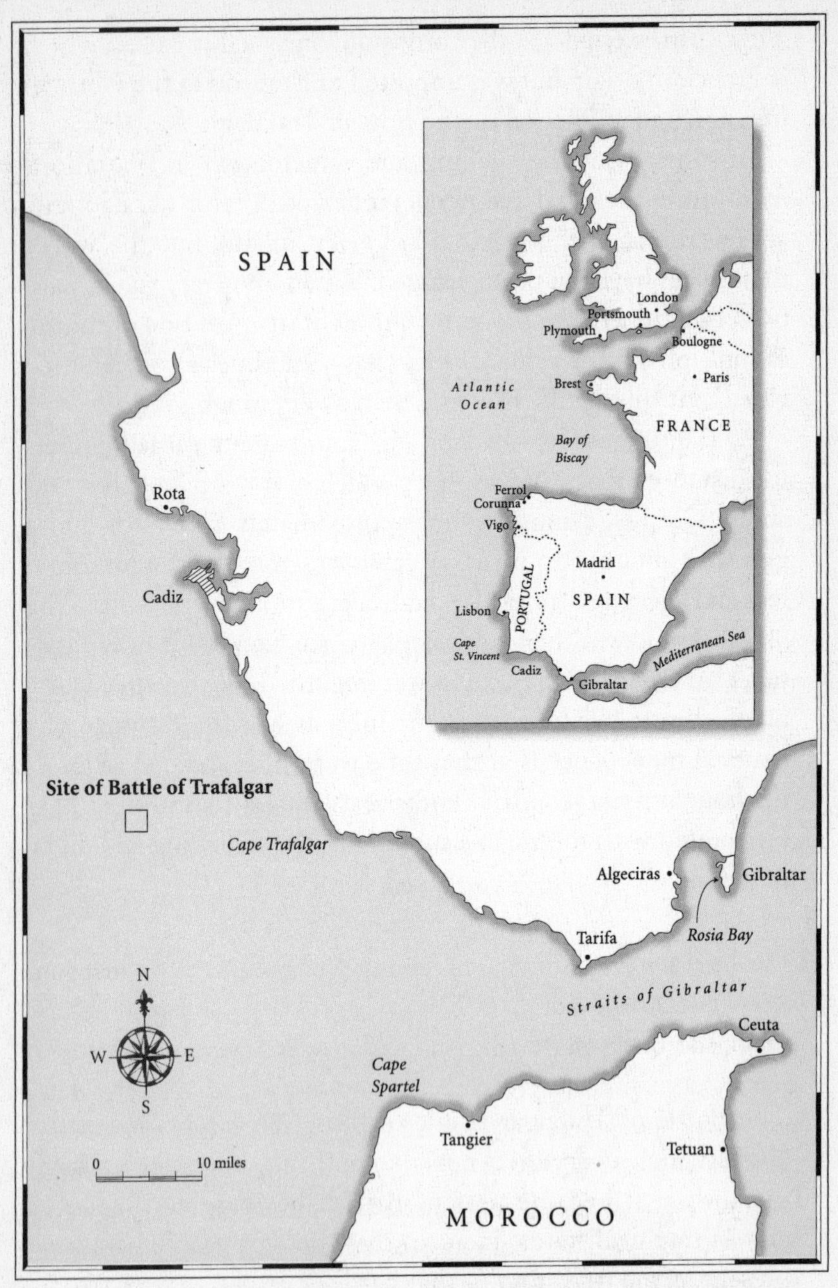

The south-western coast of Spain and the coast of North Africa, showing the site of the Battle of Trafalgar in relation to Cadiz, Cape Trafalgar and Gibraltar. The inset map marks the main places in Spain, Portugal, France and Britain that are mentioned in the text.

PROLOGUE

Opening Fire

The first shots from the French ship *Fougueux*[*] fell short, but the enemy fleet sailed steadily closer, slowly reducing the range. Then, just after noon on Monday 21 October 1805, the *Fougueux* fired the first broadside at the nearest British ship, which was the *Royal Sovereign* – the Battle of Trafalgar had begun. The master-at-arms of the *Fougueux*, Pierre Servaux, made a vivid record of how the battle unfolded:

> The *Fougueux*, a man-of-war of seventy-four guns, fired the first gun in the fleet. As she did so, she hoisted her colours. She continued her cannonade, firing on the English flagship, which was a greatly superior vessel in size, height, guns and the number of her crew. Her main-deck and upper-deck guns, in fact, could fire right down on to our decks, and in that way all our upper-deck men employed in working the ship, and the infantry marksmen posted on the gangways, were without cover and entirely exposed. We had also, according to our bad habit in the French Navy, fired over a hundred rounds from

*French word for 'Ardent'.

our big guns at long range before the English ship had practically snapped a gun lock. It was, indeed, not until we found ourselves side by side and yardarm to yardarm with the English flagship [the *Royal Sovereign*] that she fired at all. Then she gave us a broadside from fifty-five guns and carronades, hurtling forth a storm of cannon-balls, big and small, and musket shot. I thought the *Fougueux* was shattered to pieces – pulverised.[1]

Although the shock of the *Royal Sovereign*'s first broadside had quite literally knocked the *Fougueux* sideways, the damage was largely confined to the upper decks and rigging, as Servaux quickly realised:

The storm of projectiles that hurled themselves against and through the hull on the port side made the ship heel to starboard. Most of the sails and rigging were cut to pieces, while the upper deck was swept clear of the greater number of the seamen working there and of the soldier sharpshooters. Our gun decks below had, however, suffered less severely. There, not more than thirty men in all were put out of action. This preliminary greeting, rough and brutal as it was, did not dishearten our men. A well-maintained fire showed the Englishmen that we, too, had guns and could use them.[2]

The *Fougueux* could still manoeuvre and let fly further broadsides, so that soon the *Royal Sovereign* was also suffering heavy damage:

The English ship having come up to us, made to break the line between us and the *Santa Ana*.* The Spanish ship, in fact, during our action with the English leader, had not fired a single shot, but had kept stolidly on and continued her course without shortening sail,

*Spanish for 'St Ann'.

thus giving an easy passage through to the enemy. After that, however, by the smart handling of our captain, we managed to come within our proper distance of her [the *Santa Ana*]; as a fact, indeed, almost with our bowsprit over their poop. By this manoeuvre we had the enemy's ship on the port quarter in such a way that whilst we could only receive a few shots from their stern guns, they were exposed to our whole broadside, raking the enemy, end-on, along all their decks. We soon saw the English vessel's mizzenmast go by the board, and then her rudder and steering gear were damaged, making the ship unmanageable. Her sails flapped loose in the wind, and her sheets and running rigging were cut to pieces by our hail of shot. For some time she ceased firing. We, for our part, now redoubled our efforts and we next saw her main topmast come down. At that moment the English ship hoisted two signal flags at the foremast. It made us think that she was calling for help. And we were not wrong.[3]

Servaux's account continues with a description of how his ship, the *Fougueux*, came under an increasingly devastating attack:

After a very little time two fresh English men-of-war came up and began to attack us; the one on the starboard quarter, the other at the stern. Under their fire, we held out for more than an hour, but they almost overpowered us with their terrible storm of round shot and a fusillade of bullets that carried death among our men. Our mizzen-mast was now shot by the board, while our spars were shot from the masts and were lying in wreckage along the sides of the ship. Then, too, fire broke out in the stern walk and the poop. We tried our best, in spite of the hail of shot, to put the fire out, and with hatchets to cut adrift the mass of wreckage from the fallen masts, yards and cordage. It lay along the ship's sides by the gun-tiers and was endangering the ship and exposing her to the most imminent risk of destruction by fire. At this moment the captain ordered me to climb outboard and see if the wreckage of the mainsail was not in danger of being set on fire from the main-deck guns. I obeyed; but as I clambered from the gangway into the chains,* one of the enemy fired her whole starboard broadside. The din and concussion were fearful; so tremendous that I almost fell headlong into the sea. Blood gushed from my nose and ears, but it did not prevent my carrying out my duty. Then our mainmast fell. Happily it was shot through some ten or twelve feet above the deck and fell over to port. At once we cut away the shrouds [ropes bracing a mast] to starboard; but it was with great difficulty that in the end we were able to clear ourselves. Our fire was well maintained all this time, though the great superiority of the heavy guns of the English ships, and their very advantageous position, decimated our men in a fearful manner. More than half the crew had by this time been struck down, killed or wounded. Then, at length, our last remaining mast went, falling forward on to the fore part of the ship. Our flag, however, was still flying. It was the only thing left above the deck. All the same, neither our brave captain, nor a single one of our men, had a thought of lowering it.[4]

At this point the arrival of the *Temeraire*† decided the outcome, and Servaux described how his own battered ship fell to the British:

Now, however, yet another English ship, the *Temeraire* of 100 guns, came down to attack us. Borne alongside of us with the current, she fell on board us. At once a broadside burst from her upper deck guns and main battery, with a hot small-arms fusillade, fired right down into us. It swept our decks clear. Even then, though, our men rallied; with cries of 'up lads and at 'em' repeated all over the ship, some sixty to eighty of them swarmed up on deck, armed with sabres and axes. But the huge English three-decker towered high above the *Fougueux*,

*The chains were originally called 'channels' – horizontal wooden planks jutting out from the sides of the ship, to which some of the rigging was fixed.
†French for 'Reckless'.

and they fired down on us as they pleased with their musketry until, at length, they themselves boarded us. From two to three hundred of them suddenly rushed on board us, entering the ship from their chains and main-deck ports. Our captain fell dead, shot through the heart with a musket bullet. The few men who were left could make no resistance in the face of numbers. Resistance was out of the question, while still the enemy's murderous fire from the gangways continued. We were obliged to give back and yield, though we defended the decks port by port. So the *Fougueux* fell into the power of the English.[5]

In just a few hours of bloody battle off Cape Trafalgar, the world changed completely, not just for those on board the *Fougueux*, but for all those French and Spanish who had so recently been securely blockaded in the southern Spanish port of Cadiz.

ONE

INVASION

> Let us be masters of the Channel for six hours, and we are masters of the world!
>
> Napoleon Bonaparte, July 1804[1]

From 1793 to 1815 there were only thirteen months of peace between France and Britain. Theoretically three different wars were fought in this period, but in reality those wars were separated by nothing more than an armed truce. When the French Revolution degenerated into the 'Reign of Terror' in 1793, the British Government became increasingly uneasy, but what turned British public opinion against the revolutionary regime was the execution of the French king and queen. Britain immediately joined an alliance of Continental nations in a war against France. From then until Napoleon's final defeat in 1815, Britain was part of a kaleidoscopic coalition of countries trying to contain France's attempts to build a European empire. As soon as one coalition collapsed, Britain tried to build another, financed from the profits of rapidly expanding trade networks. Such sustained support for its European allies put a severe strain on Britain's resources, initially forcing tax reforms and ultimately leading to the first ever levying of an income tax in 1799. The war with France became much more violent and intense, and until the 1914–18 war usurped the title, the period from 1793 to 1815 was known as 'The Great War'.

The contest between France and Britain was essentially one between two states in the process of building empires. In France this was a conscious policy, at first to spread revolutionary ideology by conquest, but later driven by Napoleon's personal ambition. In Britain, the pursuit of the wealth and other benefits that derived from its colonies was paramount, and initially the acquisition of territory was far less important than establishing trading links. Chasing their separate goals, neither state considered how this would affect other countries unless forced to do so. On the Continent, France threatened, bullied and tried to subvert the governments of its neighbours, while at sea Britain used naval might to take whatever was needed without any thought that this might be alienating allies who could be useful in the future.

In France, undemocratic revolutionary government had been replaced by the dictatorship of Napoleon; in Britain King George III had the larger share of power, although the country was nominally governed by Parliamentary democracy. By his skilful use of patronage, however, the king was adept at subverting Parliamentary attempts to curb his actions; he bribed men with honours, positions, rewards and pensions, or intimidated them by threats to withdraw such privileges. Most other states in Europe also had hereditary monarchies, and many were linked in loose confederations or empires by virtue of the fact that their rulers came from the same family. In all cases, including Britain, no account was taken of the general population unless it rose in rebellion – in which case it was invariably repressed with brutal force if the rulers still had power to do so. While European governments pursued their own self-interests, the people they governed often had different agendas;

smuggling to avoid taxes and trade bans, and even fraternisation between opposing armed forces were commonplace.

Although most attention was concentrated on events on land during this period, Britain was nevertheless locked in an ongoing struggle with France for naval supremacy, acutely aware of the seaborne danger. The Combined Fleet of France and its allies, most notably the Dutch, became a serious rival to British naval power and threatened the trade that financed the European resistance to aggressive French expansion. In 1797 the Dutch were defeated by the British Navy at the Battle of Camperdown off the coast of Holland, and a fleet from Spain, also an ally of France, was similarly defeated at the Battle of St Vincent off the coast of Portugal. With these two successes, Britain gained control of the Atlantic, but a French fleet still had naval supremacy in the Mediterranean. This allowed Napoleon to mount an invasion of Egypt in 1798, but after Nelson's destruction of the invasion fleet at the Battle of the Nile only a few weeks later, the French Navy was in complete disarray. For a time Britain had unchallenged control of the seas.

Maintaining naval supremacy was Britain's long-term goal, since to protect and build a global commercial empire, it had to guard oceanic trade routes. While France was preoccupied with war on the Continent, Britain was seizing French colonies and strategic bases to augment its own trading network. Underlying all the Continental wars at this time was the conflict of interests between France, which was building a land-based empire in Europe, and Britain, which was accumulating a global empire based on trade. In this struggle of newly emerging empires, France's position was not helped by Napoleon being first and foremost a soldier. He understood and relied on his armies, but did not understand the strengths and weaknesses of his navy, nor did he trust his naval officers. Yet he knew well enough that a trading empire was as important to France as it was to Britain. Napoleon had a better grasp of the political situation than he did of the state of his navy, and although he counted ships and men and analysed their positions, he took little notice of how unprepared they were for the task in hand.

In 1800, Sweden, Denmark and Russia declared a state of armed neutrality to defend their trade from the Baltic to France, denying such trade to Britain. At the same time a change of government in Britain led to a peace treaty with France – the Treaty of Amiens, of 25 March 1802 – but it was the uneasy calm before the storm. Because the declaration of armed neutrality had effectively cut Britain off from the Baltic, a source of many essential naval supplies, a British fleet responded the following year by destroying the force of Danish ships in the harbour at Copenhagen and so removed the threat to British ships en route to the Baltic. By the time of Trafalgar, the only substantial number of extra warships available to Napoleon were those left to the Spanish Navy after the British victory at the Battle of St Vincent in 1797. Even with these Spanish ships and a lavish shipbuilding programme that Napoleon was pushing to its limits, any attempt to invade England had no margin for error.

War broke out again between Britain and France in April 1803, just a few months before Napoleon crowned himself emperor. Britain established a blockade of French ports less than a month later, and once Spain actively joined the war on Napoleon's side in October 1804, Spanish ports also had to be blockaded. During the French Revolution, Spain's royal family had been incensed at the execution of Louis XVI and began an invasion of France. This was repulsed, and the French counter-attacked, forcing the Spanish to sign a peace treaty in 1795. The treaty was very unpopular throughout Spain, and as it effectively made the Spanish Government a French puppet and Spain a passive ally of France, resentment continued to simmer.

While Britain began once again to build up its navy,

Napoleon made preparations to invade that country. In terms of overall strategy, he was only too aware that a better opportunity was unlikely to present itself. Despite the renewal of war, Britain's Continental allies were still recovering from the previous conflict with France and were in no hurry to form another coalition against Napoleon. France itself had been exhausted by the war and was in no position to fight on several fronts at once. With a temporary peace on the Continent, though, Napoleon could spare enough troops for an invasion of Britain. A successful invasion might stop or at least delay the formation of a hostile coalition, but he knew that he had to act quickly because British diplomats were already lobbying hard to form an anti-French alliance. Ever tempted by the bold, single-stroke solution, Napoleon threw everything into his invasion plans.

Over 100,000 troops were gradually concentrated in camps spread along 75 miles of French coastline around Calais and Boulogne. Many of the camps were plainly visible from the cliffs of Dover, causing a rising tide of panic in southern England. This French army was occupied in training and drilling in order to keep the soldiers busy and to alleviate the atmosphere of feverish suspense. At Boulogne, a huge flotilla of landing craft was being assembled, with the aim of amassing two thousand boats to carry an invasion force across the English Channel as soon as a French fleet of warships could guarantee its safe passage.

Not since the time of the Spanish Armada had Britain been seriously threatened by invasion. From the early 1790s the increasing apprehension among the British population often lapsed into paranoia and panic, but, as the possibility of invasion became more real, something close to hysteria gripped the people and the government. Now that France had passed through a revolution and had killed its king, it was totally under the thumb of Napoleon – and Napoleon was intent on destroying England: 'I know not, in truth, what kind of precaution will protect her [England] from the terrible chance she runs. A nation is very foolish when it has no fortifications and no army to lay itself open to seeing an army of 100,000 veteran troops land on its shores. This is the masterpiece of the [French invasion] flotilla! It costs a great deal of money, but it is necessary for us to be masters of the sea for six hours only, and England will have ceased to exist.'[2] Napoleon was so confident of success that, to save time, he had already ordered dies to be prepared in Paris: as soon as Britain was overrun, medals celebrating his triumph could be struck. The reverse side of the medal bore the legend 'Invasion of England, Struck in London 1804.' In the event, only four trial pieces were actually made from these dies.

The British people did not know what to expect from an invasion, but they feared the worst and generally regarded Napoleon as an ogre. Then, and for decades to come, nursemaids on the southern coast of England frightened children with this chilling rhyme:

Baby, baby, naughty baby,
Hush, you squalling thing, I say;
Hush your squalling, or it may be
Bonaparte will pass this way.

Baby, baby, he's a giant,
Tall and black as Rouen steeple;
And he dines and sups, rely on't,
Every day on naughty people.

Baby, baby, he will hear you
As he passes by the house,
And he, limb from limb, will tear you
Just as pussy tears a mouse.[3]

It was not just children who were frightened of the possibility of a French invasion. The British Government now looked more seriously at its provisions for defending the country. Preparations for defence had effectively begun as early as 1790 when the government's Board of Ordnance surveyed the county of Kent in order to produce a detailed map that could be used by the defending troops. This map, with a scale of one inch to one mile, was published in 1801 and was the first Ordnance Survey map. There followed a series of adjoining maps that gradually covered the whole country – forerunners of the maps still in use today. Kent had been chosen as the first area to be mapped because, it was reasoned, an invading force from the Continent would want to minimise its time at sea for fear of attack by the British Navy and so would use the shortest, most direct route; the coast of Kent was therefore assumed to be the likeliest landing place.

Napoleon was aiming for an invading army of at least 160,000 trained and experienced troops, although eventually it numbered over 200,000. About half were stationed in the coastal camps, ready to embark, with the rest further inland because there was not room for them nearer the ports. In theory this army was dwarfed by a British force of over 500,000, but the vast majority of these men were inexperienced and largely untrained local militias and volunteers, recently raised to support the regular troops who were already deployed to defend the coast. Another pressing problem was the fact that these militias and volunteers were spread throughout the British Isles. To combat an invasion, they needed to be collected together quickly and in sufficient numbers to meet the threat. It was hoped that an invading force would be spotted as soon as it left the shelter of the Continental ports, giving time for a warning to be passed by signal flags from ship to ship, then to Deal in Kent and finally to London via the telegraph. A telegraph system already linked Deal with the Admiralty building in

Whitehall, and similar telegraphs also connected the Admiralty with Portsmouth in Hampshire and with Chatham in north Kent. These consisted of chains of semaphore stations set up on hilltops, each within sight of the next one in the chain, so that a message coded into semaphore signals could be repeated, station to station, from one end of the chain to the other. The telegraphs were supplemented by smaller chains of signal posts, using a much simpler system of a white flag, meaning 'all is well', and a red flag for an alarm, as well as chains of beacon fires that would blaze from hilltops to warn of invasion.

On 7 August 1803, Betsey Fremantle, wife of Thomas Fremantle who was to be captain of the *Neptune* at Trafalgar, recorded in her diary:

> Went to walk on the walls [at Portsmouth], where we were not a little surprised at seeing a great concourse of people on the beach, the yeomanry out, guns frequently fired, signals made, the tellegraphes at work and many sails in sight. On enquiring I was told it was supposed the French were effecting a landing as numbers of the flat bottom boats were seen making towards the shore. This created a very great alarm . . . every precaution taken, as if really the French were approaching. I felt much alarmed myself, but as everything appeared quiet towards twelve o'clock, we went to bed in hopes some mistake created this great bustle.[4]

Her diary entry for the next day recorded that a fleet of coastal trading vessels had triggered the emergency, having been becalmed on the far side of the Isle of Wight from Portsmouth. The beacons, the signal posts and even the telegraphs were relatively crude systems of communication, spreading little more than alarm – detailed information travelled more slowly, carried by couriers on horseback.

With the early-warning systems in place, the other method of gaining time to collect together defensive forces was to slow down the advance of any invading army. This was done by reinforcing the physical defences in vulnerable coastal areas and by building obstacles between the beachheads and the primary objective of any invasion: London. The government decided to concentrate on the south-east and east coasts and started by strengthening existing fortifications, with further fortifications added at particularly vulnerable points. This still left long stretches of coastline with no permanent defences close to the beach, and so the solution was to build a string of Martello Towers. These were based on a fortification at Martello (sometimes called Mortello) in Corsica, where a round stone tower 40 feet high and 45 feet in diameter at the base, with walls 15 feet thick, housed a few cannons and a small garrison. In 1794 this squat tower had impressed the British Navy when a small body of French troops not only held out against a strong attack, but badly damaged some of the British ships during the fighting.

In the spring of 1805 a programme of building was begun that in three years would result in 73 towers being built on the coasts of Britain. By 1812 the total had reached 103 (of which only 43 survive today), and almost all were positioned along the south and east coasts of the mainland. Once in place, the Martello Towers were a very powerful coastal defence, providing strongpoints that an invasion force would find difficult to capture, but could not afford to ignore. Thought to offer such good protection, they were used not only in Britain but also in Ireland, the Channel Islands, North America and South Africa. By the time of Trafalgar in October 1805, however, the towers and other coastal defences were merely a shambolic scatter of unfinished forts, towers, barracks and building sites.

The River Medway and the Thames Estuary already had strong fortifications that had been put in place after an attack by the Dutch Navy in 1667 when their ships had sailed up the Thames and into the Medway, taking possession of the unfinished fort at Sheerness and capturing or destroying several British warships in the process. Part of the defences, called the Chatham Lines, defended the Royal Naval Dockyard at Chatham from attack, and these were now strengthened, principally by a massive expansion of the redoubt (now known as Fort Amherst) that was situated near the town. The medieval castle at Dover in Kent was also enlarged and strengthened with ramparts more suitable for defence against cannon fire and with artillery batteries to protect the harbour, while further fortifications were constructed to protect the castle's weak points on its landward side. These defences, begun in 1804, were also still very vulnerable by the time of Trafalgar.

Another perceived point of weakness in Kent was Romney Marsh, since its wide flat beaches were ideal for landing an invasion force. It would have been possible to flood the marsh, making it an impassable obstacle, but too many people lived and worked there. Instead, it was decided to block the route from the beaches to London with a canal that could be used as a defensive ditch. This ran in a northerly loop from one part of the coast to another, cutting off Dungeness and the marsh around it from the rest of the country. The canal was planned to be 62 feet wide at the surface and 9 feet deep, with the excavated material forming a defensive rampart on its inland side as well as a roadway for the rapid movement of troops. Known as the Royal Military Canal, it actually varied in width and depth, and at its narrowest was hardly more than half the planned width. Started in October 1804, it was finished five years later – a very short time for the construction of a canal that was 28 miles long – but once again, it had no defence capability by the time of Trafalgar and was not really effective until it was fully complete.

All these coastal defences were designed to slow down and reduce the numbers of an invasion force, allowing more men to be gathered to oppose it, but around London itself other protective measures were planned. A defensive line was to run on the north of the city from the River Thames at Battersea Bridge through Chelsea to the Paddington Canal and then on to Hampstead, Highgate and the marshes around the River Lea. To the south a similar line was planned from the Thames at Wandsworth towards Tooting and Streatham and then through the Norwood Hills, Sydenham and up to Deptford, with outworks on Shooter's Hill and Blackheath. A floating bridge was to span the Thames approximately on the line of the modern Blackwall Tunnel in order to connect Blackwall with Greenwich. In all, this provided a perimeter around London of over 30 miles in circumference, well outside the city in what was then open countryside. To construct permanent defences around this line would have taken time and would have been extremely costly, so it was decided that everything was to be put in place ready to construct ramparts and ditches and to defend them with artillery. A register was drawn up of men such as labourers, smiths, carpenters and even gardeners, so that in an emergency they could be rapidly conscripted to build the defences. Materials and tools were also stockpiled. The positions of the earthworks were surveyed and marked out on the ground with stakes, but no actual work was intended unless an invasion took place. It was calculated that an invasion force would not be strong enough to besiege a 30-mile-long perimeter around London and would have to attack a particular section. The gamble was that while the coastal defences were delaying the invaders, this section could be identified in time so that all available resources could be concentrated in the threatened area to construct and man the ramparts. No trace of these planned defences remains today.

The government was not relying totally on fortifications thrown up at the very last minute in the face of an advancing enemy, since in 1804 it also began the construction of an alternative administrative centre to London. This was situated at

Weedon Bec in Northamptonshire, a place about as far from the sea as it is possible to be in mainland Britain, and was chosen as a last stronghold against invasion. At Weedon Bec storage buildings, barracks, magazines and a royal pavilion to house the royal family were built, and from here the government hoped to organise the last-ditch defence of Britain.

During the years that all these preparations were being pushed forward on land, Britain was still relying on the 'wooden walls' of its warships to defend the country. Lord St Vincent, then head of the Admiralty, had noted in 1801: 'Our great reliance is on the vigilance and activity of our cruisers at sea,'[5] and this held true. While the French and Spanish fleets were kept in port by a British blockade, the fate of the country lay on a knife edge, but if sufficient warships managed to evade this blockade, unite and then take control of the English Channel, Britain would be invaded. Both sides were well aware of the precarious situation, and as Napoleon said, 'There is but one step from triumph to a fall. I have seen that in the greatest affairs, a little thing has always decided great events.'[6] Yet the odds were in Napoleon's favour; if prevented from invading, he lost very little, as long as he was still in a position to try again. It was clear that Britain needed to lift that threat by destroying or capturing a sufficiently large part of the French Navy to prevent it escorting an invasion fleet across the Channel. At all costs, Britain must win a decisive battle against the French Navy – and that battle would be Trafalgar.

TWO

BEFORE THE BATTLE

> I was in truth bewildered by the account of Sir Robert Calder's Victory, and the joy of the event, together with the hearing that *John Bull* was not content, which I am sorry for . . . and it most sincerely grieves me, that in any of the [news]papers it should be insinuated, that Lord Nelson could have done better. I should have fought the Enemy, so did my friend Calder, but who can say that he will be more successful than another?
>
> Letter from Nelson to Captain Fremantle, 16 August 1805[1]

To someone swimming in a calm sea, the furthest distance visible was less than a mile at best. From the deck of one of the vessels in Nelson's fleet, the view was substantially improved, but from the lookout station on the mainmast of a warship, over 100 feet above the waves, the furthest horizon was nearly 14 miles away, and the highest sails of another ship could be seen up to 20 miles off. With this advantage, British ships on patrol outside the Spanish port of Cadiz could keep a close watch on the fleet in the harbour without ever needing to sail within range of the enemy shore batteries.

The city of Cadiz, about 75 miles north-west along the

Spanish coast from Gibraltar, lay at the end of an isthmus and was built on an island, which was originally cut off from the mainland by a narrow channel. The entrance to the harbour was to the north, and the Bay of Cadiz, behind the isthmus and the city itself, provided shelter from the south-westerly winds and the Atlantic swell, but the scatter of small islands and sandbanks made navigation especially difficult for ships under sail. Cadiz was originally established as a port by the Phoenicians, perhaps as early as 1100 BC, and was occupied successively by the Carthaginians, the Romans and the Moors before being taken from the Muslims in the thirteenth century. In 1812 it would have a brief moment of glory as the capital of Spain, after the French had been driven from the Iberian peninsula, and Spain's first constitution was declared at Cadiz, but primarily it was a major Spanish port and naval base.

From the sea, the city was impressively exotic to British eyes, as described by Charles Pemberton, a young seaman from Pontypool in South Wales who missed the Battle of Trafalgar but was in a ship blockading the same port three years later:

What a sight it was when the whole magnificence of the scene was unfolded – laid out to the gaze! When, at the distance of about three miles from Cadiz lighthouse, making that a centre, the eye ranged along an outstretched foreground of some twenty-five miles (for I won't call the *sea* foreground, though it is the nearest object in the picture), from point Chipiona on the one hand, towards Cape Trafalgar in the S.E.; the former dwindling off into a low, fine line, as it projected into the sea, and the blue-vapour-looking hills about Seville rising over it; the latter (towards Cape Trafalgar) leaving the slopes and hillocks of sand, where the waves gently and sportively broke, and rising into a perpendicular and dark, rocky wall, against which the billows dashed angrily ... then, to an Englishman who has never seen an assemblage of houses and churches, all built of pure white stone, and shining beneath a warm sky, the city of Cadiz is an object which fills him with wonder, delight, and admiration; looking, as it does from this point of view, like a gathering of marble palaces: he knows not of the narrow and filthy streets, and the thousands of abominations which beset the passenger at every step within its walls: he sees nothing but beauty, grandeur, and splendour.[2]

In October 1805, just before Trafalgar, Vice-Admiral* Lord Nelson was maintaining a blockade of Cadiz, with most of his ships out of sight in the hope of tempting the Combined French and Spanish Fleet, under the command of Vice-Admiral Pierre-Charles-Jean-Baptiste-Silvestre de Villeneuve, to leave the safety of the harbour. Nelson was hoping for a decisive battle, but at the very least he wanted to prevent Villeneuve escaping into the Mediterranean, where the French fleet might be able to evade him and eventually return to the English Channel as part of an invasion force. Spain had formally entered the war on Napoleon Bonaparte's side just a few months earlier, after a long period of spurious neutrality during which Spanish ports nevertheless provided supplies and shelter for the French Navy. Once the Spanish ships were at Napoleon's disposal, they were used to strengthen the main French fleet, although most were kept in port by the British blockade.

Villeneuve had been stuck in port since August, unable to slip past the British ships that were blockading not just Cadiz but many other French and Spanish ports in an attempt to keep the enemy ships inactive, not least to prevent an invasion of Britain. By early 1805 Napoleon, now 'Emperor of the French' after a coronation the previous December, had already set in motion several strategies for an invasion that were later modified or rejected. On at least one occasion British Intelligence agents found out about part of such a plan, which

*Admirals outranked vice-admirals, who in turn outranked rear-admirals, but the term 'admiral' was loosely used to refer to all three ranks and to equivalent ranks in foreign navies.

was abandoned because the element of surprise was lost, but mostly Napoleon's plans had to be set aside because he did not understand the problems of war at sea anywhere near as well as he did the deployment of armies on land. He was used to organising grand projects that relied on the fast and reliable transmission of orders to move large armies across the landscape, and he wanted to use the same approach for the dispositions of his warships. It was a policy doomed to failure, because he did not allow for the vagaries of contacting fleets at sea. This was done through despatches carried by relatively small, lightly armed ships that relied on speed and manoeuvrability rather than firepower to elude capture. Speed of communication at sea seldom approached that on land, mainly because it was far more difficult to find a ship and deliver messages than for a despatch rider on land to take orders to an army. Lines of communication at sea were also at the mercy of wind and weather, and it was common practice to send duplicate despatches in different ships to increase the chances of the information reaching its destination. In such circumstances, close central control of naval operations was impossible – a fact that Napoleon repeatedly failed to grasp.

As on land, Napoleon also frequently countermanded his own orders by sending one messenger ship to follow another, without any thought that only one, or possibly none, might reach their destination in time. While trying to impose tight control on his ships at sea through a constant stream of orders, he produced more chaos than if he had left his admirals to their own devices. After so many abandoned invasion plans, he still failed to learn from his mistakes, blaming his subordinates instead.

His latest plan was for Vice-Admiral Honoré-Joseph-Antoine Ganteaume to lead his fleet from Brest on the north-west tip of France to Martinique in the West Indies. In the meantime Vice-Admiral Villeneuve was to take his fleet from Toulon on the south coast of France, collect the Spanish admiral Frederico

Carlos Gravina with five Spanish warships from Cadiz, and rendezvous with Ganteaume at Martinique. These combined forces would next attack British possessions in the West Indies, thereby drawing British ships away from Europe to deal with this threat. They would then return to take control of the English Channel so that the invasion of Britain could take place.

Napoleon's whole strategy was based on deceiving the British; Ganteaume was to leave Brest unseen so that British ships would be occupied looking for him; a large enough fleet was to stay at Cadiz to ensure that the British maintained the blockade and so could not rapidly reinforce their fleet in the Channel; and Villeneuve was to sail for the West Indies in the hope of inducing a large part of the British Navy to give chase. It was a strategy that would work well enough with armies on land, but it was far too complicated and too precise to have much chance of working at sea. Because he did not trust his admirals, Napoleon also issued increasingly detailed and rigid orders in an attempt to force them to do exactly what he wanted.

On 30 March 1805, Villeneuve's fleet had sailed from Toulon, setting in motion a train of events that would culminate in the Battle of Trafalgar nearly seven months later. The first part of Villeneuve's mission was successful; he avoided the British blockade, and Nelson only found out that he had gone four days later. Villeneuve sailed south-west along the coast of Spain and through the Straits of Gibraltar, reaching Cadiz on 9 April. Here he sent a despatch to Admiral Gravina to say that he thought Nelson's fleet was already in pursuit and there was no time to lose, to which Gravina replied that he would set sail immediately. Villeneuve pressed on towards Martinique, but when Gravina's fleet tried to set sail, the cables of some ships were found to be entangled, causing a delay of several hours. As a result only one Spanish ship caught up with Villeneuve – the rest eventually joined him at Martinique on 26 May, ten days after his arrival.

To the British, this French initiative was a disaster. A large force of French and Spanish ships had evaded the blockade and now their whereabouts were unknown. Once informed of Villeneuve's escape, Nelson first thought that the destination was within the Mediterranean. He immediately sailed to Sicily in the hope of picking up news of the French fleet – but Villeneuve had sailed west, past Gibraltar, and it was only on 18 April, when Villeneuve had already reached the West Indies, that Nelson learned the direction that the French had taken. Guessing their destination correctly this time, Nelson acted on his own initiative, sent the Admiralty in London a despatch informing them of his intentions and led his fleet westwards in hot pursuit.

In Brest, Ganteaume saw no hope of managing to slip from the port unseen, and although he sent Napoleon repeated requests for permission to attack the British blockade, he was consistently refused. In the end, his fleet never did sail to rendezvous with Villeneuve. As news of events reached the Admiralty and filtered through to the various squadrons blockading French and Spanish ports, these squadrons were redeployed and reinforced to make the blockade as tight as possible and also to guard against any action that Villeneuve's fleet might take on its return.

Nelson's squadron arrived at Barbados on 4 June, and by the 7th Villeneuve, who had already captured a British outpost and a convoy of fifteen merchant ships, received word of Nelson's arrival. Villeneuve also received revised orders from Napoleon, changing the plans yet again. He was now supposed to stay a further twenty-five days, allowing time for Ganteaume to arrive, which would keep his squadron in Martinique until 22 June. Villeneuve was not inclined to wait. Having achieved the primary aim of his mission in drawing a large British force away from Europe, he ignored every other order and set sail for home on 11 June, accompanied by Admiral Gravina and his ships. Nelson continued to cruise through the islands trying to find him – it would be another four days before the news reached him and he could renew the chase.

On 22 July, moving slowly on a light wind through intermittent fog off Cape Finisterre on the west coast of Spain, Villeneuve's squadron came in sight of a British fleet* commanded by Vice-Admiral Sir Robert Calder. When both sides realised what had happened, they made hasty preparations for battle, as Villeneuve later reported:

We steered towards the Enemy, who steered towards us in a long Line . . . The fog began to disperse. As soon as my Signal was seen by Admiral Gravina, he immediately obeyed it with much resolution, and was followed by all the Vessels of the Fleet. As soon as he closed, he engaged the Enemy's Ships, which had already begun their movement before the Wind. But the fog then became so thick that it was impossible to see any thing, and each Ship could scarcely see the Vessel next to it. The Battle then began almost along the whole line. We fired by the light of the Enemy's fire almost always without seeing them . . . An excessively thick fog covered the whole Van and Rear of the Squadron, and prevented us from executing any movement. As far as I could see, all the advantage of the Combat was with us. The fog did not abate during the remainder of the evening. During the night the two Squadrons [French and Spanish] remained in sight, making Signals to keep together. I thought, however, I perceived that the Enemy retreated. As soon as the day broke we saw them much to leeward† of us . . . At the first peep of dawn, I made Signal to bear down upon the Enemy, who had taken their position at a great distance; and endeavoured, by every possible press of sail, to avoid renewing the Action. Finding it impossible to force them to a re-engagement, I

*At the time of Trafalgar there was no real difference between the terms 'fleet' and 'squadron' except when referring to 'The Fleet' as a whole, which was divided into three squadrons (the red, white and blue). When used more generally, the terms fleet and squadron were interchangeable and have been used as such throughout this book.
†Downwind

thought it my duty not to remove any further from the line of my destination, but so to shape my course as to effect, agreeably to my instructions, a junction with the Squadron in Ferrol.[3]

A letter from an anonymous British officer on board one of the ships in Calder's squadron gives a rather different view:

About two [in the afternoon] we were considerably within gun-shot of the Enemy's advanced Squadron . . . Thus the Action commenced: our leading Ship, the *Hero*, 74 [74 guns], tacked immediately the Enemy opened their fire on us, and commenced a heavy cannonading on them in return. It continued with unremitting fury for three hours and a half, when we saw (on clearing of the fog at intervals) the French Line to windward, and two Ships disabled, although we could not at the time distinguish whether they belonged to the Enemy or us . . . Had the weather been clear, I have no hesitation in saying they would have been completely defeated – but the fog prevented our Ships getting near enough (they not being discernible but at intervals) and the French being to windward were too wise to come nearer to us.[4]

Two Spanish ships, the *San Raphael* and the *Firma*, were captured, and the combined French and Spanish squadron generally had the worst of the battle, with some of the ships being badly mauled. For two days afterwards both squadrons hovered in the fog, unwilling to join battle again but equally unwilling to leave the scene. It was not until 25 July that they both sailed off in different directions. The Spanish had taken the brunt of the conflict; at one point their six ships had engaged the entire British force of fifteen warships, their bravery making a deep impression on the British crews. Although this was technically a British victory, Villeneuve was not stopped in his tracks, but was allowed to sail on to the shelter of Vigo Bay in north-west Spain. Calder was later censured for failing to do more to hinder the enemy fleet – immediately before Trafalgar he had to return to Portsmouth to face a court martial, leaving Nelson's fleet short of a warship.

When news of Calder's confrontation with Villeneuve reached Britain, *The Times* put on a brave face, using convoluted compliments in a report published on Saturday 10 August: 'We should regret if Lord Nelson were deprived of the chief honours of a victory which his extraordinary sagacity and unparalleled activity have well deserved; but we should lament exceedingly, if any sentiment of exclusion should interfere, and render it less decisive than we expect. We are persuaded none can. That great Commander is too rich in laurels, to be impoverished by the dropping of a few leaves, from his many wreaths, upon his companions in arms.'[5]

The same report relayed the news that Nelson's fleet had reached Gibraltar from the West Indies on 19 July. Nelson calculated that his ships had travelled over 6600 miles in pursuit of Villeneuve. It was a bitter irony that in his haste to catch up with his quarry, he had unknowingly overtaken him, reaching the Mediterranean even before Villeneuve's encounter with Calder. Nelson went ashore at Rosia Bay in Gibraltar on 20 July 1805, the first time he had set foot on land for over two years, having last set sail on 16 June 1803. During this time he had been blockading the French Mediterranean ports and from the beginning of 1805 he had been occupied with chasing Villeneuve's fleet across the Atlantic. Now that the French and the Spanish fleets had eluded him, Nelson returned to England for leave that was long overdue.

When Napoleon received news of Villeneuve's clash with Calder, he was furious: '"What a chance Villeneuve has missed", he exclaimed! "He could, on arriving at Brest from the open sea, have played prisoners' base with Calder's squadron and dealt with Cornwallis, or, with his 30 ships, defeat the English and gain a decided supremacy."'[6] This might have been true for Nelson or one of the other top British admirals, but Villeneuve was constrained and unnerved by an endless succession of detailed orders from an erratic emperor.

Villeneuve's fleet was now in a weakened state, already damaged by storms on the way to and from the West Indies and further battered in the encounter with Calder's squadron. The ships were low on food and water and had many sick or wounded men. As Vigo had no resources to refit the fleet or cope with large numbers of men needing hospital treatment, Villeneuve only stayed long enough to deal with the most pressing repairs. The fleet left there on 27 July to sail north along the Spanish coast to Corunna and Ferrol, where it stayed until 11 August. By this time Napoleon had heard more accurate reports of the events in the West Indies and the battle with Calder. In his critical tirade he made unfavourable comparisons between the performance of Villeneuve and the French Navy, and that of Admiral Gravina and his Spaniards. Revising his invasion plans yet again, Napoleon sent orders for Villeneuve to sail with the Combined French and Spanish Fleet to meet him at Boulogne, where he was waiting with an invasion army of over 160,000 men ready to embark for England.

Villeneuve therefore left the shelter of Corunna and Ferrol, knowing that any number of British fleets might be out searching for him. On sighting a group of ships two days later, he did not stop to find out whether they were hostile or not, but headed straight for Cadiz – an option sanctioned in one of Napoleon's earlier sets of orders. Villeneuve's fleet reached the safety of Cadiz without mishap on 21 August, but Napoleon did not receive the news until two weeks later. 'That is certainly treason,' he ranted. 'That is unspeakable . . . Villeneuve is a wretch who must be sent packing in disgrace . . . he would sacrifice everything provided he saved his own skin.'[7]

At this time Vice-Admiral Cuthbert Collingwood was stationed off Cadiz with a small force to ensure that the ships blockaded in the harbour did not slip out to join a larger fleet.

He was as surprised as Napoleon to find out Villeneuve's destination, as he related in a letter to his sister:

We were close to the light house of Cadiz when at 6 o'clock in the morning we discovered first 6 sail, and soon after 26. I soon made out what they were, and called in any detached ships – jogging off slowly as people do when they are sullen. For as the Spaniards had eight sail in the port, 4 of them ready to come in a moment, and I was exactly between the two, I did not chuse to shew any alarm which might rouse their activity. The Combined Fleet [led by Villeneuve] had run down about 2 hours when 16 sail of them parted from the rest and gave chase to us . . . I had only 3 [war]ships, *Dreadnought*, *Colossus*, and *Achilles*, with the *Niger* frigate. We ran until we had the gut of Gibraltar open and then put an impudent face on our shabby weak state. We shortened sail* and I sent the *Colossus* (an excellent sailor) to reconnoitre them more closely . . . Whether they suspected by these movements that we had discovered a reinforcement or were afraid of being drawn through the Streights and separated from the body of their fleet, I do not know, but soon after, they all hauled off and made the best of their way to Cadiz.[8]

His bluff having succeeded, Collingwood immediately sent a message to the Admiralty, giving the position of Villeneuve's fleet, but it would take nearly two weeks for the news from Cadiz to reach London. The day after Collingwood sent it, Napoleon made a crucial decision. He may have been relatively ignorant about naval warfare, but he did have an instinct for timing and he realised that time was running out. He knew that England was building and financing a coalition of forces against him in Europe and had signed a pact with Austria. If he could invade Britain, the supply of money would be cut

*Made some sails shorter, so reducing the overall area of sail exposed to the wind and thus reducing speed.

and the coalition would collapse. Failing this, he would have to move his invasion army eastwards to destroy the elements of the coalition while they were individually weak enough to defeat. If he did not move quickly, France itself could be invaded from the east.

Throughout the summer of 1805, as Napoleon became increasingly frustrated by his own navy, which seemed to be deliberately obstructing his plans, he grew more and more concerned about the situation on the Continent. The French treasury was almost exhausted, the French people wanted peace, and the longer he continued to delay, the greater was the possibility that he would be deposed. On 26 August, nearly two months before Trafalgar, Napoleon made his decision – the invasion of England must wait. In early September, Napoleon learned that his instinct had been correct, as the Austrian Army was already heading for Munich. Using the troops marshalled around Boulogne and those gathering inland, he planned to take this army of 200,000 men into Germany, right across to Austria and into Italy, to prevent the Russian armies joining up with those from Austria. He must defeat each of the European powers individually, before they had a chance to unite into an overwhelming force. Only when he had a firm grip on Continental Europe could he again afford to turn his attention directly to England; until then, the invasion would be postponed. By the time of Trafalgar, the French troops on the Channel coast had already broken camp and marched eastwards. In London, although it was not known that the invasion had been deferred, it was obvious that some major strategy had been set in motion. A feeling of fear and anxiety prevailed, and the newspaper reports from the Continent were all 'darkness and despondency'.[9]

On 19 August 1805, two days before Collingwood sent his message to the Admiralty, Viscount Horatio Nelson set foot in England and headed straight for Merton. These were his last days with Emma Hamilton, widow of Sir William Hamilton, who had been British Ambassador to the court of the Kingdom of the Two Sicilies at Naples (a kingdom comprising the whole of southern Italy as well as Sicily itself). The relationship between Nelson and Emma has often been portrayed as that of a vulnerable hero seduced by a calculating courtesan – a view that stemmed largely from the Victorian need to explain away a 'fault' in an otherwise exemplary man. The truth was somewhat different.

Nelson had married his wife, Frances, in 1787, and their early years together were blighted by his inability to obtain another post because he had fallen out of favour with some of the Lords of the Admiralty. He finally went back to sea in 1793 and did not see his wife for four years. When he returned in July 1797 he was a changed man, white-haired and haggard with stress and pain, having just lost his right arm. Frances nursed him back to health, in what was probably their happiest time together, and he returned to duty the following year. Yet while Frances remained devoted to her husband, the idea that Nelson himself was happy in his marriage until he met Emma is also something of a myth.

When he first met Emma at Naples in 1793, he seems to have been much more focused on the political situation. Considering that at the time Emma was thought to be one of the most beautiful women in Europe, if not *the* most beautiful, her initial impact on Nelson seems disappointing. There is no record of his making any appreciable impression on her either, but he impressed Sir William: 'On Sir William Hamilton's returning home, after having first beheld Captain Nelson, he told his lady that he was about to introduce a little man to her acquaintance, who could not boast of being very handsome. "But," added Sir William, "this man, who is an English naval officer, Captain Nelson, will become the greatest man that ever England produced. I know it, from the few words of conversation I have already had with him. I pronounce, that he will one day astonish the world."'[10] While this story may have been later embellished to make Sir William appear more prescient than he actually was, there is much more evidence at this point of a strong mutual respect and good working relationship between Sir William and Nelson than of any sort of relationship between Nelson and Emma. After a few days, Nelson left Naples and was not to meet Emma again for nearly five years; indeed, a few months later he was involved in a liaison with an Italian opera singer at Livorno.

Nelson next met Emma when he was returning victorious after the Battle of the Nile in 1798. He was then nearly forty-three years old and had changed dramatically. As a result of the recent battle, he was still suffering from concussion, a bruised face and a wound over his left eye. These were the least of his injuries, since he had been wounded in the back at the siege of Bastia in Corsica in 1794. That same year he had lost the sight of his right eye when it was grazed by a stone flung up by a cannon-ball at the siege of Calvi, also in Corsica, and his right arm had been amputated in 1797 after his elbow was shattered by a musket-ball in a battle at Santa Cruz, Tenerife. All this was on top of problems from an abdominal hernia resulting from a lesser wound, the legacy of various fevers and recurrent bouts of malaria. Emma, too, had changed. The majority of her surviving portraits were painted when she was in her early twenties, but in 1798 she was thirty-three and had put on weight (some observers already regarded her as fat). Her features no longer had the first flush of youth, and her enemies described them as coarse – she was still beautiful, but had lost some of her brilliance. At this time, Sir William Hamilton was sixty-eight, worn out by his diplomatic duties, and becoming prone to illness.

After the Battle of the Nile, Nelson stayed with the Hamiltons to recover from his wounds and during this time a deep love affair developed between him and Emma, to which

Sir William tactfully turned a blind eye. Although an apparently unlikely couple, they had more in common than was instantly obvious. Coming from poor and humble backgrounds (he was a son of a country parson who, through his wife, was related to the gentry; she was a blacksmith's daughter), both Nelson and Emma had seized every opportunity to enhance their careers – with many enemies jealous of their success. Both were intelligent and able (as well as having diplomatic skills, Emma was a good linguist and had a talent for acting and singing), and both maintained a public persona that did not entirely fit their real characters. There was a bond of mutual understanding as well as love between them.

At the end of 1798, as a French army swept through Italy, Nelson evacuated the Hamiltons and the royal family of the Kingdom of the Two Sicilies from Naples to Palermo. Nelson himself stayed on in this area of the Mediterranean, but after several hints from his superiors to return home, he eventually had to be recalled to England. He travelled overland through Europe accompanied by the Hamiltons on a journey that came to resemble a celebrity tour; everywhere he was greeted as a hero following his victory over Napoleon in Egypt. The party arrived in London in November 1800, and Nelson was reunited with his wife, but he rapidly realised that the marriage was over. Although she had heard reliable reports of Nelson's relationship with Emma, Frances Nelson still loved her husband, but he could no longer face living with her. By the end of February the following year, he put into action a formal separation from his wife, giving her a settlement of half his income: £1800 a year. There was no possibility of a divorce, because this would require an Act of Parliament, for which it was necessary to prove cruelty. Although in the short time that he had been back in England, he had rebuffed his wife at every turn and had generally behaved badly towards her, there had been no physical cruelty and mental cruelty was not then recognised.

Two weeks after Nelson completed the financial settlement on his wife, he was back at sea, although he returned to England briefly in June 1801. He then joined the fleet protecting the Channel, but on 1 October an armistice was signed between Britain and France, and so on 22 October, just four years before Trafalgar, Nelson was in England once again. While he had been away, Emma, acting as his agent, had bought and furnished a house and grounds for him at Merton in Surrey. She had also borne him a child – a daughter named Horatia. It must be assumed that Sir William knew about this, but if so, he was one of only very few. Her birth was kept so secret that even after Nelson publicly acknowledged the child as his, nobody suspected that Emma was the mother.

For over a year Nelson and the Hamiltons lived together in relative harmony at Merton, but Sir William, now in his seventies, was growing increasing frail. In April 1803 he died, with Nelson and Emma at his bedside – both genuinely grieved at his death. In some ways, it was the end of an idyll. Emma's share of Sir William's legacy did not adequately provide for her needs, and even that amount was reduced because she was cheated out of part of it by one of his relatives. Pleas for Sir William's hard-won pension to be transferred to her, or for her to be granted a pension in her own right, met prevarication and silence – it was a foretaste of how she would be treated after Nelson's death. A month after Sir William died, Nelson was ordered to prepare for sea. He sailed on 16 June 1803, returning to Merton only on 20 August 1805, after failing to find Villeneuve in the chase across the Atlantic and back. Nelson and Emma had just twenty-five days together, before he left Merton on Friday 13 September to set sail on his final voyage that ended at Trafalgar.

THREE

THE STAGE IS SET

What think you, my own dearest love? At this moment the Enemy are coming out, and as if determined to have a fair fight; all night they have been making signals, and the morning showed them to us getting under sail. They have thirty-four sail of the line, and five Frigates. Lord Nelson, I am sorry to say, has but twenty-seven sail of the line with him; the rest are at Gibraltar, getting water . . . I want him to have so many as to make the most decisive battle of it that ever was, which will bring us a lasting Peace, I hope, and some prize-money.

The start of a letter from Captain Blackwood in the frigate *Euryalus* to his wife Harriet, written on 19 October 1805[1]

With Villeneuve in harbour at Cadiz and all the major elements of the French and Spanish navies accounted for, the Admiralty redeployed its forces to tighten the British cordon. As yet unaware that ships were being despatched to strengthen his fleet and that Nelson was on his way to take command, Vice-Admiral Collingwood awaited instructions and reinforcements from Britain. In the meantime he had to continue the tedious vigil outside Cadiz, pretending to send signals to an imaginary fleet, while the crews of his ships maintained the monotonous daily routine of sailing up and down the Spanish coast.

Being continuously at sea took its own toll of the men, but having to remain constantly vigilant greatly added to the stress of everyone aboard. When on blockade duty off Brest in August 1803, Collingwood had written to his father-in-law: 'I am lying off the entrance of Brest harbour to watch the motions of the French fleet. Our information respecting them is very vague, but we know they have four- or five-and-twenty great ships, which makes it necessary to be alert and keep our eyes open at all times. I therefore bid adieu to snug beds and comfortable naps at night, never lying down but in my clothes . . . We hear no news here, and cannot be in more complete seclusion from the world, with only one object in view – that of preventing the French from doing harm.'[2] Being at sea for such long periods also caused a dangerous deterioration in the ships, and four months later Collingwood was complaining to his father-in-law about the state of his own flagship:

I came in from sea [to Cawsand Bay, near Plymouth in Devon] with orders to refresh my ship's company, and, poor creatures, they have been almost worked to death ever since. We began by discovering slight defects in the ship; and the farther we went in the examination, the more important they appeared, until at last she was discovered to be so completely rotten as to be unfit for sea. We have been sailing for the last six months with only a sheet of copper* between us and eternity.[3]

The French and Spanish ships in Cadiz harbour were not much better off, so in an attempt to boost morale Villeneuve exaggerated to his men the weaknesses of the blockading British ships: 'Nothing should astonish us in the appearance of an English squadron; their 74-gun ships do not have 500 men

*The copper sheathing covering the bottom of the ship.

on board; they are worn out through cruising for two years; they are not braver than us, and have infinitely less grounds for enthusiasm and love of country; they are skilful at manoeuvring; but in a month we shall be as skilled. Finally, everything is coming together to give us confidence of the most glorious success and of a new era for the seamen of the empire.'[4] Despite Villeneuve's remarks on the state of the British vessels, the French ships and their crews were themselves in poor condition after their recent journey to the West Indies and back.

When new, British ships were often reckoned to be inferior to French and Spanish ones, although the differences between the ships of the three navies were much less obvious than the similarities. Ship design was always a compromise – a trade-off between speed, strength, stability, carrying capacity and manoeuvrability. Many of these qualities were determined largely, or wholly, by the shape of the hull, and it was mainly subtle differences in hull structure that distinguished ships of different nations. In general, French ships were built for speed, while the British placed more emphasis on strength. The French and Spanish vessels tended to be better designed, so that whenever one of their ships was captured, improvements would be copied and used in the construction of new British ships. The French and Spanish themselves copied from each other, as well as imitating any improvements made by British shipbuilders, so that the ships of the three navies eventually became very similar.

The actual methods of construction were one of the main reasons why ships deteriorated so quickly. Curved pieces of timber were usually cut from suitably shaped branches and trunks, selected before the trees were felled. Often these pieces, and many others, were taken straight from the forest to the shipyard, and without any effective preservatives such unseasoned wood had a limited lifespan. A ship took several years to build, and for most of that time both the interior and the exterior timbers were exposed in all weathers, with a consequence that some ships were badly rotten even before they were launched. Because the causes of wood rot were then unknown and attempts at preservation relied on trial and error, most ships were kept at sea by constant repairs and refitting, whose cost far outweighed the initial sum spent on building the ship.

During the blockading duties, just about the only thing the sailors had to break the boredom was the twice-daily issue of grog – with their dinner at noon and their supper at four o'clock. Grog was originally one part rum to four parts water with the addition of lemon juice and brown sugar – a drink invented by Admiral Edward Vernon in 1740 in an attempt to reduce drunkenness by diluting the rum, with lemon juice being added to help prevent scurvy. Because his nickname was 'Old Grogram', from the grogram* that he habitually wore, the name 'grog' transferred to the drink. At the time of Trafalgar, the rum allowance was a quarter of a pint at a time (a total of half a pint per day), but this was in 'wine measure', which was roughly one-fifth less than an imperial half-pint and equivalent to the modern US half-pint. Each serving was usually topped up with three-quarters of a pint of water to make a full pint, but might be watered down further or withheld as a punishment. Sailors in the sickbay were not allowed grog or tobacco, which made them reluctant to report sick.

Grog was the favourite drink among sailors, but it was really a substitute for beer. Their official allowance was a 'wine measure' gallon (a US gallon, roughly four-fifths of an imperial gallon, or 3.785 litres) of beer a day. This was brewed by the Admiralty and was mainly drunk in port and on short voyages. Because beer did not keep well, it was drunk first on longer voyages, and when supplies ran out, grog was issued instead. In the Mediterranean especially, wine was often substituted instead of

*A waterproof cloak made of grogram fabric – a mixture of mohair, wool and silk, often stiffened with gum.

beer according to the ratio of one pint of wine to one gallon of beer. Spanish wine was particularly favoured by the authorities, but not always by the sailors, who preferred beer or grog. Red wine had the derogatory nickname 'black strap' and was of poor quality, full of sediment and very unpopular. To be stationed in the Mediterranean, where this wine was commonly served to the seamen, was known as being 'black-strapped'. The more acceptable fiery white Spanish Mistela wine was pronounced 'Miss Taylor'.

Apart from keeping up morale, these alcoholic drinks were much more palatable than the water, while the addition of rum or wine to the water went some way towards disinfecting it. The few men who abstained from alcohol drank tea or cocoa – no one drank the water undisguised if they could avoid it. The water was generally collected from rivers, without any attempt to filter or purify it, and was stored in wooden casks that were reused again and again. After a few days in a cask, the water was putrid, but it often grew sweet and drinkable once more. After a few more weeks of storage in the hold it became stagnant and slimy with fronds of green algae, and it stank, as William Badcock recorded when aboard the *Montague* in 1801: 'We . . . sailed for Coron, in the Morea [Greece], to procure wood, water, and fresh provisions, of which we stood very much in need, the scurvy having begun to make its appearance from our long continuance at sea upon bad salt[ed meat] and other food of the worst quality. The bread was full of maggots and weevils, the flour musty, and swarming with insects, the water so putrid, thick and stinking, that often I have held my nose with my hand while I drank it strained through my pocket handkerchief.'[5]

The other luxury on which sailors relied was tobacco, which, like liquor, was issued free. Sailors received 2 pounds per month, in the form of dried leaves complete with stalk, and they usually prepared the leaves by soaking them in rum and then tightly rolling them in a canvas sheet. This package was completely bound with a length of wet cord, producing a cigar-shaped object about 1 foot long, called a 'perique' or 'prick'. As the cord dried, it tightened the package and compressed the rolled tobacco, which matured while stored in this way. Tobacco was largely chewed because the only place below decks where smoking was permitted was in the galley, and opportunities to smoke on deck were infrequent, particularly during bad weather. Apart from the effect of the nicotine, the raw, hot, bitter taste produced by chewing the tobacco relieved some of the seamen's craving for different flavours that arose from the bland and boring diet they endured on long voyages. A quid of tobacco would last all day, could be kept overnight and was good for a second day's chewing.

The food, like the drink, was passable in port and in the early stages of a voyage, but rapidly deteriorated, and unless they themselves were skilled in food preparation, the sailors only had the ship's cook to cater for them. In port sailors were issued with bread that would be recognisable as such today, but at sea their bread ration was in fact ship's biscuits, baked so hard that even when fresh they had to be soaked to soften them before there was any chance they could be eaten. These biscuits were defined as 'a sort of bread much dried, to make it keep for the use of the navy, and is good for a whole year after it is baked'.[6] This was an optimistic view; the reality was closer to Jeffrey Raigersfeld's recollection of what it was like when he was a midshipman a few years before Trafalgar: 'The biscuit that was served to the ship's company was so light, that when you tapped it upon the table, it fell almost into dust, and thereout numerous insects, called weevils, crawled; they were bitter to the taste, and a sure indication that the biscuit had lost its nutricious particles; if, instead of these weevils, large white maggots with black heads made their appearance, then the biscuit was considered to be only in its first state of decay; these maggots were fat and cold to the taste, but not bitter.'[7] This degree of infestation was more prevalent in warm and hot climates, but whatever the temperature, the biscuit went through a slow transformation from an inedible rocklike substance made from wheat flour, pea flour and sometimes bone dust, to an unpalatable honeycomb, home to beetles and maggots – a deterioration that could be measured by the stages in the life-cycle of weevils.

While the biscuits tended to become hollow and to crumble with age, the meat (salt beef and salt pork) became harder and harder to the point where sailors could carve it into fancy articles such as little boxes, and it was capable of taking a high polish, like fine-grained wood. This was because it was frequently several years old and had been preserved by being caked in salt; it had to be soaked in water for a day before cooking and even then was very salty. The only official vegetable issued to sailors was peas, although other vegetables were substituted when available. Nelson, who had suffered various illnesses, particularly during his early years in the navy, insisted on good food supplies, emphasising onions and citrus fruits, and this policy helped win the admiration of his crews, keeping the men happier and improving their health and their effectiveness as a fighting force. In a letter to Sir William Hamilton in 1798, Nelson wrote from his ship in the Mediterranean fleet: 'Mr. Littledale is, I suppose, sent up by the Admiral [Earl St Vincent] to victual us, and I hope he will do it cheaper than any other person; but if I find out that he charges more than the fair price, and has not the provisions of the very best quality, I will not take them; for, as no Fleet has more fag [drudgery] than this, nothing but the best food and greatest attention can keep them healthy. At this moment, we have not one sick man in the Fleet.'[8]

After chasing Villeneuve and his fleet from the Mediterranean to the West Indies, Nelson was able to boast that he had not lost a single officer or man through sickness during the entire trip. By contrast, on reaching Martinique, then held by the French, Villeneuve's fleet immediately landed one thousand sick men, and more were to follow; when his fleet sailed back to England after less than a month in the West Indies, it left behind over a thousand men buried there who had died of various illnesses. On the morning of the Battle of Trafalgar, after months at sea, out of the many thousands of seamen and marines manning the British fleet, only 186 men were reported sick.

An allowance of oatmeal for each sailor was mainly used for breakfast – boiled in water with animal fat to produce a greasy gruel called 'skillagree'. There were also small allowances of sugar, as well as of butter and cheese, which quickly became rancid on long voyages. Items that were officially condemned as unfit, such as rancid butter, were still strictly accounted for; they would either be kept in store to be returned to the victuallers, or would be passed to the boatswain and charged to his budget. The boatswain had the responsibility for maintaining the rigging, and rancid butter would be rubbed into the hemp ropes to help waterproof them and keep them supple, because sunlight dried them out and made them brittle. The smell of rancid butter on the ropes was nothing compared to that of the cheese, which bred long thin red worms as it deteriorated. Because its smell was believed to endanger the health of the crew, cheese was the only item that was invariably thrown overboard once it was condemned as unfit for use.

Mondays, Wednesdays and Fridays were meatless days, when cheese or dried peas were served with duff, a kind of pudding made from flour, suet and currants or raisins. On Sundays the diet was enlivened by a slightly more elaborate pudding made from crushed biscuit, currants, raisins and any other available delicacies. This was the pinnacle of the cook's culinary expertise; food was otherwise merely boiled in large vats on a wood-fired stove. The cook had to be frugal with the fuel supply, except after a battle when there were plenty of wood splinters. Meat was seldom cooked as well as it needed to be, and due to its very poor quality it was more fat and gristle than meat. The sailors called it 'junk', which at that time was the technical term for old rope or cable that had been condemned as unserviceable. Boiling the meat left a thick salty scum of fat on the water, known as 'slush'. This was skimmed off, and half was used to waterproof the rigging; the other half was the cook's official perk, which he sold to tallow merchants, relying on this 'slush fund' to supplement his meagre wages.

The officers could afford to pay for extra food to supplement their diet, and this included livestock, which was the only way of providing fresh meat, eggs and milk at sea. It was not unusual for goats, chickens, geese, and even pigs and cows, to be penned in various places on board navy ships; space was also taken up with storage of their fodder. The livestock was bought and loaded aboard by the captain and other officers, but sometimes permission was granted to members of the crew to have their own animals in the ship. Even when the fresh food ran out, the officers' diet was better because they had their own cooks who could prepare the rations in imaginative ways, adding spices to improve the flavour.

Usually the officers dined off china, drank from real glasses and often had silver cutlery, but equipment for the seamen varied. In some ships earthenware plates and bowls as well as pewter cutlery were available, but these were very vulnerable. For the most part, wooden bowls, plates and tankards were used, and an individual sailor might possess only one or two wooden vessels along with a basic knife and a wooden or pewter spoon. Beakers made from animal horn were commonly used for drinking. For easy storage, the wooden plates were frequently square rather than round, which gave rise to the phrase 'a good square meal', although with the poor standard of food the phrase may originally have been an ironic comment. The square wooden plates were flat, with a raised rim called a 'fiddle' that stopped food slipping off. Any sailor pushing his allowance to the limit, with his plate so full that the food overlapped the rim, was said to be 'on the fiddle'. The men ate in small groups known as 'messes', sitting around tables that were set between the cannons – usually wooden boards suspended by ropes from the deck above, which were stowed against the side of the ship when not in use. Only the officers had chairs and proper tables; seamen sat on chests, casks or anything else to hand.

The official allowance of food on board ship should have been adequate, but because the purser, who was the officer in charge of provisions in each ship, frequently cheated the sailors in order to make a profit, the ration was often short. The purser's main duty was the purchase and issue of supplies, and since his own wages depended on the efficiency of his budgeting, he was generally suspected of profiteering at the expense of the crew even when not guilty of this. The purser was seldom a popular man. Since a proportion of the food that was served was unpalatable, if not outright inedible, hunger was not uncommon, and men supplemented their diet however they could. Sometimes fish could be caught, but rats were always available, as Midshipman Raigersfeld also recalled:

> The captain of the hold [a seaman who was responsible for that part of the ship when he was on duty] used to catch rats, (of which there was an abundance in the ship,) in the night, and by eight in the morning, generally four or five rats were ready cleaned and spread out as butchers dress sheep for the inspection of amateurs; and those who purchased the rats for a relish, had only to pepper and salt them well, broil them in the galley, and they were found nice and delicate eating; so that this captain of the hold's fishing, for he caught them by a hook and line, became a source of profit. As to the rats, they fed off the best of the ship's provisions, such as biscuit, flour, peas, &c. and they were full as good as rabbits, though not so large.[9]

Unknowingly, those who ate rats helped ward off the appalling disease of scurvy. The time of Trafalgar was still an age of primary discoveries. Much of the world was not properly mapped or explored, naval journals contained lively correspondence about whether or not mermaids existed, and although different theories had developed, in practical terms medicine and surgery were still at the level reached by the Romans two thousand years earlier.

Effective methods of preventing scurvy had only just come into widespread use, and for over a hundred years the disease had caused havoc among crews on long voyages. After several months or sometimes only a few weeks at sea, sailors began to develop the symptoms. At first they complained of weakness, a lack of energy and generally feeling unwell, which was followed by bleeding around hair follicles, particularly on the legs and arms, bleeding gums, loose teeth and offensive breath. As the disease developed, large purple patches on the skin were followed by open sores, and the men became so feeble that they were unable to stand or even raise their limbs. Most horrific of all in warships, wounds would not heal properly and old wounds opened up – even fractures in bones that were not completely knitted could break again. Without effective treatment, sufferers from scurvy eventually died, and up to a few years before Trafalgar, such treatment had still not been positively identified. Almost every sailor had suffered from the disease to some degree, even Nelson; in later life he appeared unable to smile except with his mouth closed, probably because scurvy had caused his teeth to rot.

During the Seven Years War (from 1756 to 1763), with Britain fighting against the French and Spanish, it was calculated that approximately ninety thousand British seamen had died from scurvy while only about fifteen hundred were killed in battle. By trial and error it was eventually established that scurvy could be prevented and cured by giving the seamen citrus fruit. This discovery was not officially recognised until 1795, when a daily issue of lemon or lime juice was ordered for all British Navy ships – the use of 'limey' as a nickname for British sailors arose from this order. Some admirals used concentrated juice, which was easier to store but not as effective. With his personal experiences of the disease, Nelson provided his ships with fresh lemon juice whenever possible, and so his crews did not suffer from scurvy when supplies could be obtained.

The means of preventing scurvy might have been found, but the cause of the disease was still a mystery, and like other diseases triggered by malnutrition, such as rickets, it occurred on land as well as at sea. Today it is known that scurvy only affects humans, some primates and guinea pigs, since all of them lack an enzyme that converts a type of sugar known as gluconate to an essential substance called ascorbate. Humans obtain ascorbate from food, which circulates in the blood as ascorbic acid, but without a regular source of ascorbate in the diet, the level of ascorbic acid in the blood falls to zero within a few weeks and scurvy develops. Over the decades in which naval surgeons closely studied the disease in attempts to find a cure, they noticed that those seamen who regularly supplemented their diet by eating rats were much less prone to scurvy than seamen who stuck to their rations. This was because rats synthesise ascorbic acid from their food and so were a source, albeit inadequate, of the substance that protects against scurvy.

Contact with rats could in itself be dangerous: not from eating them, but from catching lice and fleas off their fur. One of the main differences between the officers and the sailors aboard ships at this time was their living conditions and, to a lesser extent, their standards of hygiene. Despite frequent attempts to cleanse ships, sailors were often infested with lice and fleas. These parasites lived in dirty clothes and bedding, though this was not peculiar to the navy, or even life on board ship, but was very common on land as well. The importance of hygiene in the prevention of disease was then unknown, and although people kept themselves and their clothes clean as a matter of pride and a mark of respectability, personal cleanliness was a luxury that only the well-to-do could afford.

Lice and fleas were carriers of a fever that had several names (gaol fever, hospital fever, army fever and ship fever), all reflecting the conditions in which it was prevalent: wherever large groups of people were living in close proximity. The disease is now known as typhus, and in the confined space of a sailing warship it spread rapidly. Those who were infected developed a very high temperature with a rapid pulse, and usually became delirious, often dying within three days. Medical theories in the nineteenth century were at an early stage, with many diseases, including scurvy and typhus, being attributed to foul-smelling air, of which there was an abundance on board ships. Dirty clothes were actually suspected as a cause of typhus, not because they contained lice and fleas (which were not considered a health hazard), but because of the noxious stench the clothes gave off. Thorough cleaning of a ship and the washing or destroying of all dirty clothes and bedding proved to be an effective solution to the spread of typhus, but only if the rats on the ship were destroyed at the same time; otherwise they continued to harbour disease-ridden lice and fleas and reinfected the crew. The situation was not helped by the fact that most of the sailors regularly slept in their clothes for warmth and to save time when they were called from their hammocks to work the ship. What clothes they did take off before sleeping went under their pillow or their blankets to prevent them being stolen.

By the time of Trafalgar, many naval surgeons understood the practical need for basic hygiene, even though they were unaware of the role played by lice and fleas. Most crews were infested with such parasites without any great harm being apparent, but often the introduction of new crew members, particularly those who had been recruited from prisons, introduced typhus into the resident lice and flea populations, and so the disease spread throughout the ship. Those naval surgeons who were aware of the importance of hygiene tried to persuade the captains of their ships to order the regular washing of clothes, the airing of bedding and the routine cleaning of the ship, but apart from resistance to changes in traditional routines, there were also practical difficulties – the main one being the shortage of fresh water.

It was official navy policy that fresh water, which had to be carried in casks, was reserved for drinking and cooking. Rainwater was used when available, but it was difficult to collect in any quantity; generally sea-water was used for all washing purposes, and the results were poor. Soap was very scarce, and in any case it did not lather properly because of the salt in the sea-water. To add to the difficulty, rinsing clothes in sea-water left a salt residue that attracted damp so that they were never fully dry, irritating and chafing the skin. Since clothes washed in sea-water were so uncomfortable to wear, there was a natural resistance among the crew to washing their clothes, and a similar attitude applied to personal hygiene – most sailors simply did not wash often, or at all, while they were at sea. At this period there was a widespread belief that bathing was harmful because it leached natural oils from the body, so anyone who bathed regularly or was fastidious about washing was regarded as a dangerous eccentric. Consequently, sailors on land did not stand out as particularly dirty in a society where bad breath, rank unwashed hair and body odour were common – as long as they were neat and tidy and their clothes relatively clean.

Clothes were bleached by soaking them in urine before washing them, and tubs for the collection of urine for this purpose were placed in the bows by the seamen's toilets. These toilet facilities were primitive in the extreme and did not help the tendency of the men to suffer from constipation owing to the blandness of their diet. In the larger ships the captain had his own private toilet in a small cubicle at one end of the stern gallery, which ran across the width of the stern and had a row of windows giving light into the captain's cabin. This cubicle was known as a quarter gallery, and on the decks below similar quarter galleries were provided for the officers. These toilets merely consisted of a seat with a hole over a vertical waste pipe or over an open drop to the sea, and at the very least they were draughty. In smaller ships, with no room for these facilities in the stern, the officers probably used chamber pots or buckets, which their servants emptied. Midshipmen and warrant officers used a similar cubicle called a roundhouse, located right up in the bows of the ship in the part called the beakhead. This area extended on either side of the bowsprit (below which was the ship's figurehead) and was floored over with wooden gratings. There were usually two roundhouses, one on either side, and again they had a seat with a hole over a clear drop to the sea. One roundhouse was often reserved for the use of men in the sickbay. In larger ships there were about twelve other seats with holes in this area (fewer in the smaller ships), and they were arranged in an equal number on each side of the bow. They did not have the privacy and shelter provided by the roundhouses and were completely exposed to the weather and the sea spray. Never pleasant to use, these toilets were dangerous in rough weather and high seas.

Probably taking the name from the nearby catheads,* beakhead and figurehead, the general name for toilets was 'heads', and 'going to the heads' meant going to the toilet. The most basic method of all was not to use such facilities, but for the men to relieve themselves while hanging from the shrouds (the rigging steadying each mast) at the points where they were secured to the side of the ship. In these places, wooden ledges known as the 'chain-wales', 'channels' or, more commonly, 'chains', provided footholds, and the lee (downwind) side of the ship was chosen, because the wind tilted the ship over in this direction, giving a clear drop to the sea. The tubs for the collection

*Catheads were wooden beams projecting on each side of the bow, from which ropes were used to heave up and secure the anchor once the anchor cable had been hauled in.

of urine for use as bleach were placed near the roundhouses in the bow. Elsewhere in the ship – on the decks well above the waterline – were a number of pissdales ('dale' being an old word for 'drain'). These were simple basins or troughs made of lead, copper or sometimes wood, fitted to a bulkhead (an internal wooden wall or partition), with a pipe taking the waste through the side of the ship.

Toilet paper was not invented until several decades after Trafalgar, but newspapers, other scrap paper and sometimes even books were recycled for cleaning after defecation, although all paper was relatively expensive at this time, since it was still being made by hand. The first machine in Britain for mass-producing paper had only been built in 1803, and as yet industrialisation had made no impact on the price of paper. On land only the well-off and the rich could afford to buy newspapers on a regular basis; the majority of people were too poor, and in any case many were illiterate. (As late as the 1820s, advertisements for professional letter-writers – who would write letters and read the replies for a fee – were a common sight in London.) In rural areas, any suitable vegetation was used, while in towns those who had no paper would employ scraps of rag or fibres. On board ship, the officers commonly recycled paper, but the seamen would probably have made use of scrap fibrous material such as tow (unwashed, uncombed wool or flax), which was a general-purpose cleaning and packing material, or even oakum (unpicked rope fibres). In some ships a sponge rinsed in a bucket of sea-water may have been provided.

In theory the seamen were supposed to use the heads on the lee side, so that waste fell clear of the ship into the sea, but with less than twenty toilets for nearly a thousand men on the larger ships, and similarly inadequate provision on smaller ships, this rule was of necessity ignored. Particular problems developed during prolonged bad weather, when the hatches were battened down for days at a time and anyone on the upper decks risked being washed overboard. Buckets could not be emptied until the weather improved, and it was not uncommon for a guard to be posted at the gratings above the hold to prevent the sailors relieving themselves there. It is hardly surprising that the surgeons recorded a rise in 'costive complaints' at such times.

On top of all the hardships of day-to-day life, the discipline was brutal. Although there were mild punishments such as the stopping of grog, tobacco and privileges, or being put in irons for a time, most punishments involved beatings. The petty officers carried canes or lengths of rope with which to beat any sailor who stepped out of line, and a routine punishment was flogging with a cat-o'-nine-tails – a rope with the end separated into nine strands, each knotted along its length. Anything over a dozen lashes – which was a common punishment – left a man's back looking like mangled meat, and in practice the number of lashes was entirely at the discretion of the captain, who might order many times that number. For some crimes a seaman was flogged through the fleet – rowed in a boat to each ship in turn, alongside which he was given a number of lashes. Few survived this treatment, and those who did seldom lived long, even if their lacerated backs healed properly. Ultimately a sailor could be hanged, but a court martial had to be held before this sentence could be passed. The older punishments of ducking (repeatedly plunging a man into the sea on the end of a rope slung from one of the yards, and then hauling him up again) and keelhauling (pulling a man on the end of a rope down one side of the ship, underneath, and up the other side), both of which sometimes drowned the victim, had been abandoned by the British Navy some years earlier, although they were still sometimes practised by the French. Worst of all was the arbitrary nature of the discipline, which was in the hands of individual captains and their officers. Some commanders, like Collingwood, did not believe in flogging and rarely sanctioned it, although his ships were well disciplined and efficient. Other captains were too lax, letting their officers bully the crew, and some were downright tyrants.

By modern standards, life in the navy at the time of Trafalgar was dangerous, degrading and harsh, but in comparison with life on land in Britain it was not much worse. A seaman had somewhere to live, he had food provided, albeit of poor quality, was not afraid of losing his job, and had easy access to largely free medical treatment – sailors only had to pay for the treatment of illnesses considered to be self-inflicted, such as venereal disease. A sailor received an average of 365 gallons of beer a year, or equivalents in wine or grog, when the average annual consumption of beer on land was less than 35 gallons, and his free issue of 24 pounds of tobacco a year was massive compared to the average annual consumption of just over 1 pound. Even after the depredations of pursers who gave short measure, a sailor's rations were often more plentiful than he could hope to get ashore.

An equivalent labourer on land was in fear of losing his job, had to pay for his own food, drink and housing at relatively high prices, and seldom had any money to spare for medical treatment, even if he could find a physician to treat him. Most doctors plied their trade in towns, and favoured the middle and upper classes who could afford their fees. An agricultural labourer at this time might earn anything between £3 and £10 a year, a maid around £5 a year and a schoolmaster £10–12. A quartern loaf (4 pounds of bread) cost about one shilling, so anyone earning less than £4 10s a year could not even afford 1 pound of bread per day, which was the nominal free ration for seamen. Even the bread itself was not much better ashore; it might not have weevils, but much of it was dark in colour because it had been made with adulterated flour, and it often had a foul taste. During this period the traditional British preference for white bread was born, since in many cases the whiter the bread, the less the flour had been adulterated. By comparison with a skilled or semi-skilled labourer on land, the pay of an able seaman (the top rank of sailors) at £14 12s 6d per annum after deductions was relatively good, and even the lowest grade of unskilled sailor earned £10 11s 6d a year.

Life on land could also be brutal, and this was reflected in the popular pastimes. The *Morning Post* for 5 January 1805 carried the advertisement: 'Cocking, to be Fought on Monday, January 7, 1805, and continue all the week, at the Cock Pit Royal, South side of St. James's Park [London], the Gentlemen of Suffolk, and the Gentlemen of Hampshire's MAIN OF COCKS, for Five Guineas the battle, and One Hundred Guineas the odd. To begin fighting each day precisely at Half-past Five o'clock.'[10] Bull-baiting was also still a legal popular sport (it was not outlawed until 1835), and bare-knuckle prizefights between two men or two women were common spectacles.

The law of the land could be just as hard as discipline at sea; hanging was the punishment for over two hundred offences, ranging from murder to stealing a sheep, and for treason a man could be hung, drawn and quartered. In 1803, Colonel Edward Despard was given such a sentence for plotting to assassinate King George III, despite Nelson appearing as a character witness at his trial. As he had not seen the man for twenty-three years, Nelson's testimony was ignored as irrelevant, but he also passed on a petition from Despard to the Prime Minister, as a result of which the sentence was commuted to hanging, with the body beheaded after death. Counterfeiting coins was one of the offences categorised as treason; men found guilty of this crime were usually hanged, but women were burned at the stake. The last woman to be executed in this way was Margaret Sullivan, who was strangled and burned at the stake in London in 1788. The law changed the following year, and by the time of Trafalgar the sentence for such a crime had been reduced to hanging or transportation. Capital punishment for forgery of anything except wills and powers of attorney to transfer stock was only abolished in 1832, when minor offences such as stealing a sheep were also made lesser crimes.

George III had a great dislike of capital punishment and commuted as many death sentences as he could; of the 350 people sentenced to death in 1805, only sixty-eight were hanged, but of these just ten had been convicted of murder. Public whippings and public imprisonment in the pillory were still common punishments in 1805, and the prisons were so overcrowded, filthy and disease-ridden that imprisonment often proved fatal as well. Suicide was illegal, and successful suicides were still punished, as an item in the *Morning Post* for 27 April 1810 recorded: 'The Officers appointed to execute the ceremony of driving a stake through the dead body of *James Cowling*, a deserter from the London Militia, who deprived himself of existence, by cutting his throat, at a public-house in Gilbert Street, Clare Market, in consequence of which, the Coroner's Jury found a verdict of Self-murder, very properly delayed the business until twelve o'clock on Wednesday night, when the deceased was buried in the cross roads at the end of Blackmoor Street, Clare Market.'[11]

Life in the navy might be hard, but other attractions existed apart from the security and pay. Bounties were often offered to entice men to join, and there was always the possibility of a share of prize money (awarded for the capture and sale of enemy ships, known as 'prizes'), which could be enough to make officers very rich and gave a good boost to the seamen's wages. Some men were lured by the prospect of travel. In an age when people seldom went anywhere beyond the nearest market town and those from another county were commonly dubbed 'foreigners', travel was an indulgence of the rich. Especially in coastal areas, many men succumbed to the romance of going to sea and were sadly disillusioned within days, if not hours, of being afloat. Except for the prospect of prize money, itself balanced by the dangers of battle, merchant ships offered just about all the same attractions as the navy, but with the added benefit of higher pay and less rigid discipline.

In time of war, when the navy expanded its fleet and when seamen to crew the ships were in short supply, a form of conscription called impressment was used. After 1793, all British seamen and boatmen working on rivers, between the ages of eighteen and fifty-five, were liable to be pressed (conscripted), although there were a few exemptions. On shore, an Impress Service employed gangs of men to forcibly carry off seamen to the ports for service in the navy. These press-gangs were not particular, taking both exempt men and those who were not seamen. The captain of each ship was responsible for finding a crew, and if ordinary recruitment and an allocation of men from the Impress Service did not provide enough, they could send their own press-gangs on shore, commanded by an officer under a warrant from the Admiralty. As a result, many men were forced to serve in the navy against their will, forming a hard core of discontent that occasionally led to disturbances and even mutiny.

Resentment was caused by the press-gangs on land as well, since husbands and fathers were wrenched from their families, frequently leaving them in financial difficulties quite apart from causing them emotional distress. Families had no idea when, if ever, they would see their men again, and in some cases only found out that they had been taken by the press-gang when they returned years later – the men just disappeared. Local magistrates saw the press as a way of ridding themselves of petty criminals and beggars, but the only criminals that the navy would willingly take were smugglers (who were usually good seamen) and those imprisoned for debt (a hazard that befell even 'people of quality'). Since each captain wanted a competent crew, he was reluctant to take any but experienced seamen, and certainly did not want the absolute dregs of the lowlife scavenged from the prisons.

Press-gangs also operated in foreign ports, and in particular there was much bitterness at men being taken from American ports and ships. The United States of America was not yet thirty years old at the time of Trafalgar, and Americans could not easily be distinguished from the British, even by their accents. Documentary evidence of exemption on grounds of nationality was sometimes deliberately ignored, giving rise to an American component within the British Navy. This included men of African ancestry (both free men and slaves) from America and the West Indies, adding to those native British men of African heritage.

At Trafalgar, the British ships were manned by a mixture of nationalities, but the proportion of foreign nationals to British varied from ship to ship. Some vessels had virtually all-British crews, while about 10 per cent of the *Victory*'s crew came from outside the British Isles: twenty-two Americans, one Brazilian, two Canadians, two Danes, seven Dutch, four French, three Germans, nine Italians, six Maltese, two Norwegians, one Portuguese, four Swedes, two Swiss, two from India, and five from the West Indies. Such a mixture was due partly to the press-gangs and partly to volunteering. French men serving in the British Navy were usually royalist volunteers, opposed to the revolutionary and then Napoleonic regimes in France.

It is now difficult to assess just how many willing volunteers served in the navy, since efforts were made to persuade men supplied by the press-gangs to volunteer in return for advances on pay or a bounty. Some men who were registered in the muster books as 'volunteers' had made the best of a bad situation by agreeing to serve voluntarily, after having been forced on board. At the time of Trafalgar, less than half of a crew might be officially registered as recruits rather than pressed men, but the real number might be under a third. The proportions varied enormously from ship to ship, since captains with a reputation for being fair to their crews and lucky in capturing prizes would attract many volunteers. Ultimately, what mattered was not the origin of the seamen, but how skilled and efficient they were and how well they worked as a team. It was this that gave the British Navy superiority over the French and Spanish; the crews of British ships had more training, practice and experience, and so could work much faster and more efficiently.

Although seamen were in short supply, there was never any trouble recruiting officers. A naval career was a frequent choice of the younger sons of the aristocracy, who had no hope of inheriting their fathers' estates, and it offered a chance of advancement for the gentry and the more 'respectable' layers of the lower classes. A few officers even worked their way up from the lowest rank of seaman, having originally been conscripted by a press-gang. The navy was much more popular with the people of Britain than the army, since sailors were not regularly billeted in civilian homes nor were they called out to deal with civil disturbances. Following the series of naval successes before Trafalgar, which were boosted by propaganda in England, the navy was seen as the saviour of Britain – the army, full of criminals and sometimes little more than an unruly rabble, was regarded as a dangerous nuisance. For a young man 'of good background', the navy offered the chance of riches, fame and elevation to the highest social circles in the land. Nelson was a friend of the Duke of Clarence (later King William IV), who had served under Nelson twenty years before Trafalgar, first as a midshipman and then as a captain.

In the British Navy there were always more officers than ships for them to serve in, but the same could not be said for the French. The structure of command in the French Navy had been effectively destroyed by the French Revolution. The sharp class-division between the officers, who were aristocrats, and the seamen, who came from the lower classes, had been denounced; most aristocratic officers had either been executed, imprisoned or exiled, or else had fled the country. By the time of Napoleonic rule in France, the best naval officers were those aristocrats who had survived, often reinstated after being freed from prison or exile. Villeneuve, the forty-two-year-old commander-in-chief of the French and Spanish fleets at Trafalgar, was one of the few aristocrats to have survived the revolution without being forced from his position, because he had supported the revolution and renounced his aristocratic origins. Attempts to make up officer numbers by transferring captains from merchant ships were unsuccessful, since these captains had no experience of fighting. Officer training schools had only been established in the early 1800s and were not yet making an impact on the supply of competent officers.

The French Navy was also lacking in competent seamen. France had a well-established system of conscription for sailors, which did not cause the same popular disapproval as the press-gangs in England, because the French Army also had conscription, so people were accustomed to the idea. The only conscription in Britain was for the militias, a form of home defence whose men could not be compelled to serve outside the country. On paper, the French system looked more efficient, yet the people found many ways to oppose or circumvent conscription. Ultimately the British system of forcibly taking men from other ships and from the streets of sea ports often proved more effective. The fighting capacity of the French Navy had also suffered from the abolition in 1793 of the specialist corps of gunners, because it was regarded as elitist, leaving French ships short of trained and experienced gun crews. The corps of gunners had later been reinstated, but many of the original members were dispersed, and it would take years to build up the corps to its former level of efficiency. Generally, discipline in the French Navy was poor, manning levels were low and morale even lower. It had a fleet of sound ships, but not enough good crews to sail them.

The Spanish also had trouble manning their ships and relied on conscription, but because there were always too few seamen to be conscripted, any available men were taken. The Spanish

Navy was short of funds, and partly for this reason its ships spent little time at sea, so that the crews lacked training and experience. Although many of the officers were experienced and had not been subject to the problems that beset the French during the revolution, the Spanish officers were aristocrats and relatively old-fashioned in their outlook in comparison with the British and the French. The Spanish Navy also carried a high proportion of soldiers (around 30 per cent of the crew, whereas marines on a British ship made up only about 20 per cent), and this often hampered the sailors, particularly when army officers interfered in the running of the ship. Spanish crews were widely recognised as brave but badly trained and inexperienced, particularly compared with British crews, and so their morale was correspondingly low.

Having just sailed to the West Indies and back, Villeneuve had been painfully conscious of all these difficulties when he sailed into Cadiz on 21 August 1805, taking command of additional Spanish ships for his Combined French and Spanish Fleet, but he had other, more urgent, worries. He needed to find provisions for his ships, but had insufficient funds to buy them, and the French agent in the port warned that credit had been exhausted. It was many days before arrangements were patched together and authorisation came from Madrid allowing Villeneuve provisions, gunpowder and shot, and even then the Spanish were obstructive. The ships themselves were in poor condition, with not only spars and rigging needing repair, but one vessel had a damaged stern from a collision, two were leaking badly, and others needed new sails. The crews were decimated by illness; Villeneuve himself was unwell with a stomach complaint, probably triggered by stress; and to make matters worse, men began to desert now that they were in port. Villeneuve tried his best to deal with the problems, working hard to get his ships ready for sea, but despite everything he did, he remained severely short of men, particularly experienced seamen, to man the fleet. He was now following a set of orders that instructed him to take the initiative against the enemy whenever possible, but as yet his fleet was in no condition to do so. In mid-September another set of orders arrived, instructing him to carry troops to Naples, capturing whatever enemy ships and convoys he encountered on the way, while maintaining control of the Mediterranean for as long as possible. Villeneuve began preparations immediately.

By this time, Nelson was a few days away from assuming command of the blockading British fleet off Cadiz, after barely a month of shore leave in England. He arrived from Portsmouth in the *Victory* late on 28 September 1805, to take over as commander-in-chief from Collingwood, and he made the effort to meet all his commanders as soon as possible. He explained to them his plan of action for the battle that he knew was coming, since such a large number of ships as the Combined French and Spanish Fleet would soon stretch the resources of Cadiz to breaking point if the British blockade was maintained. This battle plan, which was a radical departure from traditional naval strategy, he later referred to as the 'Nelson Touch' when writing to Emma Hamilton:

> I joined the Fleet late on the evening of the 28th of September, but could not communicate with them until the next morning. I believe my arrival was most welcome, not only to the Commander of the Fleet, but also to every individual in it; and, when I came to explain to them the 'Nelson Touch', it was like an electric shock. Some shed tears, all approved – 'It was new – it was singular – it was simple!'; and, from Admirals downwards, it was repeated – 'It must succeed, if ever they will allow us to get at them! You are, my Lord, surrounded by friends whom you inspire with confidence.' Some may be Judas's; but the majority are certainly much pleased with my commanding them.[12]

In a battle, the tactics of a sailing ship were dictated by

weather conditions, even down to which side of an enemy vessel was attacked. Being downwind from an enemy was regarded as a defensive position, because a ship only had to hoist more sails to escape, while being upwind was an attacking position. Warships at that time were essentially floating platforms from which to fire cannons, and the most efficient theoretical shape is circular, giving equal firepower in all directions with no point weaker than any other. This was possible on land with round forts and circular towers such as Martello Towers, but sailing ships needed to be long and narrow to move through the sea. A warship's firepower was therefore concentrated along the sides, as there was no room to fire more than a few cannons over the bow of a ship or from the stern. A standard tactic was for a ship to try to sail at right angles to the

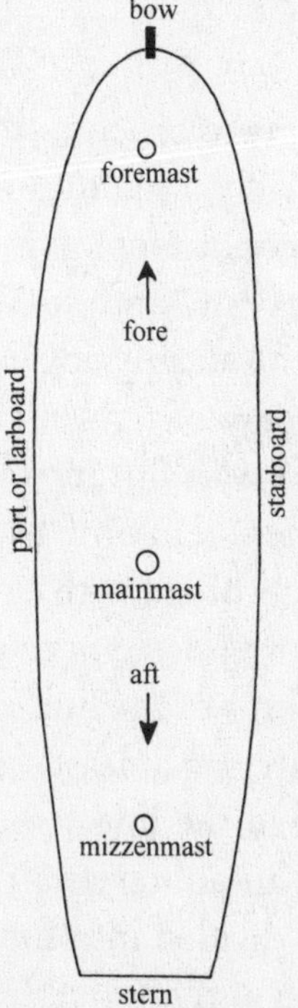

Basic plan of a ship

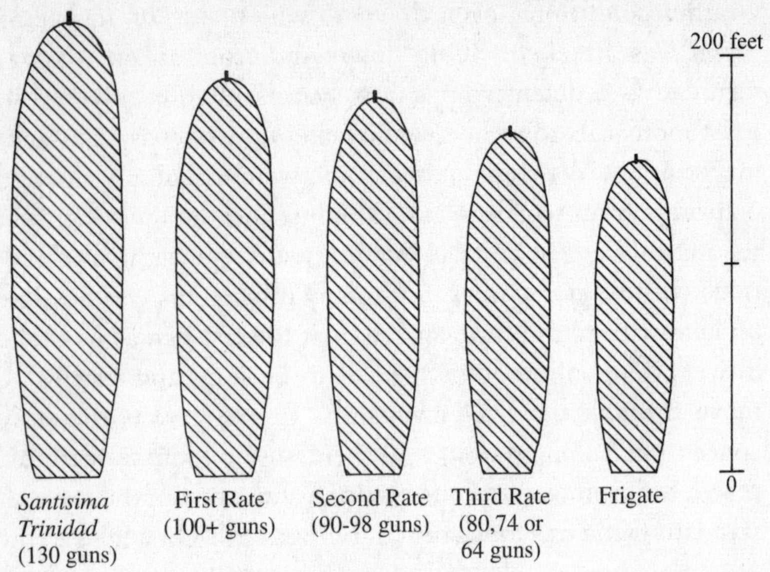

Diagram to show an approximate comparison of ship sizes

bow or stern of an enemy in order to fire a full broadside, while being in danger from only a handful of the enemy's guns. By this action, one ship could employ more than ten times the firepower of its opponent, and so vessels were constantly manoeuvring to gain this deadly advantage.

The traditional strategy of fighting at sea was for opposing sides to each form their warships into a line, bow to stern, parallel with their opponent's line of battle. The lines of ships would then pound each other with broadsides at close range until individual ships surrendered or retreated. The biggest warships were known as 'ships of the line' – so called because these were the battleships, carrying at least sixty-four guns (cannons), that traditionally formed the line of battle. The modern term 'battleship' is actually an abbreviation of 'line of battle ship'. Ships of the line were divided into first rates, carrying at least one hundred guns (such as the *Victory*), second rates, carrying at least ninety guns (such as the *Temeraire*), and third rates, carrying sixty-four, seventy-four or eighty guns (such as the *Belleisle*). Other ships might be classified as fourth rates, fifth rates or sixth rates according to the number of guns they carried. Frigates were usually fifth or sixth rates, while others such as schooners and cutters were not rated at all.

Nelson assumed that the two opposing fleets would be so large that it would take all day to form two parallel lines of battle. Instead, he proposed that the British fleet be divided into two columns that would sail through the single enemy line, breaking it into three parts. The foremost ships of the French and Spanish line would therefore be cut off and would have to turn and sail back to join the battle, by which time the British ships, temporarily outnumbering the enemy, should have control of the situation, since in the resulting confusion individual ships could choose their own targets.

Enormous risks were involved in this strategy. The two columns of British ships would be under fire from the French and Spanish as soon as they were in range. Sailing at right angles to the enemy line, the British ships would only be able to use the bow-chasers (a handful of guns pointing forwards in the bows) until they actually smashed through that line, during which time they would be very vulnerable and liable to sustain great damage. Nelson was gambling not merely on slow and inaccurate fire from the French and Spanish, but also on the overwhelming superiority in seamanship, gunnery and morale of his own sailors. The long months of patrolling and blockade duty that had so wearied the British crews had provided one benefit: as well as constant exercise in sailing the ships, the crews had had plenty of time to practise and perfect their gunnery, so that by now they had reached the highest pitch of speed and accuracy. In a memorandum written in the *Victory* on 9 October, Nelson summed up his vision of the coming conflict:

Something must be left to chance; nothing is sure in a sea fight beyond all others. Shot will carry away the masts and yards of friends as well as foes, but I look with confidence to a victory before the van of the enemy [foremost part of their line] could succour their rear, and then that the British Fleet would most of them be ready to receive their twenty sail of the line, or to pursue them should they endeavour to make off . . . But, in case signals can neither be seen or perfectly understood, no captain can do very wrong if he places his ship alongside that of an enemy.[13]

Once the plan of attack was settled, and every commander in the fleet knew what he would be doing, there was nothing left but to wait for the Combined Fleet to come out of Cadiz. Yet again, the initiative was with Villeneuve – all the British could do was watch and wait, as the tedious blockade dragged on.

In Cadiz, the situation was at best uneasy. There was no love lost between the French and Spanish crews, and frequent violent brawls on the dockside left several men dead and many injured. The hostility between the French and Spanish was well known, and reports from Spain had even reached *The Times* in London:

Cadiz, *Sept.* 14. – The scarcity occasioned by the arrival of the Combined Fleet continues to be severely felt; recourse has been had to Seville, and a supply of corn, wine, etc., demanded; even the fountains at Puerta Santa Maria have been put in requisition for the use of the fleets. Our Admiral Gravina loudly accuses Villeneuve of treachery in the late action [with Calder's fleet], and has solicited leave to resign. Between the sailors animosities have arisen to the highest pitch, and scarce a night passes but the dead bodies of assassinated Frenchmen are found in our streets.[14]

The French tended to despise the Spanish, who in turn mistrusted the French. When the Combined Fleet finally sailed out to meet the British, the Spanish ships were interwoven with French vessels in the line of battle. According to Villeneuve, this was done so that both glory and blame might be shared equally, but a suspicion arose that it was really to reduce the chance of one fleet deserting the other.

The Spanish admirals had requested a council of war, and on 16 October they met to discuss the situation with Villeneuve. By this time they already knew that the British fleet had increased in strength (as six ships sent to reinforce the blockade had arrived some days earlier), and news had reached Cadiz that the legendary Nelson was now commander-in-chief. It was not a pleasant meeting. The Spanish felt that it would be stupid to sail with a weak fleet under Villeneuve, a commander they thought incompetent to fight a superior fleet, purely for the sake of the foreign tyrant Napoleon, but they dared not put this into words. In fact, Villeneuve's only major success had been seven years earlier, when he had saved two warships and two frigates by leading them away from the Battle of the Nile before Nelson's fleet could destroy them. That battle had lost the French their naval supremacy in the Mediterranean, and from then until his foray to the West Indies, Villeneuve had achieved nothing of note. The French themselves were divided over what action to take, and a heated argument ensued. Eventually a document was agreed upon, and the minutes of the meeting were witnessed and signed by all those present. In effect, they decided to wait for a more favourable time to sail – in direct disobedience of Napoleon's orders to sail immediately for Naples.

Two days later everything changed. Villeneuve was now adamant that the fleet must sail straightaway and was frantically harassing his subordinates to complete their preparations. The Spanish and most of the French were amazed at the transformation and, at a loss to account for it, were carried along in the frenetic activity. What had actually triggered Villeneuve's change of behaviour was the arrival of news from Madrid that Vice-Admiral François-Etienne Rosily was on his way, by order of Napoleon, to take command of the fleet. After issuing a succession of orders that Villeneuve had found impossible to carry out, Napoleon now took the view that Villeneuve had repeatedly failed him and had been unnerved by the British opposition. The emperor sent him an unambiguous set of orders, but the next day changed his mind about Villeneuve's position. Hot on the heels of the courier carrying these orders, Rosily was being sent to replace Villeneuve and to ensure that Napoleon's plan was carried out: the Combined Fleet was to sail into the Mediterranean, link up with other Spanish ships and create a powerful diversion.

In danger of being superseded at any moment, Villeneuve was desperate to sail before his replacement could arrive, knowing that it was the only chance to save his career and perhaps his life. Not a cowardly man, he preferred to risk death in battle rather than the loss of his honour from the disgrace he knew Napoleon would heap on him. It has often been wrongly said that Nelson sailed into the Battle of Trafalgar seeking his own death; if any man entered the fight looking for an honourable release from his problems, it was Villeneuve.

Rosily did not arrive in time. After a week of thunderstorms, 18 October was a fine day, and Villeneuve gave orders to sail from Cadiz, but the wind was too weak and the ships could not move out until the following morning. The fleet leaving port on the morning of Saturday 19 October was immediately spotted by the British scout ships, and Nelson was alerted, as Henry Walker, a young midshipman serving in the *Bellerophon*, described in a letter to his mother in Preston, Lancashire:

> Lord Nelson took the command of our fleet on the 29th of September, and though we had, before that, no doubt of success in the event of an action, yet the presence of such a man could not but inspire every individual in the fleet with additional confidence. Everyone felt himself more than a match for any enemy . . . and as we

knew the combined fleet had positive orders to put to sea, every eye was anxiously fixed towards the shore, and every signal that was seen flying on board our repeating frigates was expected to convey the welcome intelligence. We were not long kept in this state of suspense, for about nine in the morning on the 19th October, a ship was observed firing guns and making signals for the enemy's fleet being getting under way.[15]

The patrolling British ships outside Cadiz harbour were mostly frigates. Although armed with thirty-two to forty cannons, they did not usually take an active part in pitched battles, but with their extra speed and manoeuvrability were used for scouting, carrying messages and rescuing larger warships disabled during the fighting. That morning, Midshipman Hercules Robinson on board the frigate *Euryalus* noticed that he was 'so close to Cadiz as to see the ripple of the beach and catch the morning fragrance which came out of the land'.[16] Closer inshore still was the frigate *Sirius*, and at daybreak the lookout could see topsails being set on the French and Spanish ships, which was an indication that they were preparing to sail. Immediately signal flags were hoisted on the *Sirius* to display the message: 'Enemy have their topsail yards hoisted.'[17] On board the *Euryalus* Captain Henry Blackwood, who was in charge of the frigates watching Cadiz, waited to see if this was a false alarm, but soon the *Sirius* was sending another message in the stilted code of the signal flags: 'Enemy's ships are coming out of port.'[18] In the *Euryalus* Robinson could see that 'as the sun rose . . . we saw the fleet inside [Cadiz harbour] let fall and hoist their topsails, and one after another slowly emerge from the harbour mouth'.[19]

Captain Blackwood immediately instructed the frigate *Phoebe* to sail to within signalling distance of the warship *Defence*, in order to complete the chain of ships that would carry the news to Nelson. From the *Euryalus*, where Blackwood collated the information sent by the other patrolling ships, messages were passed to the *Phoebe*, then relayed to the *Defence*, which in turn passed them to the *Agamemnon*. The *Agamemnon* repeated these messages to the *Colossus*, which then passed them to the *Mars*. Stationed 50 miles out from Cadiz, Nelson's fleet finally received the news from the *Mars*, which could only just be seen. The first signal was spotted by First Lieutenant William Pryce Cumby on board the *Bellerophon*: 'The *Mars* at this time was so far from us that her topgallant masts alone were visible above the horizon; consequently the distance was so great for the discovering of the *colours* of the flags that Captain Cooke said he was unwilling to repeat a signal of so much importance unless he could clearly distinguish the flags himself, which on looking through his glass he declared himself unable to do.'[20] The *Mars*, receiving no acknowledgement of the signal, realised that it could not be read and substituted the equivalent 'distance signal'. This was a clearer but more cumbersome set of flags and shapes that were used when the usual signals were unintelligible because the distance was too great or because the wind was blowing the flags at an awkward angle. Now justified in his identification, Cumby was at last given permission to repeat the message, but before he could do so, Nelson's flagship, the *Victory*, actually acknowledged the signal sent by the *Mars*. The *Bellerophon* therefore missed the honour of being the ship that passed the momentous news to the commander-in-chief, much to the irritation of Cumby, who grumbled: 'I had the mortification to be disappointed in my anxious wish that the *Bellerophon* should be the first to repeat such delightful intelligence to the Admiral.'[21] The message reached Nelson at half past nine in the morning, nearly two hours after Blackwood had sent it.

Nelson reacted to the news immediately, and the *Victory* displayed signal flags for 'General chase, south-east'. Quite literally, the chase was now on, for the British fleet had to catch the French and Spanish ships before they could either escape out to sea or retreat back into port. The wind was very light, but Nelson could only guess what conditions might be like 50 miles away at Cadiz. With a time delay of at least one and a half hours each way for every message, it would be a minimum of three hours before he received a reply to any query, by which time the situation could have changed dramatically. In the absence of fast communications, he had to deduce the likely course of the enemy ships. Making the assumption that they would be sailing for the Straits of Gibraltar to escape into the Mediterranean, he ordered the fleet south-east – if this decision was wrong, he would have sent the British fleet in the wrong direction. In the event he was right, but it would still take the main body of Nelson's ships two days to catch up with the Combined French and Spanish Fleet, during which time the British frigates dogged their every move in case Villeneuve should escape again.

For the thousands of men in the ships of the British fleet, anxiety at the thought of an imminent battle was tempered by excitement, because it brought the possibility of promotion for the officers, while everyone had the chance of prize money, which would be shared out among the men of the ship or ships that captured the prize. For everyone, too, a battle brought relief from the deadening monotony of month after month of patrol and blockade, as well as the possibility of time ashore afterwards. On board the *Neptune*, William Badcock summed up the mood: 'All hearts towards evening beat with joyful anxiety for the next day, which we hoped would crown our anxious blockade labours with a successful battle.'[22]

A few hours after ordering Villeneuve's fleet to be chased, Nelson wrote his last letter to Emma Hamilton, which was left open on his desk in his cabin in the *Victory* and was delivered to Emma after his death by Captain Hardy. The letter read:

Victory, October 19th, 1805, Noon, Cadiz, E.S.E., 16 Leagues

My dearest beloved Emma, the dear friend of my bosom. The signal has been made that the Enemy's Combined Fleet are coming out of Port. We have very little wind, so that I have no hopes of seeing them before to-morrow. May the God of Battles crown my endeavours with success; at all events, I will take care that my name shall ever be most dear to you and Horatia, both of whom I love as much as my own life. And as my last writing before the battle will be to you, so I hope in God that I shall live to finish my letter after the Battle. May Heaven bless you prays your

Nelson & Bronte*[23]

At the same time, Nelson wrote a letter to Horatia (now four and a half years old), in which he acknowledged that he was her father:

Victory, October 19th, 1805

My dearest Angel,

I was made happy by the pleasure of receiving your letter of September 19th, and I rejoice to hear that you are so very good a girl, and love my dear Lady Hamilton, who most dearly loves you. Give her a kiss for me. The Combined Fleets of the Enemy are now reported to be coming out of Cadiz; and therefore I answer your letter, my dearest Horatia, to mark to you that you are ever uppermost in my thoughts. I shall be sure of your prayers for my safety, conquest, and speedy return to dear Merton, and our dearest good Lady Hamilton. Be a good girl, mind what Miss Connor says to you [Ann Connor was one of several women who acted as governess to Horatia]. Receive, my dearest Horatia, the affectionate parental blessings of your Father,

Nelson & Bronte[24]

*The name Bronte used by Nelson (who usually omitted the accent over the e) was derived from the fact that he was made Duke of Brontë in Sicily by King Ferdinand of the Two Sicilies as a reward for his services during the evacuation and subsequent recapture of Naples after it was taken over by revolutionaries sympathetic to France. Patrick Brontë, the father of the novelists the Brontë sisters, changed his name from Brunty as a tribute to Nelson.

All through Saturday 19th and Sunday 20th, the British frigates tracked the Combined French and Spanish Fleet as it headed south-east, while the rest of the British fleet struggled to intercept. Nelson found time to add a few lines to his letter to Emma, explaining the situation:

October 20th. In the morning, we were close to the Mouth of the Straits [of Gibraltar], but the wind had not come far enough to the Westward to allow the Combined Fleets to weather the Shoals off Trafalgar; but they were counted as far as forty Sail of Ships of War, which I suppose to be thirty-four of the Line, and six Frigates. A group of them was seen off the Lighthouse of Cadiz this morning, but it blows so very fresh and thick weather, that I rather believe they will go into the Harbour before night. May God Almighty give us success over these fellows, and enable us to get a Peace.[25]

Sometime after receiving this letter, Emma wrote on it: 'Oh, miserable, wretched Emma, Oh, glorious and happy Nelson.'[26]

Villeneuve realised it was unlikely that battle could be avoided, and he also predicted how the British led by Nelson would attack, writing in the final instructions to his commanders before the battle:

The enemy will not content themselves in forming a line of battle parallel to ours and in engaging us in an artillery duel, whose success often belongs to the most skilful, but always to the more fortunate; they will seek to surround our rearguard, in crossing our line and in concentrating on those of our vessels that they will have cut off [from our main force] with groups of theirs in order to surround them and crush them. In that case, it is more from his own courage and his love of glory that a commanding captain should take counsel, rather than from the signals of the Admiral who, perhaps himself engaged in the battle and surrounded by smoke, no longer has the means of making any [signals].[27]

At this last minute, Villeneuve was stating that individual commanders should act on their own initiative once a mêlée had developed. This principle lay at the very core of the 'Nelson Touch', and Nelson had patiently instilled the idea in his own commanders during many tactical discussions in the days before the battle. He allowed and, indeed, expected his subordinates to use their own initiative, at the same time reducing the fleet's dependence on uncertain methods of communication. Villeneuve, by contrast, had included the idea almost as an afterthought in his final set of orders. Although he knew his enemy and was not a particularly incompetent commander, he found it impossible to meet or deflect the unrealistic demands of Napoleon and was all too well aware of the shortcomings of his own fleet. In an ironic echo of Nelson's own advice to his captains, Villeneuve emphasised that success or failure would depend on the performance of each individual ship: 'Every commanding captain who is not under fire will not be at his post; the captain of any ship who is not as close to the enemy as the ship next ahead or next astern will not be at his post, and a signal to recall him to his post will be a stain on his honour.'[28]

Yet even as the Combined Fleet left its safe haven and was first sighted by the British, the glass was dropping and a heavy sea swell was building in the Atlantic and sweeping in from the west. A storm was brewing. If Villeneuve had waited just a little longer, it would have hampered the British and might have allowed him to slip through their fingers. In reality, he knew that there was virtually no chance of avoiding the blockade and escaping into the Mediterranean – for him, the confrontation off Cape Trafalgar seemed inevitable. He decided to risk everything in battle rather than sink back into the obscurity from which he had so recently been promoted.

FOUR

INTO ACTION

> This manner of entering the battle was contrary to the most simple wisdom, because the English ships coming at us one by one, at a very slow speed, should each have succumbed in turn to the superior forces which faced them, but Nelson knew his own squadron, and ours.
>
> Report of Lieutenant Pierre-Guillaume Gicquel des Touches of the *Intrépide*[1]

On the day of the battle, dawn broke just before six in the morning. It was barely a month after the equinox, but the days were now noticeably shortening; there were less than eleven hours of daylight ahead. For sixteen-year-old Midshipman Hercules Robinson from Dublin, serving in the *Euryalus*, a 36-gun frigate that had shadowed the French and Spanish fleet throughout the night, it was 'the beautiful misty sun-shiny morning of the 21st October; the sea like a mill-pond, but with an ominous ground-swell rolling in from the Atlantic'.[2] He noted that the dawn brought 'the delight of us all at the idea of a wearisome blockade about to terminate with a fair stand up fight, of which we well knew the result'.[3] This was the decisive battle for which the British had been longing, and which now seemed inescapable. The two fleets were in sight of each other, only 9 miles apart, with the British fleet upwind from their enemy and slowly closing the gap.

On board the British ship *Neptune*, William Badcock recorded the scene at first light: 'It was my morning watch; I was midshipman of the forecastle, and at the first dawn of day a forest of strange masts was seen to leeward. I ran aft and informed the officer of the watch. The captain was on deck in a moment, and ere it was well light, the signals were flying through the fleet to bear up and form the order of sailing in two columns. The wind had moderated considerably in the night, but still our fleet, which consisted of twenty-seven sail of the line, four frigates, a schooner, and cutter, was much scattered.'[4] As Badcock watched from the *Neptune*, 'All sail was set, and the different ships tried to form the line in two divisions [columns], but the lightness of the wind, and the distance of the sternmost from the van, prevented anything like speed in the manoeuvre; in short, the line never was properly formed, for the brave and gallant chiefs of each division [Nelson and Collingwood] were too eager to get into battle to wait for this.'[5]

The British fleet was to the west-north-west of the Combined Fleet, and the lookouts had a clear view of the masts of the French and Spanish ships silhouetted against the pre-dawn light on the horizon, but it was some minutes before anyone in the French and Spanish fleet became aware of their enemy. Villeneuve immediately gave the signal instructing the Combined Fleet to form a line of battle. This was not an order for the ships simply to form a line, but rather to sort themselves out into a predetermined order: seven leading ships (the van) under the control of the Spanish Vice-Admiral Ignacio María de Álava y Navarrete; seven ships in the centre controlled by Villeneuve; seven ships in the rear controlled by the French Rear-Admiral Pierre-Etienne-René-Marie Dumanoir Le Pelley;

and a separate reserve group of twelve ships directed by the Spanish Admiral Frederico Carlos Gravina.

In the best of conditions this was a complicated manoeuvre, but with a light west-north-west wind and an increasing sea swell, which made the ships roll heavily from side to side, the process of each ship finding its proper place in the line proved painfully slow. Here, Nelson's foresight gained the British an advantage. He had told his commanders that in the approach to the enemy, their order of sailing would be the order of battle, so that in comparison with the French and Spanish fleet, the British ships were arranged in battle formation from the start. They also had the advantage that such an arrangement tended to sort each line by the sailing abilities of individual ships, with the faster ones to the front and the slower ones to the rear, so that the speed of the slower ships did not dictate the progress of the whole line, as happened with the Combined Fleet.

The Combined Fleet was at this point sailing approximately south-eastwards from Cadiz, towards the Straits of Gibraltar, with the British fleet bearing down on them from their southern side and already formed into two loose columns for the battle, which put pressure on the French and Spanish seamen to complete their manoeuvres and prepare to meet the British attack. Villeneuve was very conscious that he had been caught in an awkward position. He was only about 12 miles off Cape Trafalgar,* and although the wind was light, there were dangerous shoals between his fleet and the Cape. His ships were taking far too much time to form the line of battle, and every minute took them further from the safety of Cadiz and gave the British a better chance of cutting off their retreat.

After nearly two hours, the Combined Fleet was still in disorder. At eight o'clock Villeneuve gave the signal for the fleet to

*A name definitely derived from an Arabic word, but whose precise meaning remains uncertain.

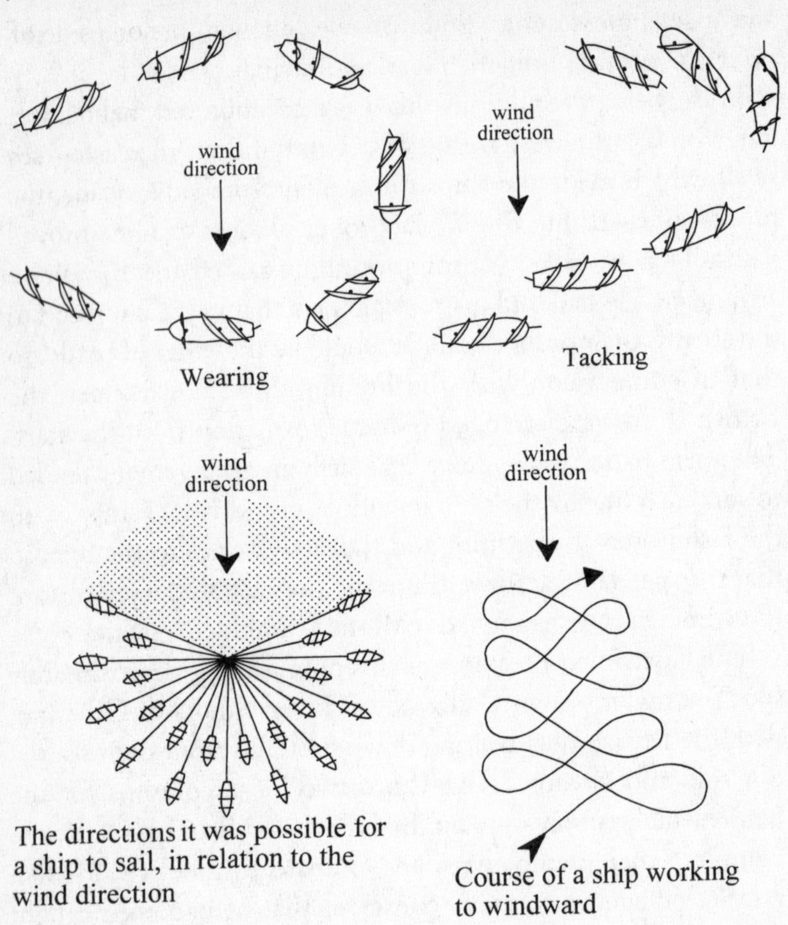

Diagrams of various aspects of sailing vessels and their limited manoeuvrability due to their dependence on wind power

wear together and form a line of battle on the opposite tack in inverse order. 'Wearing' a ship was a manoeuvre that turned the ship to sail in almost the opposite direction – 'on the opposite tack'. It was a slow method of turning and needed a wider turning circle than the alternative method of tacking, but it was safer and required less skill and co-ordination on the part of the crew. In wearing, the stern of the ship passed through the direction of the wind, so that instead of blowing on one side of the ship, it now blew on the other side, allowing the ship to steer in another direction. Because the direction from which the wind was blowing was always to the rear of the sails, it was relatively easy to maintain the ship's momentum. The quicker, but more skilful, method was called 'tacking', which turned the bow of the ship through the direction of the wind. This meant that there came a point during the turn when the wind blew directly against the front of the sails, tending to stop the ship. If enough momentum had not already been built up, or if the crew were not quick enough in hauling the sails round in order to pick up the wind in the back of the sails again, the ship would be stopped or even blown backwards.

Villeneuve's signal meant that each ship should turn immediately so that the line was reversed; the last ship would now become the leading ship, and the line would be sailing back towards Cadiz, rather than away from it. Despite choosing the safest option for turning the fleet, confusion resulted, and Captain Don Cosmé Churruca of the *San Juan Nepomuceno*, who was one of the best Spanish officers, turned to his second-in-command with the comment: 'The fleet is doomed. The French Admiral does not understand his business. He has compromised us all.'[6] The ships took different amounts of time to complete the manoeuvre, with the result that initially they began to sail too close to each other. As captains tried to compensate for this, gaps appeared in the line, and some ships were still trying to find their correct station in a line that was becoming chaotic.

From a distance, it was not at all clear what was happening, and the British believed the Combined Fleet was trying to 'wear in succession' – that is, each ship was turning one after the other, starting with the leading ship. For their manoeuvre to be mistaken for wearing in succession is an indication of the disorder afflicting the French and Spanish ships. In the last entry in his private diary, Nelson wrote:

At daylight saw the enemy's Combined Fleet from East to E.S.E.; bore away; made the signal for Order of Sailing, and to Prepare for Battle; the enemy with their heads to the Southward: at seven [actually eight o'clock] the enemy wearing in succession. May the Great God, whom I worship, grant to my Country, and for the benefit of Europe in general, a great and glorious Victory; and may no misconduct in any one tarnish it; and may humanity after Victory be the predominant feature in the British Fleet. For myself, individually, I commit my life to Him who made me, and may his blessing light upon my endeavours for serving my Country faithfully. To Him I resign myself and the just cause which is entrusted to me to defend. Amen. Amen. Amen.[7]

By ten o'clock, the gap between the two opposing fleets had been narrowed to about 5 miles, and the British were pressing hard to intercept their enemy. They held the attacking position, with the wind behind them, and were sailing towards the Combined Fleet that was gradually forming into a line of battle while heading back in the general direction of Cadiz. Villeneuve now gave a signal for 'the leading ship to keep the wind, to be followed by a successive movement of other vessels',[8] probably with the intention of speeding up the formation of the battle line. The reserve group of French and Spanish ships, commanded by Admiral Gravina, was sailing in a line upwind (to the west) of the main body of the Combined Fleet, and to the south-east of the oncoming British ships. This line was the 'Squadron of Observation' – a strategic reserve of ships that could see what was happening along the line of battle and sail quickly before the wind to help any part of the line that needed reinforcements. Whether Gravina misunderstood the intention of Villeneuve's signal or whether he acted on his own initiative is unclear, but instead of keeping to the west of the battle line of the Combined Fleet, he now led his ships to join the line at the rear.

All thirty-three French and Spanish battleships were now ranged in a long ragged line, without any outlying battleships to provide rapid support wherever it was needed, an error that could only aid the British. Within this line, where some ships were sailing faster than others, there was a danger of their running into each other; to avoid this, some of the faster ships had to steer a more easterly course to run partly alongside a slower ship in front. From some of the British ships it looked as if the Combined Fleet was forming two parallel lines of battle, and some eyewitnesses described it as such.

The twenty-seven battleships of Nelson's fleet continued directly towards the evolving battle line in two straggling columns that were still sorting themselves out. The *Neptune* tried to take the lead from the *Victory*, but Nelson would not stand for that, as Midshipman William Badcock on board the *Neptune* witnessed:

> The old *Neptune*, which was never a good sailor, took it into her head to sail better that morning than I ever remember to have seen her do before. About ten o'clock we got close to the *Victory*, and Captain Fremantle had intended to pass her and break the enemy's line, but poor Lord Nelson himself hailed us from the stern-walk of the *Victory*, and said, '*Neptune*, take in your studding-sails* and drop astern; I shall break the line myself.' A signal was then made for the *Temeraire* (98) [98 guns] to take her station between us and the *Victory*, which consequently made us the third ship in the van of his lordship's column. At this period the enemy were forming their double line in the shape of a crescent. It was a beautiful sight when their line was completed: their broadsides turned towards us, showing their iron teeth.[9]

Because the wind was so light, the manoeuvrings of the two fleets were happening in slow motion. It had already taken four hours to close the gap by 4 miles, so there was plenty of time for the British ships to get ready for the battle ahead. From the

*Extra sails rigged on the outer edges of the normal sails so as to maximise speed in light winds.

moment that the marine drummer was given the order to summon all hands to their battle stations, it could take as little as twenty minutes for a warship to be fully prepared. Since this procedure involved dousing the galley fires, with the prospect of no more hot food until after the battle, it was a delicate judgement on the part of the commanding officers as to when to give the order. Once it was given, the result was a complete transformation of the ship. On the upper decks tightly rolled hammocks were lashed into netting above the sides of the ship to provide added protection from bullets. Above them, slack netting was rigged as an obstacle to boarders, and more nets were spread to try to prevent falling debris and bodies from injuring men on the deck. Chains were used to secure the yards to prevent them falling if the rigging that held them to the masts was shot away. (The yards were the horizontal spars of wood to which the sails were fixed, and so keeping them in place also helped prevent the sails from falling.) Apart from the obvious danger of falling masts and yards, the sails and rigging posed a hazard to those below. On a second-rate ship of 74 guns, the total weight of masts and yards was around 70 tons, the rigging, pulley blocks and other fittings weighed nearly 50 tons, and the sails alone weighed around 8 tons. When part of a mast was shot away in battle, the falling wood, sails and rigging could have a combined weight of many tons – lethal to those beneath it, and a heavy, tangled obstacle that had to be cleared from the deck.

On those decks above the water-line, the bulkheads were removed along with any canvas screen partitions, which meant that the captain and officers lost their cabins for the duration of the battle. Any other obstructions, such as furniture and the chests, boxes and bags that contained the belongings of the seamen, were also removed, either to the hold or into boats towed behind the ship. If time was pressing, anything at all that was in the way was jettisoned. On board the *Ajax*, for instance, among the many items simply thrown overboard in the haste to prepare for the battle were six wooden ladders, ten cot frames (from the officers' hanging beds, which were known as 'cots'), a grinding stone, a set of screens that had formed the walls of cabins, four sails and 30 feet of the copper pipe that was used as the funnel for the galley stove. It was not uncommon for some seaman's or even officer's possessions to be thrown overboard in the rush to clear the ship – if he survived the battle, he might only be left with the clothes he was wearing. Possessions could also be hung in out-of-the-way places above the deck. On board the *Tonnant*, several 'Windsor chairs forming part of the ward-room furniture were suspended by a rope passed from the main to the mizzen mast'.[10] After the battle, the surgeon Forbes Chevers kept what was left of his as a souvenir; it 'had part of its legs shot away, and another bullet had passed completely through its thick oaken seat'.[11]

Animals were removed from the ship if they were likely to escape from their pens or if they were in wooden cages, such as hen coops. Where possible, the ship's boats were lowered and loaded with the goats, sheep, chickens, pigs and even cows, and these boats were then towed behind the warships. If time was short, the animals were simply thrown overboard to fend for themselves. Animals left on board or towed behind in the boats were as liable to be wounded or killed in battle as were members of the crew – and those thrown overboard inevitably drowned.

This 'clearing for action' provided an unobstructed view for the officers commanding each gun deck, although that would not last beyond the second or third broadside, by which time the whole deck would be filled with choking smoke from the guns, gradually blackening everyone and everything. The lack of ventilation was not helped by the fact that the gap between decks was so small that even in the largest ships there were few places where the men could stand fully upright. In smaller ships the situation was even worse.

Much more important than improving visibility, the decks were cleared of anything that might produce splinters when hit by a cannon-ball, which is why the boats were lowered and hen coops removed. At a close range of 30 yards or less, even the relatively small cannon-balls from 18-pounder guns could penetrate oak planks 30 inches thick – the approximate thickness of a first-rate ship just above the water-line. When this happened, they sent a shower of splinters across a distance of over 30 yards – more than enough to injure or kill anyone in the way. During the battle, many ships would be firing at a range considerably less than 30 yards, sometimes touching the side of the enemy ship with the muzzles of the guns, and it would not just be 18-pound shot that would be fired, but 24-pound and 32-pound shot. The planking of the sides of ships at the level of the gun decks was much less than 30 inches, and at close range with a high charge of gunpowder a cannon-ball would enter through one side of the ship, spraying deadly wood splinters, before it carried on across the deck and through the opposite wall of the ship, destroying anything and anyone in its path. For this reason, as the range became shorter the gunners reduced the amount of gunpowder in the cartridges to try to avoid the shot passing through both sides of the target; it would do far more damage by ricocheting around the cramped space of a gun deck in the enemy ship.

On board the larger ships were a few carronades, made by the Carron Iron Company at Falkirk in Scotland. These were powerful but short-ranged guns of varying calibres. The largest, carried only in first-rate ships, fired a 68-pound cannon-ball – the *Victory* carried two of these. Firing heavier shot with a reduced charge, which made the cannon-ball travel more slowly, the carronades punched larger holes in the sides of ships, spreading hundreds more splinters across the enemy decks. At close range, these guns were devastating – they were nicknamed 'smashers' – and were one tangible tactical advantage that the larger British battleships had over their French and Spanish counterparts.

Below the water-line, where the dangers of shot penetrating the hull were far less, the bulkheads were more substantial and were left in place during the battle. Before the fighting started, any young children on board were taken down to the orlop deck or to the hold for safety. The boys (other than any who were midshipmen and therefore officers) and the women often worked as 'powder monkeys' during the battle, carrying charges of gunpowder from the magazines to the gun decks, although some women acted as assistants to the surgeons.

It was actually against regulations for women to be aboard warships at sea, unless they were carried as passengers by invitation of the captain or were part of the small quota of soldiers' wives officially allowed to accompany them aboard troopships, but these regulations were frequently ignored. Some captains and officers had their wives living on board with them, and one or two were reprimanded for doing so, but most of the women and some of the children on board a warship were the families of the specialist warrant officers, such as the carpenter and gunner. These men were not usually paid off at the end of a voyage, like the majority of the crew, but often stayed with the ship, including the times it was in port. Because their rank was certified by an Admiralty warrant, this tied them to the ship for the lifetime of that vessel, even when it was not in service. Although they were the lowest in the hierarchy of officers, they often each had a small canvas-sided cabin about 8 feet square, which, being on a gun deck, also housed a cannon. Nevertheless, this gave them more room and more privacy than the ordinary sailors, who were only allowed a space 14 inches wide in which a hammock was slung. In reality, a little extra space was available for much of a voyage, since approximately half the sailors were on duty at any one time.

Some captains, through religious bigotry, enforced the regulations about women very strictly, but on many ships they turned a blind eye to their presence. Because officially they did not exist, these women rarely appear in records relating to British Navy ships, and almost never in the crew lists and logbooks, but it is likely that there were at least a handful of women and their children on the majority of larger warships.

Washing clothes was one way that women on board navy ships could earn a little money. Knowing the problems of washing with sea-water, women often resorted to the illicit use of fresh water for washing, which sometimes came to the attention of the authorities. Less than ten years before Trafalgar, Rear-Admiral Sir John Jervis, who was in charge of the Mediterranean Fleet at that time, felt compelled to issue a warning:

Memorandum H.M.S. *Victory*, at sea, 14th July, 1796

There being reason to apprehend that a number of women have been clandestinely brought from England in several ships, more particularly in those which have arrived in the Mediterranean in the last and present year, the respective Captains are required by the Admiral [Jervis] to admonish those ladies upon the waste of water, and other disorders committed by them, and to make known to all, that on the first proof of water being obtained for washing from the scuttle-butt [drinking water cask] or otherwise, under false pretences, in any ship, every woman in the fleet who has not been admitted under the authority of the Admiralty or the Commander in chief will be shipped for England by the first convoy, and the officers [of the fleet] are strictly enjoined to watch vigilantly their behaviour, and to see that no waste or improper consumption of water happen in the future.[12]

The order did not have much effect, since a year later Jervis felt compelled to issue another threat: 'Observing, as I do with the deepest concern, the great deficiency of water in several ships of the squadron, which cannot have happened without waste by collusion, and the service of our King and Country requiring that the blockade of Cadiz, on which depends a speedy and honourable peace, should be continued, an event impracticable without the strictest economy in the expenditure of water, it will become my indispensable duty to land all the women in the squadron at Gibraltar, unless this alarming evil is immediately corrected.'[13] The reply to this from Nelson, also at that time a rear-admiral and serving under Jervis, sheds light not only on Nelson's benign attitude to his crews, but also on the number of women aboard the ships: 'My dear Sir, The history of women was brought forward I remember in the Channel Fleet last war. I know not if your ship was an exception, but I will venture to say, not an Honourable [captain] but had plenty of them, and they always will do as they please. Orders are not for them – at least, I never yet knew one who obeyed.'[14]

On first-, second- and third-rate ships, a triangular area at the stern of the ship was partitioned off from the rest of the hold and was known as the 'lady's hole'. The name derived not from the women on board, but from the fact that the seaman in charge of the gunroom (the junior officer's mess) was called 'the lady of the gunroom'. He used this awkward space for storage, but in some instances it may also have been used to keep non-combatants such as women and children out of the way during battles, because it was thought to be the safest place in the ship.

During the Battle of Trafalgar, women were probably working as powder monkeys on board many of the ships, but their names are unknown because their presence was not officially recognised. The only female powder monkey of the Napoleonic Wars about which any amount of reliable information has survived is Ann Hopping, who later remarried to become Ann Perriam (also known as Nancy Perriam). She was the wife of a gunner's mate and, although not at Trafalgar, she took part in several other major battles. Her life at sea was summarised in an article in *The Times* in 1863:

There can be but very few spectators, and still fewer actors, left of the events in which Mrs. Ann Perriam, took a busy part. Aged 93 [in 1863], she was a married woman in the year 1795, a date anterior to that which some great-grandfathers among us first saw the light of day. At that time her first husband, Edward Hopping, was serving as a seaman on board Her Majesty's Ship *Crescent*, commanded by Captain Sir James Saumarez. Upon the ship putting into Plymouth for repairs, after a long cruise on the coast of France, she proceeded thither to meet her husband, and, at his request, was allowed to accompany him to sea. At that time, a certain number of women of good character were allowed to sail with their husbands. Upon Sir James Saumarez's subsequent removal to the *Orion*, Hopping and his wife followed him. Mrs. Perriam served on board the latter ship five years, and during that time witnessed and bore her part in, besides many minor engagements, the following great naval battles:- at L'Orient, on the 23rd of June, 1795; off Cape St. Vincent, on the 14th of February, 1797; and at the glorious battle of the Nile, won by Nelson on the 1st of August, 1798. Mrs. Perriam's occupation while in action lay with the gunners and magazine men, among whom she worked preparing flannel cartridges for the great guns. Her recollection of the share which she took in these great events is still vivid, and at the advanced age of 93, the veteran heroine can recall with pride and interest incidents of the hard-won fights in which she discharged a man's – more than a woman's – part. It may be mentioned that her brother fought also in the same ship, with 12 other young men from Exmouth [in Devon], her native place, who volunteered especially for service under Sir James Saumarez, one of whom died an Admiral. Of this number Ann Perriam is the sole survivor. Indeed, the number of those who fought at St. Vincent or the Nile can be very few now. After the loss of her second husband, Ann Perriam maintained herself honestly by selling fish in the streets of Exmouth. In her 80th year increasing debility compelled her to discontinue that occupation. Having outlived all her friends and children, and possessing but scanty means in her declining years, she is not surrounded by those comforts which her busy life and strange services should have secured her.[15]

Ann Perriam died in 1865 at the age of ninety-six and was buried in the churchyard at Littleham, just outside Exmouth.

Although the exact location of her grave has been lost, it is thought to be near to that of Nelson's wife, Frances. So much information has survived about Ann because she had a semi-official position as seamstress, making and mending clothes for Captain Sir James Saumarez who commanded the *Crescent* and later the *Orion*. There is even a picture of her that was published in the *Illustrated London News* in 1863 – the only picture in existence of a woman known to have worked as a powder monkey aboard ship during the Napoleonic Wars. Most women who were on board the British ships at Trafalgar remain nameless, but Jane Townshend later applied to the Admiralty for the Naval General Service Medal for her part in the battle, although she was refused. Several other women later claimed to have been at Trafalgar, and it is likely that they were present, but their claims are, as yet, unverified.

During battles, women also helped the surgeon on the orlop deck, which was immediately above the hold. In earlier ships, the orlop was not a continuous deck, but overlapped the hold like a mezzanine floor. It was once thought that the name 'orlop' was a corruption of the word 'overlap', but it is in fact derived from a similar Old German word meaning 'the deck above the hold'. The part of the orlop deck towards the stern was known as the cockpit, where the midshipmen normally lived, taking their meals at a large table. In the preparations for battle, this table was taken over by the surgeon as an operating table, but if there was no table, the midshipmen's sea chests were lashed together and covered with tarpaulin instead. The surrounding deck was also covered with tarpaulin or old canvas sails, on which the wounded men would be laid, in order to reduce the amount of blood soaking into the deck timbers. As on the gun decks, sand was also spread to help the surgeon keep his footing while he operated, once the floor had become greasy with spilt blood. Buckets of sand were placed to catch the blood flow during operations, but these could never be totally effective.

The surgical instruments, all the personal property of the surgeon, were sharpened and laid out ready for use. A surgeon might have several sets of instruments but, since the causes of infection were unknown, there was no concept of hygiene. Although he might change to a fresh knife or saw because the one he was using was blunt, the instruments were not sterilised and at best they might be quickly wiped on the surgeon's blood-soaked apron to remove any pieces of flesh that were clogging the blade. A small portable stove was set up to heat water to warm the amputation knives, a requirement introduced by Nelson. When his right arm was amputated after being hit by a musket-ball at Tenerife in 1797, he found that the cutting of his flesh with a cold knife was more excruciating than the sawing of his bone, and so he ordered that amputation knives should in future be warmed before use.

Near the operating table, buckets were lined up to collect the amputated flesh and bone, and the surgeon gave final instructions to his assistants, who were known as 'loblolly boys'. It is not certain where this name originated, but one of the words for the gruel served to sailors in the sickbay was 'loblolly', from which the men who served it to the sick sailors may have taken their name. In addition to his assistants, the surgeon might be given a few seamen to help bring the wounded down to the cockpit, but during a battle these men were often wounded themselves or were diverted to other tasks. The surgeon's assistants then had to help the wounded from the upper decks in the odd moments when they could be spared from more urgent duties, such as holding down patients while the surgeon carried out operations. The purser was also usually stationed in the cockpit, doing what he could to help the wounded men.

Being below the water-line, the orlop deck had no gunports or windows. It was dark, stifling and claustrophobic. Lanterns and candles were carefully set to provide as much light on the operating table as possible, but they did little to disperse the surrounding gloom. By contrast, the preparations for battle on the dark gun decks involved the opening of all the gunport lids, where the decks now blazed with light. The guns were loaded and run out to their firing positions, the racks of cannon-balls were filled up, and fire buckets were placed ready for use. The gun decks themselves were wetted and sprinkled with sand to provide a better footing for the gun crews when the surface became slippery with blood. A lantern was positioned by each gun to provide some light once the fighting began and the decks filled up with black smoke from the guns. Containers of fresh water were placed by the masts for the men to drink and to clear the taste of the gunpowder fumes from their parched throats.

Marines, meanwhile, were stationed by doorways and hatches to prevent men from deserting their posts in the midst of battle, and on the upper decks the rest of the marines hurried to positions along the sides of the ship, ready to provide musket fire and to repel boarders. The marksmen among them climbed to vantage points, such as the mast-heads*, from where they could fire on to the decks of enemy ships. All this furious activity of preparing a warship for battle was carried out against the background of the routine work needed to sail the ship and manoeuvre it into position. With sailors running in all directions to accomplish their allotted tasks, the potential for confusion was limitless, but eventually everything was done and everyone was at their proper station – the calm before the conflict now began.

Before the end of the medieval period, it had been common practice to commandeer merchant ships in time of war, filling them with troops who did the actual fighting, but this had given way to navies of specially designed warships that carried cannons. It was this sudden leap in technology that set European navies on the road to Trafalgar. From being merely a

*The top of a lower section of a mast, to which the next (higher) section is joined.

transport for soldiers, warships became weapons in their own right, capable of destroying other ships or land-based fortifications without any troops leaving the ship. Naval strategy rapidly changed from an emphasis on ramming and boarding to the concerted use of artillery to disable an enemy before they were close enough to ram or board. In the two centuries leading up to Trafalgar, this was the situation that had prevailed. By trial and error, the design of ships and cannons gradually improved, as did the quality of gunpowder, and at the time of the battle, wooden sailing warships had reached the very peak of technical perfection, with the expertise of the best seamen leaving little room for more advances. Trafalgar was to be the last major pitched battle between two large fleets of sailing wooden warships. Within sixty years the first iron battleship was launched, causing a race between European navies for more powerful guns to destroy enemy battleships and ever-thicker armour to protect them. In the meantime the development of steam engines broke the reliance on wind power and changed naval tactics for ever. With the advent of iron and steam, the advantage lay firmly with the fleet that had the best technology; no longer could the sheer skill, professionalism and endurance of the ships' crews, as at Trafalgar, produce a decisive victory in the face of unfavourable odds.

Although the ships were cleared for action in great haste, because this was how the crews had practised the manoeuvre in order to be ready for any emergency, with hindsight the sailors found they had plenty of time – perhaps too much time. William Robinson, a seaman on board the *Revenge* who had volunteered five months before the battle, later remembered:

As the enemy was thus driven to risk a battle, they exhibited a specimen of their naval tactics by forming themselves into a crescent, or half-moon, waiting for our approach; which did not take place until ten minutes of twelve o'clock, so that there was nearly six hours to prepare for the battle, while we glided down to them under the influence of a gentle breeze . . . During this time each ship was making the usual preparations, such as breaking away the captain and officers' cabins, and sending all the lumber below – the doctors, parson, purser and loblolly men were also busy, getting the medicine chests and bandages out; and sails prepared for the wounded to be placed on, that they might be dressed in rotation, as they were taken down to the after cockpit. In such a bustling, and it may be said, trying as well as serious time, it is curious to notice the different dispositions of the British sailor. Some would be offering a guinea for a glass of grog, whilst others were making a sort of mutual verbal will, such as, if one of Johnny Crapeau's [actually 'Crapaud', the French word for 'toad' and the seamen's slang for a Frenchman] shots . . . knocks my head off, you will take all my effects; and if you are killed, and I am not, why, I will have yours, and this is generally agreed to. During this momentous preparation, the human mind had ample time for meditation and conjecture, for it was evident that the fate of England rested on this battle.[16]

In every ship the officers did their tour of the decks, both to ensure that everything was ready and also to encourage the crews. On board the *Victory*, 'Lord Nelson went round the decks and said "My noble lads, this will be a glorious day for England who ever lives to see it. I shan't be satisfied with 12 ships this day as I took at the Nile." '[17] Then, with the galley fires being doused, the sailor John Brown recalled that the crew were 'piped to dinner and ate a bit of raw pork and half a pint of wine'.[18] In the *Ajax*, where there had been such a hurry to clear for action that many things had been thrown overboard, a deceptive hush spread through the ship, as Lieutenant Samuel Ellis of the marines observed:

I was sent below with orders, and was much struck with the preparations made by the blue-jackets [sailors], the majority of whom were stripped to the waist; a handkerchief was bound tightly round their heads and over their ears, to deaden the noise of the cannon, many men being deaf for days after an action. The men were variously occupied: some were sharpening their cutlasses, others polishing the guns, as though an inspection were about to take place instead of a mortal combat, whilst three or four, as if in mere bravado, were dancing a hornpipe; but all seemed deeply anxious to come to close quarters with the enemy. Occasionally they would look out of the [gun] ports, and speculate as to the various ships of the enemy, many of which had been on former occasions engaged by our vessels.[19]

In the magazine, the gunner and his mates filled and stacked gunpowder cartridges, working cautiously and wearing felt slippers to reduce the risk of static electricity causing an explosion. The floors of the magazines were usually also covered with felt or a rough kind of woollen cloth called 'fearnought'. Larger ships had a main magazine where cartridges were filled with gunpowder, as well as subsidiary magazines where filled cartridges could be stored ready for use. The number of magazines depended on the size of ship. They were usually built below the water-line, and slightly below the level of the deck, so that there were a few steps down from the deck to the door. This enabled the magazines to be flooded with water from specially built tanks in an emergency, a precaution against fire taking hold elsewhere in the ship. If the fire reached inside, the magazine would explode long before it could be flooded. The magazines were almost completely wrapped in one-inch canvas or felt that could be soaked with water to keep out sparks, and the entrance was hung with woollen tassels that brushed against anyone passing through and discharged static electricity harmlessly outside the room. Such precautions had been developed by trial and error, since scientists at this time still did not fully understand electricity. When the ship was cleared for action, a screen of wet blankets was also set up outside the entrance to keep out sparks, and often these had a hole through which cartridges could be passed and then carried to the guns.

The gunner and his mates had to empty their pockets of any steel or metal that could create a spark before entering the magazine, where all the tools for handling or measuring the gunpowder were made of wood, lead or brass. Having been sealed off from the rest of the ship as much as possible, the magazines were hot, stuffy and dark. No lantern could be allowed inside, and the magazines were lit by light cupboards or light rooms. Lanterns were placed in these cupboards so that the light from them shone through thick glass windows into the magazine and avoided the risk of explosion. The walls of the magazine were painted white to maximise the effect of what little illumination was available, but even so the light was very dim and did little to dispel the darkness. After about 1780 most walls of the lower decks were painted white; before that time they had often been painted red.

Cartridges were made by filling flannel bags with the correct amount of gunpowder. Originally paper bags had been used for this purpose, but it was found that the back end of the paper did not burn when the gun was fired, so that successive firings of a cannon built up a wad of paper in the barrel which was difficult to remove and eventually blocked the touch-hole. This hole at the rear end of the cannon led through the barrel to the cartridge and was filled with a trickle of gunpowder that acted as a fuse to fire the gun – any paper blocking the hole prevented the cannon from firing.

The weight of a cartridge depended on the size of the gun in which it was to be used, as well as the range of the target and the quality of the gunpowder. A rough rule of thumb was a quarter to a third of the weight of the shot for maximum range, so that a cartridge for a cannon firing shot weighing 24 pounds would contain 6–8 pounds of gunpowder, and a 32-pounder would need 8–10 pounds of gunpowder. For shorter ranges, the amount of gunpowder was reduced, so that in a battle fought at close range, a cartridge for a 24-pounder cannon might have less than 5 pounds of gunpowder.

Each gun was kept supplied with cartridges by a powder monkey. This was an unskilled job that merely required stamina and endurance in handling the heavy cartridges. The skilled members of the gun crews were sailors, but marines could be assigned to them to make up numbers. The role of powder monkey was given to the least useful member of each gun crew (often a marine) as well as to boys and women. The powder monkeys carried the cartridges in bulky tubular containers of wood, metal or sometimes leather, with close-fitting lids to keep out any sparks and reduce the risk of explosion. These containers could be 20 inches tall and carried one or more cartridges, depending on the size of the charge. How the powder monkeys were organised seems to have varied from ship to ship, but on the larger ships, having each powder monkey running with single cartridges from magazine to gun and back again would have added greatly to the confusion and would probably have caused congestion outside the magazines. It is therefore likely that the powder monkeys worked in teams, passing the cartridges from hand to hand. Such supply chains would have been easily disrupted by enemy fire, since a break in the chain when two or three powder monkeys were wounded or killed could stop several guns firing for a time. On smaller ships, with fewer guns and shorter distances to be covered, each individual gun may well have had its own powder monkey running to and from the magazine.

Preparations on board the French and Spanish ships followed broadly the same course as on the British ships, because everything was largely dictated by the layout of the ships themselves, which was very similar in all three navies. In his fictional account of the battle based on interviews with Spanish survivors, Benito Pérez Galdós gave a vivid vignette of preparations in the *Santísima Trinidad* through the eyes of a new recruit:

Early in the morning the decks were cleared for action, and when all was ready for serving the guns and working the ship, I heard some one say: 'The sand – bring the sand.' . . . A number of sailors were posted on the ladders from the hatchway to the hold and between decks, and in this way were hauling up sacks of sand. Each man handed one to the man next to him and so it was passed on without much labour. A great quantity of sacks were thus brought up from hand to hand, and to my great astonishment they were emptied out on the upper deck, the poop, and the forecastle, the sand being spread about so as to cover all the planking; and the same thing was done between decks. My curiosity prompted me to ask the boy who stood next to me what this was for. 'For the blood,' he said very coolly. 'For the blood!' I exclaimed, unable to repress a shudder.[20]

The twenty-seven battleships of the British fleet were facing thirty-three French and Spanish ones that carried a total of at least 2640 guns – approximately 490 more than the British. Although in raw figures the British fleet was outnumbered, no one on either side had any illusions about the relative strengths of the two fleets. What counted was not the number of guns, but how rapidly they could be fired. From the point of view of a gun crew, once the gun was fired they had to race to prepare the gun for firing again, but incoming fire could disrupt this preparation in many ways. Members of the gun crew could be killed or put out of action by shot, splinters or shrapnel; the supply of powder to the guns could be interrupted; the gun could be damaged or dismounted (the barrel knocked off the wooden gun carriage); and the tools to work the gun destroyed. If the gun crews could achieve a sufficiently rapid rate of fire, they could effectively prevent the enemy gun crews from completing the loading and firing cycle, or even drive the gun crews from their guns and so stop an opposing ship from firing back. British sailors had months – often years – of experience in firing guns under all manner of sailing conditions, and so even those French and Spanish crews who had not been confined to harbour by the blockade were nowhere near as efficient as the

British. In terms of manpower, too, the British were outnumbered since the French and Spanish ships were carrying about thirty thousand men (almost double the seventeen thousand manning the British ships). However, many of these were soldiers who were useful only in providing small-arms fire and in boarding to capture ships – generally they got in the way of the sailors and hindered the efficiency of the gun crews.

As was happening in the British ships on the morning of the Battle of Trafalgar, once the French and Spanish ships were cleared for action, their commanders carried out inspections and tried to encourage the men. In the French ship *Fougueux*, 'Captain Baudoin made an inspection of all the batteries and the different posts; the whole crew showed the greatest desire to fight, and it was to shouts of "Long live the Emperor! Long live our Captain!" that he was received in all parts of his vessel.'[21] Fifes and drums continued to play throughout the Combined Fleet, and in each Spanish ship a large wooden cross, blessed by the chaplains on board, was hauled up to a place of prominence, hanging from a boom. The devoutly Catholic Spanish fleet and the nominally atheist French fleet were about to clash with their Protestant enemy, but this was one battle where the conflicting beliefs of the opponents played less than a minor role, since the attitudes of the people of the three nations were more determined by politics than religion.

The British hated the French, did not want to be ruled by Napoleon and were suspicious of their revolutionary politics, but there was much less animosity towards the Spanish, who had recently been allies. Nevertheless, although they recognised the courage of the Spanish seamen, the British had no great respect for their abilities. The French hated the British and distrusted and despised the Spanish. In turn, many of the Spanish felt that their country had been drawn unwillingly into the war and had been forced to support the wrong side. Even among the admirals there was a great deal of suspicion and distrust, with the Spanish worried about the motives of the French, who in turn questioned the loyalty of the Spanish. The French and Spanish fleets might be combined, but they were anything but united. It was yet another factor in favour of the British.

At ten minutes to eleven Nelson sent another signal informing his commanders: 'I intend to push through the end of the enemy's line to prevent them getting into Cadiz.'[22] It had been five hours since the opposing fleets had first sighted each other, but still they were not within range and would not be so for another hour. As the gap was narrowed with oppressive slowness, the ships were creeping towards Cadiz as well as towards each other, and Nelson was worried that even at this late stage Villeneuve's fleet might escape back into port. As he assessed the situation, he was conscious of the rising sea swell from further out in the Atlantic, which was a sign of approaching bad weather. Fearing a storm and knowing the nearness of the dangerous shoals along the Spanish coast, he was already making plans for beyond the battle. Ten minutes later he sent another signal to all the ships: 'Prepare to anchor after the close of day.'[23]

Another half-hour crawled by as the crews, with little else to do, studied the opposing fleet and tried to judge when they would come within range. Nelson now prepared to send his final signals before the battle began. His ships were using a combination of an old signal code invented by Admiral Lord Howe in 1790 and a new code invented by Sir Home Popham in 1800, which had been expanded three years later. The signals were transmitted by flags that each represented a number, used in conjunction with other flags that modified the message or indicated which code was being used. The message was read by checking what each number represented in a code book. Sir Home Popham's improvements allowed numbers to stand for the root of a word and relied on those reading the message to supply the ending. The number 49, for example, meant 'agree', leaving the reader to judge whether 'agree', 'agreed', 'agreeing', 'agreement', or 'agreeable' made the most sense in the context. Words outside the set vocabulary could be spelled out using a system where each number represented a letter of the alphabet, but this was time-consuming and might result in a message having to be sent in several instalments because it was not possible to fly all the required flags at once.

At twenty minutes to midday, Nelson asked Lieutenant John Pasco, who was in charge of signals in the *Victory*, to send the message that became the most famous signal in naval history. The message was altered before sending, and shortly after the battle a historian claimed that the original message was: '*Nelson* confides [has confidence] that every man will do his duty.' This is an attractive suggestion, since it would be in character for Nelson to send such a personal message, knowing the effect it would have on the crews who respected and loved him. However, the only eyewitness in support of this suggestion was Lieutenant George Brown, who was assisting with the signals, and he was not wholly certain what changes had been made nor who had suggested them. Lieutenant Pasco himself had a different story:

His lordship came to me on the poop, and after ordering certain signals to be made, about a quarter to noon, he said, 'Mr. Pasco, I wish to say to the Fleet, ENGLAND CONFIDES THAT EVERY MAN WILL DO HIS DUTY;' and he added, 'you must be quick, for I have one more to make, which is for Close Action.' I replied, 'If your Lordship will permit me to substitute the *expects* for *confides* the signal will soon be completed, because the word *expects* is in the vocabulary, and *confides* must be spelt.' His Lordship replied, in haste, and with seeming satisfaction, 'That will do, Pasco, make it directly.' When it had been answered by a few Ships in the Van, he ordered me to make the signal for Close Action, and to *keep it up*: accordingly I hoisted No. 16 [meaning 'Close Action'] at the top-gallant mast-head, and there it remained until [it was] shot away.[24]

FIVE

FIRST SHOT

'I shall go at them at once, if I can, about one-third of their line from their leading ship.' He then said, 'What do you think of it?' Such a question I felt required consideration. I paused. Seeing it, he said, 'but I'll tell you what *I* think of it. I think it will surprise and confound the Enemy. They won't know what I am about. It will bring forward a pell-mell battle, and that is what I want.'

Nelson explaining his tactics to Captain Richard Keats during the last time that Nelson was in England[1]*

Gradually the French and Spanish ships had formed their long line of battle that ran roughly north–south, stretching over 4 miles along the Spanish Atlantic coastline between Cape Trafalgar to the south and Cadiz to the north. The British fleet, divided into two relatively parallel columns, was heading north-eastwards at right angles to the enemy line, but the different speeds of their ships began to have an effect. Both columns were strung out, and the slower ships were struggling to keep

*Keats's ship was due to be part of the fleet off Cadiz, but was delayed and missed the battle.

up. The *Africa*, which had been separated from the British fleet overnight, was sailing south to join the rest of the ships, but still had a long way to go and was almost parallel to the leading ships of the Combined Fleet. As the British columns closed in, the heavy sea swell and light almost westerly winds pushed the centre of the enemy line further away from them, so that the French and Spanish ships ended up sailing in an arc.

With all sails set to catch every breath of the light winds, but still only crawling along, slower than a man could swim, the first British ship that would eventually come within range was the *Royal Sovereign* with Collingwood on board. This was leading the south (or lee) column of ships towards the enemy line, while the north (or weather) column was led by the *Victory*, Nelson's flagship. These two columns would try to slice through the French and Spanish ships, but for the moment there was little to be done except continue to wait until the line was cut.

This was a nerve-twisting time for the crews on both sides. With the ships already cleared for battle, they could only watch and wait as the enemy grew steadily closer. Soon, even those without telescopes could make out individual figures in the rigging and on the decks of the oncoming ships, then the colour of their clothes became visible, followed by flames from cannons and muskets as the marksmen and gunners tested the range. Most of those on the gun decks could do little of practical worth except adjust the bandages and handkerchiefs tied round their heads and over their ears against the noise. If they survived the slaughter, the thunder of their guns would leave them deaf for days afterwards, and some men would never regain their hearing. The bravado and excitement of the earlier preparations were now replaced by a tense silence. The immense importance of the Battle of Trafalgar and subsequent events led eyewitnesses to concentrate on the battle and its aftermath, rather than the final minutes before it began, and none gives such an accurate impression of this period of anxious unreal calm before a conflict as Charles Pemberton, in his description of a battle at Madeira in 1808:

Everything was now in order, fires extinguished, fearnaught screens round the hatchways for passing powder from the magazines. Shot racks drawn from under their peaceable coverings, and arrayed ready for their work; guns cast loose, crowbars for pointing the guns lying at hand on the deck; tompions [plugs in the barrels of cannons to keep out water] out all ready for a game of thunder . . . there was something in the orderly stillness of lying there for half an hour with all this preparation for destruction and death, that made me think there might be worse places than the counting house after all [Pemberton had run away from being apprenticed as a clerk]. There was no noise, no laugh, no show of hilarity, yet was there some interjectorial jesting bandied about, which called up grim smiles, but no laugh, no cachination, no chirruping. Men, shirtless, with handkerchiefs bandaged tightly round their loins and heads, stood with naked brawny arms folded on their hairy and heaving chests, looking pale and stern, but still hushed; or glancing with a hot eye through the [gun]ports. All these matters were to me ugly, dismal, throat pinching; I felt a difficulty in swallowing.[2]

Only five minutes had passed since Nelson had sent his famous signal that had roused a ragged cheer through the British fleet as ship after ship managed to read the flags, but the sentiment met a mixed reception. In the *Bellerophon*, Midshipman Henry Walker noted that 'this was received on board our ship with three cheers, and a general shout of "No fear of that" ',[3] but in the *Ajax*, Lieutenant Ellis of the marines felt a more personal message from Nelson would have been better appreciated:

I was desired to inform those on the main-deck of the Admiral's signal. Upon acquainting one of the quartermasters of the order, he assembled the men with 'Avast there, lads, come and hear the

Admiral's words.' When the men were mustered, I delivered, with becoming dignity, the sentence – rather anticipating that the effect on the men would be to awe them by its grandeur. Jack [the sailors], however, did not appreciate it, for there were murmurs from some, whilst others in an audible whisper, muttered, 'Do our duty! Of course we'll do our duty! I've always done mine, haven't you? Let us come alongside of 'em and we'll soon show whether we'll do our duty.' Still, the men cheered vociferously – more, I believe, from love and admiration of their Admiral and leader than from a full appreciation of this well-known signal.[4]

The tension was mounting on both sides. To break the monotony, at about a quarter to midday, Villeneuve gave the order to open fire as soon as the enemy was in range. This was met with cheering and shouts of 'Long live the Emperor!' throughout the Combined Fleet. In his flagship the *Bucentaure*,* Villeneuve paraded the Imperial Eagle around the deck, followed by his officers. Captain Jean-Jacques Magendie later stated in his official report: 'It is impossible . . . to show more enthusiasm or desire to fight than was done and proved by all the officers, sailors and soldiers of the *Bucentaure*, each one of them putting their hands between those of the Admiral and renewing their oath, and upon the eagle entrusted to us by the Emperor, to fight to the very last, and shouts of "Long live the Emperor!, Long live Admiral Villeneuve!" were once again repeated . . . each of us resumed our post; the Eagle was put on display at the foot of the mainmast.'[5] All the French ships flew the red, white and blue tricolour flag, and the Spanish hoisted the red and gold flag of Spain, as well as their wooden crosses. Each French ship also had a lozenge-shaped escutcheon on the stern, painted with

*The French version of the traditional name given to the state barge used by the Doge of Venice, ultimately derived from the Italian *buzino d'oro*, meaning golden barge.

three horizontal lines of blue, white and red as a recognition mark. Throughout the Combined Fleet, as in the British one, extra national flags were lashed to various masts in case the main flags were shot away, since striking the flag, the naval term for lowering it, was a signal of surrender.

The flags flown by the British ships were the new Union Jacks and White Ensigns. Ireland had been officially united with Great Britain to form the United Kingdom just four years previously, and the red X-shaped cross of St Patrick had been incorporated in the national flag. Technically, the flag should only be called a 'jack' when it is in the form of a small flag flown from a jackstaff at the bow of a ship and should otherwise be known as a 'Union Flag', but the incorrect usage has become universal. The White Ensign had the red cross of St George and, in the upper corner, the design of the Union Jack. Looking back from the *Neptune*, which was hard on the heels of the *Victory* and the *Temeraire* in the northerly column, Midshipman Badcock could see throughout the fleet that, 'union-jacks and ensigns were made fast to the fore and fore-topmast-stays, as well as to the mizzen-rigging, besides one at the peak, in order that we might not mistake each other in the smoke, and to show the enemy our determination to conquer . . . our two lines were better formed, but still there existed long gaps in Vice-Admiral Collingwood's division. Lord Nelson's van was strong: three three-deckers (*Victory*, *Temeraire*, and *Neptune*), and four seventy-four's . . . the bands playing "God save the King", "Rule Britannia", and "Britons strike home".'[6] In those ships where the captain had invested his own money on musical instruments to form a band, stirring patriotic tunes were now ringing out to help relieve the tension.

Since the ships in both fleets were very similar in form, through the fog of battle it was easy to mistake a friend for an enemy. Most of the British ships were painted with the 'Nelson chequer', so that the black hull had a yellow band at the level of each row of gunports. The lids of the gunports were also painted black so that when they were closed it produced a chequered effect. Many of the British ships had been freshly painted since Nelson had arrived three weeks ago, as admiring captains spent their own money on a new colour scheme for their ship to emulate that of their new commander-in-chief. Although Nelson did not order this repainting, he was rightly concerned about the problems of 'friendly fire', and William Robinson in the *Revenge* said later: 'Often during the battle we could not see for the smoke, whether we were firing at a foe or a friend, and as to hearing, the noise of the guns had so completely made us deaf, that we were obliged to look only to the motions [hand-signals] that were made.'[7]

With his customary attention to detail, Nelson had earlier ordered the *Africa* and the *Belleisle* (meaning Beautiful Island) to paint the hoops* on their masts yellow, because they were the only ships in the fleet with black hoops, the colour normally used by the French. It would be one more way of telling friend from foe – until the masts themselves were shot away. Now, as the fleets began to approach each other, Midshipman Badcock in the *Neptune* managed to make out the paintwork on the enemy ships: 'Some of them were painted like ourselves – with double yellow sides; some with a broad single red or yellow streak; others all black; and the noble *Santissima Trinidada* (138), with four distinct lines of red, with a white ribbon between them, made her seem to be a superb man-of-war, which indeed she was. Her appearance was imposing; her head splendidly ornamented with a colossal group of figures, painted white, representing the Holy Trinity, from which she took her name.'[8]

Five more minutes had dragged by, after nearly six hours of waiting, as the British fleet strained sails and rigging to catch up

*Reinforcing iron bands around those lower masts built as a composite of several tree trunks rather than a single piece of wood.

with the French and Spanish fleet, each final minute seeming to go on for ever. The nerves of the sailors were so stretched that the battle, when it started, seemed at first to be a relief. Again Charles Pemberton, talking of the later battle at Madeira, described the grimness of the last few minutes of peace before the fighting:

If we had gone at it at once, without this chilling prelude, why I dare say I should have known very little about that thing which we call fear . . . 'Stand to your guns!' at last came in a peal through the perfect stillness from the captain's speaking trumpet; it swept fore and aft with such clear force, as though it had been spoken within a foot of the ear, and seemed to dash down into the holds, and penetrate to the very keel. The instant change this produced was magical. 'Take good aim! Ready the first *platoon*!' Ready? Aye, every one *was* ready; stern, fixed, rigid in soul – pliant, elastic in body. 'Captains of the guns, watch the falling of the first shot, and point accordingly.' Not a word was replied; even the everlasting 'ay, ay, sir' was refused now.[9]

Particularly on the lower decks, which would become unbearably hot once the guns began to fire, many sailors wore only trousers as they went into battle. A few men still wore the old-fashioned petticoat breeches, which were very wide breeches reaching to around the knee, often worn with a canvas kilt over the top and stockings on the feet. Many men in the gun crews took off their shoes so that their bare feet might make a better grip on the deck, and in any case many seamen only wore shoes for climbing the rigging or as part of their 'best' clothes for going on leave. There was no uniform for seamen, but generally they wore shirts and short jackets with a large handkerchief tied around the neck. Long pigtails and a variety of hats were fashionable among seamen, but marked them out as sailors when they were ashore. A pigtail might be greased or tarred to waterproof it, and some men without long hair added to the length of their pigtail with strands from old rope.

The uniform of the marines was a red jacket with tails, white waistcoat and breeches, with a white belt or cross-belts over the shoulders. Naval officers had a blue jacket with tails, similar white waistcoats and breeches, and generally also a cocked hat, which was worn with the two pointed ends over the shoulders, rather than the later fore-and-aft style when the hat was positioned at right angles to the line of the shoulders. The wearing of beards was against regulations, but many seamen had large sideburns. Although the officers were clean shaven, on some ships the men only shaved once a week in order to look smart for Sunday. Some men had pierced ears and wore gold earrings, partly due to the superstition that this practice improved the wearer's sight. Tattoos were also very popular, descriptions of which were usually entered in the muster book with other details such as colour of hair and eyes in order to help identify the sailors if they deserted.

Like the men, many of the officers paid close attention to their dress as they went into battle. Some put on clean clothes, probably for luck, while others, perhaps through experience, felt that dirty clothes delayed wounds from healing – even though the causes of infection were still unknown at this time. Collingwood, on board the *Royal Sovereign*, which was leading the southern column, had more practical reasons for choosing particular clothes: 'meeting Lieutenant Clavell, [Collingwood] advised him to pull off his boots. "You had better," he said, "put on silk stockings, as I have done: for if one should get a shot in the leg, they would be so much more manageable for the surgeon."'[10] It was good advice, as both men were to be injured in the battle, and Collingwood was to suffer a bad leg wound from a wood splinter.

At noon Nelson ordered his final signal to the fleet to be hoisted: 'Engage the enemy more closely,'[11] and the signal flags were left in position as a reminder to the British fleet. Nelson's work was now done. He had devised the plan of attack and set it in motion. Against the traditions of all three navies involved in the battle, he had deliberately made provision for each and every one of his commanders to act on their own initiative once the fighting had begun – unlike the French and Spanish captains who would be hampered by the custom of waiting for specific directions from their commander-in-chief. As the flags of Nelson's last signal unfurled, the first British ship finally came into range, and the French ship *Fougueux* let loose the first broadside of thirty-seven guns at the *Royal Sovereign*, followed soon after by the fifty-six-gun broadside of the Spanish ship *Santa Ana*. The *Royal Sovereign*, carrying one hundred guns on three decks, with a broadside of fifty guns, was one of the largest ships in the British fleet but, being neither fast nor elegant under sail, was nicknamed the 'West Country Waggon'. Now the closest vessel to the enemy line of battle, the *Royal Sovereign* would soon come under fire from other ships as well, but with only a very small number of guns that could be moved to fire forwards, there was little chance of returning fire until the enemy line was actually reached. The line was still about 1000 yards away, and with the light wind it would take another ten minutes to sail that distance – ten minutes that would drag by for the crew as increasingly they had to suffer casualties from cannon-balls, splinters, shrapnel and, eventually, musket shot, before they could fire any guns in return.

On board the British ships everyone was aware that when they did reach the enemy line, they would have to fire rapid broadsides to do as much damage as possible in the first few minutes. The very best that gun crews could achieve was one co-ordinated broadside a minute, but individual gun crews were doing well if they could fire three rounds in five minutes or less. This rapid rate of fire could not be maintained for very long, since each gun weighed around three tons and required a crew of at least six men to handle it. When the ship was firing from only one side, crews from the opposite side crossed over to help, doubling the number of each gun crew, but despite this, as the men grew tired and their numbers were depleted by casualties, the rate of fire slackened. Even when this was not the case, rapid firing made the guns too hot for safety, and they had to be allowed to cool before the next cartridge was loaded.

If the French and Spanish gunnery had been as fast and as accurate at long range as the British, the *Royal Sovereign* would have been hit by more than sixteen broadsides from the *Fougueux* and the *Santa Ana* in the time that it took to reach the line – over seven hundred cannon-balls, enough to completely destroy the ship – but the *Fougueux* and the *Santa Ana* produced nothing like such devastating fire-power. Even though other ships besides the *Fougueux* and the *Santa Ana* opened fire as the *Royal Sovereign* approached the Combined Fleet, only a relatively small proportion of the shots hit their target. The

Plan of the two opposing fleets at noon on 21 October 1805 (after Taylor 1950). The British fleet is approaching the Combined French and Spanish fleet from the south-west. The ships are numbered as follows:

1 *Victory*
2 *Temeraire*
3 *Neptune*
4 *Leviathan*
5 *Conqueror*
6 *Britannia*
7 *Ajax*
8 *Agamemnon*
9 *Orion*
10 *Prince*
11 *Minotaur*
12 *Spartiate*
13 *Royal Sovereign*
14 *Belleisle*
15 *Mars*
16 *Tonnant*
17 *Bellerophon*
18 *Colossus*
19 *Achilles*
20 *Revenge*
21 *Defiance*
22 *Dreadnought*
23 *Swiftsure*
24 *Polyphemus*
25 *Thunderer*
26 *Defence*
27 *Africa*
28 *Euryalus*
29 *Scipion*
30 *Intrépide*
31 *Formidable*
32 *Mont-Blanc*
33 *Duguay-Trouin*
34 *Héros*
35 *Bucentaure*
36 *Redoutable*
37 *Neptune*
38 *Indomptable*
39 *Fougueux*
40 *Pluton*
41 *Algésiras*
42 *Aigle*
43 *Swiftsure*
44 *Argonaute*
45 *Achille*
46 *Berwick*
47 *Neptuno*
48 *Rayo*
49 *San Francisco de Asís*
50 *San Agustín*
51 *Santísima Trinidad*
52 *San Justo*
53 *San Leandro*
54 *Santa Ana*
55 *Bahama*
56 *Montañes*
57 *Argonauta*
58 *San Ildefonso*
59 *Principe de Asturias*
60 *San Juan Nepomuceno*
61 *Monarca*

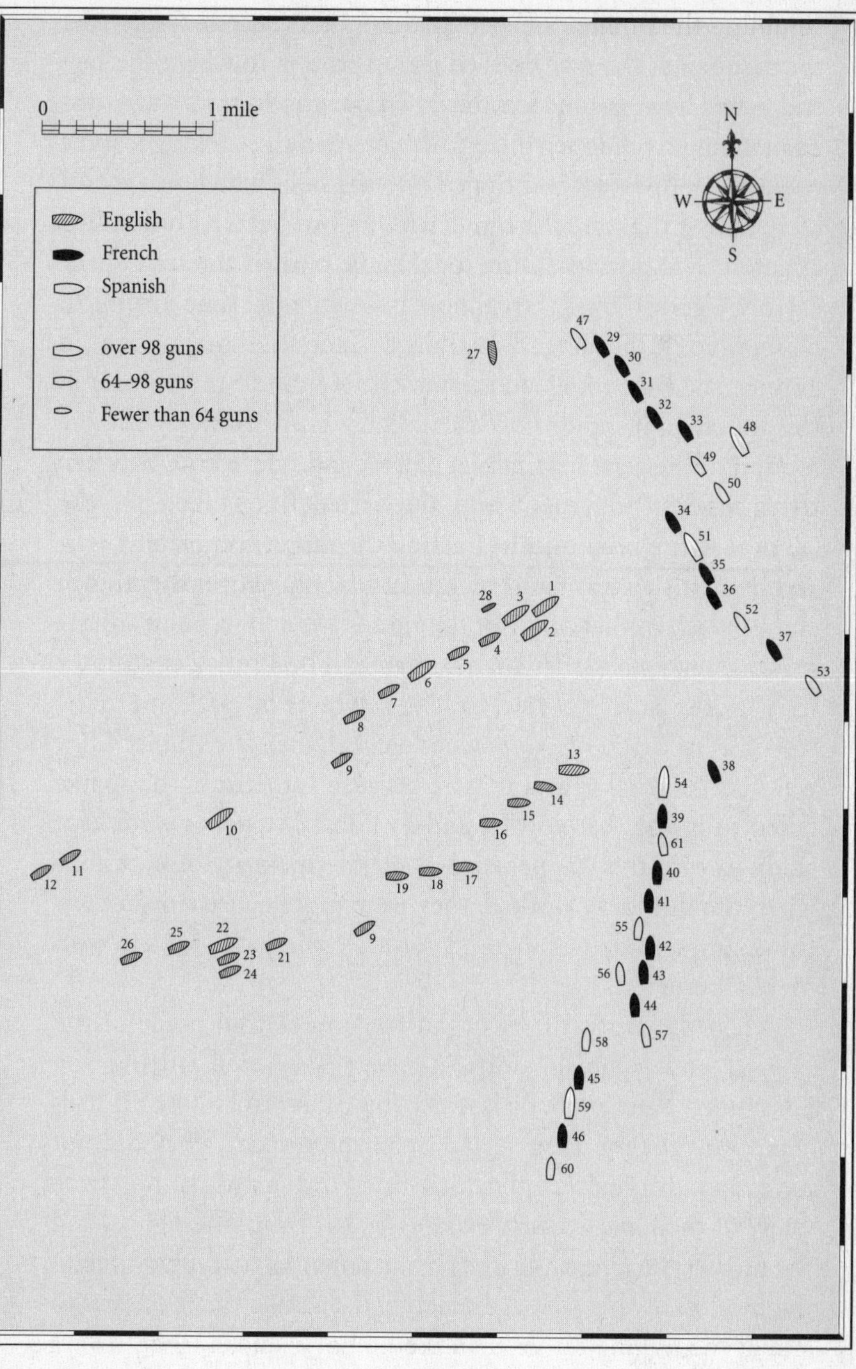

0
1 mile
N
W
E
S
English
French
Spanish
over 98 guns
64–98 guns
Fewer than 64 guns

cannons, which were muzzle loading, had a narrow hole (the touch-hole) at the rear that led right through to where the cartridge had been rammed home down the gun barrel. A wire was pushed down the touch-hole to break open the cartridge, and a trickle of gunpowder was tipped into the hole, which was set off by touching the top of the hole with a slow-burning fuse called a match. The powder in the touch-hole burned through to the cartridge and so fired the cannon, but while the time for this to happen could be judged fairly accurately by an experienced gunner, the time in which the match set light to the powder in the touch-hole tended to vary. On a ship rolling with the motion of the waves, a fraction of a second's difference between the gunner's judgement and the actual time taken for the cannon to fire often meant missing the target completely.

The British ships had a technical advantage over the French and Spanish in that many of their guns were fired using a flintlock mechanism rather than a match. The flintlocks struck a flint against a piece of steel to send a shower of sparks on to the top of a little pan of gunpowder against the touch-hole. They were not as reliable as a match, because sometimes the sparks failed to ignite the powder, and so lighted matches were kept ready in case this happened, but on the majority of occasions when the flintlocks worked, they were more consistent in their firing times, so that a practised gunner could judge his aim with more accuracy.

When the British fleet began to come within range of the French and Spanish ships, a heavy sea swell hitting the Combined Fleet more or less side-on caused the most difficult conditions for the French and Spanish gunners. They did not have the advantage of flintlock-firing mechanisms, nor were many of them particularly experienced at firing their guns, and the further the range, the greater the potential inaccuracy due to the motion of the ship. A French and Spanish tradition was to aim at the rigging rather than the hull of a ship, a tactic always

Rear-Admiral Lord Nelson wearing all his decorations and honours. At this point in his life he was effectively blind in his right eye, but the visible damage to that eye was slight, and he is correctly portrayed without an eye-patch (which he never wore)

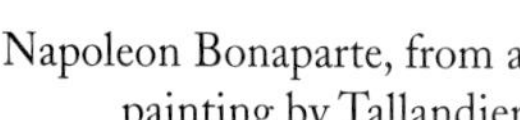

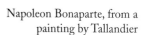

Napoleon Bonaparte, from a painting by Tallandier

A near-contemporary print showing sailors drinking grog below deck, sitting around a table hung from ropes from the deck above

Ann Hopping (later known as Ann or Nancy Perriam), who worked on board several naval ships, shown here at the age of ninety-three. This is the only known picture of a woman who was on board British Navy ships around the time of Trafalgar

Vice-Admiral Villeneuve, who was in overall command of the Combined French and Spanish Fleet. Engraved by Gilles Louis Chretien after a portrait by Edme Quenedey

Vice-Admiral Lord Collingwood, who took over command of the British fleet after the death of Nelson. Collingwood maintained the blockade of Spanish and French Mediterranean ports after the battle and was destined never to set foot in Britain again. He died at sea in 1810, having hardly been ashore since before the battle

Spanish Admiral Frederico Carlos Gravina, captain of the *Principe de Asturias* and Villeneuve's second in command during the battle

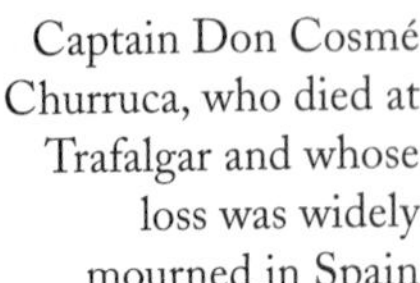

Captain Don Cosmé Churruca, who died at Trafalgar and whose loss was widely mourned in Spain

Nelson and his officers sitting around a table on board the *Victory* just before the battle discussing the plan of attack, including the 'Nelson Touch'. Coloured etching by James Godby after an original by William Marshall, and published on the day of Nelson's funeral

Nelson giving instructions for his famous signal before the battle – 'England expects that every man will do his duty' – at twenty minutes to midday on board the *Victory*. Painting by Thomas Davidson

The Combined French and Spanish Fleet blockaded in Cadiz harbour just before the battle. Watercolour from the journal of William Pringle Green, a Master's Mate of the *Conqueror*

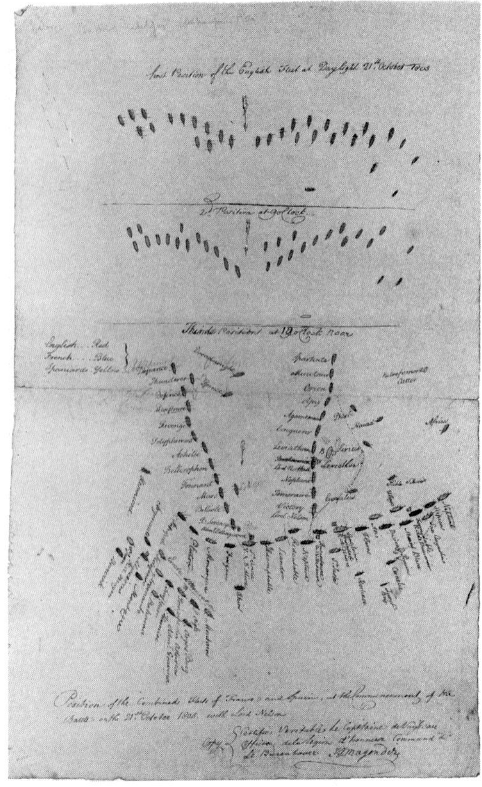

A plan of the approach of the British ships and also the very start of the battle. A copy of an original drawing by Captain Magendie of the *Bucentaure*

A cartoon of a British seaman, moments before the battle, praying that the enemy's shot will be shared like the prize money, with most going to the officers

Captain Jean-Jacques-Etienne Lucas, whose ship the *Redoutable* had the best-trained sharpshooters, one of whom killed Nelson

Dr William Beatty, the surgeon on board the *Victory*, who attended the mortally wounded Nelson. Portrait by Arthur William Devis

Nelson's column (on the left) and Collingwood's column (far right) approach the line of French and Spanish ships at about midday. Aquatint engraving by Thomas Sutherland after an original by Thomas Whitcombe

A view from the French and Spanish side as their line of ships is cut by Nelson's flagship, the *Victory*, at a quarter to one. In the foreground, left to right, are the *Redoutable*, *Victory*, *Bucentaure* and *Santísima Trinidad*. Painting by Nicholas Pocock

adopted by pirates whose purpose was to disable ships by bringing down masts and rigging to prevent the escape of their prey without endangering valuable cargoes. The problem with this strategy was that even using special shot, such as two cannon-balls joined by a chain or an iron bar, it was more difficult to hit the masts and rigging of a ship than it was to hit the hull. While this tradition was not universally observed by all the ships of the Combined Fleet, and certainly not once they were at point-blank range, some ships do seem to have followed this tactic at the beginning of the battle; in the heavy swell the gunners were lucky if any of their shots damaged the rigging of the advancing British ships. Ironically, since the British fleet could not bring more than a handful of guns to bear on the French and Spanish ships until they had sailed within very close range, the advantage of having flintlocks on their guns was initially of no use to them.

By modern standards of engineering, the barrels of cannons were not precision made, but there was much more of a problem with the shot. However near to perfectly spherical a cannon-ball had been when first cast, after it had been stored in the hold of a ship, rusted and had the rust chipped off with a hammer, it was not always a close fit in the cannons. A loose fit meant a loss of range and power, but care was taken that the shot would not jam in the barrel, causing the gun to explode. To avoid this, each shot was carefully measured with a ring that was the same size as the bore of the gun in which it was to be used. An 18-pound shot was approximately 5.29 inches in diameter, a 24-pound shot was about 5.8 inches, and a 32-pound shot was around 6.4 inches.

As well as solid iron cannon-balls, various kinds of special shot were used to damage rigging. Grape-shot (a collection of iron balls in a canvas bag) and canister (a tin filled with musket-balls) were used against groups of men, such as potential boarders, since the containers disintegrated on firing, allowing the bullets to spread out; grape-shot and canister effectively turned cannons into giant shotguns. Below decks, the thunderous noise of the shot smashing its way through the sides of the ship, and the repeated impacts that made the ship itself tremble, were enough to produce terror in anyone who had a few seconds to spare to dwell on what was happening. On the upper decks, open to the air, there was a different sort of horror. The cannon-balls fired from the cannons did not travel at high velocity; if the eye managed to spot them, their flight through the air was just slow enough to be visible. They made a peculiar hissing and screaming noise, while musket-balls produced a more muted version that was sometimes described as like the sound of canvas being torn.

Until they experienced a sea battle, it is unlikely that the sailors, French, Spanish or British, understood the risks they ran. Cannon fire was devastating, because cannon-balls would slice through any number of men who were in the way. When a cannon-ball struck anything made of wood, the resulting splinters were just as deadly as musket-balls; when the amount of gunpowder was reduced in an attempt to make the shot pass through only one side of the ship, it could ricochet around the enclosed space below deck to cause maximum damage. Anyone hit by a shot from a cannon rarely survived, although there were cases where men were brushed by a ball as it passed. Because the ball was so hot it often set their clothes alight and invariably left them with a severe burn. Occasionally the shock of the pressure wave from a passing ball could instantly kill a man, without leaving a mark on his body. During the battle, Midshipman George Westphal in the *Victory* was talking to Thomas Whipple, Captain Hardy's clerk, when a cannon-ball just missed them. Westphal was unhurt, although he was later wounded and lay near Nelson in the cockpit, but Whipple was killed instantly, without even a bruise on his body, to the amazement of all who witnessed it.

As the *Royal Sovereign* inched towards the enemy line minute by minute, more ships began firing as the range narrowed. Soon not just the *Santa Ana* and the *Fougueux*, but also the *San Justo*, the *San Leandro*, the *Monarca*, the *Pluton* and the *Algésiras* were all firing. In order to create a smokescreen that might drift with the wind in front of the ship to spoil the aim of the enemy gunners, the *Royal Sovereign* fired a few guns on the starboard side, which at that moment was the downwind side. Then, in both the *Royal Sovereign* and the *Belleisle* (which, being immediately behind, was now also under heavy fire), the officers were ordered to ensure that the men lay down at their posts and were kept quiet to minimise casualties and panic.

On both sides of the conflict, the officers had a paternalistic attitude to their men and a strong sense of honour and chivalry. They led from the front, winning the respect of their crews by an exaggerated disregard for their own safety. While the sailors had no qualms about seeking any available protection from the lethal showers of enemy missiles, it was a point of honour among the officers that they paced the deck proudly in all their finery and did not flinch at the bullets and cannon-balls ricocheting around them. This obsessive adherence to duty had been taken to extremes at the Battle of the Nile, where Admiral Brueys, commanding the French fleet, had both his legs shot away and was wounded in the head. He was propped in an armchair on the quarterdeck and continued to issue orders until he was hit by another cannon-ball that almost cut him in two. He still insisted on staying on deck, but died shortly afterwards. Further down the French line of battle at the Nile, in another ship, Admiral Dupetit-Thouars lost first one arm, then another, and finally one of his legs was shot off. He ordered his men to prop him up in a bran barrel, and he too continued to command his ship until the last.

On board the *Royal Sovereign*, as the enemy line drew closer, fifty-two-year-old Captain Edward Rotheram, the son of a physician from Newcastle-on-Tyne, was pacing the deck in an unusually large cocked hat. When someone suggested it made a tempting target for snipers and he should take it off or change it, he replied: 'Let me alone. I've always fought in a cocked-hat, and I always will.'[12] From the deck of the *Victory* at the head of the northern column, which was still not in range of the French and Spanish guns, Nelson could also see clearly his old friend and rival Collingwood on board the *Royal Sovereign*, commenting admiringly, 'See how that noble fellow Collingwood carries his ship into action.'[13]

At eight minutes past midday the *Royal Sovereign* was almost at the enemy line, thirty-five minutes ahead of the *Victory*. Collingwood knew how much Nelson had wanted to lead the fleet into action and so voiced his satisfaction to the captain of the *Royal Sovereign*: 'Rotheram, what would not Nelson give to be here!'[14] The *Royal Sovereign* steered between the *Santa Ana* and the *Fougueux*; in a last attempt to close the gap, the *Santa Ana* slowed down while the *Fougueux* tried to catch up, having set extra sails to increase speed. It was too late. Only the bowsprit of the *Fougueux* covered the gap, and Collingwood ordered Rotheram to steer straight for it and break it away. To avoid this, at the very last moment the *Fougueux* slackened speed, and the *Royal Sovereign* sailed slowly through the gap at eleven minutes past midday, unleashing a broadside into the stern of the *Santa Ana* from guns loaded with three shot each. It was the type of death-blow that Nelson's strategy had been designed to bring about.

SIX

SECOND STRIKE

> He was a youth of not more than twelve or thirteen years of age . . . Killed on the quarter-deck by a grape-shot, his body greatly mutilated, his entrails being driven and scattered against the larboard* side.
>
> Report of the death of a midshipman in the British ship *Revenge*[1]

The first broadside of the *Royal Sovereign* against the *Santa Ana* put fourteen guns of the Spanish ship out of action and killed or wounded many of the crew: 'El rompio todos [It smashed everything],'[2] as one of the officers on board the *Santa Ana* reportedly described the havoc that resulted. The broadside had sent over one hundred cannon-balls plus grape-shot – a total of nearly 1½ tons of scorching-hot iron – ripping its way the whole length of the gun decks of the *Santa Ana*. It said

*The term 'larboard' for the left-hand side of the ship when looking from the stern towards the bow was at this time gradually being superseded by the term 'port', and both terms were in use. Eventually the term larboard was abandoned, because it could be confused too easily with starboard, the term for the right-hand side of the ship.

much for the courage of the remaining Spanish crew that they were able to respond at all, let alone unleash a similarly fierce broadside that made the *Royal Sovereign* heel over as that ship drew alongside.

Because no detailed Spanish records from this ship have survived, the experiences of the men in the *Santa Ana* remain unknown, but the view from the *Royal Sovereign* shows it to have been a dogged and determined conflict between two evenly matched ships:

In [first] passing the *Santa Ana*, the *Royal Sovereign* gave her a broadside and a half into her stern, tearing it down, and killing and wounding 400 of her men; then, with her helm hard a-starboard, she ranged up alongside so closely that the lower yards of the two vessels were locked together. The Spanish Admiral [Don Ignacio de Álava], having seen that it was the intention of the *Royal Sovereign* to engage to leeward, had collected all his strength on the starboard; and such was the weight of the *Santa Ana*'s metal, that her broadside made the *Sovereign* heel two strakes* out of the water. Her studding-sails and halliards† were now shot away . . . In about a quarter of an hour, and before any other English ship had been enabled to take a part in the action, Captain Rotheram, whose bravery on this occasion was remarkable even among the instances of courage which the day displayed, came up to the Admiral [Collingwood], and shaking him by the hand, said, 'I congratulate you, Sir: she is slackening her fire, and must soon strike [surrender].' It was, indeed, expected on board the *Royal Sovereign*, that they would have had the gratification of capturing the Spanish Admiral in the midst of a fleet of thirty-three sail, before the arrival of another English ship, but the *Santa Ana*, though exposed to a tremendous loss from the unremitting fire of the

*The horizontal planks forming the ship's hull.

†Derived from 'haul yard', a rope used for raising or lowering parts of the rigging such as yards, spars, sails and even flags and signals.

Sovereign, and unable to do more than to return a gun at intervals, maintained the conflict in the most determined manner, relying on the assistance of the neighbouring ships, which now crowded round the English vessel, hoping, doubtless, to destroy her before she could be supported by her friends.[3]

With the muzzles of the British guns almost touching the *Santa Ana*, whose yardarms had become entangled with those of the *Royal Sovereign*, the relentless and bloody process of battering the opponent into submission began in earnest. In the *Royal Sovereign*, George Castle, a midshipman from Durham, was 'stationed at the heaviest guns in the Ship, and I stuck close to one gun and poured it into her [the *Santa Ana*], she was so close, it was impossible to miss her . . . I looked once out of our stern ports – but I saw nothing but French and Spaniards round [us] firing at us in all directions – it was shocking to see the many brave seamen mangled so, some with their heads half shot away, others with their entrails mashed lying panting on the deck, the greatest slaughter was on the quarter deck* and Poop.'[4]

The other British ships were still sailing towards the line and could do nothing but watch as the *Royal Sovereign* came under fire, not just from the *Santa Ana*, but also from the *Fougueux*, the *Indomptable*, the *San Leandro* and the *San Justo*. This set up a terrifying crossfire, but as the French and Spanish gunners were still aiming too high, a number of shots were seen to collide in mid-air, while others passed over the *Royal Sovereign* to fall harmlessly in the sea or even to hit the *Santa Ana*. In the *Royal Sovereign*, as spent shot and debris from the rigging were falling around them, the officers continued to pace the deck and

*The quarterdeck was the aftermost deck, except in larger ships, which had a poop – a smaller deck above and behind it. The quarterdeck was the place from which officers controlled the ship and was thus an obvious target.

talk among themselves, as if they were merely discussing the weather, and Collingwood was eating an apple with every appearance of enjoying it. He did, though, ask his captain of the marines to remove his men from danger:

The Admiral [Collingwood] now directed Captain Vallack, of the Marines, an officer of the greatest gallantry, to take his men from off the poop, that they might not be unnecessarily exposed, but he remained there himself much longer. At length, descending to the quarter-deck, he visited the men, enjoining them not to fire a shot in waste, looking himself along the guns to see that they were properly pointed, and commending the sailors, particularly a black man, who was afterwards killed, but who, while he stood beside him, fired ten times directly into the port-hole of the *Santa Ana* . . . During such an action, it is impossible that the actual time of any particular occurrence can be satisfactorily ascertained . . . There is, accordingly, great diversity of opinion as to the exact period during which the *Royal Sovereign* was engaged alone. Admiral Collingwood considered it to be twenty minutes, while others believe that it considerably exceeded that time.[5]

Several eyewitnesses later wrote down their memories of this dreadful day, but in common with the official ships' logbooks, no two accounts agree on the timing of any significant event. Not only were the pocket watches possessed by the officers generally unreliable, but they were not synchronised with one another and, in the heat of battle, were not frequently consulted. The official time on board ships was still measured by sand-glasses, a large one that had to be turned every four hours and a smaller one in which the sand took half an hour to run out. The official logbooks recorded the *Royal Sovereign* as first opening fire at times varying between twenty to twelve and seventeen minutes past twelve, while the explosion that later destroyed the French ship *Achille* was recorded at times ranging from ten minutes past five to seven o'clock – a difference of nearly two hours.

The second ship in Collingwood's column was the *Belleisle* – originally a French ship called the *Formidable*, built by the French in 1793 and captured and renamed two years later. Only three minutes behind the *Royal Sovereign*, the *Belleisle* was the next British ship to come under heavy fire. Lieutenant John Owen of the marines related the tense approach to the French and Spanish line:

Seven or eight of the enemy's ships opened their fire upon the *Royal Sovereign* and *Belleisle*, and as we were steering directly for them we could only remain passive, and perseveringly approach the post we were to occupy in this great battle. This was a trying moment. Captain Hargood had taken his station at the forepart of the quarterdeck, on the starboard side, occasionally standing on a carronade slide [special gun carriage for a carronade], whence he issued his orders for the men to lie down at their quarters, and with the utmost coolness directed the steering of the ship. The silence on board was almost awful, broken only by the firm voice of the captain, 'Steady!' or 'Starboard a little!' which was repeated by the master to the quartermaster at the helm, and occasionally by an officer calling to the now impatient men, 'Lie down there, you sir!' As we got nearer and nearer to the enemy the silence was, however, broken frequently by the sadly stirring shrieks of the wounded, for of them, and killed, we had more than fifty before we fired a shot; and our colours were three times shot away and rehoisted during the time. Seeing that our men were fast falling, the first lieutenant ventured to ask Captain Hargood if he had not better show his broadside to the enemy and fire, if only to cover the ship with smoke? The gallant man's reply was somewhat stern but emphatic: 'No, we are ordered to go through the line, and go through she shall, by —!' This state of things had lasted about twenty minutes, and it required the tact of the more experienced officers to keep up the spirits of those around them, by observing that 'We should soon begin our work', when . . . our energies were joyfully called into play by the command, 'Stand to your guns!'[6]

Also on the poop deck with Lieutenant Owen was Paul Harris Nicolas from Looe in Cornwall, another lieutenant of the marines. Just sixteen years old, he vividly described his recollections of the carnage and fear as the *Belleisle* gradually became involved in the first battle he had ever experienced:

The shot began to pass over us and gave us intimation of what we should in a few minutes undergo. An awful silence prevailed in the ship, only interrupted by the commanding voice of Captain Hargood, 'Steady! starboard a little! steady so!' echoed by the master directing the quartermasters at the wheel. A shriek soon followed, – a cry of agony was produced by the next shot, – and the loss of the head of a poor recruit was the effect of the succeeding, – and, as we advanced, destruction rapidly increased. A severe contusion in the breast now prostrated our Captain, but he soon resumed his station. Those only who have been in a similar situation to the one I am attempting to describe, can have a correct idea of such a scene. My eyes were horror-struck at the bloody corses [corpses] around me, and my ears rang with the shrieks of the wounded and the moans of the dying. At this moment, seeing that almost every one was lying down, I was half disposed to follow the example, and several times stooped for the purpose, but – and I remember the impression well – a certain monitor seemed to whisper 'Stand up and do not shrink from your duty!'. Turning round, my much esteemed and gallant senior [Lieutenant Owen] fixed my attention; the serenity of his countenance and the composure with which he paced the deck, drove more than half my terrors away, and joining him I became somewhat infused with his spirit, which cheered me on to act the part it became me. My experience is an instance of how much depends on the example of those in command when exposed to the fire of the enemy, more particularly in the trying situation in which we were placed for nearly thirty minutes, from not having the power to retaliate.[7]

The *Belleisle* tried to cut through the same gap as the *Royal Sovereign*, firing broadsides into both the *Santa Ana* and the

Fougueux on the way but, in turning northwards, the starboard side of the *Belleisle* was grazed by the *Fougueux*. The two ships, each with seventy-four guns, became locked together side by side, as Lieutenant Nicolas described:

It was just twelve o'clock [actually over ten minutes later] when we reached their line. Our energies became roused, and the mind diverted from its appalling condition, by the order of 'Stand to your guns!' which, as they successively came to bear, were discharged into our opponents on either side, but as we passed close under the stern of the *Santa Ana,* of 112 guns, our attention was more strictly called to that ship. Although until that moment we had not fired a shot, our sails and rigging bore evident proofs of the manner in which we had been treated: our mizentopmast was shot away, and the ensign had been thrice rehoisted; numbers lay dead upon the decks, and eleven wounded were already in the surgeon's care. The firing was now tremendous, and at intervals the dispersion of the smoke gave us a sight of the colours of our adversaries. At this critical period, while steering for the stern of *L'Indomptable* (our masts and yards and sails hanging in the utmost confusion over our heads), which continued a most galling raking fire upon us, the *Fougueux* being on our starboard quarter, and the Spanish *San Juste* on our larboard bow, the Master earnestly addressed the Captain: 'Shall we go through, sir?' 'Go through by ——!' was his energetic reply. 'There's your ship, sir; place me close alongside of her.' Our opponent defeated this manoeuvre by bearing away in a parallel course with us within pistol shot . . . the *Fougueux* ran us on board the starboard side, and we continued thus engaging.[8]

In this position, the *Belleisle* and the *Fougueux* pounded each other at point-blank range for nearly an hour.

The *Mars*, which was third in line after the *Belleisle* and the *Royal Sovereign*, had steered more to the south, taking a shorter route, and so reached the line of French and Spanish ships moments after the *Belleisle*. The *Mars* and the French ship *Pluton*, both with seventy-four guns, now began to exchange broadsides at point-blank range. The *Pluton* had overtaken the Spanish *Monarca* to engage the *Mars*, leaving a gap in the line between the *Monarca* and the next ship, the French *Algésiras*. Following the *Mars*, the *Tonnant* passed through this gap at about twenty minutes past midday, firing the port broadside into the *Monarca* and the starboard broadside into the *Algésiras* before turning northwards alongside the *Monarca*.

Fifth in Collingwood's column, behind the *Tonnant*, was the *Bellerophon* (known to the sailors as the 'Billy Ruffian'), which came under fire from at least five ships on the dangerous approach to the French and Spanish line. A few minutes before reaching the line, and with several men already injured or killed, the *Bellerophon* opened fire, as much to boost morale among the crew as in hope of disabling an enemy, as First Lieutenant William Cumby reported:

> On going round the decks to see everything in its place and all in perfect order before I reported to the Captain [John Cooke] the ship in readiness for action, the fifth or junior lieutenant . . . Lawrence Saunders, who commanded the seven foremost guns on each side of the lower deck, pointed out to me some of the guns at his quarters, where the zeal of the seamen had led them to chalk in large characters on their guns the words 'Victory or Death', a very gratifying mark of the spirit with which they were going to their work . . . It had been Captain Cooke's original intention not to have fired a shot until we were in the act of passing through the enemy's line, but finding that we were losing men as we approached their ships from the effect of their fire, and also suffering in our masts and rigging, he determined on opening our fire a few minutes sooner, from the double motive of giving our men employment, and at the same time of rendering the ship a less ostensible mark to be shot at by covering her with smoke.[9]

The *Bellerophon* was heading for the *Bahama*, nearly half a mile to the south of where the *Royal Sovereign* had cut the line. On passing behind the Spanish ship, the gunners fired a broadside into the stern, while at the same time firing from the other side at the Spanish ship *Montañes* to the south. As the *Bellerophon* turned northwards alongside the *Bahama*, the French ship *Aigle* appeared unexpectedly out of the bank of gunsmoke that was gradually enveloping this hot spot of the battle. As neither the *Bellerophon* nor the *Aigle* had time for evasive action, they collided and became locked together. A duel began, described by Cumby on board the *Bellerophon*:

At half-past twelve we were engaged on both sides, passing through their line close under the stern of a Spanish seventy-four [the *Bahama*], into whom, from the lightness of the wind being still farther lulled by the effect of the cannonade [it was widely believed that cannon fire reduced the speed of the wind], we fired our carronades three times, and every long gun on the larboard side at least twice. Luckily for us, by this operation she had her hanging magazine blown up and was completely beaten, for in hauling up to settle her business to leeward we saw over the smoke the top-gallant sails of another ship close under our starboard bow, which proved to be the French seventy-four, *L'Aigle*, as the name on her stern showed us, and although we hove all aback to avoid it, we could not sufficiently check our ship's way to prevent our running her on board with our starboard bow on her larboard quarter, our foreyard locking with her mainyard . . . By the Captain's directions I went down to explain to the officers on the main and lower decks the situation of the ship with respect to this new opponent, and to order them to direct their principal efforts against her. Having so done, as I was returning along the main deck, I met my poor messmate Overton the Master carried by two men, with his leg dreadfully shattered, and before I reached the quarter-deck ladder, having stopped to give some directions by the way, I was met by a quartermaster, who came to inform me that the

Captain was very badly wounded and, as he believed, dead. I went immediately on the quarterdeck and assumed the command of the ship – this would be about a quarter past one o'clock . . . we were still entangled with *L'Aigle*, on whom we kept up a brisk fire, and also on . . . the *Monarca*, who by this time was nearly silenced, though her colours were still flying.[10]

The Spanish ship *Monarca* was now under fire from the *Bellerophon*. Earlier on, the *Tonnant* had continued to engage both the *Algésiras* and the *Monarca* until, at about five minutes past one, the *Monarca* had pulled away out of range with nearly half the crew of over six hundred men killed or wounded. Nearby, the French ship *Swiftsure* had also suffered as the first British ships cut the line. Captain C. E. L'Hospitalier-Villemadrin, commander of the French *Swiftsure*, described the initial action around his vessel:

A plan of the opening phase of the battle at 12.45 p.m. (after Taylor 1950). The leading ships of both British columns have cut the French and Spanish line of battle.

1 *Victory*
2 *Temeraire*
3 *Neptune*
4 *Leviathan*
5 *Conqueror*
6 *Britannia*
7 *Ajax*
8 *Agamemnon*
9 *Orion*
10 *Prince*
11 *Minotaur*
12 *Spartiate*
13 *Royal Sovereign*
14 *Belleisle*
15 *Mars*
16 *Tonnant*
17 *Bellerophon*
18 *Colossus*
19 *Achilles*
20 *Revenge*
21 *Defiance*
22 *Dreadnought*
23 *Swiftsure*
24 *Polyphemus*
25 *Thunderer*
26 *Defence*
27 *Africa*
28 *Euryalus*
29 *Scipion*
30 *Intrépide*
31 *Formidable*
32 *Mont-Blanc*
33 *Duguay-Trouin*
34 *Héros*
35 *Bucentaure*
36 *Redoutable*
37 *Neptune*
38 *Indomptable*
39 *Fougueux*
40 *Pluton*
41 *Algésiras*
42 *Aigle*
43 *Swiftsure*
44 *Argonaute*
45 *Achille*
46 *Berwick*
47 *Neptuno*
48 *Rayo*
49 *San Francisco de Asís*
50 *San Agustín*
51 *Santísima Trinidad*
52 *San Justo*
53 *San Leandro*
54 *Santa Ana*
55 *Bahama*
56 *Montañes*
57 *Argonauta*
58 *San Ildefonso*
59 *Principe de Asturias*
60 *San Juan Nepomuceno*
61 *Monarca*

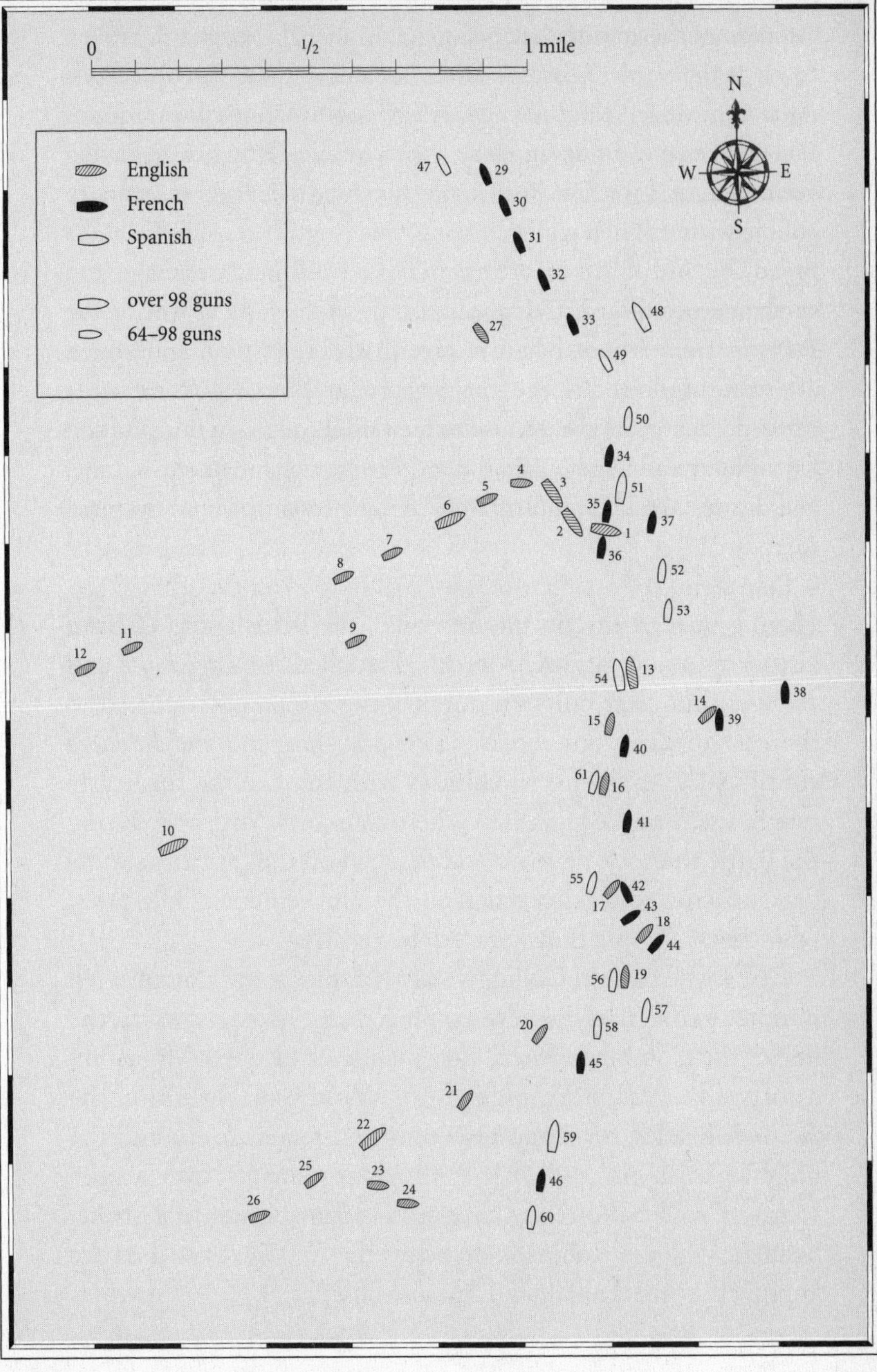

0
1/2
1 mile
N
W
E
S
English
French
Spanish
over 98 guns
64–98 guns
47
29
30
31
32
48
27
33
49
50
34
4
3
51
5
35
6
37
2
1
7
36
8
52
53
9
11
12
13
54
38
14
39
15
40
61
16
41
10
55
42
17
43
18
44
56
19
57
20
58
45
21
59
22
25
23
46
24
26
60

At midday, the engagement was general, and the rearguard, broken towards the *Algésiras* by 12 vessels, including three three-deckers. At 12.05, a vessel [the *Bellerophon*] having wanted to cut in front of the *Aigle*, engaged this ship [the *Aigle*]. While getting clear, having veered astern, I was forced to mask this ship [the *Aigle*] so as not to collide with it. Then while crossing, this English vessel delivered a broadside and killed 17 of my men, and did much damage and came and positioned itself abeam of me to leeward, as well as the *Defence*, from whom I had received two broadsides, and which afterwards followed closely the *Bahama*, and the *Aigle* then had a three-decker vessel abeam, also to leeward. I fought in this position for an hour and a half against the *Colossus*, which had crossed me, and during which I was dismasted of my mizzenmast and my main topmast.[11]

Having opened fire on the *Swiftsure*, the British ship *Colossus* also came under attack from the French ships *Argonaute* and *Bahama*, but after only ten minutes the *Argonaute* retreated to the east to carry out repairs. The *Swiftsure* and the *Bahama* continued to exchange broadsides with the *Colossus* for nearly two hours. The *Colossus* 'had a hen-coop on board, and during the battle the cock flew out and perched on the captain's shoulder and crowed loudly, much to the amusement of the crew, who cheered while they kept up the fighting'.[12]

Being well back in Collingwood's column, it was not until ten minutes to one that the newly built *Revenge* managed to cut the line of the Combined Fleet. Commanded by Robert Moorsom, a forty-five-year-old captain from Whitby in Yorkshire, the *Revenge* headed for a gap between the French *Achille* and the huge Spanish three-decker *Principe de Asturias*, over a mile south of where the *Royal Sovereign* had made the first strike. Seaman William Robinson on board the *Revenge* described the approach to the French and Spanish line:

It fell to our lot to cut off the five stern-most ships and, while we were running down to them, of course we were favoured with several shots, and some of our men were wounded. Upon being thus pressed, many of our men thought it hard that the firing should be all on one side, and became impatient to return the compliment: but our captain had given orders not to fire until we got close in with them, so that all our shots might tell: – indeed, these were his words: 'We shall want all our shot when we get close in: never mind their firing: when I fire a carronade from the quarter-deck, that will be a signal for you to begin, and I know you will do your duty as Englishmen'. In a few minutes the gun was fired, and our ship bore in and broke the line, but we paid dear for our temerity, as those ships we had thrown into disorder turned round, and made an attempt to board. A Spanish three-decker [the *Principe de Asturias*] ran her bowsprit over our poop, with a number of her crew on it, and, in her fore rigging, two or three hundred men were ready to follow; but they caught a Tartar,* for their design was discovered, and our marines with their small arms, and the carronades on the poop, loaded with canister shot, swept them off so fast, some into the water, and some on the decks, that they were glad to sheer off. While this was going on aft, we were engaged with a French two-deck ship on our starboard side, and on our larboard bow another, so that many of their shots must have struck their own ships, and done severe execution.[13]

A fierce conflict was taking place between the leading ships of Collingwood's column and the ships of the Combined Fleet, but Nelson in the *Victory* only managed to cut the line of French and Spanish ships five minutes before the *Revenge*, at a quarter to one (over half an hour later than the *Royal Sovereign*), to open up a second area of fighting. His ragged column of ships was heading to a point about half a mile north-west from where the line had already been cut, on a course roughly parallel to

*To 'catch a tartar' was to be surprised by an unexpectedly powerful opponent.

that of the column led by the *Royal Sovereign*. The *Victory*, launched in 1765 and almost the oldest ship in the British fleet (only the *Britannia* and the *Defence* were older), had not come within range of the Combined Fleet until some ten minutes after the *Royal Sovereign*, when at a distance of about 1000 yards. The French ship *Héros* immediately opened fire, followed shortly after by the Spanish *Santísima Trinidad* (the *Most Holy Trinity*) and the French *Bucentaure*. In the French ship *Redoutable*, Captain Jean-Jacques-Etienne Lucas observed that these ranging shots were falling short and waited a few minutes before he opened fire. Sailing slowly on, unable to reply, the *Victory* also gradually came within range of the ships at the head of the French and Spanish line that were under the control of Rear-Admiral Dumanoir, and at a quarter past midday these leading ships opened fire as well.

The *Victory* now began to suffer a great deal of damage, mainly to sails and rigging, as many of the French and Spanish gunners were aiming high, although their aim was adversely affected by the sea swell that was growing more pronounced. The swell soon made the long-range firing from the five leading French and Spanish ships very inaccurate – so much so that after a few minutes they switched their fire to the *Africa*. One of the smallest of the British battleships, carrying sixty-four guns, the *Africa* was sailing south-east, roughly parallel with the line of the Combined Fleet, still attempting to join the British attack after having become separated from the fleet overnight. Nelson had signalled 'make all possible sail', intending the *Africa* to take up a proper station within his column of ships, but Captain Henry Digby, in an interpretation of orders reminiscent of Nelson himself, sailed the *Africa* down the French and Spanish battle line, trading broadsides with every ship that he passed. Born in Bath in 1770, the son of the Dean of Durham, Digby was a colourful character who had already made a fortune from the enemy ships he had captured. By the time of Trafalgar he had acquired over £60,000 in prize money, much of it from his share in the taking of the *Santa Brigada*, with its cargo worth over a million dollars.* On that occasion he claimed to have been woken from his sleep by a recurring dream that advised him to change course: he did so, and intercepted the Spanish treasure ship.

The gap between the *Victory* and the line was narrowing, and the French and Spanish gunners were improving their aim and causing devastation, as was related by the surgeon on board the *Victory*, Dr William Beatty:

At fifty minutes past eleven [it was actually about twenty-five minutes later] the Enemy opened their fire on the Commander in Chief. They showed great coolness in the commencement of the battle; for as the *Victory* approached their line, their ships lying immediately ahead of her and across her bows fired only one gun at a time, to ascertain whether she was yet within their range. This was frequently repeated by eight or nine of their ships, till at length a shot passed through the *Victory*'s main topgallant sail; the hole in which being discovered by the Enemy, they immediately opened their broadsides, supporting an awful and tremendous fire.[14]

More shots shredded rigging and several sails and also brought down parts of masts or bounced across the upper decks. One shot smashed the wheel, leaving the ship out of control. Lieutenant John Quilliam and the master, Thomas Atkinson, rushed down to the gun room two decks below, where the tiller, a massive horizontal wooden beam, was swinging free. This beam moved the rudder to steer the ship and was normally operated by cables and pulleys from the wheel. They now had to quickly organise a team of men to control the tiller, and from

*Dollar was the English name for the Spanish peso or piece of eight, equivalent to eight Spanish reals.

then on the *Victory* had to be steered by forty seamen hauling on the huge beam. These men were completely blind as to what was ahead of the ship and relied on directions that were shouted down to them, but amid the noise of battle, the order sometimes had to be carried by messengers running down the ladders between decks. Throughout the rest of the battle, Atkinson and Quilliam ensured that the ship could be steered in response to messages sent down from the upper decks.

With the *Victory* still not in a position to aim a broadside at the enemy, the situation on the upper decks was becoming increasingly dangerous, as Beatty noted:

In a very short time afterwards, Mr Scott, Public Secretary to the Commander in Chief, was killed by a cannon-shot while in conversation with Captain Hardy. Lord Nelson being then near them, Captain Adair of the Marines, with the assistance of a seaman, endeavoured to remove the body from His Lordship's sight: but he had already observed the fall of his Secretary; and now said with anxiety, 'Is that poor Scott that is gone?' and on being answered in the affirmative by Captain Adair, he replied 'Poor fellow!'.

Lord Nelson and Captain Hardy walked the quarterdeck in conversation for some time after this, while the Enemy kept up an incessant raking fire. A double-headed shot struck one of the parties of Marines drawn up on the poop [deck] and killed eight of them; when His Lordship, perceiving this, ordered Captain Adair to disperse his men round the ship, that they might not suffer so much from being together. In a few minutes afterwards a shot struck the forebrace-bits on the quarterdeck, and passed between Lord Nelson and Captain Hardy; a splinter from the bits bruising Captain Hardy's foot, and tearing the buckle from his shoe. They both instantly stopped, and were observed by the Officers on deck to survey each other with inquiring looks, each supposing the other to be wounded. His Lordship then smiled, and said: 'This is too warm work, Hardy, to last long,' and declared that 'through all the battles he had been in, he had never witnessed more cool courage than was displayed by the *Victory*'s crew on this occasion.'

The *Victory* by this time, having approached close to the Enemy's van, had suffered very severely without firing a single gun: she had lost about twenty men killed, and had about thirty wounded. Her mizzen topmast, and all her studding-sails and their booms, on both sides were shot away; the Enemy's fire being chiefly directed at her rigging, with a view to disable her before she could close with them. (The Enemy's fire continued to be pointed so high throughout the engagement, that the *Victory* did not lose a man on her lower deck, and had only two wounded on that deck, and these by musket balls).[15]

Captain Thomas Masterman Hardy was a long-standing friend of Nelson's and one of his closest comrades, despite being very different in personality. Born into a Dorset farming family in 1769, Hardy first went to sea at the age of twelve. At times he served in both the British Navy and in merchant ships, before taking up a full-time naval career in 1790. Hardy was described as reserved, unemotional and dependable, and Nelson relied on his quiet strength. In a famous incident, when both Nelson and Hardy were in the British frigate *Minerve* off Gibraltar, being chased by two Spanish battleships, a man fell overboard. Hardy took some men in a boat to try to rescue him, but the man drowned. The Spanish ships were now gaining on the *Minerve*, and the sailors were unable to row fast enough to catch up with the frigate – it looked very likely that Hardy and the boat's crew would be taken prisoner. When Nelson saw the problem, he exclaimed, 'By God, I'll not lose Hardy: back the mizen top-sail.'[16] The *Minerve* actually stopped to allow the boat to catch up, a manoeuvre that puzzled the Spanish. Possibly suspecting a trap, the leading Spanish battleship slowed down to allow the other battleship to catch up, which provided enough time for Hardy to get on board the *Minerve* and the British frigate to escape. Hardy would survive Trafalgar and eventually become

First Sea Lord at the Admiralty, spending his final years as governor of Greenwich Hospital, where in 1839 he was buried, with a miniature of Nelson placed in his coffin at his request.

On board the British ship *Neptune*, sailing north-eastwards close behind the *Victory*, the officers also refused to take cover from the firing, and Midshipman Badcock described how 'during the time we were going into action, and being raked by the enemy, the whole of the crew, with the exception of the officers, were made to lie flat on the deck, to secure them from the raking shots, some of which came in at the bows and went out at the stern. Had it not been for the above precaution, many lives must have been sacrificed.'[17]

Watching from the deck of the *Bucentaure*, Vice-Admiral Villeneuve was certain that the *Victory* was heading straight for him or for the *Santísima Trinidad*, which was next in line, and that if the leading ships of the line under Dumanoir did not turn immediately to provide reinforcement, they would reach the *Bucentaure* too late. Villeneuve hoisted a signal, but instead of sending a message direct to the leading ships to turn back and help those under attack, the message ordered any ship that was not already engaged to take steps to join the action – despite the fact that in his written instructions before the battle, Villeneuve had stated that if this signal had to be hoisted it was a sign of disgrace to those ships not already engaged. As the signal gave no precise instructions and was not a direct order to any particular ship, Dumanoir ignored it, continuing to wait for a specific order from Villeneuve. It was not forthcoming.

This reliance on orders from a central command proved a recurring weakness in the French and Spanish navies where, by tradition, commanders of individual ships awaited orders transmitted in flag signals that could be hidden by smoke, cut down by enemy fire, or merely misunderstood. When Nelson, who had abandoned centralised control for a more flexible approach, sent his most famous signal, Collingwood – on seeing the flags fluttering yet again above the deck of the *Victory* – exclaimed before reading the message, 'I wish Nelson would stop signalling, as we know well enough what we have to do!'[18] It is quite possible that Villeneuve's crucial signal was hidden by smoke from most of his fleet, as only Commodore Esprit-Tranquille Maistral in the nearby French ship *Neptune* seems to have responded. At about half past twelve, the *San Justo* and the *San Leandro* decided to leave the action around the *Royal Sovereign* and headed northwards in the direction of the *Neptune*, in order to reinforce the ships now threatened by Nelson's column.

For whatever reason, although Dumanoir should have acted on Villeneuve's signal, he continued to lead the foremost ships of the line – three Spanish and five French – away from the fighting. This controversial action would result in him being blamed for the eventual outcome of the battle, and he was subsequently court-martialled, but acquitted. Irrespective of whether it was his fault or not, Dumanoir's failure to act was the turning point of the battle. Nelson was certainly relying on those leading ships having difficulty in turning and therefore being unable to help the rest of the battle line until it was too late, so the longer Dumanoir led his ships away from the line, the more chance the British fleet had of winning. With the lack of understanding between Villeneuve and Dumanoir, strategically the Combined Fleet had already lost the battle, although it was less than thirty minutes since the first shot had been fired. Now the British commanders needed to make good the victory.

Although Villeneuve believed that the *Victory* was heading straight for the *Bucentaure*, from on board the *Victory* it looked as if it was going to be very difficult to cut the French and Spanish line without ramming, since the gaps between the *Bucentaure*, the *Santísima Trinidad* in front and the *Redoutable* following behind were too small to pass through. Captain Hardy consulted Nelson as to which ship should be rammed, and Nelson replied, 'It does not signify which we run on board of [ram]; go on board which one you please, take your choice.'[19] Hardy continued to steer straight ahead, a course that would force the *Victory* through the gap between the stern of the *Bucentaure* and the bow of the *Redoutable*.

Just as the actions of Villeneuve and Dumanoir had already decided the outcome of the conflict, the decision just taken aboard the *Victory* sealed Nelson's fate. On board the *Redoutable*, one of the most disciplined and efficient ships of the Combined Fleet, Captain Lucas was preparing to meet the *Victory*. Knowing he had little chance of training his crew to match the British standards of gunnery, Lucas had taken the deliberate decision to concentrate on training them in musketry and the boarding of enemy ships, as he explained in his subsequent report:

Ever since the *Redoutable* was fitted out, nothing on board had been left to chance in instructing the crew in all kinds of exercise; my ideas were always turned towards fighting by boarding enemy ships. I was counting so much on its success that every thing had been set up to undertake it with advantage. For all the captains of guns I had had canvas pouches made that could hold two grenades. The cross-belts of these pouches carried a tin tube containing a small match. In all our exercises, I made them throw a large quantity of pasteboard grenades, and I often led the grenadiers ashore in order to explode iron grenades in front of them; they were so used to throwing them that on the day of the battle our topmen were hurling two at a time. I had on board one hundred carbines fitted with long bayonets; the men for whom they were intended had been so well trained in using them that they climbed right up to the middle of the shrouds in order to open fire. All the men carrying cutlasses were instructed in sword practice every day, and the pistol had become a familiar weapon for them. The boarding grapnels were thrown on board with such skill that they succeeded in catching hold of a vessel that might not even have been actually touching us. In the preparations for action, each person went to his post completely armed and with his weapons loaded; he placed them near his gun in nettings nailed between each beam. Finally, the crew themselves had such confidence in this method of fighting that they often urged me to board the first ship which we came up against.[20]

Although relatively accurate rifles were used by some of the sharpshooters in both fleets, there were too few of them to make any difference to the conflict. The sharpshooters' most common weapon was a smooth-bore musket – not accurate, but powerful at close range. Muskets used on board British ships were slightly shorter versions of the 'Brown Bess' musket used by the army, with a barrel 36–38 inches long, rather than the 42-inch version that was used on land. This made them easier to use in a confined space, although the reduced barrel length affected their accuracy at long range. French and Spanish muskets were very similar, while carbines had a shorter barrel still.

All these guns were muzzle loading, using prepared paper cartridges in a cumbersome and time-consuming ritual. The tubular paper bag of the cartridge, containing the correct amount of gunpowder and a musket-ball, was securely tied with thread. Loading the gun began with biting off the end of the cartridge that had the musket-ball and keeping the ball in the mouth. Gunpowder was poured down the touch-hole that would carry the spark from the flintlock to the main charge, and the flintlock itself was primed with a little gunpowder. The rest of the powder was poured down the barrel. The ball was spat out and rammed down the barrel after it, and the paper from the cartridge was rammed down last of all to stop the musket-ball and the powder falling out when the gun was pointed downwards. The ramrod was removed, the flintlock cocked, and the musket could now be fired. A similar process was used to load pistols, so no single man could maintain a rapid rate of fire without others loading the weapons for him. Because of this, pistols were used in pairs, and had heavy butts, often with metal knobs, so that when they had been fired they could be held by the barrel and used as clubs. For the same reason, muskets had a heavy wooden stock (shoulder-piece) and could be fitted with a 17-inch-long bayonet.

Musket-balls were of lead, about three-quarters of an inch in diameter, and weighed about an ounce. As the musket barrel had a smooth bore, anything that would fit down it could also be fired. On land, soldiers who still had powder left frequently resorted to firing stones when they ran out of bullets, and men could be killed by ramrods, buttons and even wads of chewed tobacco fired from these guns. At a range of 40 yards, which was not uncommon when ships were fighting side by side, musket-balls could pass through oak planking 2 inches thick. Compared with modern guns, muskets were low-velocity weapons, with a normal musket-ball travelling at approximately 600 feet per second. At this speed, it was the relatively large size and weight of the ball that caused the damage – bruising and tearing flesh to create substantial wounds, and breaking bones or being deflected off bones to inflict more destruction elsewhere in the body. If musket-balls passed through the body without hitting bones or major blood vessels, they left uncomplicated wounds that responded well to the medical treatment then available, and many men survived multiple musket-shot wounds of this type. More often, however, a musket-ball would shatter a bone and itself break up, with individual pieces of lead causing further injury. Such an internal wound was frequently fatal, while a limb broken by musket shot usually had to be amputated.

Muskets were notoriously inaccurate. On land, when using the longer version of the musket, a man firing at a stationary target 2 feet in diameter was doing well to hit it at a distance of 100 yards. The musket was considered useless at distances of over 150 yards, although the bullet still had the power to kill at distances beyond this. On board ship, aiming a shorter, less accurate weapon at a moving target, while firing from a position that was also in motion, reduced the accuracy much further. Muskets were usually fired at groups of men, because more often than not the ball would hit a man next to the one being targeted. Another drawback to using muskets aboard ship was the flash of flame, not only from the muzzle, but also back up the touch-hole at the rear of the gun. The firing mechanism was on the right-hand side, so that a right-handed man would hold his cheek against the left-hand side for sighting, so as not to be burned and blinded. Guns for left-handed people had to be made specially and were not issued by the navy; every man fired a musket with his right hand on the trigger and his left supporting the barrel. Worse than the danger to the musketeer was the danger to the sails and rigging from the muzzle flash, which could easily set the tar and grease weatherproofing alight. For this reason, Nelson disliked having men shooting from the masts and rigging, since the one thing most likely to destroy a ship was fire. The French ship *Achille*, which caught fire later on in the battle and eventually blew up, was set alight by the musketeers firing from the rigging.

Muskets were generally used by the marines or, in French and Spanish ships, by the soldiers who served in place of marines, while seamen detailed to form boarding parties were issued with pistols. These were simple, robust weapons, which had a metal clip on one side so that they could be hooked on a belt to be easily withdrawn and fired. Men on both sides also used grenades – hollow cast-iron balls 3–4 inches in diameter, with a hole through which they were filled with about 3 ounces of gunpowder. A hollow wooden fuse was then hammered into the hole. This fuse was filled with combustible material and waterproofed on the outside with sealing wax, and it was supposed to burn for about 6 seconds, being lit just before the grenade was thrown. So that the enemy did not have time to put out the fuse, grenades were not supposed to be thrown too early, but since the rate at which the fuses burned was variable, the judgement of just when to throw them was difficult and dangerous.

In British ships, one man from each gun crew was designated a boarder, although custom varied from ship to ship. Some commanders were more keen on the tactic than others, but none had the enthusiasm of Captain Lucas of the French ship *Redoutable*. The men assembled for boarding were generally issued with either pistols and a cutlass, a cutlass and a tomahawk, or a pike. The pistols were for close-range use, at a distance of 3 or 4 yards, and once fired they were dropped so that the cutlass could be drawn for use. The cutlass has been illustrated many times in cartoons with an exaggeratedly wide and curved blade as a trademark of the pirate, but navy cutlasses at the time of Trafalgar were simple swords with a blade around 28 to 29 inches long and a hilt guard. The blade was straight with a single edge and had a constant width of just over an inch for the whole of its length. It was a essentially a long knife, which seamen used to slash and stab at their opponents. Tomahawks were axes with a broad, slightly curved blade, on the back of which was a sharp spike. They could be weapons, but were more often used for cutting away obstacles to boarding or were struck into the side of the ship to form hand- and footholds for climbing. Officers who led boarding parties had their own swords and pistols, while midshipmen were armed with shorter swords called 'dirks'.

Pikes were spears with an iron head set on a wooden shaft about 7–8 feet long. Rather awkward weapons, they were more suited to defending a ship against boarders than to being carried by attackers. Various specialist weapons were even more effective against boarders, such as musketoons, which were large-bore muskets that could fire a ball of around 5–7 ounces in weight, or swivel guns, which were small cannons mounted so that they could be aimed in almost any direction by one man. They fired grape-shot and canister that could destroy a boarding party in seconds, and if there was time cannons on the upper deck could also be trained on boarders. With such defences, boarding was at best a risky tactic, unless the opposing crew had been decimated and demoralised by cannon fire first. What Captain Lucas of the *Redoutable* proposed to do was use his musketeers, instead of gunnery, to drive the enemy from the upper decks of the *Victory* and give his boarding parties a chance of gaining a foothold.

As he watched the approach of the *Victory*, Lucas noted that

the *Redoutable* began firing with a shot from the lower battery, which carried away the fore-topsail of the *Victory*, which was still steering towards the foremast of the *Redoutable*; then shouts of joy were repeated from every deck; our firing was well sustained; in less than ten minutes this same vessel had lost its mizzenmast, its fore topmast and its main topgallant mast. I still pursued the [French] *Bucentaure* so closely that they hailed me several times from the stern gallery that I was about to collide with them; actually the bowsprit of the *Redoutable* did graze the stern, but I assured them that there was nothing to fear. The damage to the *Victory* did not alter in any way the audacious manoeuvres of Admiral Nelson; he still persisted in wanting to cut the line in front of the *Redoutable* and was threatening to collide with us if we dared to try to stop him; the nearness of this three-decker, followed closely by the *Temeraire* of the same size, far from intimidating our fearless crew, on the contrary only made their courage grow. To prove to the English Admiral that we did not fear his boarding us, I had the grapnels hoisted at all the yards. Finally, the *Victory* not having managed to pass astern of the French Admiral [in the *Bucentaure*], collided with us on the port side, outflanking us from the stern, so that our poop was abeam and at the level of their quarterdeck.[21]

Despite the assertion of Lucas, at a quarter to one the *Victory* did at last manage to cut the line by crossing behind the stern of the French flagship *Bucentaure*. On board the *Bucentaure*, Admiral Villeneuve tried to rally his men. He seized the Imperial Eagle and held it up for the sailors to see, boldly shouting: 'I am going to throw this on board the English ship. We will go and fetch it back or die!'[22] It was not to be, for the *Victory* did not range alongside the *Bucentaure* as Villeneuve expected, but in passing, one of the *Victory*'s carronades, loaded with a cannon-ball and a keg of five hundred musket-balls, devastated the crowd of men on the *Bucentaure*'s upper deck. At the same time the *Victory* fired a broadside of double- and treble-shotted guns through the stern of the French ship, disrupting the lower gun decks and dismounting twenty guns. The ships were so close that the officers on the *Victory*'s quarterdeck were covered in dust blown from the *Bucentaure*'s stern as the *Victory*'s cannons shattered the woodwork.

While the *Victory* was breaking through the line, the French ship *Neptune*, which had responded to Villeneuve's signal for support and was immediately east of the *Bucentaure*, fired a broadside into the bows of the *Victory*, causing a great deal of further damage. The French *Neptune* then managed to avoid being rammed by the *Victory* and continued northwards, while the *Victory* collided instead with the *Redoutable*. These two ships became locked together, and the momentum of the *Victory* carried them both out of the line, with their bows swinging round eastwards as if heading for the Spanish coast.

Behind the *Victory*, the *Temeraire* approached the line, firing at the *Héros*, the *Santísima Trinidad*, the *Bucentaure* and the *Redoutable*. Instead of passing through the same gap as the *Victory*, the *Temeraire* went further south to break the line between the French ships *Neptune* and *Redoutable*, coming under fire as well from the Spanish ships *San Justo* and *San Leandro*. Already the damage to the *Temeraire*, caused especially by the *Neptune*, was becoming serious, with masts and rigging brought down.

Near the *Victory*, the British ship *Neptune*, which had kept close to the *Temeraire*, but to the north rather than directly behind, turned southwards and opened fire first at the Spanish ship *San Agustín*, then the French *Héros* and finally the Spanish *Santísima Trinidad*. With four decks carrying 130 guns, the *Santísima Trinidad* was the largest ship at the battle and was thought to be the largest in the world at that time, standing out as a prestigious ship in any battle line – an obvious target for captains and crews hungry for honour, glory and prize money. Its sheer size made the *Santísima Trinidad* unwieldy and, with a mixed crew of around one thousand sailors and soldiers, quick manoeuvring was very difficult.

After receiving broadsides from the *Héros* and the *San Agustín*, the British ship *Neptune* was severely damaged, but managed to pass behind the French flagship *Bucentaure*, firing a broadside into the stern at close range, just as the *Victory* had done fifteen minutes earlier. A mêlée of ships was developing, and in the wake of the British *Neptune*, the *Leviathan* fired another broadside into the *Bucentaure* before also engaging the *Santísima Trinidad*. In this small area of sea around the *Bucentaure*, British, French and Spanish ships were manoeuvring slowly in the light winds, trying to identify neighbouring ships through the drifting banks of gunsmoke and firing at any enemy ship within range.

The *Africa* under Captain Henry Digby now reached the *Santísima Trinidad*, and although the Spanish vessel towered far above, this did not prevent the *Africa* joining in the fight and letting fly another broadside. The crew of the *Santísima Trinidad* were putting up a valiant resistance, but the sheer weight of incoming shot from the various British assailants was gradually destroying the vast ship. Even so, on board the *Britannia*, still some distance away, Lieutenant Lawrence

Halloran of the marines witnessed the terrible effects of just one shot received from the *Santísima Trinidad*:

a shot struck the muzzle of the gun at which I was stationed (the aftermost gun on the larboard side of the lower deck), and killed or wounded everyone there stationed, myself and Midshipman Tompkins only excepted. The shot was a very large one, and split into a number of pieces, each of which took its victim. We threw the mangled body of John Jolley, a marine, out of the stern port, his stomach being shot away; the other sufferers we left to be examined. The gun itself was split, and our second lieutenant Roskruge, who came down at that moment with some orders, advised me to leave the gun as useless. He had scarcely left us, when he was brought down senseless with a severe wound in his head . . . [he died later, without regaining consciousness]. Amongst the wounded who suffered at my gun was a man named Pilgrim, an Italian, who was stooping to take up a shot for the gun, when it was split, and both his arms were blown off [Pilgrim survived and was later given a pension].[23]

In the *Conqueror*, Midshipman William Hicks had a lucky escape:

I was aide-de-camp to Sir I. Pellew [the captain], and had just reported to the first lieutenant that I had obeyed an order which he had commanded me to convey to the officers on the lower deck, and had walked a few yards from him, when I saw a grape shot which had struck a canister case close by. I took it up and put it in my pocket. Turning round I saw the first lieutenant [Robert Lloyd] and sixth [lieutenant, William St George] lying close by me. I ran to them, saying 'I hope you are not seriously hurt', and lifting Mr. Lloyd's head the blood gushed into my shoes. Both were dead.[24]

Later in the battle Hicks, who was seventeen years old and came from St Columb in Cornwall, was himself wounded, but he survived and served in the navy until the close of the Napoleonic Wars, after which he studied for ordination, ending his days as the rector of Halstead in Essex.

Although the *Santísima Trinidad* attempted to escape from the ring of fire set up by the British ships, the masts were already shot through, and another officer in the *Conqueror* watched as the *Santísima Trinidad* 'gave a deep roll with the swell to leeward, then back to windward, and in her return every mast went by the board, leaving an unmanageable hulk on the water. Her immense topsails had every reef out, her royals were sheeted home but lowered, and the falling mass of the square sails and rigging, plunging into the water at the very muzzles of our guns, was one of the most magnificent sights I ever beheld.'[25]

Now unmanoeuvrable, the *Santísima Trinidad* was severely hampered by the masts, rigging and sails draped over the side, dragging in the water and covering the gunports. The fighting ceased, and some witnesses reported that a Union Jack was waved from the Spanish ship in token of surrender. Captain Digby of the *Africa*, the smallest ship in the circle, was quick to send an officer to take charge of the huge prize, but when Lieutenant John Smith climbed on board, he was greeted with elaborate Spanish courtesy and informed that the ship had not surrendered, had no intention of doing so and had merely paused in firing to supply the guns with more powder. The lieutenant and his party were politely sent back to their ship, but the fighting did not recommence because it was obvious that the *Santísima Trinidad* was now a drifting hulk. The British gunnery had been more destructive than was apparent, and the pumps aboard the Spanish vessel were already losing the battle against the water rising in the hold. The British ships moved on to seek other opponents.

SEVEN

SLAUGHTER

> There was one ship so close to us that we could not run out our guns their proper length. Only conceive how much we must have smashed her, every gun was trebly shotted for her.
>
> Midshipman Richard Roberts of the *Victory* describing the encounter with the French ship *Redoutable*[1]

It was now a few minutes past one o'clock, just over an hour after the battle had begun. At the heart of the fighting, where the two British columns had cut the French and Spanish line, the flow of blood from the decks into the gutters and out through drain holes had left scarlet streaks down the sides of the ships. The sea itself was taking on a dull crimson cast alternately lit by flashes from the muzzles of the cannons and shaded by the pall of dust and smoke.

The British, French and Spanish ships were now shuffling positions in a kaleidoscope of fire, smoke, wreckage and blood, while the battle line of the Combined Fleet continued to degenerate into a confused mass as one after another of the British ships slid through it. Those British ships reaching the line were no longer running before the wind, which itself was very light, but were manoeuvring at very slow speeds, sometimes less than one mile per hour, to aim at selected targets. It often took many minutes for a vessel to be turned to fire efficiently at a particular ship – time enough for crushing damage to be inflicted – so all the ships inched through the banks of gunsmoke, struggling to tell ally from enemy, while seizing any chance to catch an opponent at a disadvantage. Yet only about half the ships on either side were engaged in the action. To those still outside the conflict, what was left of the middle of the French and Spanish line – where the fighting was most intense – looked like an erupting volcano with great flashes of flame emerging from a shroud of smoke and airborne debris.

Rear-Admiral Dumanoir with the leading ships of the French and Spanish line – representing a quarter of the fleet – continued to sail away northwards. In the meantime, the slowest-sailing ships of the British fleet were still desperately struggling to catch up and reach the now disintegrating line so as to support their leaders. This meant that some ships fought in the battle for a much longer time than others, and afterwards crews would taunt each other on shore, 'Oh! you belong to one of the ships that did not come up till the battle was nearly over.'[2]

With the *Victory* so close, Captain Lucas feared that there might be an attempt to board his own ship, the *Redoutable*. Relying more on his own plan of boarding the *Victory* than on his gunners, he ordered the gunports to be closed on the side against the *Victory* in order to stop the British gaining access. His musketeers kept up a constant fire with bullets and grenades, concentrating on the *Victory*, but in the middle of this growing chaos, where the noise was by now deafening, all the officers continued to pace the decks, frequently choked and blinded by smoke, largely ignoring the increasing carnage and destruction around them. The guns of the *Victory* were continuing to pulverise the hull of the *Redoutable*, and behind the shredded wooden wall of the French ship there was devastation – few men were left on the lower decks who had not been hurt. This did nothing to diminish the musket fire that was raking the upper decks of the British flagship.

Before the battle, some discussion had taken place among the officers about the decorations on Nelson's coat, which some thought might identify him as an important target for enemy sharpshooters, but no one had found an opportunity to suggest that the admiral should change into something less conspicuous. In fact, Nelson's dress was the same as always: a white neckerchief, white waistcoat, breeches, stockings and shoes with buckles, on top of which was his uniform coat with four stars. He had a plain cocked hat with a green eyeshade sewn on to it above his good left eye. Nelson never wore an eyepatch – his blind right eye, with which he could only distinguish light from dark, had been damaged but not destroyed. Afraid that his good left eye was deteriorating, he protected it with this eyeshade. The stars on his coat were sequin facsimiles of the four orders of chivalry that he had been awarded, and the wearing of such decorations was not unusual at this time. The sea air had tarnished the sequins, and the stars no longer resembled the bright jewels they represented, but controversy still continues about whether they attracted the attention of a sharpshooter, whether they could be properly seen from the *Redoutable*, or even whether Nelson deliberately wore the coat to attract snipers because he had a death-wish.

Nelson knew very well that the risks were great, but he did nothing to increase them, even if he also did little to reduce them. He was a fatalist, but he did not *want* to die; he merely wanted to do his duty in the battle and then retire to a quiet life with Emma Hamilton and their daughter Horatia. This is not to say that he might not have had a premonition of his death. Before every major battle he fought, there are indications that he thought he might be killed (which was nothing more than a realistic assessment on his part), but this time it was slightly different. Some years before, a fortune-teller had told him that she could see nothing of his life beyond the year 1805. If she had also prophesied fame and fortune, which he had already achieved, he might have been more inclined to believe her apparent prediction about his death. He had certainly mentioned the fortune-teller to his sister, Catherine Matcham, not long before Trafalgar, so the prophecy had not been forgotten. While Nelson seemed certain of success in the battle, he may also have been certain of his own death; as he said goodbye to Captain Blackwood, who was leaving the *Victory* to return to the *Euryalus* after a final conference of commanders just minutes before the battle began, Nelson took his hand and said, 'God bless you, Blackwood. I shall never speak to you again.'[3]

At a quarter past one Nelson was shot by a sharpshooter on board the *Redoutable*. He and Captain Hardy were walking on the quarterdeck of the *Victory*, with Hardy a little ahead. When Hardy turned to walk back, he saw Sergeant James Secker of the marines and two seamen supporting Nelson. He had fallen at the point where only minutes before his secretary, Scott, had been killed, and whose blood now covered Nelson's clothes. Hardy hurried over and said that he hoped Nelson had not been badly wounded, to which Nelson replied, '"They have done for me at last, Hardy." "I hope not," answered Captain Hardy. "Yes," replied His Lordship, "my backbone is shot through."'[4] Hardy ordered the seamen to carry the admiral down to the cockpit, where he greeted the surgeon with: 'Ah, Mr. Beatty! you can do nothing for me. I have but a short time to live: my back is shot through.'[5]

The cockpit was already full of casualties, lying in the shadows cast by the dim lanterns that provided the only light. The constant groaning was punctuated by frequent screams of pain, and even in the half-light the scene made an indelible impression on Nelson's chaplain, also called Scott, like the secretary who had been killed:

Dr Scott's duties confined him entirely to the cockpit, which was soon crowded with wounded and dying men, and such was the horror that filled his mind at this scene of suffering, that it haunted him like a shocking dream for years afterwards. He never talked of it. Indeed the only record of a remark on the subject was one extorted from him by the enquiries of a friend . . . The expression that escaped him at the moment was, 'it was like a butcher's shambles'. His natural tenderness of feeling, very much heightened by the shock on his nervous system, quite disqualified him for being a calm spectator of death and pain, as there exhibited in their most appalling shapes. But he suppressed his aversion as well as he could, and had been for some time engaged in helping and consoling those who were suffering around him, when a fine young lieutenant was brought down desperately wounded.[6]

This was Lieutenant William Ram, an Irishman from County Wexford, just twenty-one years old. He had been stationed on the quarterdeck when a deflected shot from the *Redoutable* erupted through the deck, spewing splinters into the men standing there. Several men were killed outright. Ram, who had multiple wounds,

was not aware of the extent of his injury, until the surgeon's examination, but on discovering it, he tore off with his own hand the ligatures that were being applied, and bled to death. Almost frenzied by the sight of this, Scott hurried wildly to the deck for relief, perfectly regardless of his own safety. He rushed up the companion ladder – now slippery with gore – the scene above was all noise, confusion, and smoke – but he had hardly time to breathe there, when Lord Nelson himself fell, and this event at once sobered his disordered mind. He followed his chief to the cockpit.[7]

The surgeon, Dr Beatty, did what little he could for Nelson, and afterwards wrote one of the more detailed and reliable accounts of what happened next:

His Lordship was laid upon a bed, stripped of his clothes, and covered with a sheet. While this was effecting, he said to Doctor Scott, 'Doctor, I told you so. Doctor, I am gone,' and after a short pause he added in a low voice, 'I have to leave Lady Hamilton, and my adopted daughter Horatia, as a legacy to my Country.' The Surgeon then examined the wound, assuring His Lordship that he would not put him to much pain in endeavouring to discover the course of the ball; which he soon found had penetrated deep into the chest, and had probably lodged in the spine. This being explained to his Lordship, he replied, 'he was confident his back was shot through.' The back was then examined externally, but without any injury being perceived; on which His Lordship was requested by the Surgeon to make him acquainted with all his sensations. He replied, that 'he felt a gush of blood every minute within his breast: that he had no feeling in the lower part of his body: and that his breathing was difficult, and attended with very severe pain about that part of the spine where he was confident that the ball had struck, for', said he, 'I felt it break my back.' These symptoms, but more particularly the gush of blood which His Lordship complained of, together with the state of his pulse, indicated to the Surgeon the hopeless situation of the case, but till after the victory was ascertained and announced to His Lordship, the true nature of his wound was concealed by the Surgeon from all on board except only Captain Hardy, Doctor Scott, Mr. Burke, [the purser] and Messrs. Smith and Westemburg, the Assistant Surgeons.[8]

At a quarter past one, when Nelson had been shot and was being carried below, the fierce exchange of small-arms fire was unceasing on the upper decks of the *Victory*. Years later in France, a book was written that purported to be the life story of a retired army sergeant, Robert Guillemard, who was claiming not only to be the man who had shot Nelson but also the man who later witnessed the death of Villeneuve. The book was published in 1825 by a hoaxer called Lardier, a naval accountant, and although he confessed five years later that it was all fiction based on the rumours current at the time, the story still persists today.

In England in 1863, a controversy of a different sort arose in the newspapers – the identity of the 'avenger of Nelson'. The officers remaining on deck after Nelson was wounded assumed that the shot had been fired from a platform at the mizzentop of the *Redoutable*, and they proceeded to concentrate their fire at that point. The arguments in the newspapers prompted a statement, in the *Kentish and Surrey Mercury*, from Captain John Pollard, who had been a nineteen-year-old midshipman on board the *Victory*. Pollard, a Cornishman from Cawsand, claimed that he himself and not Edward Collingwood had avenged Nelson:

I was on the poop of the *Victory* from the time the men were beat to quarters before the action till late in the evening. I was the first struck, as a splinter hit my right arm, and I was the only officer left alive of all who had been originally stationed on the poop. It is true my old friend Collingwood (who has now been dead some years) [Edward Collingwood, midshipman] came on the poop after I had for some time discovered the men in the top of the *Redoutable*; they were in a crouching position, and rose breast-high to fire. I pointed them out to Collingwood as I made my aim; he took up a musket, fired once, and then left the poop, I concluded [he did this] to return to the quarter-deck, which was his station during the battle. I remained firing at the top till not a man was to be seen; the last one I discovered coming down the mizzen rigging, and from my fire he fell also. John King, a quarter-master, was killed while in the act of handing me a parcel of ball cartridge long after Collingwood had left the poop. I remained there till after the action was over, and assisted in superintending the rigging of the jury mast.* Then I was ushered into the ward-room where Sir Thomas Hardy and other officers were assembled, and [was] complimented by them on avenging Lord Nelson's death.[9]

*Anything used as a temporary mast in an emergency.

It is impossible to know whether the man who shot Nelson was among those killed by Midshipman Pollard, but in spite of his efforts, the intense small-arms fire from the *Redoutable* continued to take its toll of the men on the upper decks of the *Victory*. The number of shots fired at the quarterdeck actually ploughed up the surface of the planking. As seamen carried the wounded below and the dead were left where they fell, Captain Hardy, Captain Adair of the marines and a handful of others were the only men still left alive on the upper decks. Dr Beatty noted that 'the *Redoutable* commenced a heavy fire of musketry from the tops, which was continued for a considerable time with destructive effect to the *Victory*'s crew; her great guns however being silent, it was supposed at different times that she [the *Redoutable*] had surrendered; and in consequence of this opinion, the *Victory* twice ceased firing upon her by orders transmitted from the quarter deck.'[10] Captain Hardy later said that the *Victory* had ceased firing in order to put out fires aboard the *Redoutable*. Whatever the true reason, Captain Lucas assumed that the *Redoutable* was gaining the upper hand and ordered his eager men to board the *Victory*, about five minutes after Nelson had been carried below.

Lucas recounted the attempt and the events leading up to it:

> We continued to fire our guns for some time [after running alongside the *Victory*, although other witnesses said that the gunports of the *Redoutable* were already shut to prevent boarding], we managed to load some guns by means of swabs with rope handles; several were fired with the breeching tackle fully extended [as far inboard as the breeching tackles would allow, so that the muzzles did not protrude through the gunports], not being able to hoist them through the gun ports which were blocked by the side of the *Victory*, and by means of the firearms placed in our batteries we so prevented the enemy from loading theirs that he ceased to fire at us . . . What a day of glory for the *Redoutable*, if we only had to fight the *Victory*! At last, the batteries

of the *Victory* no longer being able to reply to us, I noticed that they were about to come on board, the enemy forming groups on their upper decks. I ordered the trumpet sounded, a signal recognised in our exercises as summoning the boarding parties. They came up in such good order, the officers and midshipmen at the head of their companies, that one might have said it was only a practice run. In less than a minute our upper decks were covered with armed men who rushed to the poop deck, on to the nettings and into the shrouds; it was impossible for me to pick out the bravest men. They then engaged in a furious musketry fire in which Admiral Nelson fought at the head of his crew [Nelson had actually already been wounded and taken below some minutes before]; our firing became so superior that in less than fifteen minutes we silenced that of the *Victory*; more than two hundred grenades were thrown aboard this ship with the greatest success, the upper decks were strewn with the dead and wounded men, and Admiral Nelson was killed by our musket fire. Almost immediately, the upper decks of the enemy vessel were cleared, and the *Victory* completely ceased to fight us, but it was difficult to get on board because of the movement of the two vessels and the greater height of the *Victory* because of its third deck. I ordered the slings of the mainyard to be cut and for it to be lowered to act as a bridge. Midshipman Yon and four sailors succeeded in boarding the *Victory* by means of the anchor, and informed us that there was nobody in its batteries, but at the moment when our brave men were going to rush forward to follow them, the three-decker *Temeraire*, which had without doubt noticed that the *Victory* was no longer fighting and was inevitably going to be taken, came close against our starboard side and riddled us with shot at point-blank range from all its artillery.[11]

The bias and errors in Lucas's account arise partly from his desire to present the actions of his crew in the best possible light in a report that might be read by Napoleon, but mainly – as with so many of the eyewitness reports – they result from the inevitable confusion of later recalling a battle that was to last nearly six hours. He had misjudged the state of the *Victory* and the reason for the cessation of fire, but the hand-to-hand fighting was nevertheless fierce, leaving eighteen men of the *Victory*'s crew dead, including Captain Adair of the marines, and twenty more were wounded. The attempt at boarding was repulsed in less than five minutes, and although the arrival of the *Temeraire* was decisive, the *Victory* would have eventually fought off the attack, but probably with much greater loss of life among the British crew.

In the confusion of fighting, it began to be difficult telling friend from foe, of which Captain Eliab Harvey of the *Temeraire* was very aware as he described this particular action:

I can give you no other account of this part of this most glorious day's work than what immediately concerned the *Victory* or myself. We were engaged with the *Santísima Trinidad* and the other ships for perhaps 20 minutes or more, when for a minute or two I ceased my fire, fearing I might from the thickness of smoke be firing into the *Victory*, but I soon saw the *Victory* close on board a French ship of two decks, and having the ship under command, notwithstanding we had suffered much in our masts and sails &c. &c., I placed the ship so as to give this *Redoutable* a most severe dressing by raking of her fore and aft.[12]

Harvey, forty-seven years old and from Chigwell in Essex, was an experienced seaman who had served during the American War of Independence, and who was also the Member of Parliament for Essex. He had taken command of the *Temeraire* at the renewal of war with France in 1803 with a completely new crew after the ship had been paid off, following a mutiny the year before. The ship was known to sailors as 'The Saucy *Temeraire*', only being named 'The Fighting *Temeraire*' in 1838 by the artist Turner, who gave that title to his painting of the ship being towed to the breaker's yard.

In the *Redoutable*, Lucas ordered the remnants of his boarding parties to man the guns against the *Temeraire*, but already the lower gun decks were a shambles. Now trapped in the crossfire between the *Victory* and the *Temeraire*, the French gunners on board the *Redoutable* stood no chance. The *Victory*'s surgeon, Dr Beatty, noted that the lieutenants on the lower gun decks, who could now see nothing but the side of the *Redoutable* with all the lids of the gunports closed, adapted their fire to the difficult conditions:

The starboard guns of the middle and lower decks were depressed, and fired with a diminished charge of powder, and three shot each, into the *Redoutable*. This mode of firing was adopted by Lieutenants Williams, King, Yule, and Brown, to obviate the danger of the *Temeraire*'s suffering from the *Victory*'s shot passing through the *Redoutable*, which must have been the case if the usual quantity of powder, and the common elevation, had been given to the guns. A circumstance occurred in this situation, which showed in a most

A plan of the battle at 1.15 p.m. (after Taylor 1950). As more British ships reach the French and Spanish line, the battle becomes a series of conflicts between pairs of ships and small groups.

1 *Victory*
2 *Temeraire*
3 *Neptune*
4 *Leviathan*
5 *Conqueror*
6 *Britannia*
7 *Ajax*
8 *Agamemnon*
9 *Orion*
10 *Prince*
11 *Minotaur*
12 *Spartiate*
13 *Royal Sovereign*
14 *Belleisle*
15 *Mars*
16 *Tonnant*
17 *Bellerophon*
18 *Colossus*
19 *Achilles*
20 *Revenge*
21 *Defiance*
22 *Dreadnought*
23 *Swiftsure*
24 *Polyphemus*
25 *Thunderer*
26 *Defence*
27 *Africa*
28 *Euryalus*
29 *Scipion*
30 *Intrépide*
31 *Formidable*
32 *Mont-Blanc*
33 *Duguay-Trouin*
34 *Héros*
35 *Bucentaure*
36 *Redoutable*
37 *Neptune*
38 *Indomptable*
39 *Fougueux*
40 *Pluton*
41 *Algésiras*
42 *Aigle*
43 *Swiftsure*
44 *Argonaute*
45 *Achille*
46 *Berwick*
47 *Neptuno*
48 *Rayo*
49 *San Francisco de Asís*
50 *San Agustín*
51 *Santísima Trinidad*
52 *San Justo*
53 *San Leandro*
54 *Santa Ana*
55 *Bahama*
56 *Montañes*
57 *Argonauta*
58 *San Ildefonso*
59 *Principe de Asturias*
60 *San Juan Nepomuceno*
61 *Monarca*

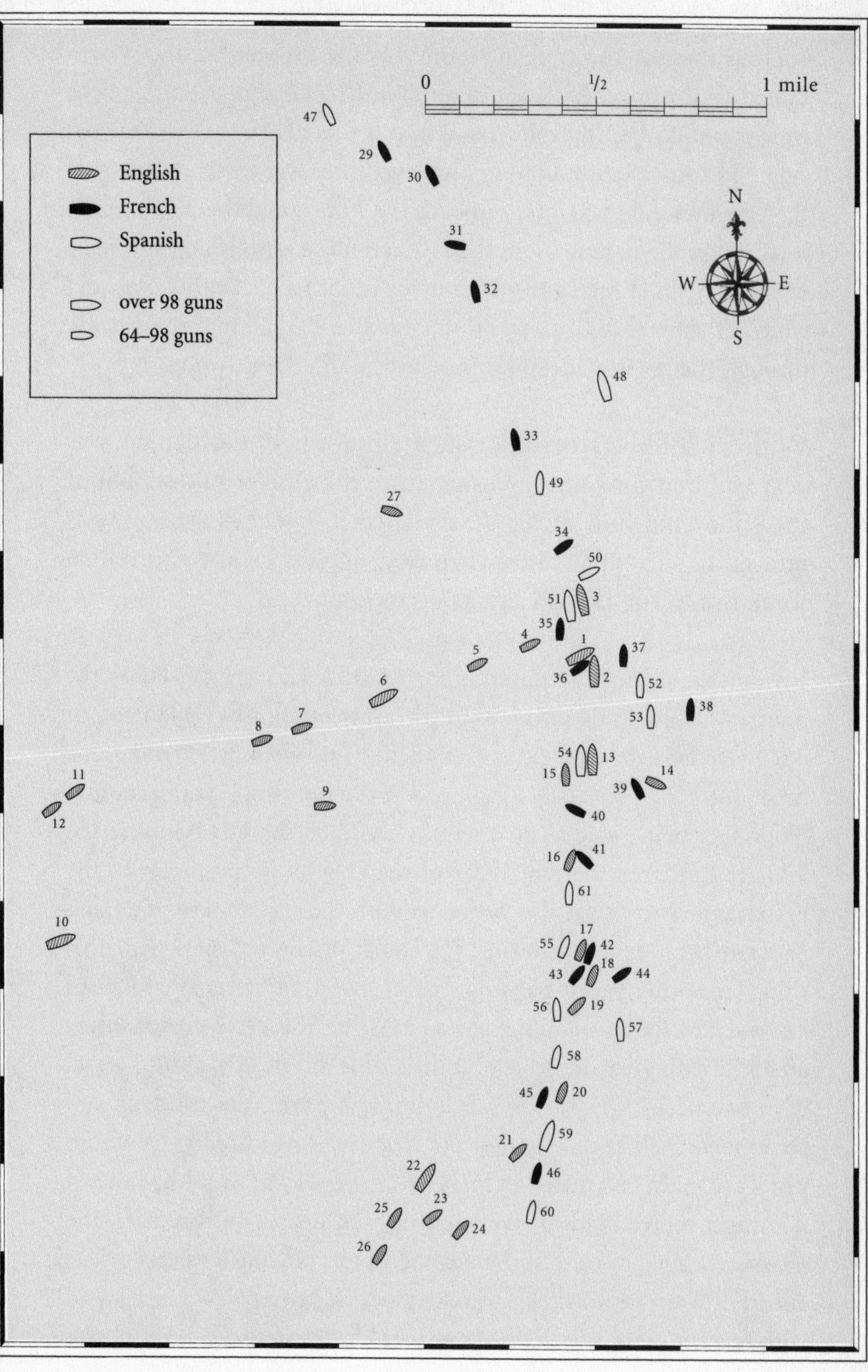

0
1/2
1 mile
English
French
Spanish
over 98 guns
64–98 guns
N
W
E
S
47
29
30
31
32
48
33
49
27
34
50
51
3
35
4
1
37
5
36
2
52
6
38
53
7
8
54
13
15
14
11
39
9
12
40
16
41
61
10
17
55
42
43
18
44
56
19
57
58
45
20
59
21
22
46
23
25
24
60
26

striking manner the cool intrepidity of the Officers and men stationed on the lower deck of the *Victory*. When the guns on this deck were run out, their muzzles came into contact with the *Redoutable*'s side, and consequently at every discharge there was reason to fear that the Enemy would take fire, and both the *Victory* and the *Temeraire* be involved in the flames. Here then was seen the astonishing spectacle of the fireman of each gun standing ready with a bucket full of water, which as soon as his gun was discharged he dashed into the Enemy through the holes made in her side by the shot.[13]

With such ferocious fire at such close range, the danger was very real that the muzzle flashes from the guns would set alight the splintered hull of the *Redoubtable* just inches away. Lucas refused to surrender, and his crew struggled valiantly to return some fire to the British ships. Lucas later recalled:

It would be difficult to describe the dreadful carnage caused by the murderous broadside of this ship [the *Temeraire*]. More than 200 of our brave lads were killed or wounded, I was wounded at the same time, but not so seriously as to prevent me remaining at my station. No longer being able to do anything more on the side opposite the *Victory*, I ordered the remainder of the crew to go promptly to the batteries and to fire at the *Temeraire* with those starboard guns that had not been wrecked during the shock of the collision with this ship. This order was carried out; nevertheless we were so weakened and we had so few cannons left to use, that the *Temeraire* counterattacked with great advantage. A little time afterwards, a third vessel with two decks, whose rating I do not know precisely, came up and positioned itself at the stern of the *Redoutable* and fired at us within pistol range. In less than half an hour our vessel was so riddled that it no longer represented more than a heap of debris. In this state, the *Temeraire* called to us to surrender and not to prolong a useless resistance. I ordered some soldiers who were near me to reply to this demand with musket shots, which was done with the greatest eagerness.[14]

The damage to the *Redoutable* became even worse, but Lucas's men remained determined:

All the guns were broken or dismounted by the shots or by [the jolt of] the collisions of these two ships. An 18-pounder gun of the second battery and a 36-pounder carronade on the forecastle,* having burst, killed and wounded many of us; on the two sides of the ship, all the lids and bars of the gunports were entirely cut to pieces; four out of our six pumps were broken, as were all our ladders in general, such that communication between the batteries and the upper decks was extremely difficult; all our decks were covered with dead men, buried beneath the debris and the splinters from the different parts of the vessel. A great number of wounded were killed on the orlop deck. Out of a crew of 643 men, we had 522 out of action, of whom 300 were dead and 222 wounded; amongst them almost all the officers. Of the 121 who remained, a large part were employed in carrying gunpowder on the orlop deck and past the water tiers,† such that the upper decks and the batteries were absolutely deserted and we could consequently no longer show any resistance. Whoever has not seen the *Redoutable* in this state will never be able to form an idea of the destruction. I know of nothing on board that was not cut up by the shot; in the middle of this horrible carnage the brave men who had not yet succumbed and those who were wounded, with whom the orlop-deck was strewn, were still crying out: 'Long live the Emperor! We are not yet taken; does the captain still live?'[15]

Nearby, the *Bucentaure*, Villeneuve's flagship, was now being pounded by the next three ships of Nelson's column to break the French and Spanish line – the *Conqueror*, the *Britannia* and the *Agamemnon*. At half past one Villeneuve hoisted a final signal, specifically ordering his leading ships, under Dumanoir,

*The deck between the foremast and the bow of a ship.
†A row, layer or rack of water casks.

to return and join the fighting. There was no response. Fifteen minutes later the *Bucentaure* became the first ship of the battle to surrender, and the captain, Jean-Jacques Magendie, reported the last minutes of the fight:

> Our rigging completely dismantled, having lost all the men on the upper decks, the 24-pounder battery entirely out of commission and abandoned through [having so many] dead and wounded men, the starboard side fouled by the masts; incapable of defending ourselves, with nearly 450 men killed or wounded [out of a crew of around 800]; not having been helped by any other vessel, everyone appearing engaged, and there being none within reach, nor any frigate to which the Admiral could move his flag; not even having a small boat in which he could embark, all of them having been crippled, as well as the one we had kept in the sea since before the battle, we were isolated in the middle of five enemy vessels that were firing very vigorously at us. At that moment I went back on to the deck, because Admiral Villeneuve had been forced to order our ship to surrender so as to avoid more brave men being killed who were unable to fight back, which was done after three and a quarter hours of the most furious fighting [actually, just over one hour] almost always within pistol range. The remains of the Eagle [which Villeneuve had earlier threatened to throw aboard the *Victory*] were thrown into the sea as well as all the signals.[16]

The *Conqueror* seized control of the *Bucentaure*, and Captain Israel Pellew sent James Atcherley, captain of the marines, in a boat to take command of the vessel. Having secured the ship, Atcherley took Vice-Admiral Villeneuve, Captain Magendie and the other high-ranking officers into his boat, but in the smoke Atcherley could no longer see his own ship, the *Conqueror*, which had moved on to join those British ships encircling the crippled *Santísima Trinidad* further north. Instead, Atcherley had his boat rowed to the badly damaged *Mars*, the only British ship visible, which was drifting in a wrecked state towards the *Bucentaure.*

The *Mars* had earlier been in Collingwood's part of the action. When the stricken Spanish ship *Monarca* had limped away southwards from the *Tonnant* and come within range of the *Bellerophon*, the port guns of the *Tonnant* were turned on the French ship *Pluton* to the north, which was still fighting the *Mars*. Five minutes before Nelson was shot, the *Fougueux* brought down the *Belleisle*'s mizzenmast. The *Belleisle*, between the *Mars* and the *Fougueux*, pulled away, leaving the *Fougueux* clear to pour the whole port broadside into the stern of the *Mars*, which caused great damage and killed the forty-one-year-old commander, Captain George Duff. As the *Mars* turned, the *Pluton*'s guns could now be brought to bear, and they fired another broadside into the stern of the *Mars*, which completed the destruction of the masts and rigging. Out of control and with the captain and twenty-nine crew killed plus sixty-nine wounded (from a crew of nearly six hundred), the *Mars* drifted slowly north-eastwards towards the *Bucentaure* and the boat carrying Atcherley and his French captives. Despite being badly damaged, the *Mars* did not surrender but, now completely unmanageable, could only drift with the wind and the current, unable to return to the fray.

Around half past one, the badly damaged *Fougueux*, having been in combat with the *Belleisle* and the *Mars*, was now close to the action of the *Victory* and the *Temeraire* against the *Redoutable*. The *Temeraire* fired a broadside at the *Fougueux*, using the starboard guns for the first time, and the *Fougueux* collided with the *Temeraire*, causing yet more problems for the stricken *Redoutable*, as Lucas noted: 'In this state, fire took hold of the rudder coating. Happily, it did not spread further, and the men succeeded in extinguishing it. The *Victory* was not fighting; it was occupied solely in extricating itself from the *Redoutable*, but we were riddled by the crossfire from the *Temeraire*, with which we had collided, and from the vessel that was firing into [the *Temeraire*] at the stern.'[17] Within ten minutes, most of the remaining serviceable guns aboard the *Fougueux* were put out of action, many men were dead, and the situation became hopeless, as Commander François Marie Bazin, second-in-command of the *Fougueux*, reported:

At the moment of collision, I noticed a French vessel [the *Redoutable*] entangled to larboard [of the *Temeraire*], but did not recognise it – it had ceased firing. Seeing that our vessel was totally crippled, with the topsail yards and the lower yards cut and in confusion, without the least breeze to enable us to steer, we were not able to avoid the collision which took place . . . at the same moment as our brave Captain Baudoin received a mortal wound and lost consciousness. I then took over the command, and I continued firing into the vessel that was right against ours. I deployed the sailors and soldiers intended for boarding to defend our ship against the enemy who were looking to board the *Fougueux*; several English sailors and soldiers paid dearly for their boldness and retreated on board their vessel, where they took up defensive positions and then for half an hour [actually a little less] used their carronades to fire grapeshot along with their musket fire to sweep across our decks, which the enemy ship dominated due to its great height. As I had received several wounds right at the beginning of the battle, I had the 1st Lieutenant called to help me in this dreadful situation. I was given the news that he was no longer alive and of his two subordinates, one was nearly dead and the other, Lieutenant Peltier, had a bullet in his leg. I asked for the fourth lieutenant, who told me that his battery was nearly out of service; Lieutenant Drudésit [the fourth lieutenant] let me know that he had no more than 15 men and all his guns were wrecked; everyone that I had in the shrouds and on the deck were killed or wounded.[18]

Although the *Redoutable* still refused to surrender, at five minutes to two the flag of the *Fougueux* was struck, at almost the same time as the *Monarca* surrendered to the *Bellerophon* over half a mile to the south-west. In the moments before that,

Bazin in the *Fougueux* first ensured that no sensitive papers fell into the hands of the English:

> Seeing that the enemy were coming on board, and several were killed in the batteries and on the deck, but having then so few people to fight the enemy who had already succeeded in taking possession of the deck, I ordered the firing to cease and I next went into the captain's cabin to remove the lead box containing the secret papers, which I myself threw into the sea, and appearing on the quarterdeck, I saw the enemy had seized it [the *Fougueux*]. I fell into their hands, and they took me prisoner. I was immediately led on board their ship. Our colours were hauled down and gradually the carnage ceased.[19]

With the possible exception of the *Redoutable*, the *Fougueux* suffered the worst casualties of any ship in the entire battle.

EIGHT

Visions of Hell

> A shot took off the arm of Thomas Main, when at his gun on the forecastle; his messmates kindly offered to assist him in going to the surgeon, but he bluntly said, *'I thank you, stay where you are; you will do more good there.'* He then went down by himself to the cockpit. The Surgeon (who respected him) would willingly have attended him, in preference to others whose wounds were less alarming; but Main would not admit of it, saying *'Avast, not until it comes to my turn, if you please.'* The Surgeon soon after amputated the shattered part of the arm, near the shoulder, during which, with great composure, smiling, and with a steady clear voice, he sang the whole of 'Rule Britannia'.
>
> A letter from Captain Bayntun of the *Leviathan*, recording the injuries of Thomas Main[1]*

On all the gun decks of those ships in the midst of the conflict, the sailors were working in a suffocating stench of gunpowder smoke, blood, sweat and burnt and torn skin. Here and there the

*Thomas Main died later from a fever at Gibraltar when his wound had almost healed.

throat-catching tang of vomit added bitterness to the fumes. Despite having stripped off their shirts before the battle began, they were almost overpowered by the heat of the guns in the confined space. Many men were now smoke-blackened and covered with dust, streaked by the rivulets of sweat running down their faces and bodies. In the cramped gun decks the noise of the battle could be felt as much as heard: a maddening sensation of pressure on the skull, which added to the sense of detachment induced by the deafening noise and reduced visibility:

At every moment the smoke accumulated more and more thickly, stagnating on board between-decks at times so densely as to blur over the nearest objects, and often blot out the men at the guns from those close at hand on each side. The guns had to be trained as it were mechanically by means of orders passed down from above, and on objects that the men fighting the guns hardly ever got a glimpse of. In these circumstances you frequently heard the order on the main and lower deck to level the guns 'two points abaft the beam', 'point blank', and so on. In fact, the men were as much in the dark as to external objects as if they had been blindfolded, and the only comfort to be derived from this serious inconvenience was that every man was so isolated from his neighbour that he was not put in mind of his danger by seeing his messmates go down all round. All that he knew was that he heard the crash of the shot smashing through the rending timbers, and then followed at once the hoarse bellowings of the captains of the guns, as men were missed at their posts, calling out to the survivors, 'Close up there! close up!'[2]

Moving the guns became more and more difficult as men lost their balance on the slippery deck. Although sand had been spread on the decks to reduce the amount of slipping and sliding as the gun crews hauled the cannons into position, and many men were working in bare feet for a better grip, the sand could no longer cope with the quantity of blood, and the deck was slick with shredded flesh. As casualties were carried below, each man had to work harder to compensate for the dwindling numbers in each gun crew, and many of the survivors would later need to be treated for hernias. The rate of firing inevitably slowed, but at such close range accuracy was much less of a problem. Instead, the weary gun crews tried to maintain a steady rhythm.

As the gun was fired, the recoil thrust it back from the gunport against the breeching rope, which was passed round the back of the gun and through metal rings fixed on either side of the gunport. When the guns grew hot with continuous firing, the recoil was more violent, lifting the gun carriage off the deck, sometimes so far that the gun hit the beams of the deck above. Such powerful recoils made the guns a danger to their own gun crews, and the thunder of the gun carriages falling back to the deck added to the numbing barrage of sound. If the breeching ropes were too weak, or had started to rot, they broke under such heavy recoils, and the loose flying gun caused great injury to anyone in the way.

After firing, the gun was hauled back sufficiently for the gunners to work at the muzzle. A rod with an iron spiral on the end, resembling a huge corkscrew and called a 'worm', was thrust down the barrel, turned and withdrawn to remove any remains of the cartridge. A wet sponge or mop was next pushed down on a long handle of wood or rope to extinguish remaining sparks and cool any hot spots. After the sponge was removed, the cartridge was loaded into the muzzle, followed by a wad of rope yarn, and rammed home. The rammer was withdrawn and a cannon-ball loaded, with another wad rammed down on top to stop the ball falling back out of the muzzle as the ship rolled. Shot of the right size was stored near the guns in racks against the ship's sides, around hatches and towards the centre of the deck, while fresh cartridges were brought by powder monkeys as they were needed.

Once the gun was loaded, the captain of the gun primed it.

First he pushed a priming iron, much like a knitting needle, down the touch-hole to break a hole in the cartridge. He then inserted a priming tube, which was a quill from a feather or a narrow tin tube, ready-filled with gunpowder to save the time involved in pouring loose gunpowder down the touch-hole. A small amount of gunpowder was also placed in the pan of the flintlock. The gun was then run out – hauled forward by rope tackles fixed to the side of the ship – so that the muzzle stuck out clear of the gunport. The gun was aimed by physically levering the gun carriage from side to side with long crowbars, or by levering the gun itself up or down on the gun carriage and hammering in wedges to hold it in position. To fire the gun, the gunner cocked the mechanism of the flintlock and, judging the timing, pulled the lanyard that operated the trigger of the flintlock. The result was a spurt of flame from the touch-hole that burned the beams of the deck above. In the same instant, the gun kicked back across the deck as the shot left the muzzle, and the tail-end of the muzzle flash singed the sides of the gunport.

Sometimes the flintlocks misfired, because the flint broke or the powder in the pan did not catch light; in case this happened a match tub was placed near every gun. The match tubs, filled with sand or water, had notches round the rim that held slow-burning fuses called 'matches', with their burning ends suspended over the water or sand. If a flintlock failed, the gunner took one of these matches, fitted it to the end of a rod called a 'linstock', blew on the burning end until it glowed and used it to set fire to the priming tube in the touch-hole. This was done with care, since using a match made it more difficult to synchronise the firing of the gun with the movements of the ship, and the back-blast from the touch-hole could easily blow the linstock out of the hand of the gunner. Aboard the French and Spanish ships, which had few flintlocks, most of the guns were being fired with a match.

Maintaining the rhythm in each gun crew was the key to

rapid firing. First haul the gun back to get at the muzzle; scrape out any remains of the spent cartridge and sponge out the bore to extinguish sparks; load the gunpowder cartridge and cannon-ball; prime the firing mechanism; haul the cannon forwards; aim and fire; haul the gun back and start again. The short fierce conflicts of the opening moves of the battle evolved into trials of endurance as ships lay side by side, pulverising each other with broadside after broadside. The superior training and practice of the British gunners now began to tip the balance. After the first broadside, it was usual for each gun to fire again as soon as it was ready, so the broadsides gradually became ragged, but by maintaining a steady fire, the British disrupted the enemy gun crews, reducing the amount of fire being returned and lessening the number of their own casualties. In some instances, French and Spanish guns fell silent, where their crews were all killed or wounded or too few men were left to operate them. According to Captain Rotheram of the *Royal Sovereign*, sometimes when British ships were alongside and touching French ships, the French gunners lowered the gunports and abandoned their guns, knowing that they could not match the British gunners. Lieutenant des Touches, on board the *Intrépide*, later summed up the differences between the British gunners and those in the French and Spanish ships:

> The audacity with which Admiral Nelson had attacked us, and which had been so successful for him, was due to the complete contempt that he held, not without reason, for the effects of our artillery. At that time our principle was to aim at the masts, and in order to produce any real damage, we wasted a mass of missiles that, fired into the hull of the enemy vessel, would have brought down part of the crew. Also, our losses were always incomparably higher than those of the English, who fired horizontally and reached us through our wooden sides, making splinters fly up which were even more murderous than the cannon-ball itself. We were still using linstock matches that fired our

guns with despairing slowness, so that if the ship was rolling badly, as it was on 21 October, entire broadsides passed above the masts without causing the least damage. The English had rather crude flintlocks, but very much superior to our linstocks. They used . . . a horizontal fire, thanks to which, if they did not score a direct hit, they at least obtained a very effective ricochet.[3]

By now the chain of events was set. In calculating his plan for the battle, Nelson had been both right and wrong. His assumption was over-optimistic that Villeneuve would be surprised by the speed of attack and by the use of columns or lines of ships sailing directly at the enemy line, rather than forming a parallel line of battle. The French admiral had correctly predicted what Nelson's plan would be and had warned his officers accordingly, but Nelson was right that such tactics would break up the opposing battle line, causing a mêlée where British ships had the advantage – in his words, 'a pell-mell battle'.[4] Now, after nearly two hours of fighting and with Nelson himself lying fatally wounded in the cockpit of the *Victory*, his prediction was coming true. No longer was there a line of French and Spanish ships cut in two places by the British attack, but a seething cloud of smoke pierced by flashes of gunfire, masking ships that slowly milled around as the better gunnery and manoeuvrability of the British ships gradually ground their French and Spanish opponents into submission. In an area of sea nearly two miles long and roughly half a mile wide, there was now a constant exchange of gunfire within a confusion of ships – it was literally a battle of endurance as the carnage on and below decks increased. The leading ships of the French and Spanish line, which had been cut off from the battle and were still sailing away to the north-west, needed to turn round and make their way back to be of any help – a very slow task in the light winds. With the odds now in favour of the British, their task was to capture or disable as many French and Spanish ships as possible before those at the head of the line could return to reinforce them.

At a quarter to two, Rear-Admiral Dumanoir decided at long last to turn back towards the action, but the signal he gave to his ships for them to perform the manoeuvre together resulted in confusion, because there was so little wind and the sea swell was by this time quite violent. Dumanoir's ship, the *Formidable*, was forced to lower a boat to tow the ship round, and the *Scipion* did the same. The *Intrépide* collided with the *Mont-Blanc* during the turn, splitting the *Intrépide*'s foresail and breaking the *Mont-Blanc*'s jib-boom. The *Rayo*, the *San Francisco de Asís*, the *Duguay-Trouin* and the *Neptuno* all managed the turn, but very slowly. A real danger was nevertheless emerging that a sustained and co-ordinated counter-attack by these ships could carry the day, because many of the British warships were badly damaged and their crews were exhausted.

In the action that was taking place at the same time two miles to the south, the 74-gun French *Algésiras* took the opportunity to try to sail behind the 80-gun British *Tonnant* to fire a broadside through the stern, now that the Spanish ship *Monarca* had pulled away, but instead the bow of the *Algésiras* struck the middle of the starboard side of the *Tonnant*, and they became entangled. Since, with the light winds, every manoeuvre was unusually slow, Captain Laurent Le Tourneur of the *Algésiras* had time to foresee what would happen and so assembled a boarding party, as Lieutenant Philibert of the same ship later recorded in his journal:

As this ship [the *Tonnant*] persisted in its manoeuvre, we collided with it by driving our bowsprit into its mainmast shrouds. They then fired several volleys of canister shot at us, which totally carried away our rigging. Our well-sustained fire soon reduced it to the same state as ourselves. From that moment it was no longer possible to make out anything of our fleet: we could only see the *Pluton* in front of us, which was in close combat with an enemy vessel [the *Mars*]. There was also fighting behind us, but the cloud of smoke which enveloped us did not let us see anything. Our General [Rear-Admiral Magon, also aboard the *Algésiras*] gave orders to board, and everyone appointed for this went enthusiastically; although supported by a very lively volley of musket fire, nearly all of them fell victim to their courage and daring, because at that moment the enemy ship fired at us a whole volley of shot from the cannons on its upper decks and gangways. Among those brave men, we most sincerely regret the loss of Lieutenant Verdreau, an officer of great merit, who was in charge of them and who had been the first to advance.

Shortly afterwards we had three other ships within pistol range that came to engage us after having cut the line behind us. They were firing their muskets so effectively that our upper decks were swept clear in less than half an hour. We were then engaged more than ever with the enemy, who were surrounding us on all sides, in such a way that we were, so to speak, separated from our fleet, not a single vessel of which was visible to us. Our general [Magon], feeling how critical our position was becoming, went about everywhere and encouraged us by his presence, which only showed his composure and the most heroic bravery.[5]

Heroism was evident in the *Tonnant* as well, because during the action,

a man who was working one of the quarter-deck guns was shot through the great toe. He looked at his toe, which hung by a fragment of skin, and then at his gun, and then at his toe again. At last he took out his pocket knife, [and] gave it to his comrade – 'Jack, cut that bit of skin through for me.' 'No,' says the other, 'go down to the Doctor, man.' 'Damn it, I'm ashamed of going down to him for this trifle, just whip it off for me, it's only a bit of skin.' In this way they were going on, when the carronade near him took a cant accidentally, from a roll of the ship, and crushed the whole of that part of his foot.[6]

Below decks on board the *Tonnant,* where the surgeon was working, Lieutenant Frederick Hoffman found a shocking scene:

On entering the cockpit I found fourteen men waiting amputation of either an arm or a leg. A marine who had sailed with me in a former ship was standing up as I passed, with his left arm hanging down. 'What's the matter, Conelly?' said I to him. 'Not much,' replied he, 'I am only winged above my elbow, and I am waiting my turn to be lopped.' His arm was dreadfully broken by grape-shot. I regret to mention that out of sixteen amputations only two survived. This was in consequence of the motion of the ship during the gale [after the battle]. Their stumps broke out afresh and it was impossible to stop the haemorrhage. One of them, whose name was Smith, after his leg was taken off, hearing the cheering on deck on consequence of another of the enemy striking her colours, cheered also. The exertion he made burst the vessels, and before they could be again taken up he died.[7]

It was during battle that surgeons were most effective, even though they were working in appalling conditions. For much of their time on board ship, they were involved not with battle injuries, but with the daily hazards of disease and accidental injury. Men working aloft on the masts, rigging and sails frequently slipped, and many of them could not swim, nor were they encouraged to learn, since it was thought this would help them to desert. Even in calm weather a man who fell overboard was likely to drown, and in bad weather the danger was many times greater. For the day of the battle, the log of the *Conqueror* prosaically recorded: 'At 5.30, fell overboard and was drowned Aaron Crocan.'[8] Working before daybreak, the seaman Aaron Crocan was lost overboard and became the very first of the many casualties that day.

A fall into the sea or to the deck was almost always fatal, while an accident aloft could result in torn muscles and ligaments, or even broken bones. Crushing injuries, where limbs were trapped under heavy equipment, and all varieties of strains were common. The immense physical effort needed for much of the work, and the prevalence of chronic constipation due to the poor diet and primitive toilets, made hernias an occupational hazard – so much so that free trusses were provided. Unfortunately, these were made of straw and were rather crude; such was the market for an efficient hernia remedy that between 1617 and 1852 thirty-five applications were made to patent new designs for trusses.

Most of the large ships carried a surgeon, and the largest, the first rates, also carried three assistant surgeons. Smaller ships might have one or two, and the smallest might only have one man with the rank of assistant surgeon. Whatever their actual status, they were employed primarily as surgeons rather than physicians, and although they were responsible for the health of the people on board their ship, it was in surgery that their efforts were most effective. The skills of surgeons varied according to their experience and training, but all were hampered by the poor state of medical knowledge at that time. Most diseases were thought to originate from a single cause, usually evil-smelling vapours termed miasmas, although some religious surgeons thought that disease was caused by sin, and doctors had no idea why some medicines apparently worked while others did not. In reality, many medical treatments did no good at all (and, if the patient was fortunate, they did no harm either). Many patients recovered, not because they had been treated by a doctor, but because their own immune system eventually overcame the problem; in some cases faith in the doctor's skills may in itself have had a beneficial psychological effect. There was an effective treatment and preventative for malaria, and the use of bleeding or leeches was helpful for some medical conditions, but these remedies were also used in many situations where this was far from the case – in general ships' surgeons were under no illusions about the limits of their expertise.

As soon as a ship was under fire, a steady stream of casualties arrived on the orlop deck. In most ships the crew were taught the use of tourniquets, to reduce blood loss, and also elementary bandaging, but in the heat of battle such first aid was usually inadequate. This would not have mattered but for the fact that, for want of a better system, the surgeon had a strict first-come, first-tended policy. While waiting their turn to see the surgeon, some men bled to death whose wounds were otherwise not serious or complicated, but merely required competent stitching and bandaging. This fact was known to the surgeons, putting them under pressure to work as fast as possible. When an injured man was laid on the surgeon's table, his clothes were ripped and cut off around the wounds so that the surgeon could inspect them. In a matter of seconds, he had to decide whether the injuries were fatal, could be dealt with by stitching and dressing, whether amputation was necessary, if it was possible, and so on. Usually this was all decided in one hurried glance, in poor lighting, as the surgeon tried to stand steady on a deck juddering from the countershocks of outgoing and incoming broadsides, as well as the normal roll and pitch of the ship.

If amputation was decided on, there was no time lost and nothing in the way of refinement. No effective anaesthetic was known – the patient was given a swig from one of the bottles of spirits, often rum or brandy, that were ready to hand for that purpose, a leather gag was placed in his mouth to bite on, and he was held down on the table by the surgeon's assistants. A tourniquet was applied above the site of the operation, and the surgeon then took his knife and cut the flesh, muscle and sinews around the limb, right down to the bone. Some surgeons were apparently able to do this in a single swift cut, but frequently a series of cuts were needed. The flesh was then drawn back from the cut to allow the surgeon to saw through the bone as high up on the limb as possible to leave an overlap of flesh to cover the end of the bone. Once the bone was sawn through and the amputated part discarded, the assistant released his grip, allowing the flesh to creep back over the end of the bone, and the tourniquet was loosened just enough to allow the arteries to bleed a little. This was done to make the blood vessels visible in the livid mass of severed flesh so that they could be tied off with waxed silk or thread ligatures – broad ones that were less likely to cut through the wall of the artery than finer ligatures. The ends of these were left long, and once the blood vessels had been secured, the tourniquet was removed. The stump was sealed with spirits of turpentine or, as a last resort, with pitch, and it was then dressed. The ends of the ligatures helped to drain fluids out of the stump as it healed – a process that took months of careful management of the wound – and as the blood vessels sealed themselves, the ligatures fell off. Nelson himself, after his arm was amputated, suffered constant pain from one ligature for months afterwards, possibly because a nerve had been tied up along with the artery.

Speed was the key to a successful amputation. Opium could be given to dull the pain afterwards but, without anaesthetic, if the operation went on too long, the overwhelming pain sent the patient into deep shock, which usually proved fatal. This restriction applied not just at sea, but to all surgeons at that time, and the most successful surgeons were the fastest ones. Robert Liston, Professor of Surgery at University College Hospital, London, had the reputation of being the fastest in England, and gamblers would often bet on the speed of an operation, many of which were performed publicly. A balance had to be struck, however, since greater speed tended to be achieved at the expense of accuracy. Even Liston on one occasion, eager to beat his personal best performance while amputating a leg, is said to have cut off one of the patient's testicles and two of his assistant's fingers at the same time. A surgeon was doing well if he managed to cut off the limb in anything approaching thirty seconds and was able to complete the operation in under two minutes – minutes that seemed but seconds for the surgeon and a lifetime for the patient. In 1846, over four decades after the battle, Liston would be the first surgeon in England to perform an amputation on an anaesthetised patient.

Men wounded on board ship had one advantage over soldiers on the battlefield: the proximity of the surgeon. Napoleon's surgeon, Dominique-Jean Larrey, found his success rate was much higher when he performed operations on the battlefield, even if he was under fire, than if he waited until the wounded were transported to a hospital away from the fighting. This was because the wound was often still numb and the patient still in the initial stages of shock, which tended to reduce their suffering during the operation. On board ship, even those who had to wait their turn might be dealt with by a surgeon sooner than soldiers wounded in land battles. Surgeons also noted that some very serious wounds did not lose much blood, apparently because the blood vessels were partially closed or had been flattened. Some men, who were so badly wounded that the surgeon could do nothing for them, lingered for several hours because of this, adding to the difficulties that the surgeon worked under as they called to him for help and grabbed hold of him if he was within reach.

A 'vision of hell' was a recurring phrase in the writings of those who witnessed the cockpit of a battleship during a battle. It was hot and airless, with every surface – walls, floor and the deck above – trembling from the recoil of the guns. In this gloomy confined space, reeking with the stench of blood and mangled flesh, from the shadows of which came the screams and moans of the wounded and dying, the little light shed by flickering candles and lanterns was focused on the surgeon. Often described as looking more like a butcher than a medical man, covered with blood and working as fast as possible to hack off mangled limbs, which were unceremoniously thrown in a tub prior to being heaved overboard, the sweating surgeon worked up to and beyond the point of exhaustion. If they were not employed as powder monkeys, it was here that any women in the ship did what they could to help. On board the *Tonnant*, where Lieutenant Hoffman had found his friend Conelly badly wounded in the cockpit, another officer noted it was 'very dark, the amputations were done by the surgeon with his two assistants holding tallow candles for the doctor to see by. Helping him were the purser and a petty officer's wife, a very big woman, who, as fast as the unfortunate wounded were operated on, lifted them off the table bodily in her arms and bore them off as if they were children to their temporary berths out of the way elsewhere.'[9]

An account of the work of Forbes Chevers, the surgeon on board the *Tonnant*, was later published by one witness:

> It may well be imagined that, with 26 killed and 50 wounded, C. [Chevers, the surgeon] had hot work in the cockpit of the *Tonnant* during the action. The place was utterly dark, half of its depth being below the water-line. C. did all his amputations by the light of tallow candles, held torch-like by two assistants, to whom he said, 'If you look straight into the wound, and see all that I do, I shall see perfectly' . . . A consequence was that, when he washed his face at the first opportunity, he found that his eyebrows had been burnt off. He received most admirable assistance from Mr. George Booth, the purser, who, having no duty elsewhere, shared the labours of the surgeon. Excellent aid was also given by a very powerful and resolute woman, the wife of a petty officer, whose name I deeply regret I cannot recall. She and Mr. Booth . . . a small but singularly agile man, carried the sailors who had been operated upon to their

temporary berths, taking them up in their arms as if they had been children, in a manner in which C. himself, a tall and very strong young man, always spoke of with expressions of wonder . . . C. described the agony suffered by strong, muscular sailors torn by splinter wounds (these wounds being generally much more formidable than those inflicted by shot) as being terrible, even to a surgeon.[10]

Between those requiring amputation, and those who could only be made comfortable in their last hours or minutes, were a number of wounded for whom the surgeon was able to do no more than dress their wounds. Burns were treated with olive oil and ointments to soothe the pain and reduce exposure to air, but little could be done for many penetrating wounds to the body or head. The surgeon would often probe a wound blindly in the hope of locating the bullet or splinter that had caused it, but unless it was sufficiently near the surface to be extracted with forceps, the bullet or splinter was left in place and the wound merely dressed to prevent blood loss. Surgeons knew from experience that opening up the chest or abdomen to remove a bullet almost always resulted in the death of the patient, who stood more chance of survival by being left alone. If the patient recovered, he usually carried the wood or lead inside him for the rest of his life, sometimes suffering later from its presence. On board the *Belleisle,* Marine Lieutenant Nicolas saw one seaman who had been shot in the head about to be dropped overboard. At the last moment he was found to be still breathing: 'he was, of course, saved, and after being a week in the hospital, the ball, which entered the temple came out of his mouth'.[11]

All too often, for those who survived surgery, the following days and weeks were the most hazardous. Tetanus was always possible and always deadly; sometimes the gangrene that amputation was meant to prevent set in anyway. Almost invariably patients had some kind of infection, brought on by the unhygienic conditions, which often resulted in a fever that could be fatal. Knowing what was involved, many seamen feared amputation more than the dangers of battle, and for some the prospect of life without all four limbs was so terrible that they deferred treatment until it was too late to be effective.

Wherever the fighting continued, more casualties were destined for the surgeons, particularly aboard the *Bellerophon* and the *Aigle*, which were still engaged in a bloody struggle. With the two ships locked together, Lieutenant Cumby prepared his men for any attempt by the French crew of the *Aigle* to board:

Our quarterdeck, poop, and forecastle were at this time almost cleared by musketry from troops on board *L'Aigle*, her poop and gangway completely commanding those decks, and the troops on board her appearing very numerous. At this moment I ordered all the remaining men down from the poop and, calling the boarders, had them mustered under the half deck and held them in readiness to repel any attempt that might be made by the enemy to board us, their position rendering it quite impracticable for us to board them in the face of such a fire of musketry so advantageously situated. But whatever advantage they had over us on these upper decks was greatly overbalanced by the superiority of our fire on the lower and main decks, *L'Aigle* soon ceasing entirely to fire on us from her lower deck, the ports [gunport lids] of which were lowered down, while the fire from ours was vigorously maintained, the ports having by my orders been hauled up close against the side when we first fell on board her, to prevent their being torn from their hinges when the ships came into contact. While thus closely engaged and rubbing sides with *L'Aigle*, she threw many hand grenades on board us, both on our forecastle and gangway and in at the ports. Some of these exploded and dreadfully scorched several of our men.[12]

The onslaught of grenades was witnessed by Midshipman Robert Patton, who recalled that it 'put upwards of twenty-five men *hors de combat*, many of whom were dreadfully scorched. One of the sufferers, in his agony, instead of going down to the surgeon, ran aft and threw himself out of one of the stern ports.'[13] Cumby himself heroically picked up one of the unexploded grenades and managed to throw it overboard while the fuse was still burning, next noticing that

> one of these grenades had been thrown in at a lower deck port and in its explosion had blown off the scuttle [hatch] of the Gunner's storeroom, setting fire to the storeroom and forcing open the door into the [gunpowder] magazine passage; most providentially, this door was so placed with respect to that opening from the passage into the magazine that the same blast which *blew open* the storeroom door *shut to* the door of the magazine, otherwise we must all in both ships inevitably have been blown up together. The Gunner, who was in the storeroom at the time, went quietly up to Lieutenant Saunders on the lower deck, and acquainting him the storeroom was on fire, requested a few hands with water to extinguish it; these being instantly granted he returned with them and put the fire out without its having been known to any person on board except to those employed in its extinction.[14]

The lucky chance that kept the fire out of the main magazine and the cool efficiency of the gunner who put out the fire, before the sight of it spread panic through the crew, saved the *Bellerophon*, which gradually subdued the *Aigle*. At half past one Cumby watched as the French vessel disengaged: '*L'Aigle* hoisted her jib and dropped clear of us, under a tremendous raking fire from us as she paid off; our ship at this time was totally unmanageable, the main and mizen topmasts hanging over the side, the jib-boom, spanker-boom and gaff shot away, and not a brace or bowline serviceable.'[15]

Just as the *Aigle* was disengaging, the two ships having fought for an hour, one of the last ships in Collingwood's column – the *Defiance* – finally broke through the line to the south. The *Defiance* chose as a target the Spanish ship *Principe de Asturias*, a three-decker of 112 guns. Although this was much larger than the 74-gun *Defiance*, the aim of the Spanish gunners proved too high, which saved many men, as Colin Campbell, an eighteen-year-old master's mate from Ardpatrick in Scotland, recorded:

> We continued running down [towards the Combined Fleet] till half past one when we began firing, but not before a great many shot had been fired at us and cut our running rigging to pieces. In ten minutes we got close alongside of the *Prince de Esturias*, Spanish three decker, and hammered away upon her within pistol shot for 3/4 of an hour when not being able to stand the little *Defiance* any longer she bore up before the wind and ran to leeward, when we got her stern to us we raked her hotly with plenty of grape and canister. The slaughter on board of her must have been very great. She ran to leeward and never re-entered the action again. She only killed one man on board of us; the whole of her shot went through our rigging and over our mastheads. They fired so high that they shot away our main-top-gallant truck. Every one of our shot told upon her and made the splinters fly.[16]

In fact, the struggle between the *Defiance* and the *Principe de Asturias* was not as simple as portrayed by Campbell, for as the *Defiance* reached the line of the Combined Fleet and attempted to pass behind the *Principe de Asturias*, the French ship *Berwick* tried to close the gap and collided with the *Defiance*. This allowed the *Principe de Asturias* to pull ahead before an annihilating broadside could be fired into the unprotected stern of the Spanish ship. The *Principe de Asturias* then manoeuvred to engage the *Revenge*, giving the battered French *Achille*, already fighting the

Revenge, the chance to withdraw. It was some minutes later before the *Defiance* caught up with the *Principe de Asturias* to join the violent turmoil that was forming around the *Revenge* and the Spanish ship *San Ildefonso*, while the British ships *Polyphemus* and *Swiftsure* were lending support from a distance.

With this newly arrived assistance in the fight with the *Achille*, there was now an opportunity for the *Revenge* to repair some of the extensive damage, as seaman William Robinson described:

After being engaged about an hour, two other ships fortunately came up, received some of the fire intended for us, and we were now enabled to get at some of the shot-holes between wind and water, and plug them up: – this is a duty performed by the carpenter and his crew. We were now unable to work the ship, our yards, sails, and masts being disabled, and the braces completely shot away. In this condition we lay by the side of the enemy, firing away, and now and

A plan of the battle at 2 p.m. (after Taylor 1950). The French and Spanish line of battle has been destroyed as the battle becomes a free-for-all. The leading French and Spanish ships that had continued sailing away have now turned back towards the battle.

1 *Victory*
2 *Temeraire*
3 *Neptune*
4 *Leviathan*
5 *Conqueror*
6 *Britannia*
7 *Ajax*
8 *Agamemnon*
9 *Orion*
10 *Prince*
11 *Minotaur*
12 *Spartiate*
13 *Royal Sovereign*
14 *Belleisle*
15 *Mars*
16 *Tonnant*
17 *Bellerophon*
18 *Colossus*
19 *Achilles*
20 *Revenge*
21 *Defiance*
22 *Dreadnought*
23 *Swiftsure*
24 *Polyphemus*
25 *Thunderer*
26 *Defence*
27 *Africa*
28 *Euryalus*
29 *Scipion*
30 *Intrépide*
31 *Formidable*
32 *Mont-Blanc*
33 *Duguay-Trouin*
34 *Héros*
35 *Bucentaure*
36 *Redoutable*
37 *Neptune*
38 *Indomptable*
39 *Fougueux*
40 *Pluton*
41 *Algésiras*
42 *Aigle*
43 *Swiftsure*
44 *Argonaute*
45 *Achille*
46 *Berwick*
47 *Neptuno*
48 *Rayo*
49 *San Francisco de Asís*
50 *San Agustín*
51 *Santísima Trinidad*
52 *San Justo*
53 *San Leandro*
54 *Santa Ana*
55 *Bahama*
56 *Montañes*
57 *Argonauta*
58 *San Ildefonso*
59 *Principe de Asturias*
60 *San Juan Nepomuceno*
61 *Monarca*

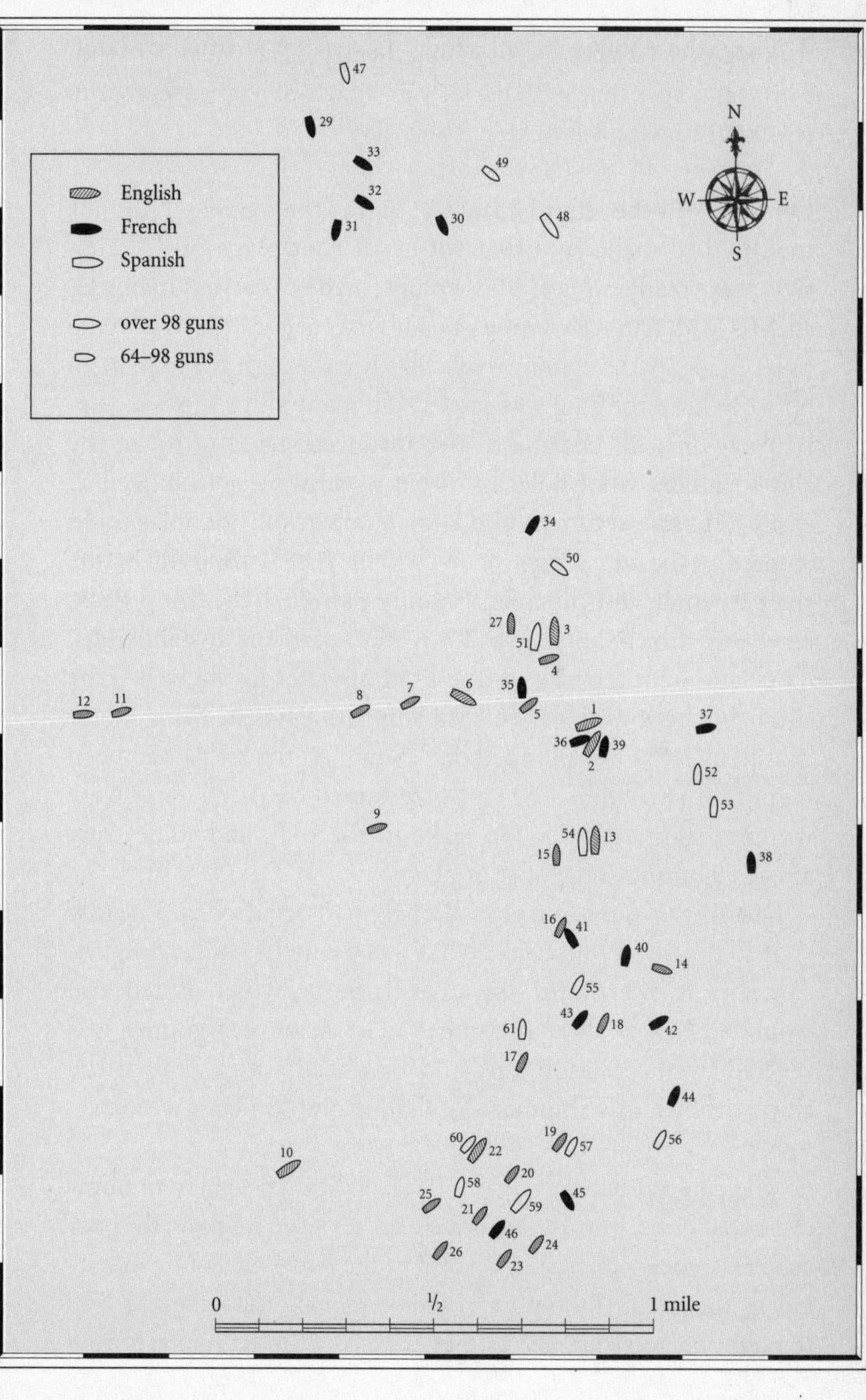

English
French
Spanish
over 98 guns
64–98 guns
N
W
E
S
0
1/2
1 mile

then we received a good raking from them, passing under our stern. This was a busy time with us, for we had not only to endeavour to repair our damage, but to keep to our duty.[17]

On board all the ships before the battle, the carpenter and his men had to make sure that sufficient shot plugs of differing sizes were ready for use. These plugs, made of various materials such as lead, felt, rolled rope or canvas, were hammered into the holes made by the cannon-balls blasting through the hull, in an effort to keep the ship watertight. On many ships this was particularly difficult because of the advanced stages of rot in the ship's timbers. Shot holes in rotten wood were not plugged so easily as in sound timber, and large numbers of shot holes could jeopardise the very structure of a rotten ship. During the battle, the carpenter and his mates mainly patrolled the orlop deck, since any shot holes so low down were particularly dangerous. They also kept a check on the level of water in the well – the sump in the lowest part of the ship from where rising water caused by leaks was pumped out. Now that the battle had been raging for two hours, the carpenter's men on many ships were working frantically to stop leaks in the hull, and some were already running short of shot plugs.

Part of the damage to the *Revenge* had occurred in a deadly shot to the lower gun deck: 'what was termed a *slaughtering one* came in at one of the lower deck ports, which killed and wounded nearly all at the gun'.[18] The head of a gunner was severed by the cannon-ball, and this head struck that of the ship's cobbler. His shipmate William Robinson later wrote:

no one doubted but that he was dead. As it is customary to throw overboard those, who, in an engagement are killed outright, the poor cobbler, amongst the rest, was taken to the port-hole to be committed to the deep, without any other ceremony than shoving him through the port: but, just as they were about to let him slip from their hands into the water, the blood began to circulate, and he commenced kicking. Upon this sign of returning life, his shipmates soon hauled the poor snob [cobbler] in again, and, though wonderful to relate, he recovered so speedily, that he actually fought the battle out; and, when he was afterwards joked about it, he would say, 'it was well that I learned to dance, for if I had not shown you some of my steps, when you were about to throw me overboard, I should not be here now, but safe enough in Davy Jones's Locker.'[19]

Another casualty also to have a lucky escape from death was a soldier with the rank of captain called Pernot on board the French ship *Pluton*:

A cannon-ball piercing the second battery killed three men and wounded several others, of whom I was one. I fell, bathed in my own blood and that of the dead men. I remained there for some time unconscious. When I came to, I recognised one of my soldiers by the sound of his voice and begged him to lead me to the surgeon's post. He told me that he would already have done it, if he hadn't believed me dead. On my arrival they dressed my wounds. Happily I had no fractures. I had received three wounds, one to the left eye which I believed I would lose, but which opened after four days; one to the left hand which would be the longest to heal; and that which caused me the greatest pain . . . the blow I received on my chest, near the collar bone, and from one shoulder to the other . . . After that, when I was laid out on a mattress, I was again wounded in the head in two places by the splinters thrown up by a cannon-ball as it passed through the orlop deck . . . What made me worse was that yet again I could not see, and that afterwards a dozen wounded men fell on my body and made me suffer considerably. They were obliged to dress my wounds again, and they put me in a room belonging to a naval officer. If I was no longer witness to the combat, and its terrible consequences, I could not help trembling at hearing it. I learned that my sub-lieutenant had been killed, as well as my first sergeant, my drummer and two other soldiers, and 23 were very badly wounded. The number of killed and wounded on our ship was put down as 400.[20]

In the British Navy, anyone who died at sea was buried at sea. The body of a sailor was sewn into one of his hammocks (he usually possessed two), with two round shot at his feet. As the hammock was sewn into the form of a shroud, it was the custom to pass the last stitch through the nose of the corpse: theoretically, if the man was not dead, the needle passing through the nose would produce a reaction. The wrapped corpse was then placed on a plank propped on the rail at the side of the ship, and after a funeral service the plank was raised, sliding the corpse off into the water. The length of the funeral service depended on the time available; during a chase, there might be an opportunity to sew the body in a hammock, but perhaps only time enough for a few words from the chaplain with a couple of sailors in attendance when every other man was needed to work the ship. After the burial, the dead man's possessions were sold off at auction, and the proceeds were sent to the man's next of kin; if a man was well liked, the bidding could be generous.

Officers sometimes had coffins made for them by the ship's carpenter, and after the Battle of the Nile, Nelson had a special coffin presented to him by the Canadian captain, Benjamin Hallowell. This coffin was made from a piece of the mainmast of the French flagship *L'Orient*, which blew up during the battle. Just before leaving for Trafalgar, Nelson had arranged for the history of this coffin, which was kept by his agents in London, to be engraved on the coffin's lid, remarking that he felt he might have need of the coffin on his return.

Amid the haste and confusion of battle every semblance of a funeral service was abandoned, and bodies were just thrown overboard as quickly as possible. Without being weighted down, they did not sink straight to the bottom, where they might decompose relatively undisturbed by predators, but floated on or under the surface. Here they were vulnerable to any carnivorous fish or animals, although the autumnal Atlantic waters off the coast of Spain were at least free of sharks. Depending on many variables, these bodies were moved by the local currents as they gradually sank, with some being swept out to sea, while others would eventually be washed up on the beaches between Cadiz and Cape Trafalgar.

In the French and Spanish ships, the dead were not so readily thrown overboard, but were generally laid anywhere that was out of the way. This arose from the Catholic tradition in those countries that placed great stress on burial in consecrated ground and did not sanction burial at sea: even though the French were nominally secular, the old ways persisted. On long voyages, sailors who died on board French and Spanish vessels were often 'buried' in the shingle ballast in the bottom of the ship until land was reached and they could be given a proper Catholic burial. This practice proved a health hazard, particularly in hot climates, and did nothing to alleviate the overpowering stench that tended to rise from the darkest depths of all ships – particularly when water from leaks had to be pumped out.

NINE

SURRENDER

> About 4 they called for quarter which we instantly gave and sent a lieutenant and 20 men to take possession of her. The slaughter on board of her was horrid, the decks were covered with dead and wounded. They never heave their dead overboard in time of action as we do.
>
> Midshipman Colin Campbell of the *Defiance*, describing the surrender of the French ship *Aigle*[1]

From the *Victory*, it could now be seen through the smoke and gloom that Dumanoir's ships over a mile to the north were at last turning. It was a manoeuvre that had been expected, and the British commanders were pleasantly surprised to have been given so much time before this threat materialised. Hardy hoisted a signal to rally the British fleet, but in the smoke and confusion it was only seen by a few ships. The *Leviathan*, the *Conqueror*, the *Neptune*, the *Ajax*, the *Agamemnon* and the *Britannia* now began to form a rough line of battle at the northern edge of the main arena of conflict to meet the new threat head on.

At about the same time, the *Redoutable* surrendered. Having been locked in combat between the *Victory* and the *Temeraire* for over ninety minutes, the French ship was all but useless. Captain Lucas decided to surrender, admitting at long last that there was no possibility of rescue and that his ship was fast filling with water:

Not being able to retaliate at all and not seeing any of our ships, which were all very far off to leeward, coming to our assistance, I only waited until I knew for certain that the leaks which the ship had sprung were so large that it could not be long before it sank, before surrendering. At the moment I was assured of this, and had ordered the colours to be hauled down, they came down of themselves as the mizzenmast fell . . . The enemy made no movement to take possession of the *Redoutable,* whose leaks were so serious that I feared the ship might sink before they could remove the wounded. I put this situation to the *Temeraire*, stating that if they delayed any longer in putting on board members of its crew to pump and to give us that help of which we had the most urgent need, it only remained for me to set fire to the *Redoutable*, whose destruction would certainly involve the *Temeraire* and the *Victory*. Immediately two officers, some soldiers and some sailors from the *Temeraire* were sent on board to take possession of the ship, but at the moment when one of the English seamen put a foot through a gunport of the second battery of the *Redoutable*, one of our sailors, who had already been wounded by a bullet in his leg, seized hold of a musketoon fitted with a bayonet and swept down on him with fury, crying 'I must kill one of them!', and running the bayonet through his hip, made him fall between the two vessels. Despite this occurrence, I succeeded in keeping the English on board, they having wanted to return to the *Temeraire*.[2]

Captain Lucas's account does not quite coincide with that of Dr Beatty, who claimed that after the *Redoutable* surrendered, the *Victory* disengaged and then took possession of the *Redoutable*, although some of the crew from the *Temeraire* later assisted: 'Messrs. Ogilvie and Collingwood, Midshipmen of the *Victory*, were sent in a small boat to take charge of the prize, which they effected. (The *Redoutable* lay alongside and still foul of the *Temeraire* for some time after this, and till several Seamen were sent from the latter to the assistance of the two Officers and men belonging to the *Victory* who had before taken possession of the prize.)'[3]

Further south, both the *Santa Ana* and the *Royal Sovereign* were by this time also in a dreadful state. They had been fighting for over two hours, but when the Spanish Vice-Admiral, Álava, was badly wounded, he decided to surrender – at about the same time as the *Redoutable*. Because the masts and rigging

A plan of the battle at 2.45 p.m. (after Taylor 1950). The British ships on the northern edge of the battle area take positions to meet the threat of the returning French and Spanish ships that have not yet been involved in the battle.

1 *Victory*
2 *Temeraire*
3 *Neptune*
4 *Leviathan*
5 *Conqueror*
6 *Britannia*
7 *Ajax*
8 *Agamemnon*
9 *Orion*
10 *Prince*
11 *Minotaur*
12 *Spartiate*
13 *Royal Sovereign*
14 *Belleisle*
15 *Mars*
16 *Tonnant*
17 *Bellerophon*
18 *Colossus*
19 *Achilles*
20 *Revenge*
21 *Defiance*
22 *Dreadnought*
23 *Swiftsure*
24 *Polyphemus*
25 *Thunderer*
26 *Defence*
27 *Africa*
28 *Euryalus*
29 *Scipion*
30 *Intrépide*
31 *Formidable*
32 *Mont-Blanc*
33 *Duguay-Trouin*
34 *Héros*
35 *Bucentaure*
36 *Redoutable*
37 *Neptune*
38 *Indomptable*
39 *Fougueux*
40 *Pluton*
41 *Algésiras*
42 *Aigle*
43 *Swiftsure*
44 *Argonaute*
45 *Achille*
46 *Berwick*
47 *Neptuno*
48 *Rayo*
49 *San Francisco de Asís*
50 *San Agustín*
51 *Santísima Trinidad*
52 *San Justo*
53 *San Leandro*
54 *Santa Ana*
55 *Bahama*
56 *Montañes*
57 *Argonauta*
58 *San Ildefonso*
59 *Principe de Asturias*
60 *San Juan Nepomuceno*
61 *Monarca*

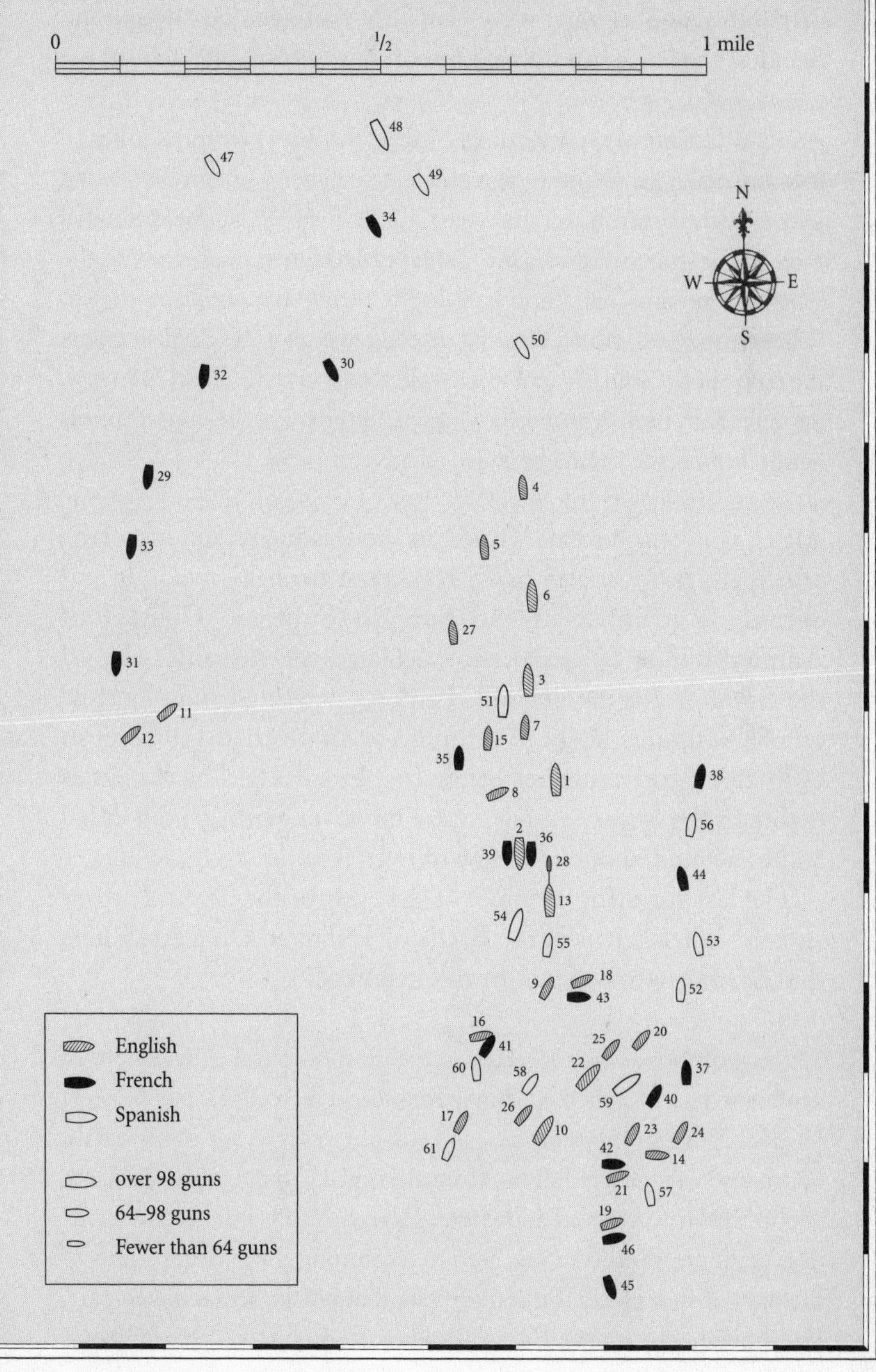

0
1/2
1 mile
N
W
E
S
48
47
49
34
50
32
30
29
4
33
5
6
27
31
3
51
11
7
12
15
35
1
38
8
2
36
39
28
56
44
13
54
55
53
9
18
43
52
16
41
25
20
60
58
22
37
59
40
17
26
10
23
24
61
42
14
21
57
19
46
45
English
French
Spanish
over 98 guns
64–98 guns
Fewer than 64 guns

of the *Royal Sovereign* were so badly damaged, Collingwood decided that his ship needed towing away from the action:

Admiral Collingwood accordingly called the *Euryalus* to take her in tow, and make the necessary signals. He despatched Captain Blackwood to convey the Spanish Admiral on board the *Euryalus*, but he was stated to be at the point of death, and Captain Blackwood returned with the Spanish Captain. That officer had already been to the *Royal Sovereign* to deliver his sword, and on entering, had asked one of the English sailors the name of the ship. When he was told that it was the *Royal Sovereign*, he replied, in broken English, while patting one of the guns with his hand, 'I think she should be called "the Royal Devil."'[4]

Álava, who was born at Vitoria in the Basque region of northern Spain in 1750, eventually recovered from his wounds and became a member of the Spanish Supreme Council of Admiralty. The Spanish later calculated the casualties aboard the *Santa Ana* as 112 men killed and 145 wounded, out of a crew of 1188 – figures likely to be more accurate than the English estimate of 400 casualties in the first broadside. The casualties on board the *Royal Sovereign* were far fewer, with 47 men killed and 94 wounded out of a crew of over 800.

The last surviving member of the crew of the *Santa Ana* was also the last survivor of the Battle of Trafalgar. On 9 April 1892 the *Tribuno* newspaper at Seville reported:

The last of those who took part in the glorious naval engagement of Trafalgar has just died at San Fernando. He was Gaspar Costela Vasquez, born in the year 1787, and was 105 years of age at his death. For many years he lived in the Convalescent Hospital of the garrison, and to the last preserved and enjoyed the use of his intellectual faculties. With great pride he was used to recounting the exciting affairs of the days of that glorious naval campaign at which he had taken part. His funeral, which took place yesterday afternoon, was attended by a very numerous following, composed of the principal officers, and of troops of the naval and military forces.[5]

The surrender of French and Spanish ships now took place in rapid succession, with the *Santa Ana* being followed a few minutes later by the *Algésiras* and then the *San Juan Nepomuceno*. In the battle between the *Tonnant* and the *Algésiras*, the French ship was also smashed into submission, with the numerous casualties including Charles-René Magon, the forty-one-year-old Rear-Admiral from Paris, whose death was described by Lieutenant Philibert:

> Fighting with the same forces and still caught alongside the *Tonnant*, our foremast snapped close to the deck; it had already received several shot and was carried away by the fall of the mizzenmast from the English ship. The few men who remained on our upper decks were still defending them with determination. Several times the English vainly tried to gain control; all those who came on board were killed. At 3 o'clock, our captain (the brave M. Le Tourneur) was very seriously wounded in the shoulder: Lieutenants Morel and Plassan were also seriously wounded at the same time. The firing from the batteries continued with the greatest briskness, and in an incredible way considering our situation; everywhere we were retaliating against the enemy: to starboard, to larboard and with stern-chasers . . . our general [Magon], who had already received two wounds from a bullet in his right arm and a splinter in his thigh, not having wished to give in to our urgent entreaties to go below in order to have his wounds dressed, even though losing much blood, was hit in the chest and died instantly. Our 18-pounder battery was almost deserted, several guns were wrecked. We then brought together all our forces in the 36-pounder battery, which continued to be employed on both sides with the same vigour. The *Tonnant*, with whom we were entangled, set fire to our boatswain's storeroom with burning wads covered in sulphur, and killed three of our men there.[6]

The *Tonnant*'s fire hose was played on the side of the *Algésiras*, which was so close that the discharge from both their broadsides was in danger of setting the ship alight. So great was the turmoil in such a close conflict that other eyewitnesses reported Rear-Admiral Magon as variously being cut in half by a cannon-ball, killed by grape-shot as he was carried below, or struck down with a tomahawk in his hand as he led men to repel a British boarding party. Napoleon was especially affected by his death, declaring, with tears in his eyes: 'With money and timber, I will have other ships, but the loss of Rear-Admiral Magon is irretrievable.'[7]

The *Algésiras* struggled on after Magon was killed and Captain Le Tourneur was wounded, but the ship was becoming unmanageable and surrendered at half past two, as Lieutenant Philibert reported:

> our main mast and mizzenmast fell and fouled nearly all the guns in our two starboard batteries. Two ships, one being a three-decker, then attacked us more closely. Not seeing any help coming from our fleet, we made a final effort with those guns of our 36-pounder battery which were still capable of being fired at the enemy, and we had the satisfaction of seeing that some lucky and well-aimed shots totally crippled the three ships that had been the last to engage us, and in particular the *Tonnant* (which lost the mainmast and mizzenmast), which the guns in our bow, triple-shotted and fired at point-blank range, greatly damaged at the water-line at the stern and also at the bow. The last shots from the enemy did so much damage to us, that they forced us to cease firing, and 66 men from the *Tonnant* were sent on board our ship and took control.[8]

On board the *Tonnant*, Lieutenant Hoffman recalled that

> the crew were then ordered with the second lieutenant to board her. They cheered and in a short time carried her. They found the gallant

French Admiral Magon killed at the foot of the poop ladder, the captain dangerously wounded. Out of eight lieutenants five were killed, with three hundred petty officers and seamen, and about one hundred wounded [actually about 77 killed, and 142 wounded]. We left the second lieutenant and sixty men in charge of her, and took some of the prisoners on board when she swung clear of us. We had pummelled her so handsomely that fourteen of her lower deck guns were dismounted, and her larboard bow exhibited a mass of splinters.[9]

Almost straightaway, the *Tonnant* was in a position to take possession of another ship that was drifting closer, as Hoffman reported: 'After she cleared us another Spanish three-decker drifted nearly on board of us. We received her fire, which shot away the gaff. We returned her salute with interest, and her foremast went about four feet above her deck. We cheered and gave her another broadside, and down came her colours.'[10] This ship was not in fact a three-decker, but the 74-gun, two-decker *San Juan Nepomuceno*, which had originally been attacked by the *Dreadnought* when that ship first reached the battle just after half past one. Until he had moved to the *Royal Sovereign* ten days before, the *Dreadnought* had been Collingwood's flagship, and under his influence the crew had developed a rate of firing one full broadside every three minutes. It took a further fifteen minutes of broadsides from the *Tonnant* for the guns of the *San Juan Nepomuceno* to fall silent, most of them having been dismounted from their gun carriages. With only the mainmast standing, and with 150 wounded and 100 killed out of a crew of nearly 700, the Spanish ship surrendered to the *Tonnant*. Among the dead was the captain, Don Cosmé Churruca. Born in the small Basque country village of Motrico, Churruca became well known through his involvement in scientific expeditions to South America and the Caribbean, as well as his distinguished service in the war years leading up to Trafalgar. As a famous navigator and explorer, he was hailed as a hero in Spain for his voyages of discovery, much as

Nelson was lionised for his military victories in England, and ironically Churruca also had a dislike for the French and for Napoleon. He was forty-five years old at the time of his death and had married only five months before; his loss was widely mourned.

The *Dreadnought* moved off from the *San Juan Nepomuceno* and, from the nearby *Tonnant*, Lieutenant Hoffman watched as his own ship sent 'the only boat that we thought would float, to take possession of her, but she had not proceeded more than a few yards when down she went, leaving the fourth lieutenant and her crew paddling like sea nondescripts'.[11] Lieutenant Benjamin Clement could not swim, but, as he later wrote to his father,

> the two men that were with me could, one a black man, the other a quarter-master: He was the last man in her, when a shot struck her and knocked her quarter off, and she was turned bottom up. Macnamara, the black man, staid by me on one side, and Maclay the quarter-master on the other, until I got hold of the jolly boat's fall [rigging to raise and lower the boat between the deck and the water] that was hanging overboard. I got my leg between the fall, and as the ship lifted by the sea so was I, and as she descended I was ducked. I found myself weak, and thought I was not long for this world. Macnamara swam to the ship, and got a rope and [swam] to me again, and made it fast under my arms, when I swung off, and was hauled into the stern port.[12]

Lieutenant Hoffman, who witnessed the rescue, thought that Clement 'was nearly drowned, and had it not been for a black man, who took him on his back, he must have sunk. This man he never lost sight of, and left him a handsome legacy when he died.'[13] Shortly afterwards the *Dreadnought* sent a boat and took possession of the Spanish ship.

By half past two, after two and a half hours of so much carnage, there were still warships from Nelson's column that had not yet joined in the battle. The *Spartiate* and the *Minotaur*, both very slow ships, were heading as fast as they could directly towards the action, while the *Orion* had veered south-eastwards towards where Collingwood's column had originally cut the line. The chaotic pattern of ships was again beginning to resolve into distinct groups as the final critical point of the battle approached. Around the periphery, the small fast scout ships hovered, watching the battle: the British frigates *Naiad*, *Phoebe* and *Sirius*, the schooner *Pickle* and the cutter *Entreprenante*, as well as the French frigates *Hermione*, *Hortense*, *Cornélie*, *Thémis* and *Rhin* and the brigs *Argus* and *Furet*.

Just as the British frigate *Euryalus* was about to take in tow the crippled *Royal Sovereign* at the centre of the action, the *Orion* at long last reached the battle line, in time to help the *Colossus* against the Spanish ship *Bahama* and the French ship *Swiftsure*. Seeing this, the *Swiftsure* tried to sail northwards, coming between the Spanish *Bahama* and the British *Colossus* and masking the *Bahama*'s guns. It was the advantage that the *Colossus* had been looking for and, after firing several broadsides into the *Swiftsure*, the *Colossus* concentrated fire on the *Bahama*, forcing the vessel to surrender – just moments after the surrender of the *San Juan Nepomuceno*.

The *Colossus* then turned back to the *Swiftsure*, firing into the stern and rapidly bringing about the surrender of the French vessel. The action was later recorded by Captain Villemadrin, commander of the *Swiftsure*, in his official report:

At last the odds were almost equal, when at 2.30 a three-decker [the *Orion*] passed me at the stern and, as it was then almost calm, it had the time to deliver three broadsides, which brought down my main-mast, carried away part of the taffrail,* the helm,† and dismounted

*Ornate rail at the stern of the ship.
†Literally, the entire steering apparatus, but here referring to the ship's wheel.

most of the guns of the 2nd battery, and killed many people. In this cruel position, the senior surgeon twice sent me a midshipman from the 1st battery to warn me that he could no longer receive any wounded, that the space cleared in the hold and the orlop-deck were packed full. I then sent to the 1st battery all the men that I had available, both from the 2nd battery and the upper decks, in order to keep firing. At 3 o'clock I lost my foremast but I continued to fight right up to 3.40, no longer having any hope of being saved, only observing the fleet at a great distance and no longer having in range the *Achille*, which caught fire an instant later, and with 5 feet of water in the hold, I gave orders to cease fire and surrendered. I cannot say exactly how many men I lost, but it could be as many as 260 to 300 men killed or wounded [there were in fact nearly 500 casualties out of a crew of about 700].[14]

The badly mauled *Colossus* took possession of both the *Swiftsure* and the *Bahama*, while the *Orion* headed northwards in the direction of Dumanoir's ships.

One of the next French ships to surrender was the *Aigle*, yet it looked as if the British ship *Belleisle* might have to surrender first. Having disengaged from the *Bellerophon* at half past one, the *Aigle* came into contact with the *Belleisle* fifteen minutes later. The mainmast of the *Belleisle* was brought down, followed by the foremast at half past two. Although the vessel was totally dismasted and in a terrible state, the captain refused to give up, as Marine Lieutenant Owen later recalled:

About two o'clock the mainmast fell over the larboard side, and half-an-hour afterwards the foremast, also, fell over the starboard bow. Thus was the *Belleisle* a total wreck, without the means of returning the fire of the enemy except from the very few guns still unencumbered by the wreck of the masts and rigging. Every exertion, however, continued to be made for presenting the best resistance, and offering the greatest annoyance to the enemy; guns were run out from the sternports on each deck, and all that intelligence could suggest, and discipline effect, was done. Our loss was, however, becoming severe: the first and junior lieutenants had both been killed on the quarter-deck early in the action, and about the same time the Captain was knocked down and severely bruised by a splinter, but refused to leave the deck. As we were lying in this dismasted state, surrounded by the enemy's ships and not having seen the colours of a friendly ship for the previous two hours, the Captain, seeing me actively employed in my duty, was kind enough to bring me a bunch of grapes, and seemed pleased when I told him that our men were doing nobly, and that the ship had been greatly distinguished.[15]

Around three o' clock, other British ships came to help the beleaguered *Belleisle*, after the vessel had been in action for nearly three hours, as Owen reported:

To our great joy, at half-past three the *Swiftsure*, English 74, came booming through the smoke, passed our stern, and giving us three cheers, placed herself between us and the French ship which had been so long more attentive to us than was agreeable; shortly afterwards the *Polyphemus* took the enemy's ship off our bow, and thus we were at length happily disengaged after nearly four hours of struggle, perhaps as severe as ever fell to the lot of a British man of war.[16]

The damage to the *Belleisle* was considerable: 'The only British ship totally dismasted. Her hull was literally knocked to pieces: scarcely a spot in her sides, bows, or stern, appeared untouched; – all her ports, port-timbers, chain-plates, channels, &c., were cut to pieces, and she was exceedingly leaky from shot holes.'[17] Thirty-three men on board were killed and ninety-three wounded, which was a relatively small number of casualties out of a crew of some six hundred men, considering the length of time that the *Belleisle* had been under fire and the amount of damage to the ship itself.

Having drifted away from the *Belleisle* much earlier, at half past two the *Aigle* engaged the *Defiance*, which had not long left off fighting the *Principe de Asturias*. From the *Defiance* the French *Aigle* 'appeared to have been severely handled by some other ship. She was, however, quite ready for action, and defended herself most gallantly for some time.'[18] Half an hour later, it looked as if the *Aigle* was finished, and so boarders were sent from the *Defiance*, led by James Spratt, a forty-six-year-old master's mate from Harrel's Cross in Ireland: 'at length her fire began to slacken, and Captain Durham thinking she surrendered, called up his boarders to take possession. The boats were found to be all shot through, upon which Mr. Spratt . . . took his cutlass between his teeth, called to the boarders to follow, leapt overboard, and swam to *l'Aigle*.'[19] He managed to clamber aboard and 'fought his way courageously through the different decks, and was soon after seen on the Enemy's poop, with his hat on the point of his cutlass, rallying the boarders to his assistance who were then anxiously waiting for the ships to close. He attempted to haul down the French colours, but was attacked by several grenadiers whom he repulsed with success.'[20]

Spratt was next attacked by a French soldier, who lunged at him with the bayonet on his musket, but Spratt struck the bayonet downwards with his cutlass. However, the musket went off, and the musket-ball struck just below his knee, shattering both bones in his leg. Two more soldiers attacked him, but he managed to get to the side of the ship between two guns and hold them off until other boarders came to his rescue. They managed to throw ropes to the *Defiance*, and Spratt, 'holding his bleeding limb over the railing, called out, "Captain, poor Jack Spratt is done up at last." Captain Durham managed to warp alongside,* and this gallant fellow was slung on board. The boarders being thus repulsed, and many of them having swum back to the *Defiance*, Captain

*Pull the two ships together using ropes.

Durham hauled off and engaged the *Aigle* again, she having rehoisted her colours, and after a cannonade of half an hour she struck [surrendered].'[21]

While the *Aigle* was being battered into submission, Spratt was taken to the surgeon, who, convinced that he could not survive without surgery, applied to Durham for permission to amputate after Spratt had refused to go ahead – no doubt well aware that his chances of survival would be remote. The captain 'replied that he could not give such an order, but that he would see Mr. Spratt, which he managed to do in spite of his own wounds and, upon remonstrating with him, Mr. Spratt held out the other leg, (certainly a very good one) and exclaimed, "Never; if I lose my leg, where shall I find a match for this." He was a high-spirited young Irishman, and one of the handsomest men in the service. He was safely landed at Gibraltar, where he remained seventeen weeks in the hospital.'[22] The injury left him lame in the wounded leg, but he remained a strong swimmer. After returning to England, he was put in charge of the telegraph station at Dawlish in Devon and died at nearby Teignmouth on 15 June 1852, at the age of eighty-one.

A loud cheer erupted from the crew on board the *Victory* every time a French or Spanish ship surrendered. The *Aigle* did not surrender alone, as at almost the same time there was cause to celebrate the surrender of three more ships: the French *Berwick* and the Spanish *Argonauta* and *San Ildefonso*. The enthusiastic display of cheering could be heard by Nelson down in the surgeon's cockpit above the din of the battle, as Dr Beatty recorded:

> The *Victory*'s crew cheered whenever they observed an Enemy's Ship surrender. On one of these occasions, Lord Nelson anxiously inquired what was the cause of it, when Lieutenant Pasco, who lay wounded at some distance from His Lordship, raised himself up, and told him that another ship had struck, which appeared to give him much satisfaction. He now felt an ardent thirst, and frequently called for drink,

and to be fanned with paper, making use of these words: 'Fan, fan,' and, 'Drink, drink.' This he continued to repeat, when he wished for drink or the refreshment of cool air, till a very few minutes before he expired. Lemonade, and wine and water, were given to him occasionally. He evinced great solicitude for the event of the battle, and fears for the safety of his friend Captain Hardy. Doctor Scott and Mr. Burke used every argument they could suggest, to relieve his anxiety. Mr Burke told him 'the Enemy were decisively defeated, and that he hoped his Lordship would still live to be himself the bearer of the joyful tidings to his country.' He replied, 'It is nonsense, Mr. Burke, to suppose I can live: my sufferings are great, but they will all be soon over.' Dr. Scott entreated His Lordship 'not to despair of living,' and said, 'he trusted that Divine Providence would restore him once more to his dear Country and friends.' – 'Ah, Doctor!' replied his Lordship, 'it is all over, it is all over.'[23]

Nelson, Beatty noted, became increasingly agitated about the fate of Hardy, who was commanding the *Victory*:

Many messages were sent to Captain Hardy by the Surgeon, requesting his attendance on His Lordship, who became impatient to see him, and often exclaimed: 'Will no one bring Hardy to me? He must be killed: he is surely destroyed.' The Captain's Aide-de-camp, Mr. Bulkeley, now came below, and stated that 'circumstances respecting the Fleet required Captain Hardy's presence on deck, but that he would avail himself of the first favourable moment to visit His Lordship.' On hearing him deliver this message to the Surgeon, His Lordship inquired who had brought it. Mr. Burke answered, 'It is Mr. Bulkeley, my Lord.' – 'It is his voice,' replied His Lordship: he then said to the young gentleman, 'Remember me to your father.'[24]

Hardy was at last able to pay the first of two visits to see Nelson and to give him encouraging news of the battle, as Beatty related:

They shook hands affectionately, and Lord Nelson said: 'Well, Hardy, how goes the battle? How goes the day with us?' – 'Very well, my Lord,' replied Captain Hardy: 'we have got twelve or fourteen of the Enemy's Ships in our possession, but five of their van [under Dumanoir] have tacked, and shew an intention of bearing down on the Victory. I have therefore called two or three of our fresh ships round us, and have no doubt of giving them a drubbing.' – 'I hope,' said His Lordship, 'none of *our* ships have struck, Hardy.' – 'No, my Lord,' replied Captain Hardy, 'there is no fear of that.'[25]

TEN

Lost and Won

> To any other Nation the loss of a Nelson would have been irreparable, but in the British Fleet off Cadiz, every Captain was a Nelson.
>
> The opinion of Vice-Admiral Villeneuve,
> after the Battle of Trafalgar[1]

The battle was almost over. It was apparent to Nelson that his own life was almost over as well, as he confided in Hardy:

'I am a dead man, Hardy. I am going fast: it will be all over with me soon. Come nearer to me. Pray let my dear Lady Hamilton have my hair [for making mourning jewellery and mementoes] and all other things belonging to me.' Mr Burke was about to withdraw at the commencement of this conversation, but His Lordship, perceiving his intention, desired he would remain. Captain Hardy observed, that 'he hoped Mr. Beatty could yet hold out some prospect of life.' – 'Oh! no,' answered His Lordship, 'it is impossible. My back is shot through. Beatty will tell you so.' Captain Hardy then returned on deck, and at parting shook hands again with his revered friend and commander.[2]

The surgeon, Dr Beatty, now became distressed at being unable to do anything more for Nelson:

His Lordship now requested the Surgeon, who had been previously absent a short time attending Mr. Rivers [a midshipman whose leg was amputated], to return to the wounded, and give his assistance to such of them as he could be useful to, 'for,' said he, 'you can do nothing for me.' The Surgeon assured him that the Assistant Surgeons were doing everything that could be effected for those unfortunate men, but on His Lordship's several times repeating his injunctions to that purpose, he left him surrounded by Doctor Scott, Mr. Burke, and two of His Lordship's domestics. After the Surgeon had been absent a few minutes attending Lieutenants Peake and Reeves of the Marines, who were wounded, he was called by Doctor Scott to His Lordship, who said: 'Ah, Mr. Beatty! I have sent for you to say, what I forgot to tell you before, that all power of motion and feeling below my breast are gone, and *you*,' continued he, 'very well *know* I can live but a short time.' The emphatic manner in which he pronounced these last words, left no doubt in the Surgeon's mind, that he adverted to the case of a man who had some months before received a mortal injury of the spine on board the Victory, and had laboured under similar privations of sense and muscular motion. The case had made a great impression on Lord Nelson: he was anxious to know the cause of such symptoms, which was accordingly explained to him, and he now appeared to apply the situation and fate of this man to himself. The Surgeon answered, 'My Lord, you told me so before,' but he now examined the extremities, to ascertain the fact, when his Lordship said, 'Ah, Beatty! I am too certain of it: Scott and Burke have tried it already. You *know* I am Gone.' The Surgeon replied: 'My Lord, unhappily for our Country, nothing can be done for you,' and having made this declaration he was so much affected, that he turned round and withdrew a few steps to conceal his emotions. His Lordship said: 'I know it. I feel something rising in my breast,' putting his hand on his left side, 'which tells me I am gone.' Drink was recommended liberally, and Doctor Scott and Mr. Burke fanned him with paper. He often exclaimed, 'God be praised. I have done my duty,' and upon the Surgeon's inquiring whether his pain was still very great, he declared, 'it continued so very severe, that he wished he was dead. Yet,' said he in a lower voice, 'one would like to live a little longer too,' and after a pause of a few minutes, he added in the same tone, 'What would become of poor Lady Hamilton, if she knew my situation!' The Surgeon, finding it impossible to render His Lordship any further assistance, left him, to attend Lieutenant Bligh, Messrs. Smith and Westphall, Midshipmen, and some Seamen, recently wounded.[3]

Even though Nelson had been told that the battle was all but won, Dumanoir's reinforcement of eight ships was still a huge threat, especially as two further ships that had earlier ceased firing – the *San Agustín* and the *Héros* – were now also joining this force. As the British watched their approach, they gradually realised that fortune was still with them. Instead of a massed attack that might be difficult to beat off, the French and Spanish ships were dividing in two. Dumanoir's *Formidable* was leading the *Duguay-Trouin*, the *Scipion* and the *Mont-Blanc* to intercept the *Spartiate* and the *Minotaur*, which were the last ships in Nelson's column still struggling towards the battle area. Dumanoir's remaining ships were sailing straight for the battle, led by the *Intrépide*, which was out in front, with the *San Agustín* to the east and the others straggling behind. The *Leviathan* pulled out of the British line to deal with the threat from the *San Agustín*, forcing the Spanish vessel to surrender, while the *Intrépide* sailed alone down the west side of the British line, exchanging broadsides with each British ship in turn. Captain Louis Infernet, commanding the *Intrépide*, was intent on helping Villeneuve's flagship, the *Bucentaure*, which had already surrendered. They planned to rescue their admiral, not realising that by now he was safely on board the *Mars*. Lieutenant des Touches in the *Intrépide* soon saw that his ship's gallant attempt had no chance of success:

When we arrived in the wake of the *Bucentaure* and the *Redoutable*, their masts were fallen, their firing almost stopped, the heroism of their defenders alone continued an unequal and hopeless struggle against almost intact ships, whose broadsides succeeded one another without respite. It was to the most intense part of this fray that Captain Infernet led us. He wished, he said, to rescue the Admiral, to take him on board, and to rally around us the vessels which were still in a fit state to fight. The undertaking was insane, and he himself did not believe in it; it was an excuse that he was giving himself in order to continue the struggle, and so that nobody might say that the *Intrépide* had left the battle while there remained one cannon and one sail. It was noble madness which cost us very dearly, but which we did with joy: and that others should have imitated![4]

As des Touches well knew, with the support of the other ships under Dumanoir's command the attempt might have succeeded and tipped the balance of the battle, but unsupported the *Intrépide* was doomed to defeat. Having run the gauntlet of the newly formed British line, the French ship was set upon by the *Orion* and the *Africa* and suffered broadsides from other passing British ships, but nevertheless continued a determined resistance. The courageous defence of the *Intrépide* was recorded by des Touches:

I spent all the time during the battle on the forecastle, where I was in charge of the sails and the musketry; it was from there that I was due to lead my company of boarders; to lead them was my most ardent desire, which unhappily I could not fulfil. One of my worries was to prevent the masts from falling, and I succeeded for a long time in keeping the foremast standing, which still allowed us to manoeuvre a little. When the fighting was most intense, the English vessel *Orion* went in front of us in order to fire a series of broadsides at us; I arranged my men ready to board, and pointing out to a midshipman the manoeuvres of the *Orion*, I sent him to the Captain to beg him to steer so as to board. I saw to the rest, and seeing the enthusiasm of my men, I already imagined myself in charge of the English vessel, and returning with it into Cadiz, its flag hoisted beneath our colours. I was waiting anxiously, but there was no change in the *Intrépide*'s course. I rushed towards the quarterdeck, and on the way I found my midshipman lying flat on his stomach, terrified by the sight of the *Temeraire* [not the *Temeraire*, possibly the *Britannia*], which was alongside us within pistol range, battering us with fire from the upper batteries. I treated my emissary as he deserved, by giving him a kick up the backside, and I went to explain my plan to the Captain. But it was too late. The *Orion* was already passing across our bow, letting loose a murderous broadside, and the opportunity no longer presented itself.

At the moment I reached the poop deck the brave [Captain] Infernet was brandishing a little curved sabre which struck off one of the wooden balls that was part of the ornamental work by the rail. The sword passed rather too close to my face, so that I said to him, smiling, 'Do you want to cut off my head, Captain?' 'No, not yours, certainly, but the first one who talks of surrender!' Next to him was a brave infantry colonel, who had distinguished himself at [the Battle of] Marengo, but whom the broadsides from the *Temeraire* [not the *Temeraire*, possibly the *Britannia*] troubled deeply. He sought in vain to hide behind the powerful figure of our Captain, who eventually noticed it and said to him: 'Ah, Colonel, do you think I am sheathed in metal then?', and we could not stop ourselves smiling despite the gravity of the moment.[5]

While the *Intrépide*'s valiant struggle kept two British ships fully occupied, the *Leviathan* captured the *San Agustín*, and firing from the northernmost British ships forced the *Rayo*, the *Héros* and the *San Francisco de Asís* to sheer off to the east. To the west, Dumanoir's four ships were not quite fast enough to cut off the *Spartiate* and the *Minotaur*, which passed close ahead of the *Formidable*, firing broadsides before turning northwards to fire into each of the four French ships as they sailed by. These now came within range of several other British ships and were attacked by the *Victory*, the *Mars*, the *Royal Sovereign*, the *Temeraire*, the *Tonnant* and the *Bellerophon*. This was enough to deter Dumanoir from any further attempt to turn the tide of battle, but as he passed close to the west side of the main battle area, he fired into those Spanish ships that had surrendered and were now flying British flags. Captain Rotheram of the *Royal Sovereign* recorded his outrage, believing that it was

> an extraordinary and almost incredible fact, that three French ships, under a Rear Admiral, who had no share in the action, did in their flight fire for some time upon the *Santísima Trinidad*, and others of the Spanish prizes, after they had struck their colours to the English. And it is now found from the concurring testimony of several Spanish Officers of rank . . . that Rear Admiral Dumanoir was the person who led his division to the perpetration of this bloody deed, so worthy [of] the days of Robespierre, by which several hundred of the Spaniards were killed or wounded.[6]

Beatty was no less horrified by this act of treachery, noting that French ships had been Dumanoir's target as well:

> After this, the ships of the Enemy's van [led by Dumanoir] that had shewn a disposition to attack the *Victory*, passed to windward, and fired their broadsides not only into her and the *Temeraire*, but also into the French and Spanish captured ships indiscriminately, and they were seen to back or shiver their topsails for the purpose of doing this with more precision. The two Midshipmen of the *Victory* had just boarded the *Redoutable*, and got their men out of the boat, when a shot from the Enemy's van ships that were making off cut the boat adrift. About ten minutes after taking possession of her, a Midshipman came to her from the *Temeraire*; and had hardly ascended the poop, when a shot from one of those ships took off his leg. The French Officers seeing the firing continued on the prize by

their own countrymen, entreated the English Midshipmen to quit the deck, and accompany them below. The unfortunate Midshipman of the *Temeraire* was carried to the French Surgeon, who was ordered to give his immediate attendance to him in preference to his own wounded: his leg was amputated, but he died the same night.[7]

Such was the anger at what was happening that one Spanish ship offered to fight the French: 'the crew of the *Argonauta*, in a body, offered their services to the British officer who had charge of the Prize, to man the guns against any of the French ships; and they were actually stationed at the lower deck guns for that purpose, whilst the English Seamen manned those of the upper deck. The English officer on board returned all the Spanish officers their arms, and placed the most implicit confidence in the honor of the Spaniards, which he had no reason to repent.'[8] Later, when he was a prisoner of war in England, Dumanoir felt the need to write to *The Times*,* denying that he had deliberately fired at his allies who had surrendered, although he admitted that a few stray shots may have hit them. His letter did little to repair his reputation.

With the counter-attack under Dumanoir obviously failing, Hardy came to speak with Nelson for the very last time, to tell him the battle was won:

Captain Hardy now came to the cockpit to see His Lordship a second time, which was after an interval of about fifty minutes from the conclusion of his first visit. Before he quitted the deck, he sent Lieutenant Hills to acquaint Admiral Collingwood with the lamentable circumstance of Lord Nelson's being wounded. – Lord Nelson and Captain Hardy shook hands again, and while the Captain retained His Lordship's hand, he congratulated him even in the arms of Death on his brilliant victory; 'which,' he said, 'was complete, though he did not know

**The Times*, 2 January 1806.

how many of the Enemy were captured, as it was impossible to perceive every ship distinctly. He was certain however of fourteen or fifteen having surrendered.' His Lordship answered, 'That is well, but I bargained for twenty:' and then emphatically exclaimed, '*Anchor*, Hardy, *anchor!*' To this the Captain replied: 'I suppose, my Lord, Admiral Collingwood will now take upon himself the direction of affairs.' – 'Not while I live, I hope, Hardy!' cried the dying Chief, and at that moment endeavoured ineffectually to raise himself from the bed. 'No,' added he, 'do *you* anchor, Hardy.' Captain Hardy then said: 'Shall *we* make the signal, Sir?' – 'Yes,' answered His Lordship, 'for if I live, I'll anchor.'[9]

Convinced a storm was brewing, Nelson was anxious for the fleet to anchor to ride out the bad weather.

Nelson's final thoughts, Beatty recorded, were not for the battle or his fleet, but for Emma and Horatia:

The energetic manner in which he uttered these his last orders to Captain Hardy, accompanied with his efforts to raise himself, evinced his determination never to resign the command while he retained the exercise of his transcendent faculties, and that he expected Captain Hardy still to carry into effect the suggestions of his exalted mind; a sense of his duty overcoming the pains of death. He then told Captain Hardy, 'he felt that in a few minutes he should be no more,' adding in a low tone, 'Don't throw me overboard, Hardy.' The Captain answered: 'Oh! no, certainly not.' – 'Then,' replied His Lordship, 'you know what to do (alluding to some wishes previously expressed by His Lordship to Captain Hardy respecting the place of his interment), and' continued he, 'take care of my dear Lady Hamilton, Hardy: take care of poor Lady Hamilton. Kiss me, Hardy.' The Captain now knelt down, and kissed his cheek, when His Lordship said, 'Now I am satisfied. Thank God, I have done my duty.' Captain Hardy stood for a minute or two in silent contemplation: he then knelt down again, and kissed His Lordship's forehead. His Lordship said: 'Who is that?' The Captain answered: 'It is Hardy,' to which His Lordship replied, 'God bless you, Hardy!' After this affecting scene Captain Hardy withdrew, and returned to the quarter-deck, having spent about eight minutes in this his last interview with his dying friend. Lord Nelson now desired Mr. Chevalier, his Steward, to turn him upon his right side, which being effected, His Lordship said: 'I wish I had not left the deck, for I shall soon be gone.' He afterwards became very low; his breathing was oppressed, and his voice faint. He said to Doctor Scott, 'Doctor, I have *not* been a *great* sinner,' and after a short pause, '*Remember*, that I leave Lady Hamilton and my Daughter Horatia as a legacy to my Country, and,' added he, 'never forget Horatia.' His thirst now increased, and he called for 'Drink, drink,' 'Fan, fan,' and 'Rub, rub,' addressing himself in the last case to Doctor Scott, who had been rubbing His Lordship's breast with his hand, from which he found some relief. These words he spoke in a very rapid manner, which rendered his articulation difficult: but he every now and then, with evident increase of pain, made a greater effort with his vocal powers, and pronounced distinctly these last words: 'Thank God, I have done my duty,' and this great sentiment he continued to repeat as long as he was able to give it utterance.[10]

In less than half an hour Nelson died, although the precise time of death remains uncertain:

His Lordship became speechless in about fifteen minutes after Captain Hardy left him. Doctor Scott and Mr. Burke, who had all along sustained the bed under his shoulders (which raised him in nearly a semi-recumbent posture, the only one that was supportable to him), forbore to disturb him by speaking to him; and when he had remained speechless about five minutes, His Lordship's Steward went to the Surgeon, who had been a short time occupied with the wounded in another part of the cockpit, and stated his apprehensions that his Lordship was dying. The Surgeon immediately repaired to him, and found him on the verge of dissolution. He knelt down by his side, and took up his hand; which was cold, and the pulse gone from the wrist. On the Surgeon's feeling his forehead, which was likewise cold, His Lordship opened his eyes, looked up, and shut them again. The Surgeon again left him, and returned to the wounded who required his assistance, but was not absent five minutes before the Steward announced to him that 'he believed His Lordship had expired.' The Surgeon returned, and found that the report was but too well founded: his Lordship had breathed his last, at thirty minutes past four o'clock; at which period Doctor Scott was in the act of rubbing His Lordship's breast, and Mr. Burke supporting the bed under his shoulders.[11]

Dr Beatty, ever the man of science trying to define the limits of authenticity in his account, added a warning in a footnote: 'It must occur to the reader, that from the nature of the scene passing in the cockpit, and the noise of the guns, the whole of His Lordship's expressions could not be borne in mind, nor even distinctly heard, by the different persons attending him.'[12] It was left to others to take a less clinical view of the admiral's death, and the poet Southey, who wrote one of the early biographies of Nelson, concluded: 'He cannot be said to have fallen prematurely whose work was done; nor ought he to be lamented, who died so full of honours, and at the height of human fame. The most triumphant death is that of the martyr; the most awful, that of the martyred patriot; the most splendid, that of the hero in the hour of victory: and if the chariot and horses of fire had been vouchsafed for Nelson's translation, he could scarcely have departed in a brighter blaze of glory.'[13]

In the end, all the arguments about how much, if at all, Nelson had been identified as a target for French snipers, and whether or not he made himself deliberately conspicuous, are largely irrelevant. It was a quirk of fate, a phenomenon Nelson well understood, that instead of engaging the *Bucentaure*, the *Victory* became locked alongside the *Redoutable*, the one ship in the Combined Fleet that had well-trained and motivated marksmen, who had been set the task of clearing the upper decks of the *Victory* prior to boarding. Nelson had been a target insofar as he stood on deck where everyone was a target. The final irony, produced by modern research, is that from the angle that it entered his body, the bullet that killed Nelson was a stray or a ricochet and was not aimed at him at all. This most famous musket wound was caused by a ball fired at a distance of 15–20 yards. It entered the left shoulder in a downward direction, passed through the left lung, breaking two ribs and cutting through an artery and the spine, before coming to rest just below the right shoulder bone. Nelson died from internal bleeding, but the damage from the single musket-ball was such that if the artery had not been severed, the spinal injury would ultimately have proved fatal anyway.

The closing stage of the battle was almost an anticlimax. In some places ships were still carrying on a fierce and terrifying slaughter, while in others the conflict had ceased, and exhausted sailors turned their attention from manning guns to emergency repairs, trying to bring some sort of order to their slowly drifting hulks. From the *Algésiras*, which had surrendered to the *Tonnant* so long ago, Lieutenant Philibert surveyed the scene:

The smoke which had enveloped us up to then having cleared, our first glances searched for our fleet; there no longer existed any line on either side; we could see nothing more than groups of vessels in the most dreadful state, towards the place more or less where we judged that our battle fleet ought to be. We counted 17 ships from the two navies totally dismasted – their masts gone right down to the deck – and many others partially dismasted . . . Several vessels that we judged to be from our fleet were not attacking, although they appeared to be in good condition, to judge by their masts and sails. Two French ships were hugging the wind in order to reach the vanguard, but afterwards they rejoined the *Principe*, Admiral Gravina's ship, which, as far as we could see, was flying the flag for the general and unconditional recall.[14]

Gravina's ship, the *Principe de Asturias*, was in a poor state. At around half past three, the British ship *Prince* had fired two terrible broadsides into the stern. Gravina had already been wounded, and now the commander, Captain Rafael de Hore, was knocked unconscious. When he came to, he found that the colours were no longer flying, but he had them rehoisted, and as the *Prince* had now passed by, the *Principe de Asturias* limped away from the heart of the fighting.

After four and a half hours of battle, the outcome was finally decided. At about the time that Nelson died, Dumanoir ceased fire and led his four ships away to the south-south-west. This time he did not turn back. The Combined Fleet had no further reserve of unscathed ships to call on, and the threat had been completely neutralised. Nelson's strategic gamble had paid off. The superior gunnery and seamanship of the British sailors had succeeded against a larger but poorly managed fleet, and the outcome of the battle was no longer in doubt. At about five o'clock, the French frigate *Thémis* sailed in from the periphery of the battle and took the *Principe de Asturias* in tow and, with the French ships *Neptune* and *Pluton* and the Spanish *San Leandro*, they headed for Cadiz. On the way they were gradually joined by the French ships *Argonaute*, *Héros* and *Indomptable*, as well as the Spanish ships *Rayo*, *San Justo*, *San Francisco de Asís* and *Montañes*. These eleven ships and the four that Dumanoir had led away were all that escaped from the thirty-three ships of the Combined Fleet, along with all the French frigates and brigs (including the *Thémis*) that had hovered around the edge of the fighting. Although they were initially pursued by the *Conqueror*, the *Agamemnon*, the *Ajax*, the *Britannia* and the *Neptune*, these British ships were soon recalled.

There were now very few vessels belonging to the Combined Fleet that had not fled or surrendered to the British. The *Intrépide* had embarked on the abortive attempt to take back the *Bucentaure*, but was now in a desperate state, as des Touches related: 'by now the deck had become deserted, the masts brought down, our guns wrecked, and the batteries strewn with dead and dying. There could be no question of continuing a struggle in which we would have seen the rest of our valiant crew die, without causing any harm to the enemy. Our flag was lowered.'[15] By the time the *Intrépide* surrendered, it was little more than a wreck. In the words of des Touches, 'the *Intrépide* no longer had a lower mast left standing, it had lost two-thirds of its crew, and was riddled with shot holes, the port-lids ripped off, it was leaking everywhere. But at least our honour was saved, the task accomplished, duty fulfilled right to the end.'[16]

The Spanish ship *Neptuno* had attempted to follow the *Intrépide* but, being so far behind, was cut off and forced to the west by fire from the newly formed British line of battle ships. There the *Neptuno* fell foul of the *Minotaur* and the *Spartiate*, surrendering as dusk was falling, some ten minutes after the

A plan of the battle at 4.30 p.m. (after Taylor 1950). It is now obvious that the British fleet has won the battle, and those French and Spanish ships still capable of doing so retreat from the area of battle.

1 *Victory*
2 *Temeraire*
3 *Neptune*
4 *Leviathan*
5 *Conqueror*
6 *Britannia*
7 *Ajax*
8 *Agamemnon*
9 *Orion*
10 *Prince*
11 *Minotaur*
12 *Spartiate*
13 *Royal Sovereign*
14 *Belleisle*
15 *Mars*
16 *Tonnant*
17 *Bellerophon*
18 *Colossus*
19 *Achilles*
20 *Revenge*
21 *Defiance*
22 *Dreadnought*
23 *Swiftsure*
24 *Polyphemus*
25 *Thunderer*
26 *Defence*
27 *Africa*
28 *Euryalus*
29 *Scipion*
30 *Intrépide*
31 *Formidable*
32 *Mont-Blanc*
33 *Duguay-Trouin*
34 *Héros*
35 *Bucentaure*
36 *Redoutable*
37 *Neptune*
38 *Indomptable*
39 *Fougueux*
40 *Pluton*
41 *Algésiras*
42 *Aigle*
43 *Swiftsure*
44 *Argonaute*
45 *Achille*
46 *Berwick*
47 *Neptuno*
48 *Rayo*
49 *San Francisco de Asís*
50 *San Agustín*
51 *Santísima Trinidad*
52 *San Justo*
53 *San Leandro*
54 *Santa Ana*
55 *Bahama*
56 *Montañes*
57 *Argonauta*
58 *San Ildefonso*
59 *Principe de Asturias*
60 *San Juan Nepomuceno*
61 *Monarca*

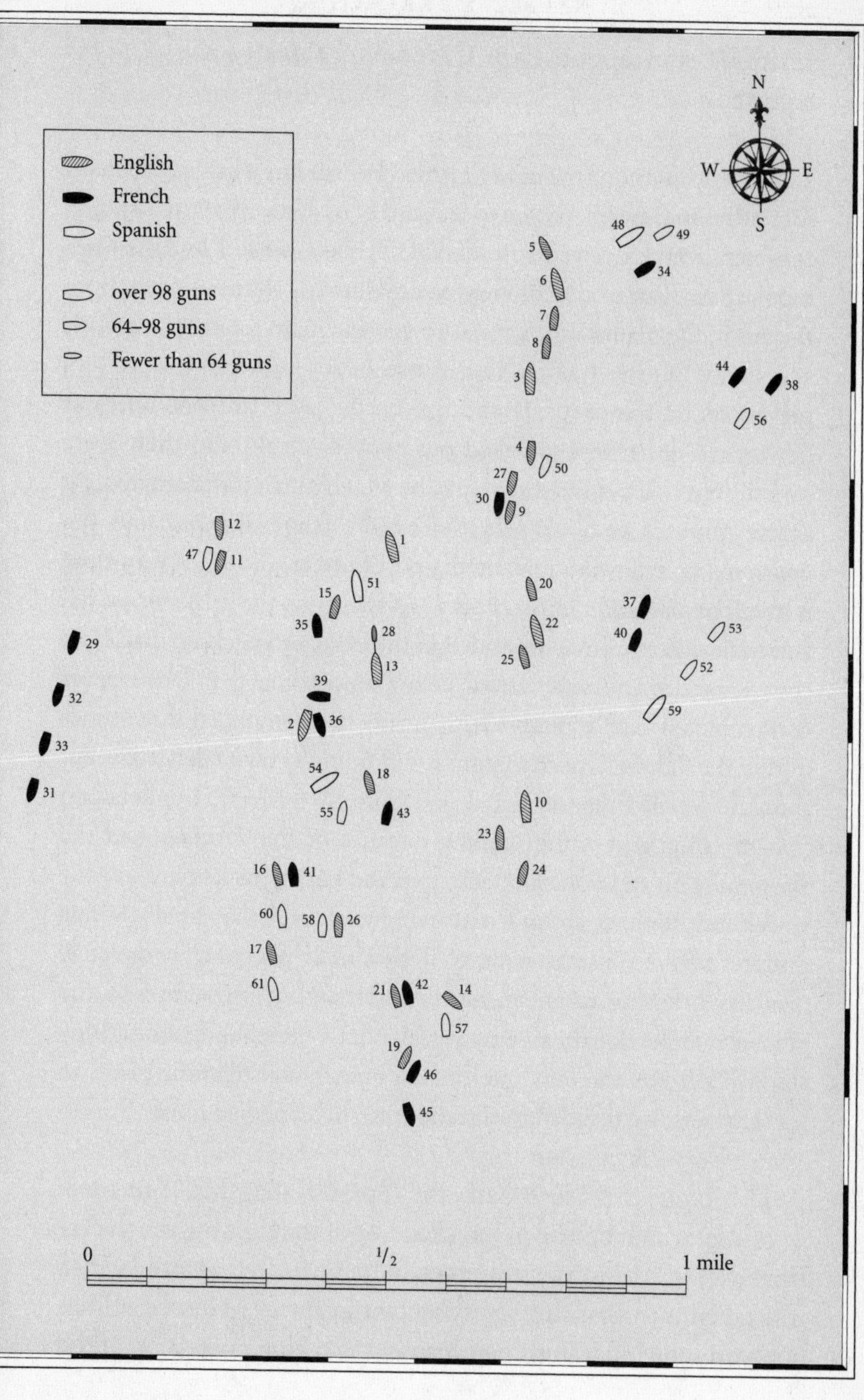

N
W
E
S
English
French
Spanish
over 98 guns
64–98 guns
Fewer than 64 guns
48
49
5
34
6
7
8
44
38
3
56
4
50
27
30
9
12
47
11
1
51
20
15
37
35
28
22
40
53
29
13
25
52
39
32
59
2
36
33
54
18
31
10
55
43
23
16
41
24
60
58
26
17
61
21
42
14
57
19
46
45
0
1/2
1 mile

Intrépide, as Captain Don Cayetano Valdés of the *Neptuno* reported:

The enemy division [the newly formed British line], having fallen off somewhat to leeward, passed to leeward of us at a very short distance, at which time I received considerable damage, since I lost the fore-topmast and part of the foremast, many shrouds were cut down from this mast; the mainstay, the foreyard and the main topmast were lost, and the mainmast was pierced in five places. All the shrouds and preventers on the port side and five on the starboard side were cut down; two guns were knocked out between decks and there were several shot holes at the water-line, by which much water entered. At a few minutes to 4 o'clock, the enemy [the *Minotaur* and the *Spartiate*] bore down on me on the port quarter, and I was very close to the *Trinidad* and the *Bucentaure*. At that time the mizzenmast fell and in its collapse I was wounded in the head and neck, so that I lost consciousness, and was carried below, something that I had never contemplated even though I had already been wounded three times during the fighting. Since that time, not from my own knowledge, but through detailed reports that I had from my officers, I understood that my ship kept within hailing distance of the *Trinidad* and the *Bucentaure* on the opposite tack; that the enemy tacked around my vessel and doubled around it to windward, and that finally, a few minutes before sunset, having 30 dead and 47 wounded, completely dismasted, having taken on much water, and overwhelmed by the greater numbers of the enemy vessels that were circling around my ship, which was the only one [of the French and Spanish Fleet] in those waters, we decided to surrender to such unequal forces.[17]

The biggest prize of all, the Spanish flagship *Santísima Trinidad*, which had been knocked out of the fighting much earlier, was the last ship to surrender, at half past five, and the wreck was taken into British possession by the *Prince*. After hostilities between individual ships had ceased, the taking possession of the prizes was an occasion for ceremony and civilities between officers from opposing ships. This was often a bizarre contrast to the bloody carnage that had prevailed only moments earlier. Marine Lieutenant Owen of the *Belleisle* described one such encounter:

A beaten Spanish 80-gun ship – the *Argonauta* – having, about this time, hoisted English colours, the Captain was good enough to give me the pinnace* to take possession of her; the Master accompanied me with eight or ten seamen or marines who happened to be near us. On getting up the *Argonauta*'s side, I found no living person on her deck, but on my making my way, over numerous dead and a confusion of wreck, across the quarterdeck, was met by the second captain at the cabin door, who gave me his sword which I returned, desiring him to keep it for Captain Hargood to whom I should soon introduce him. With him I accordingly returned to the *Belleisle*, leaving the Master in charge of the prize, on board which I had seen only about six officers, the remainder (amongst whom was the captain, wounded) and all the men below out of the way of the shot. Captain Hargood took the Spaniard to his cabin, where he shortly afterwards assembled as many of the officers as could be spared from duty, to the most acceptable refreshment of tea.[18]

Marine Lieutenant Nicolas, one of those called to take tea with the captured Spanish officer, wryly commented: 'The parching effects of the smoke made this a welcome summons, although some of us had been fortunate in relieving our thirst by plundering the Captain's grapes which hung round his cabin.'[19]

The only fighting that still continued was with the French ship *Achille*. This vessel had already been battered by the *Revenge*, and later by the *Swiftsure* and the *Polyphemus*. Towards five o' clock the *Achille* was drifting south-eastwards with a fire around one of the masts where musketeers had accidentally set the rigging alight. At this point, the British ship *Prince*, which

*A boat, usually propelled by eight oars.

was said to sail like a haystack and was the last British ship to have reached the battle, attacked the *Achille*, firing three broadsides that brought down all the French ship's masts – and with them the fire. Within minutes the flames had spread across the upper decks, and the ship was uncontrollably ablaze. It was obvious that the fate of the *Achille* was sealed, and as the *Prince* pulled away to a safe distance, boats were lowered to try to recover those who were already jumping overboard from the stricken French ship. Two British ships, the schooner *Pickle* and the cutter *Entreprenante*, sailed in very close to pick up men from the sea, but already the fire had reached some of the loaded guns, which were firing at random in the heat. At sunset, at half past five, the *Achille* blew up.

An officer on board the British ship *Defence* described the explosion as 'a sight the most awful and grand that can be conceived. In a moment the hull burst into a cloud of smoke and fire. A column of vivid flame shot up to an enormous height in the atmosphere and terminated by expanding into an immense globe, representing, for a few seconds, a prodigious tree in flames, speckled with many dark spots, which the pieces of timber and bodies of men occasioned while they were suspended in the clouds.'[20] This destruction of the *Achille*, just as night fell, marked the finality of the battle. All firing had by now ceased, and the remaining seaworthy boats were picking their way between the drifting ships in search of survivors. The sea itself was littered with wreckage and thick with splinters. Its very colour was patchy: sometimes stained with blood, sometimes stained by materials and supplies hastily jettisoned from ships; sometimes even a normal grey-green-blue colour where it was relatively untainted by the battle. Everywhere among the floating wooden debris were corpses and all manner of body parts that had been dumped overboard after surgery – some were waterlogged and sinking, having been in the water for several hours, while others continued to float half submerged. Occasionally someone still alive tried to attract the attention of one of the cruising boats that were picking up survivors and salvaging anything of any use, their oars stirring the wreckage as they tried to ride through the heavy swell rolling in from the deep Atlantic. Eventually only the dead were left on the surface of the sea, and with nightfall they were lost to sight.

In the initial stages of searching for survivors, the boats and small ships soon filled up and had to deliver their cargoes to the warships. On board the *Britannia*, Lieutenant Halloran of the marines noticed that

amongst the prisoners brought on board from one of the ships was a man in the costume and character of a Harlequin, pressed, we believe, off the stage [in Cadiz] the evening previous to the battle, without having time to change. There was also a poor woman saved from the *L'Achille* through the gunroom port as she blew up. This poor creature was brought on board with scarcely any covering, and our senior subaltern of marines, Lieut. Jackson, gave her a large cotton dressing-gown for clothing. There were also amongst the prisoners two Turks, father and son; the former had both legs amputated, and both men died the same night.[21]

The schooner *Pickle* was also picking up survivors and unloaded some from the *Achille* on board the *Revenge*, watched by one of that ship's lieutenants:

The poor fellows belonging to her [the *Achille*], as the only chance of saving their lives, leaped overboard, having first stripped off their clothes, that they might be the better able to swim to any pieces of floating wreck or to the boats of the ships sent by those nearest at hand to their rescue. As the boats filled, they proceeded to the *Pickle* schooner, and, after discharging their freight into that vessel, returned for more. The schooner was soon crowded to excess, and, therefore, transferred the poor shivering wretches to any of the large ships near her. The *Revenge*, to which ship I belonged, received nearly a hundred of the number, some of whom had been picked up by our own boats. Many of them were badly wounded, and all naked. No time was lost for providing the latter want, as the purser was ordered immediately to issue to each man a complete suit of clothes.[22]

The following morning, the same lieutenant was on duty when another lot of prisoners was brought to the *Revenge*:

I had charge of the deck, the other officers and crew being at breakfast, when another boat load of these poor prisoners of war came alongside, all of whom, with one exception, were in the costume of Adam. The exception I refer to was apparently a youth, but clothed in an old jacket and trousers, with a dingy handkerchief tied round the head, and exhibiting a face begrimed with smoke and dirt, without shoes, stockings, or shirt, and looking the picture of misery and despair. The appearance of this young person at once attracted my attention, and on asking some questions on the subject, I was answered that the prisoner was a woman. It was sufficient to know this, and I lost no time in introducing her to my messmates, as a female requiring their compassionate attention. The poor creature was almost famished with hunger, having tasted nothing for four-and-twenty hours, consequently she required no persuasion to partake of the breakfast upon the table. I then gave her up my cabin, for by this time the bulk-head had been replaced, and made a collection of all the articles which could be procured to enable her to complete a more suitable wardrobe. One of the lieutenants gave her a piece of sprigged blue muslin, which he had obtained from a Spanish prize, and two new checked shirts were supplied by the purser; these, with a purser's blanket, and my ditty bag, which contained needles, thread, etc., being placed at her disposal, she, in a short time, appeared in a very different, and much more becoming, costume. Being a dressmaker, she had made herself a sort of a jacket, after the Flemish fashion, and the purser's shirts she had transformed into an outer petticoat; she had a silk handkerchief tastily tied over her head, and another thrown round her shoulders; white stockings and a pair of the chaplain's shoes were on her feet, and, altogether, our guest, which we unanimously voted her, appeared a very interesting young woman.[23]

The French woman then told the British lieutenant how she had fled the burning *Achille*:

'Jeannette', which was the only name by which I ever knew her, thus related to me the circumstances. She said she was stationed during the action in the passage of the fore-magazine, to assist in handing up the powder, which employment lasted till the surrender of the ship. When the firing ceased, she ascended to the lower deck, and endeavoured to get up to the main deck, to search for her husband, but the ladders having been all removed, or shot away, she found this impracticable, and just at this time an alarm of fire spread through the ship, so that she could get no assistance. The fire originated upon the upper deck, and gradually burnt downwards. Her feelings upon this occasion cannot be described, but death from all quarters stared her in the face. The fire, which soon burnt fiercely, precluded the possibility of her escaping by moving from where she was, and no friendly counsellor was by with whom to advise. She remained wandering to and fro upon the lower deck, among the mangled corses [corpses] of the dying and the slain, until the guns from the main deck actually fell through the burnt planks. Her only refuge, then, was the sea, and the poor creature scrambled out of the gun-room port, and, by the help of the rudder chains, reached the back of the rudder, where she remained for some time, praying that the ship might blow up, and thus put a period to her misery. At length the lead which lined the rudder-trunk began to melt, and to fall upon her, and her only means of avoiding this was to leap overboard. Having, therefore, divested herself of her clothes, she soon found herself struggling with the waves, and providentially finding a piece of cork, she was enabled to escape from the burning mass. A man, shortly afterwards, swam near her, and, observing her distress, brought her a piece of plank, about six feet in length, which, being placed under her arms, supported her until a boat approached to her rescue. The time she was thus in the water she told me was about two hours, but probably the disagreeableness and peril of her situation made a much shorter space of time appear of that duration. The boat which picked her up, I have heard, was the *Belleisle*'s, but her sex was no sooner made known than the men, whose hearts were formed of the right stuff, quickly supplied her with the articles of attire in which she first made my acquaintance. One supplied her with trousers, another stripped off his jacket, and threw it over her, and a third supplied her with a handkerchief. She was much burnt about the neck, shoulders, and legs, by the molten lead, and when she reached the *Pickle* was more dead than alive. A story so wonderful and pitiful could not fail to enlist, on her behalf, the best feelings of human nature, and it was, therefore, not praiseworthy, but only natural, that we extended towards her that humane attention which her situation demanded. I caused a canvas screen berth to be made for her, to hang outside the wardroom door, opposite to where the sentry was stationed, and I placed my cabin at her disposal for her dressing-room.[24]

The *Revenge*, with all the prisoners rescued from the *Achille*, was now starting to sail south-eastwards in the growing darkness in an attempt to reach the safety of Gibraltar.

A more unusual rescue was witnessed on board the *Conqueror*, when a dog was found safe after all the trauma of the battle: 'A Sardinian pointer, belonging to an officer of the *Conqueror*, that, in clearing ship for action, had hastily been thrown out of one of the main-deck ports, was afterwards found to have lodged upon the rigging of the swinging boom on the side engaged, and continued there unhurt during the action; this created so strong an affection for it in the ship's company, that they requested to have him, and the dog, afterwards turned over [transferred] with his shipmates to the *Barham*, was alive in 1820.'[25]

ELEVEN

HURRICANE

> Plymouth, October 29.— The hurricane of last Friday [25th] was so tremendous, and came in such sudden squalls and flits of wind, that many persons were carried off their legs. A sentinel just relieved in the Dock-yard . . . about 3 A.M. was literally blown off with his great coat and musket into the Tamar, and was drowned before any person or boat could go to his assistance, as the tide ran twelve knots an hour.
>
> Report in *Bell's Weekly Messenger*[1]

At Cadiz itself, and along the entire coast to Cape Trafalgar, people had seen the smoke of battle on the horizon, and all the afternoon of Monday 21 October the constant dull concussions of the guns reached not just to the Spanish coast, but right into the heart of Andalusia, carried by the light onshore wind. Towards dusk the explosion on board the *Achille* was also clearly visible from Cadiz, as a witness reported:

The ships were not visible from the ramparts, but the crowd of citizens assembled there had their ears assailed by the roaring of the distant cannon; the anxiety of the females bordered on insanity; but more of despair than of hope was visible in every countenance. At this dreadful moment, a sound louder than any that had preceded it, and attended with a column of dark smoke, announced that a ship [the *Achille*] had exploded. The madness of the people was turned to rage against England; and exclamations burst forth, denouncing instant death to every man who spoke the language of their enemies. Two Americans, who had mixed with the people, fled, and hid themselves, to avoid this ebullition of popular fury; which, however, subsided into the calmness of despair, when the thunder of the cannon ceased. They had no hope of conquest, no cheering expectations of greeting their victorious countrymen, nor of sharing triumphal laurels with those who had been engaged in the conflict; each only hoped that the objects of his own affection were safe.[2]

As soon as the fighting had ceased, Captain Hardy was rowed across to the *Royal Sovereign* to bring Collingwood the dreadful news that Nelson was dead. Collingwood took command, and Hardy informed him of Nelson's last order to anchor the ships as soon as the battle was over. Disagreeing, Collingwood replied: 'Anchor, it is the last thing I should have thought of!'[3]

At the start of the battle, the opposing fleets had been at a point about 18 miles due west of Cape Trafalgar and about 22 miles south-south-west of Cadiz, a notoriously windy area of coastline. During the battle, the light winds and the strengthening westerly sea swell had continued to push the fleets slowly but relentlessly towards the coast. Now that the onshore wind was starting to gain in strength, the badly damaged ships in particular were in danger of being trapped – unable to manoeuvre out to sea to avoid the shallow waters around Cape Trafalgar. This was the situation that Nelson had foreseen, and his solution had been for the fleet to anchor in order to ride out the storm that was developing.

Collingwood was under great stress. He had survived the

battle, but he had been hit several times by flying debris, had nearly been killed by a cannon-ball and had suffered a bad leg wound. Characteristically, he did not include himself in the list of wounded that was sent back to England; it was only some months afterwards that he wrote about it to his wife, and only then in response to an anxious letter she had written after hearing a rumour that he had been wounded. He was also affected, as so many men were, by the loss of his comrades. A longstanding friend and colleague of Nelson, Collingwood found his customary reserve failed him – he was seen to shed tears when he heard the news from the *Victory*.

Nelson had led twenty-seven ships, all in good order, into the battle, and not one had surrendered. Collingwood inherited command not only of these ships and the schooner, cutter and the four frigates that had acted as observers, but also of the seventeen captured French and Spanish ships. Many were damaged, others were badly battered, and some were completely disabled. He felt the full weight of the responsibility, for on his decisions rested the fate of the surviving ships and men, and he was also conscious of the need to ensure safe passage home for the *Victory*, which was carrying Nelson's body. On top of it all he had to prepare against any possible counter-attack from the French and Spanish, since the ships that had escaped from the battle could return to renew the fighting, and other enemy ships could also attack. There was no immediate danger of the ships running aground, and because some of the disabled vessels needed urgent repairs before they were even capable of anchoring, Collingwood decided that the first priority was establishing order within the fleet after the chaos of battle. He was later criticised for making wrong decisions, as people endlessly dissected each and every moment of the battle, but in reality little more could be done.

By a quarter past six in the evening, Collingwood had transferred to the frigate *Euryalus*, because the *Royal Sovereign* no longer had any masts from which signal flags could be flown, and he immediately gave orders for all the disabled ships to be taken in tow. The smoke of battle was finally clearing, and the seamen were partially numbed by the sudden end of frantic activity. With their ears still ringing from the after-echo of the guns, in many cases surrounded by chaotic debris, the survivors slowly absorbed the fact that they were now about to trade the exhilaration and terror of combat for the hard slog of clearing up the shambles. Many of the crews were significantly under strength, having lost men killed and injured, or else having transferred to the captured ships to disarm and control the prisoners, as well as to make those ships as seaworthy as possible. Some sailors were also needed to tend the wounded while the surgeons worked their way through the casualties who were still waiting their turn. Sixteen-year-old Marine Lieutenant Nicolas in the *Belleisle* described a scene that could be mirrored in many of the surrounding ships:

> Eager inquiries were expressed, and earnest congratulations exchanged at this joyful moment. The officers came to make their report to the captain, and the fatal result cast a gloom over the scene of our triumph . . . [Our first lieutenant] was severely wounded in the thigh, and underwent amputation: but his prediction [of his own death, made some hours earlier] was realised, for he expired before the action had ceased. The junior lieutenant was likewise mortally wounded on the quarterdeck. These gallant fellows were lying beside each other in the gunroom preparatory to their being committed to the deep; and here many met to take a last look at their departed friends, whose remains soon followed the promiscuous multitude, without distinction of either rank or nation, to their wide ocean grave . . . The upper deck presented a confused and dreadful appearance: masts, yards, sails, ropes and fragments of wreck were scattered in every direction; nothing could be more horrible than the scene of blood and mangled remains with which every part was covered, and which, from the quantity of splinters, resembled a shipwright's yard strewed with gore.[4]

Nicolas and others next went down to where the surgeon was still operating in the cockpit to try to find out the fate of other sailors:

From our extensive loss – thirty-four killed, and ninety-six wounded – our cockpit exhibited a scene of suffering and carnage which rarely occurs. I visited this abode of suffering with the natural impulse which led many others thither – namely, to ascertain the fate of a friend or companion. So many bodies in such a confined place and under such distressing circumstances would affect the most obdurate heart. My nerves were but little accustomed to such trials, but even the dangers of the battle did not seem more terrific than the spectacle before me. On a long table lay several anxiously looking for their turn to receive the surgeon's care, yet dreading the fate which he might pronounce. One subject was undergoing amputation, and every part was heaped with sufferers; their piercing shrieks and expiring groans were echoed through this vault of misery . . . What a contrast to the hilarity and enthusiastic mirth which reigned in this spot the preceding evening! At all times the cockpit is the region of conviviality and good humour, for here it is that the happy midshipmen reside, and at whose board neither discord nor care interrupt the social intercourse. But a few short hours since, on these benches, which were now covered with mutilated remains, sat these scions of their country's glory, who hailed the coming hour of conflict with cheerful confidence, and each told his story to beguile the anxious moments; the younger ones eagerly listening to their experienced associates, and all united in the toast of 'May we meet again at this hour to-morrow!'[5]

In fact, the midshipmen from the *Belleisle* were lucky, as fourteen survived, only one being killed.

While those in command took stock of the losses and damage, the seamen, exhausted and shocked after six hours of intense fighting, were set to work by the surviving officers. In the *Revenge*, the sailor William Robinson recorded the dismal task:

We were now called to clear the decks, and here might be witnessed an awful and interesting scene, for as each officer and seaman would meet . . . they were inquiring for their mess-mates. Orders were now given to fetch the dead bodies from the after cock-pit, and throw them over-board; these were the bodies of men who were taken down to the doctor during the battle, badly wounded, and who by the time the engagement was ended were dead. Some of these, perhaps, could not have recovered, while others might, had timely assistance been rendered, which was impossible; for the rule is, as order is requisite, that every person shall be dressed in rotation as they are brought down wounded, and in many instances some have bled to death. The next call was 'all hands to splice the main brace', which is the giving out of a gill of rum to each man, and indeed they much needed it, for they had not ate nor drank from breakfast time: we had now a good night's work before us; all our yards, masts, and sails were sadly cut, indeed the whole of the sails were obliged to be unbent, being rendered completely useless.[6]

Just as Nelson had relied on the training and discipline of the crews in battle, Collingwood now relied heavily on their expertise as he and his captains tried to organise the drifting disorder of ships and wreckage into a coherent group once more. Some of the ships needed urgent repairs just to keep them afloat, and many needed temporary masts and rigging to restore the ability to sail and steer. On board those ships with many casualties, vinegar was heated and sprinkled through the ship to alleviate the smell of blood; only later would there be time to eradicate it completely by scrubbing down the ship with vinegar and then fumigating it with sulphur. Barely had the fighting ceased than the crews set to work – it was something that the French found hard to believe, as Captain Jean-Baptiste Prigny, Villeneuve's chief of staff, admitted: 'The act that astonished me the most was when the action was over. It came on to blow a gale of wind, and the English immediately set to work to shorten sail and reef the topsails, with as much regularity and order as if their ships had not been fighting a dreadful battle. We were all amazement, wondering what the English seamen could be made of. All *our* seamen were either drunk or disabled, and we, the officers, could not get any work out of them. We never witnessed such clever manoeuvres before, and I shall never forget them.'[7]

With the relatively light wind blowing directly onshore on the evening after the battle, the only choice was to sail north-west towards Cadiz or south-east towards Cape Trafalgar, travelling as far as possible before being blown too near the shallows during the storm that was brewing. Later that evening, the wind began to change direction and was now coming more directly from the west, making it easier to head for Cape Trafalgar and after that the safe haven of Gibraltar. Leaving Cadiz and the potential danger of renewed attack behind, Collingwood decided that the fleet should sail for Gibraltar, in the hope of passing Cape Trafalgar and being free of the coastal shoals before the peak of the storm. In the event, only two British ships, the *Naiad*, towing the *Belleisle*, managed to round Cape Trafalgar before the storm abated, and even then they narrowly escaped being wrecked on the shore, as Marine Lieutenant Nicolas on board the *Belleisle* described:

About midnight [on the 23rd–24th] a midshipman entered the ward-room, where most of our cots were swinging, to say that the captain wished the officers to come on deck, as it was probable we should be ashore [wrecked] very shortly. This awful intelligence was received with much concern, and we instantly started on our feet. Just at this crisis one of the 24-pounders [cannons] out of the stern-port broke adrift from its lashings, and the apprehension of our danger had taken such entire possession of our minds, that the crash appeared to announce the approach of our destruction. With difficulty I got on deck. The ship rolled in the trough of the sea in such a manner that the water came in through the ports and over the waist hammock-nettings, and the shot out of the racks were thrown about the decks, upon which the men, tired and exhausted, were lying. At one o'clock the roar of the elements continued, and every roll of the sea seemed to the affrighted imagination as the commencement of the breakers.[8]

They had to endure the storm, now raging at full strength, for four more hours of darkness until dawn finally broke:

The hours lagged tediously on, and death appeared in each gust of the tempest. In the battle the chances were equal, and it was possible for many to escape, but shipwreck in such a hurricane was certain destruction to all, and the doubtful situation of the ship kept the mind in a perpetual state of terror. In this horrible suspense each stroke of the bell, as it proclaimed the hour, sounded as the knell of our approaching destiny, for none could expect to escape the impending danger. In silent anxiety we awaited the fate which daylight would decide, and the thoughts of home, kindred, friends, pressed round the heart and aggravated our despair. Each brightening of the clouds, which appeared as if to mock our misery, was hailed as the long looked-for dawn, and sank our wearied hopes into deeper despondency as the darkness again prevailed. How numerous were the inquiries made to the sentry, 'How goes the time?' and when the welcome order to strike two bells (that is, five o'clock) was heard, it aroused our sinking energies, and every eye was directed towards the shore. In a few minutes 'Land on the lee bow! put the helm up!' resounded through the ship, and all was again bustle and confusion. When we got round, the breakers were distinctly seen about a mile to leeward, throwing the spray to such a terrific height that even in our security we could not behold them without shuddering. This was a period of delight most assuredly, but intense dread had so long overpowered every other feeling, that our escape from destruction seemed like returning animation, producing a kind of torpor which rendered us insensible to our miraculous preservation, and it was not until the mind had recovered its wonted calmness, that our hearts were impressed with a due sense of the merciful protection we had experienced. As the day advanced the wind abated, and the enlivening rays of the sun well accorded with our happiness. The *Naiad*, having us in tow, spread all her canvas, steering a direct course for Gibraltar.[9]

The remaining British ships, along with the French and Spanish prizes, had been sailing closer to the shore and by midnight on the 21st were in such shallow waters that they were about to be forced to anchor. Suddenly the ever-increasing wind changed direction again and began blowing more from the south. These vessels were now able to turn and work their way further from the shore, but this was a mixed blessing as now they were sailing away from Gibraltar and back towards Cadiz. In fact, their one chance of escape had been lost. The wind continued to increase, accompanied by torrential rain, squalls and lightning – it was the onset of a hurricane. For the following few days it was so overcast and dark that the sun, moon and stars could not be seen.

By noon the next day, the winds had reached gale force, and the storm, of unusual severity and persistence, continued to rage for the next seven days.* The winds fluctuated in direction and strength, eventually dropping a little on Friday 25 October, only to become worse the following day. Henry Walker, a midshipman in the *Bellerophon*, later told his mother in Preston that some twenty-four hours after the battle had ceased, 'a storm came on, such as I had never witnessed, and for the four following days we had a much severer struggle against the elements than the enemy'.[10] With the ships in such a vulnerable state after the battle, a violent storm was to prove catastrophic.

Until the wind direction changed sufficiently for the fleet to break free of the coast, the ships could only sail up and down near Cadiz, keeping as far from the treacherous shallows as possible, while the crews continued the struggle to repair the damage. The

*The modern metereological term for this type of storm is a cut-off low.

first disaster was the loss of the prize ship *Fougueux*, which had been taken in tow by the frigate *Phoebe*. Around midnight of the day of the battle, ten hours after surrendering and just as the wind started to increase, the *Fougueux* broke adrift from the tow. During the early hours of Tuesday 22 October, the *Phoebe* repeatedly tried to get a line to the *Fougueux*, but it proved impossible. The drifting ship was blown onshore and repeatedly dashed against the rocks until the vessel broke up. All that could be done was to launch boats in the hope of picking up survivors. One of the very few men who managed to escape the wreck and swim to a nearby boat was the master-at-arms, Pierre Servaux. He later recalled his final moments on board:

> The ship was in a terrible condition, cut down to a hulk, without masts, sails, or rigging left. She was, too, without a boat that could swim, while the whole vessel was as full of holes as a sieve, shattered from stem to stern, and with two enormous gaps forced in on the starboard side at the water-line, through which the sea poured in a stream. The water had risen almost to the orlop deck. Everywhere one heard the cries of the wounded and the dying, as well as the noise and shouts of insubordinate men who refused to man the pumps and only thought of themselves. The scenes of horror on board the ship that night were really the most awful and fearful that imagination might call up.[11]

Almost the whole crew of the *Fougueux* perished. Including those killed in battle, a total of 546 men were lost out of a crew of around 680. The thirty officers and men from the *Temeraire* who had originally taken charge of the prize ship also died.

After this disaster, the remaining ships managed well enough during what remained of the morning of the 22nd. On board the *Victory*, Nelson's body was prepared for his return to England for burial. As he lay dying, Nelson had specifically asked Captain Hardy not to throw him overboard, and special preparations were later made to transport his body back to England in a leaguer, which was now filled with brandy, as Beatty explained:

There was no lead on board to make a coffin: a cask called a leaguer, which is of the largest size on shipboard, was therefore chosen for the reception of the Body; which, after the hair had been cut off, was stripped of the clothes except the shirt, and put into it, and the cask was then filled with brandy. In the evening [22 October] after this melancholy task was accomplished, the gale came on with violence from the south-west, and continued that night and the succeeding day without any abatement. During this boisterous weather, Lord Nelson's Body remained under the charge of a sentinel on the middle deck.[12]

This method of preserving Nelson's body gave rise to several myths. Many sailors wrongly thought that the body had been preserved in rum, and as a consequence navy-issue rum was nicknamed 'Nelson's Blood'. It was also believed that the sentries guarding the cask used the opportunity to draw off and drink the rum inside.

A local legend from Fife in Scotland relates that a woman from that area called Mary Buick (or Buek), the wife of Thomas Watson, a seaman in the *Victory*, helped prepare Nelson's body before it was placed in the leaguer on the day following the battle. During the battle she had helped tend the wounded, and her four-year-old daughter, born aboard HMS *Ardent* during the Battle of Copenhagen, was also supposed to be in the ship. There is no evidence from navy records to support Mary Buick's story, but this and other tales of Mary's experiences while on board navy ships with her husband have persisted in her home village of Cellardyke in East Fife, occasionally being reported in the local newspapers. The research that has so far been done to test the story has verified parts of it, not disproved it.

Another woman, Mary Sperring, may also have been

involved in the preparations of Nelson's body in the *Victory*. On her death at Burnham-on-Sea in Somerset nearly six decades later, it was reported by a local newspaper that, 'AN OCTOGENARIAN, named Mary Sperring, died here [Burnham-on-Sea, Somerset] on Friday [2 December 1864]. The old lady was present with her first husband at the Battle of Trafalgar, when Nelson exterminated the navies of France and Spain. She frequently recounted many of the most stirring events of that period and was never tired of telling that she washed the blood from the shirt which the gallant Admiral wore when he received his fatal wound.'[13]

By midday on the 22nd the storm had reached gale force, and the ships under tow were becoming unmanageable. The next ship to be in serious trouble was Captain Lucas's *Redoutable*, which had surrendered over twenty-four hours earlier. Having been so badly broken during the battle, this vessel was taking in water through shot holes in the hull faster than the pumps could remove it. The *Redoutable* was being towed by the British ship *Swiftsure*, whose log for that day records a curt summary of the situation: 'At 4, the prize in tow. At 5, the prize made the signal of distress to us. Hove to, and out boats, and brought the prize officer and his people on board, and a great many of the prisoners. At a quarter past, the boats returned the last time with very few in them, the weather so bad and sea running high that rendered it impossible for the boat to pass. Got in the boats. At a quarter past 10, the *Redoutable* sunk by the stern. Cut the tow, and lost two cables of eight and a half inch, and a cable of 5 inches, with the prize.'[14]

The five hours of desperate struggle to rescue the men from the *Redoutable* was less prosaically described in Midshipman George Barker's letter home:

On the 22nd it came on a most Violent Gale of wind, the Prize in Tow seem'd to weather it out tolarable well notwithstanding her shatter'd state until about three in the afternoon, when from her rolling so violently in a heavy sea, she carried away her fore Mast, the only mast she had standing. Towards the evening she repeatedly made signals of distress to us: we now hoisted out our Boats, and sent them on board of her although there was a very high Sea and we were afraid the boats would be swampt alongside the Prize, but they happily succeeded in saving a great number, including our Lieut, and part of the Seamen we sent on board, likewise a Lieut, two midshipmen with some Seamen belonging to the *Temeraire*. If our situation was disagreeable from the fatigue and inclemency of the weather what must the unfortunate Prisoners have suffered on board . . . What added to the horrors of the night was the inability of our saving them all, as we could no longer endanger the lives of our people in open boats, at the mercy of a heavy sea and most violent Gale of Wind; at about 10.p.m. the *Redoutable* sunk, and the Hawser, by which we still kept her in Tow, (in order if the weather should moderate and the Prize be able to weather the tempestuous night) was carried away with the violent shock; this was the most dreadful scene that can be imagined as we could distinctly hear the cries of the unhappy people we could no longer assist.[15]

The *Algésiras* was also in trouble. After the French vessel had surrendered to the *Tonnant*, Lieutenant Charles Bennett and fifty seamen had taken charge, and the remaining 270 men of the original crew became prisoners. The *Algésiras* was so badly damaged, however, that Bennett's men were not nearly enough to carry out essential repairs and manage the ship, which was drifting towards the shore without a usable anchor. For much of the day on the 22nd, Bennett fired distress signals while his men cleared the decks, but no help came, and by early evening the ship was dangerously close to the shoals off Cape Trafalgar. At this point the remaining French officers decided to take back control of their ship, as Lieutenant Philibert recorded in his journal:

At 7 o'clock in the evening, everything being ready, we invited the

English officers, three in number, to enter the council chamber [probably the captain's cabin] where M. Feuillet, secretary to General Magon, who spoke the best English, told them . . . that, following the noble defence of our ship we had good cause to expect help from the English fleet, which they had asked for in vain; that thinking ourselves therefore free from the obligations that we had made when putting ourselves in their power, we had decided to take back our vessel . . . At 7.15 in the evening, we were in control of the ship, having the satisfaction of not having shed a drop of blood . . . After having disarmed the English, they were placed in the council chamber under a close watch, and their officers placed in their own room [cabin] . . . At 7.30, being south-south-west of Cadiz lighthouse, we had arranged to be served [rigged sails to catch the wind] and steered by a following wind for some time, with two topgallant sails rigged on our stumps [of masts]; we were working to set up a mizzen topgallant sail on the stump of the mizzenmast, but heavy sea having caused several of our guns to break loose, we hauled to the wind again [steered into the wind to stop the ship, in order to secure these cannons], taking advantage of this moment to attach a cable to the only bower anchor that was left. At 11 o'clock, this task having been completed, we set off and headed for Cadiz, only having on board one assistant gunner with experience [to pilot us], who had been there several times. Although the weather was then gloomy, with squalls, the sea heavy, raining continuously and a strong fresh gale from the south-west, which was making us fear we would perish before reaching some anchorage, we were sufficiently fortunate to cast our anchor to the north-east of the Cadiz lighthouse, at 2 in the morning.[16]

When the Spanish ship *Neptuno* was taken in tow by the *Minotaur*, the hawser broke, causing the prize ship to drift helplessly towards the coast, until ending up close to the *Algésiras*. The *Neptuno* was in the charge of a marine lieutenant and sixty-eight British sailors from the *Minotaur*, one of whom was a seaman called William Thorpe, who recorded the events:

22nd [October]. At daylight [we] began to release away the wreck, got the mizen mast fore yard and main top gallant mast overboard and cut away a number of loose spars and rigging. At half past three p.m. the *Minotaur* took us in tow. The wind continued to increase to a hard gale. Soon after, the hawser broke, [and] we were now left to the mercy of the waves. The gale continued to increase – the ship a mere wreck on a lee shore possessed by the enemy. At 12 [mid]night the main mast went by the board, stove in the poop and quarter deck, [and] killed one of our seamen and the Spanish captain of marines [actually the paymaster, Don Diego de Soto] who was lying asleep in his cot. We then shored up the quarter deck and the broken beams to prevent the deck falling in upon us. About three o'clock [in the morning of the 23rd] cleared away the best bower anchor* on account of seeing Cadiz light house close under our lee, having only 18 fathoms water . . . and remained in that situation till daylight.[17]

By dawn on Wednesday 23 October weather conditions had improved, and Midshipman Barker on board the British ship *Swiftsure* described how they managed to rescue several survivors from the *Redoutable* that had sunk the previous night:

Towards the morning the weather moderated and we had the good fortune to save many that were floating past on rafts—at 9 a.m. discovered a large raft ahead and shortly after another, many of the unfortunate people were seen clinging to the wreck, the merciless sea threatening almost instant destruction to them, the Boats were immediately lowered down, and we happily saved thirty-six people from the Fury of the Waves. When the Boats came alongside many of these unfortunate men were unable to get up the Ship's side, as most of them were not only fainting from fatigue, but were wounded in the most shocking manner, some expired in the Boats before they could

*The two largest anchors were carried at the bows of the ship – the best bower, on the starboard bow, was the larger of the two.

get on board, completely exhausted and worn out with struggling to preserve their lives, having been the whole of a Tempestuous Night, upon a few crazy planks exposed to every inclemency of the weather. If our Seamen had conducted themselves as brave men during the Action, now it was they evinced themselves as human, and generous, as they were Brave. When these unfortunate people came on board, you might have seen them cloathing them as well as a scanty stock would admit of, though scanty yet hard earn'd, and that in the Defence of His King, his Family, and Country at large.[18]

According to Lucas, captain of the *Redoutable*, 474 men out of a crew of 643 were killed in the battle or else went down with the ship – only 169 survived, and of these 70 were wounded.

While survivors from the *Redoutable* were being rescued on the morning of the 23rd, many of the ships of the Combined Fleet in Cadiz harbour had sailed out in an attempt to retake some of the vessels that had surrendered to the British in the battle two days previously. They took with them as many extra men as possible, so that they could take charge of any ships that they managed to capture. The raid was headed by Captain Cosmao Kerjulien, the most senior surviving French officer at Cadiz. He led in his own ship, the *Pluton*, which was barely seaworthy having been so badly damaged. The *Pluton* was accompanied by the French battleships *Indomptable* and *Neptune*, and the Spanish *Rayo* and *San Francisco de Asís*, as well as the five French frigates *Cornélie*, *Hermione*, *Hortense*, *Rhin* and *Thémis*, along with the two French brigs *Argus* and *Furet*.

When this small fleet set out from Cadiz, there was a lull in the weather. The wind was now blowing from the north-west and was ideal for a rapid approach to the British fleet, but even as the last ship cleared the harbour entrance, the wind shifted closer to the south-west and began to gain in strength once more. Around noon, the French and Spanish ships sighted part of the British fleet, which had become dispersed by the storm. Since the rain and the spray whipped up by the high winds made visibility poor, the British ships initially mistook Kerjulien's frigates for battleships and thought his force was twice as strong as it actually was. The nearest British ships abandoned the captured vessels that they were towing, including the *Bucentaure* and the *Santa Ana*, and formed up in a line of battle to meet this new threat. On board the *Euryalus*, Captain Blackwood described the situation in a letter to his wife:

> Last night and this day, my dearest Harriet, has been trying to the whole fleet, but more so to the Admiral [Collingwood] who has the charge. It has blown a hurricane, but, strange to say, we have as yet lost but one ship – one of our finest prizes – *La Redoutable*; but which I feel the more, as so many poor souls were lost. The remains of the French and Spanish fleet have rallied, and are at this moment but a few miles from us – their object, of course, to recover some captured ships or take some of the disabled English; but they will be disappointed, for I think and hope we shall have another touch at them ere long. We are now lying between them and our prizes, with eleven complete line-of-battle ships, besides more ready to come to us if we want them.[19]

As the *Bellerophon* prepared for action, Lieutenant Cumby noticed a young midshipman by the name of George Pearson. He was the fourteen-year-old son of a clergyman from Queen Camel in Somerset, and had joined the *Bellerophon* as his first ship a few months before. During the earlier stages of the battle, when their captain was mortally wounded, Cumby said that Pearson, 'ran to his assistance, but ere he reached his Captain he was himself brought down by a splinter in the thigh. As I was coming up to take command of the ship I met on the quarter-deck ladder little Pearson in the arms of a quarter-master who was carrying him to the surgeons in the cockpit. I here made an exception to my general rule of silence on such occasions and said "Pearson, my boy, I'm sorry you've been hit; but never mind – you and I'll talk over this day's work fifty years hence, depend upon it." He smiled and I passed on.'[20]

Faced with the new threat of the ships from Cadiz, Pearson was once again at work on the quarterdeck,

dragging with difficulty one leg after the other. I said to him, 'Pearson, you had better go below; wounded as you are you will be better there.' He answered, 'I had rather stay at my quarters, Sir, if you please!' On which I replied, 'You had much better go down; someone will be running against you and do you further mischief.' To this he exclaimed, the tears standing in his eyes, 'I hope, Sir, you will not order me below; I should be very sorry to be below at a time like this.' I instantly said, 'Indeed, I will not order you down, and if you live you'll be a second Nelson.' Poor fellow, he did live to be made a lieutenant some years after, and then died of fever.[21]

The British, mistaking the size of his fleet, gave Kerjulien the chance he needed, since he was actually more intent on recovering the French and Spanish ships that had been captured than on challenging the British in pitched battle. As the two opposing forces manoeuvred around each other, the French frigates managed to take the Spanish ships *Santa Ana* and *Neptuno* in tow and headed back towards Cadiz. It was the only success Kerjulien was to have, for by this time the British line of battle ships was in position to block access to their remaining prizes. The French and Spanish ships could do nothing more, and so they altered course back to Cadiz.

At the approach of Kerjulien's ships, the *Conqueror*, which had been towing Villeneuve's flagship the *Bucentaure*, cast off the tow in order to join the battle line, and the *Bucentaure* drifted helplessly towards the shore. Neither side managed to take this ship in tow again, but boats from the French and

Spanish ships rescued most of those on board, including the British crew that had been put in charge of the prize. The majority of those rescued were taken aboard the French ship *Indomptable*. Shortly after, the *Bucentaure* was driven on to the rocks of Cadiz Point and was wrecked, followed by a further tragedy when the *Indomptable* ran aground at Rota in Cadiz Bay and gradually broke up. Of over one thousand men on board, less than one hundred survived. The *San Francisco de Asís* managed to anchor outside Cadiz harbour, but under pressure from the rising wind and heavy sea the anchor cables snapped, and this ship was driven ashore and wrecked near Fort Santa Catalina. The *Rayo* was also unable to make it back into Cadiz and was forced to anchor some miles away, off the San Lucar shoals, where, tossed and rolled by the violence of the storm, all the masts snapped and fell overboard.

From Kerjulien's raiding fleet, three battleships had now been lost, and of the two ships recaptured, only the *Santa Ana* managed to get into Cadiz harbour – the *Neptuno* was not so lucky. Before being recaptured, the *Neptuno* had still been perilously close to the lighthouse at Cadiz. The British crew in charge of the prize ship had noticed Kerjulien's fleet coming out of Cadiz, but were powerless to do anything. William Thorpe described how later that afternoon the French frigate *Hortense* managed to take control of the *Neptuno*, with all the British on board becoming prisoners:

We then [in the morning] saw a squadron inshore consisting of 5 sail of the line, 3 frigates and a brig which proved to be the enemy. Thus situated, we expected assistance from our own fleet, but looked in vain. At 10 o'clock, rigged a spar to the stump of the main mast and another to the taffrail, set a top gallant [sail] upon each and got another to the fore mast in lieu of a fore sail. At 3 o'clock [in the afternoon], cut our cable and stood toward our own fleet with all sail we could set, but the enemy was gaining upon us fast from Cadiz. We cleared away our stern chasers and the magazine – the prisoners observing this, rose upon our people and retook the ship, in doing which they met with little opposition – indeed it would have been madness to resist. A slight resistance was made by some men who narrowly escaped with their lives. They now wore ship and stood towards Cadiz. At 4 p.m. *Le Hortense* French frigate of 44 guns took us in tow and towed us to the harbour mouth [of Cadiz] where we brought up amongst some of their disabled ships and rode till 3 o'clock the following day [the morning of the 24th] when we parted from our anchors and not having another cable bent to bring her up, they let her drive ashore.[22]

While the *Santa Ana* and the *Neptuno* were being recaptured and those on board the *Bucentaure* were being rescued before the vessel was wrecked, there were few spare boats to go to the assistance of the nearby *Algésiras*, which had been taken over by the French prisoners the night before. At daylight on the 23rd, the French crew had realised that they were in a critical position, reliant on the hastily repaired anchor to stop them being blown on to nearby rocks, as they were not fully within Cadiz harbour. Some boats from ships that had been left in the harbour tried to help, but the deteriorating weather conditions made rescue attempts almost impossible. Despite repeatedly firing distress signals, the *Algésiras* remained in the same position for the whole day, expecting the anchor to give way at any moment. In the evening, the situation worsened, as Lieutenant Philibert recorded:

At night, the weather very bad, with squalls, blowing rather freshly and in gusts from the south-west. Towards 10 o'clock we scraped the bottom with the keel on the Diamond [shoals], and thank goodness that in the violent squall which drove us, the winds turned to the east, such that we bypassed and rounded the Diamond; our anchor held well because it was on the edge of the Galera bank, but our small cable broke and we lost its anchor. At this moment, a vessel that was dragging its anchor

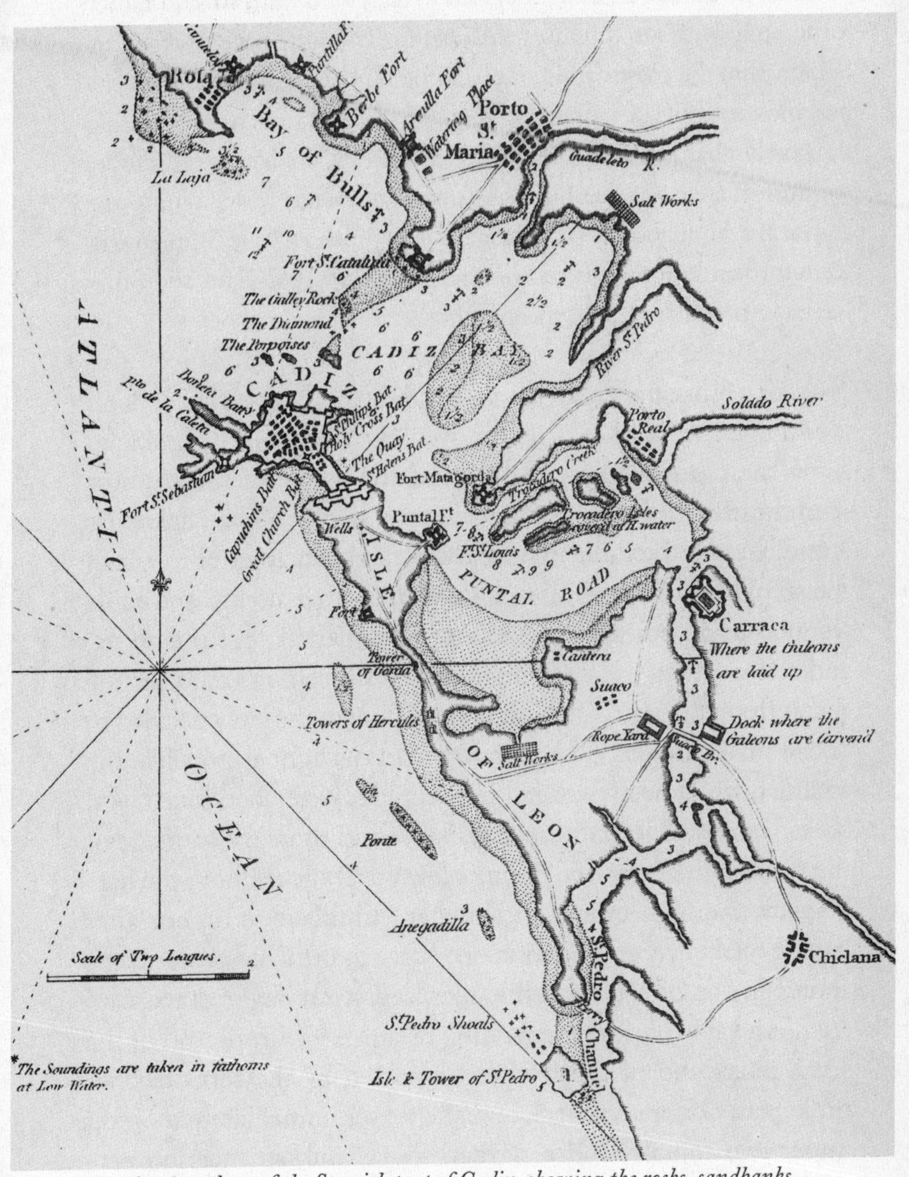

An 1809 chart of the Spanish port of Cadiz, showing the rocks, sandbanks and other hazards that made the passage into the harbour so difficult for sailing vessels

came on us broadside-on and passed to starboard, yard to yard rather fortunately without colliding with us, for it might have dragged us helplessly to the coast with it. At 10.30 [at night], the weather [becoming] increasingly bad, we still dragged [our anchor] right up to touching the bottom hard on the Galera bank; as the tide still had to fall a little, we immediately occupied ourselves with all means of lightening the ship at the stern; four 18-pounder guns, two of which were dismounted, were thrown into the sea, as well as all the shifting ballast, and other heavy objects that were in this part of the vessel.[23]

As day broke on Thursday 24 October, the crew of the *Algésiras* found that the weather had improved. Spanish boats were able to bring them a cable and anchor, and the whole of the day was spent in rowing the anchor ahead of the ship in a boat, dropping it and hauling the cable in on the capstan in an attempt to winch the ship off the rocks – all to no avail. Another anchor and cable were brought, but again it was not possible to move the vessel, and the weather was showing signs of worsening again. In the early afternoon, with the high tide imminent, the crew decided to take a final gamble. With the ship made as light as possible, the anchors, which were wedged in the rocks, were abandoned, and boats were used to pull the *Algésiras* round to take advantage of the wind in the hope of its being blown over the reef into the harbour on the high tide. As Lieutenant Philibert recorded, 'after having taken every precaution necessary to break away from [the shore] in the direction of the open sea, we brought the stream anchor away – our only remaining resource – with the aid of the small boats and of the hawser supported by the schooner, we broke away on a good tack and the vessel immediately took off under two topsails and a mizzen topgallant sail, steering perfectly. From then, we found ourselves saved.'[24]

Although the *Algésiras* had escaped safely to Cadiz, the other prizes were still very vulnerable in the storm, as they were too close to the shore. On board the Spanish *Neptuno*, which had gone on to rocks in the darkness of the early hours of the 24th, the Spanish were frantic, while the few British attempted to rescue as many as possible, as seaman Thorpe described:

At this time the confusion on board is inexpressable, it being dark, and ignorant what part of the coast we were cast upon. Expecting the ship every moment to go to pieces. The Spaniards, naturally dispirited, now showed every symptom of despair. They run about in wild disorder nor make the least effort to extricate themselves from the danger that threatened them. At daylight our people conveyed three ropes on shore – one from the cat head, one from the bowsprit and another from the fore mast head – by the assistance of which a number of men got safe on shore whilst others were employed constructing a raft for more expeditiously landing, as well as to convey such as were unwilling to risk themselves by the ropes. When the raft was completed, 20 men ventured on board and arrived safe on shore, but the raft was driven so far upon the rocks that it was found impossible to get it off again. Those on board seeing this sad disaster, far from giving way to despair, immediately set about making another, which certainly was our last resource, as we had not any more spars fit for that purpose. When finished we launched it overboard and 20 men embarked on board it who arrived safe, one Spaniard excepted who was washed off by the surf. We then made fast a rope to the raft on shore and there being one already fast from the ship, the people dragged it off to the ship. When 28 men embarked on board, all of whom arrived safe on shore, the raft was again dragged on board and 28 men embarked, one of whom was washed from the raft (a Spaniard) by the surf and perished. The raft was much damaged upon the rocks. It was again dragged off onto the ship, but fate had decreed that all who remained on board should perish. The raft, laden, shoved off from the ship side, but ere it gained the shore it upset and every soul perished. No further attempt could be made to save those unfortunate men who remained on board, all perished . . . our loss [among the

British sailors] amounted to four killed by the falling of the masts [and] rigging, and drowned.[25]

Despite all he had gone through, Thorpe had warm feelings towards the Spanish: 'Though the sufferings of our people were great, yet no imputation of cruelty or even unkindness can be alleged to the Spaniards. Those [Spaniards] who arrived safe on shore looked upon our men as their deliverers, and there were instances of gratitude and kindness that would do honour to any nation. It is with regret the Spaniard goes to war with the English whom he wishes always to consider his friends. It is from the unfortunate situation of affairs – on the continent he is compelled to cut a part so foreign to his interest and contrary to the public wish.'[26] According to the report of the captain of the *Neptuno*, Cayetano Valdés, fishing boats were later able to take more of the men off the wreck, and in the end only about twenty were drowned. Thorpe was soon marched away with the other British prisoners and may not have seen the efforts of these boats.

With no sign that the storm was abating, it was obvious that drastic action had to be taken if the whole fleet was not to be lost. After fighting a battle and then continuously struggling to keep the ships away from the shore for over sixty hours, during one of the worst storms ever recorded, the crews were completely exhausted. Many ships were overcrowded, where they had rescued survivors or taken on board prisoners, and some remained in a filthy mess. Even those prisoners not employed in pumping out or repairing the ships were worn out with enduring the constant violent motion. The wounded suffered terribly, and not all survived, as on board the *Victory* on the 27th, when the log recorded: 'Departed this life, Joseph Gordon (boy), of the wound he received on the 21st instant. Committed the body of Joseph Gordon, deceased, to the deep, with the usual ceremony.'[27] Collingwood later summed up the situation: 'The condition of our own ships was such that it was very doubtful what would be their fate. Many a time I would have given the whole group of our capture, to ensure our own.'[28]

At eight-thirty on the morning of the 24th, Collingwood sent the signal: 'Prepare to quit and withdraw men from prizes after having destroyed or disabled them if time permits.'[29] It was a difficult decision, but one for which no one criticised Collingwood. Many of the ships had already been forced to anchor, to stop themselves being washed on to the rocks around Cadiz, and the situation was so desperate that further attempts to save the captured ships were likely to result in the loss of British ones. There now began frantic efforts to get everyone off those ships that were to be abandoned. The largest of the captured ships, the *Santísima Trinidad*, which before the battle had been carrying over one thousand men, was already sinking. It is estimated that around two hundred men on board this ship had been killed during the fighting, but it is remarkable that most of those still on board were now taken off – mainly by boats from the *Prince*, the *Ajax* and the *Neptune*. A lieutenant from the *Ajax* declared that 'Everything alive was taken out, down to the ship's cat',[30] but he seems to have discounted a number of wounded who were too badly injured to move.

As on many of the ships that had been in the thick of the fighting, there had only been the few hours between the end of the battle and the onset of the storm during which wreckage could be cleared. Since then, it had been a constant struggle to keep the *Santísima Trinidad* afloat and away from the coast. The conditions in the ship were horrifying, as Midshipman Badcock from the British ship *Neptune* recorded: 'I was on board our prize the *Trinidada* getting the prisoners out of her, she had between 3 and 400 killed and wounded [the final estimate was 216 killed and 116 wounded], her beams were covered with blood, brains, and pieces of flesh, and the after part of her decks with wounded, some without legs and some without an arm;

what calamities war brings on, and what a number of lives were put an end to on the 21st.'[31]

John Edwards, a lieutenant of the *Prince*, who was sent on board the *Santísima Trinidad* to help with the evacuation and who was one of the last to leave the ship, recorded his terrible experience:

we [the *Prince*] . . . took the *Trinidad*, the largest ship in the world, in tow; all the other ships that could render assistance to the disabled [were] doing the same. Before four in the morn [on the 24th] it blew so strong that we broke the hawsers twice, and from two such immense bodies as we were, found it difficult to secure her again; however, every exertion was made, and we got her again. By eight in the morning it blew a hurricane on the shore, and so close in that we could not weather the land either way.'Tis impossible to describe the horrors the morning presented, nothing but signals of distress flying in every direction, guns firing, and so many large ships driving on shore without being able to render them the least assistance. After . . . [having endured] four days without any prospect of saving the ship or the gale abating, the signal was made to destroy the prizes. We had no time before to remove the prisoners, and it now became a most dangerous task; no boats could lie alongside, we got under her stern, and the men dropped in by ropes; but what a sight when we came to remove the wounded, [of] which there were between three and four hundred. We had to tie the poor mangled wretches round their waists, or where we could, and lower them down into a tumbling boat, some without arms, others no legs, and lacerated all over in the most dreadful manner. About ten o'clock we had got all out, to about [except for] thirty-three or four, which I believe it was impossible to remove without instant death. The water was now at the pilot deck, the weather dark and boisterous, and taking in tons [of water] at every roll, when we quitted her, and supposed this superb ship could not remain afloat longer than ten minutes. Perhaps she sunk in less time, with the above unfortunate victims, never to rise again.[32]

Even when they had managed to climb into the boats, the rescued men were not out of danger, as a seaman from the *Revenge* recalled:

On quitting the ship [the *Santísima Trinidad*] our boats were so overloaded in endeavouring to save all the lives we could, that it is a miracle they were not upset. A father and his son came down the ship's side to get on board one of our boats; the father had seated himself, but the men in the boat, thinking from the load and the boisterous weather that all their lives would be in peril, could not think of taking the boy. As the boat put off the lad, as though determined not to quit his father, sprang from the ship into the sea and caught hold of the gunwale of the boat, but his attempt was resisted, as it risked all their lives; and some of the men resorted to their cutlasses to cut his fingers off in order to disentangle the boat from his grasp. At the same time the feelings of the father were so worked upon that he was about to leap overboard and perish with his son. Britons could face an enemy but could not witness such a scene of self-devotion: as it were a simultaneous thought burst forth from the crew, which said, 'Let us save both father and son or die in the attempt!' The Almighty aided their design, they succeeded and brought both father and son safe on board our ship where they remained, until with other prisoners they were exchanged at Gibraltar.[33]

That same morning, many prisoners were rescued from the *Monarca*, a prize ship that had been in trouble from the moment the crew surrendered, because only a lieutenant, a midshipman and eight seamen could be spared from the *Bellerophon* to take over the Spanish vessel. Later, the midshipman sent an anonymous report to a Portsmouth newspaper:

Our second Lieutenant, myself, and eight men, formed the party that took possession of the *Monarca*: we remained till the morning [of the 22nd] without further assistance, or we should most probably have saved her, though she had suffered much more than ourselves [the *Bellerophon*]; we kept possession of her however for four days, in the most dreadful weather, when having rolled away all our masts, and being in danger of immediate sinking or running on shore, we were fortunately saved [on the 24th] by the *Leviathan*, with all but about 150 prisoners, who were afraid of getting into the boats. I can assure you I felt not the least fear of death during the action, which I attribute to the general confidence of victory which I saw all around me; but in the prize, when I was in danger of, and had time to reflect upon the approach of death, either from the rising of the Spaniards upon so small a number as we were composed of, or what latterly appeared inevitable from the violence of the storm, I was most certainly afraid; and at one time, when the ship made three feet [of] water in ten minutes, when our people were almost all lying drunk upon deck, when the Spaniards, completely worn out with fatigue, would no longer work at the only chain pump left serviceable; when I saw the fear of death so strongly depicted on the countenances of all around me, I wrapped myself up in a union jack, and lay down upon the deck for a short time, quietly awaiting the approach of death; but the love of life soon after again roused me, and after great exertions on the part of the British and Spanish officers, who had joined together for the mutual preservation of their lives, we got the ship before the wind, determined to run her on shore: this was at midnight, but at day-light in the morning [the 24th], the weather being more moderate, and having again gained upon the water [by pumping], we hauled our wind, perceiving a three-decker (*El Rayo*) dismasted, but with Spanish colours up, close to leeward of us: the *Leviathan*, the first British ship we had seen for the last thirty hours, seeing this, bore down, and firing a shot ahead of us, the *Rayo* struck without returning a gun.[34]

The *Leviathan* began taking the men off the *Monarca*, and the *Rayo* – one of Kerjulien's ships that had failed to make it back to Cadiz – surrendered to the *Donegal*. This vessel had just returned from Gibraltar, having been sent there for supplies before the battle began. With all but about 150 Spanish sailors removed from the *Monarca*, a fresh crew was sent on board, and both the *Monarca* and the *Rayo* were anchored, for it was impossible to try to move them until the winds died down.

Prisoners began to be taken off the *Intrépide*, another captured ship that had been under tow when Kerjulien's fleet had appeared from Cadiz the previous afternoon. The *Britannia* had abandoned the tow to join the British battle line, and now the *Intrépide* was in a hopeless position. Lieutenant des Touches, on board the French ship, had vivid memories of the situation:

> in the midst of the gloom, while the storm was still gathering strength, we had to pass through a leeward gunport more than eighty wounded who were incapable of moving into the small English boats. We succeeded in this with infinite trouble, by means of a bed-frame and capstan bars.* Afterwards, we were towed by an English frigate, which we followed while rolling from side to side and leaking everywhere. I became aware that the pumping was slowing down, and I was warned that the doors of the storeroom had been broken down, and that everyone, English and French, had rushed there to get drunk. When I arrived amongst these men, reduced to the state of brutes, a cask of brandy had just been broken, and the liquid was running over the floor and lapping against the foot of a candle which had been set up there. I only just had time to stamp out the flame, and in the darkness threatening voices rose against me . . . With kicks and punches I had the storeroom cleared, I barricaded the door, and I agreed with the English officer how to avert the danger that was threatening . . . I wished to remain on board the *Intrépide* right up to the last minute of agony for one of my friends. This was a lieutenant by the name of Poullain, with whom I was closely connected. He had

*Wooden bars fitted into sockets in the head (top) of the capstan, against which the men pushed to turn the capstan round, winding in a cable or rope.

been judged too badly wounded to survive transfer to another ship, and had begged me not to abandon him in the anguish of his final hour . . . When I had heard the last sigh of my poor friend, there remained just three of us alive in the *Intrépide*. This was a captain of artillery and a midshipman who had not wished to leave me . . . our situation in the *Intrépide* was becoming worse every minute. In the midst of these bodies and the spilt blood, the silence was no longer disturbed only by the sound of the sea, but by a subdued murmuring that the water was making as it rose in the hold and spread through the vessel. Night began to close in, and the vessel was sinking in such a way that it was easy to see that by daybreak it would have disappeared. No longer having anything to do, I had let myself fall asleep, but the artillery officer, having become nervous, gathered together wooden debris on the deck and wanted to set fire to it, preferring a quick death to the slow agony that was being prepared for us. I became aware of this plan in time and absolutely opposed it. We found a lantern that was fixed to the end of a rod, which I advised him to wave. By a lucky chance, the *Orion* passed within earshot; we hailed it and a small boat came to take us off.[35]

Afterwards the *Intrépide* was set alight, and the end of the French vessel was recorded in the *Orion*'s log: 'October 24th . . . P.M. . . . At 8, received all the prisoners from on board her (the prize). At 8.30, perceived the fire to have taken. At 9, wore round and made all sail. At 9.30, the *Intrépide* blew up. At 11, strong gales.'[36]

On the next day, Friday 25th, the weather briefly relented, but this did not prevent the loss of the French ship *Aigle*. During the battle the *Aigle* had surrendered to the *Defiance*, but although a British crew had been put on board immediately, all attempts to take the *Aigle* in tow had failed, and the ship had continued to drift to a point about 3 miles off the Cadiz lighthouse. Here the *Aigle* managed to anchor, and part of the British crew was taken off. The remaining men were overpowered by the French who took back possession of the ship.

Lieutenant Asmus Classen, who had assumed command after the captain of the *Aigle* had been killed, now took the opportunity to try to sail into Cadiz harbour. He described the chain of events leading to the vessel's loss in his official report:

In the afternoon of the third day [24th], recognising both the impossibility of receiving help and that of struggling for much longer against the storm without risking being lost with all hands; fearing, if we remained there, we would share the sad fate of the *Fougueux*, which perished at three cables' length from us,* I took the advice of my companions and it was decided that we would get under way in order to try to reach Cadiz. The winds were just pulling into the south-west very freshly; I made use of this at that very moment by cutting the cable, and I had the joy of heading under my modest sail and steering laboriously by means of a cross-bar to operate the tiller. I came to anchor, without a pilot, at the end of the shore at the entrance of the harbour, near the Spanish ship *San Justo*, and passed the night, not without anxiety, because of the breakers which appeared at low tide very close to the vessel on the starboard. At daybreak [on the 25th] our vessel scraped the bottom with force and lost the rudder after several consecutive jolts. I recognised that I was on the Diamond [shoals] and had no other option but to cut my last cable in order to make for the shore. I steered towards the right of the opening of Santa Maria entrance, where the ship is still situated, run aground on a muddy, sandy seabed.[37]

The *Monarca* and the *Rayo* were not so fortunate. They had anchored the previous night a few miles to the north, but in the early morning of the 25th the anchor cables of the *Monarca* parted, and the vessel with 150 men on board was driven on to the shoals of San Lucar and wrecked. The *Rayo* remained anchored until Saturday the 26th, but despite having survived the worst of

*About 600 yards away.

the storm, the strain on the anchor cables proved too great. This vessel was also driven on to the San Lucar shoals and wrecked, killing a great many Spaniards and some of the British crew.

In the deteriorating weather, the French ship *Berwick* was likewise driven on to the San Lucar shoals, as Captain Rotheram of the *Royal Sovereign* described:

I cannot . . . pass over in silence the heroic conduct of Captain Malcolm and his ship's company in the *Donegal* who, at the imminent hazard of being totally lost, rescued hundreds of the enemy from a watery grave . . . During the violence of the gale, when she was riding at anchor near the *Berwick*, then in possession of the English, some of the French prisoners on board of the prize, in a fit of madness, or desperation, cut the cables of the *Berwick*, by which means she immediately drove towards the dangerous shoals of St. Lucar, then to Leeward, where there was hardly a chance of a man being saved. In this situation Captain Malcolm, without hesitation, ordered the cables of the *Donegal* to be instantly cut, and stood after the *Berwick* to which he dispatched his boats with orders first to save all the wounded Frenchmen before they brought off any of the English, which order was most punctually complied with; the English were next removed, but before the boats could return, the *Berwick* struck upon the shoals, and every soul on board perished, to the number of three hundred. The wounded Frenchmen, who were thus saved, were supplied with the cots and bedding which had been prepared for our own sick and wounded, and after being treated with every kindness and mark of attention, they were sent into Cadiz by a flag of truce, with all the cots and bedding in which they had been placed, that they might suffer as little pain or inconvenience as possible in their removal . . . On the 26th of October, whilst the *Donegal* was at anchor off Cadiz, in a violent gale of wind, with upwards of 600 prisoners on deck, an unfortunate Spanish prisoner fell overboard. Notwithstanding the sea was then running so high that they had not ventured to hoist out a boat for twelve hours before, two seamen belonging to the

Donegal immediately jumped overboard after him, in hopes of saving his life, to the admiration of the Spaniards, who were lost in astonishment at so daring an act. The poor man, however, sunk and was drowned, just as one of the English seamen had nearly hold of him; a boat was immediately lowered and fortunately the two gallant fellows [John Thompson and John Carter] were got safe on board.[38]

The *San Agustín* was too badly damaged to survive the journey to Gibraltar and was set on fire, and shortly afterwards the *Argonauta* was scuttled. What Nelson had begun, the weather had finished. On the day of the battle, only the *Achille* had blown up and sunk; in the week that followed a further fourteen ships of the Combined French and Spanish Fleet were wrecked or sank, while only four captured ships remained in British possession (the *Bahama*, the *San Ildefonso*, the *San Juan Nepomuceno* and the *Swiftsure*). As Nelson lay dying, Captain Hardy had informed him that fourteen or fifteen enemy ships had surrendered, to which Nelson answered, 'That is well, but I bargained for twenty!'[39] In all, the Combined Fleet had actually lost nineteen ships by now – the storm had almost granted Nelson's wish, but the cost in human life was terrible, and further losses were to come. As Collingwood put it: 'I can only say that in my life I never saw such efforts as were made to save these ships, and would rather fight another battle than pass through such a week as followed it.'[40]

On board the *Pluton*, which had led Kerjulien's counterattack from Cadiz on the 23rd and eventually managed to return to the shelter of the harbour, a wounded French soldier by the name of Pernot recorded his experience of the dreadful weather that followed the battle:

During these unhappy days and nights, occasional cannon shots here and there were all that could be heard. I was told that these were vessels that had lost their masts and, hurled ashore, were calling for help. But it was not possible to take them off. Attempts had been made; several rowing boats and dinghies that had been sent for this purpose had capsized or sunk. The poor wretches were condemned to perish. Very few men escaped the disaster. The wounded were shrieking. When the tide was out, they dragged themselves along on those limbs that were not maimed, and sought to avoid the death that they found further on. All of this presented the most hideous and heartbreaking sight.[41]

In Cadiz itself, the anxiety and anger had turned to despair once the weather worsened on the first evening:

The storm that succeeded the battle tended only to keep alive, through the night, the horrors of the day, and to prepare them for the melancholy spectacle of the ensuing morning, when the wrecks of their floating bulwarks were seen on shore, and some, that had escaped the battle and the storm, entering the bay to shelter . . . When the first emotions had subsided, the people of Cadiz strongly manifested their contempt of the French, whom they accused of having deserted them in the hour of battle; and the attention of Lord Collingwood to the wounded Spanish prisoners induced them to contrast the conduct of their generous enemies with that of their treacherous allies.[42]

In the days that followed the battle, most people were kept from the shore by the weather, but it was not many hours before wreckage and bodies began to be washed on to the beaches and into Cadiz harbour. Some were still alive, and a local doctor devised a technique of reviving them by pumping tobacco smoke into their lungs with bellows, so that they vomited and coughed up the sea-water. The majority of those washed ashore were already dead, however, and the Spanish authorities organised mounted patrols along the coast, with burying parties set up at various points. As the men on horseback discovered corpses, they told the nearest burying party, which dug holes and buried the bodies where they came ashore. One was identified by British prisoners as that of Lieutenant William Ram of the *Victory*. It was his deliberate removal of tourniquets in order to bleed to death more quickly once he knew he could not be saved that had almost unhinged the *Victory*'s chaplain, Dr Scott. Ram's body had been thrown overboard while the battle was still raging, and it was washed up on the Spanish coast a few days later. The British prisoners who found Ram obtained permission from the Governor of Cadiz to give him a Christian burial in the town.

As more days passed and the bodies of those killed in the battle were joined by those drowned in the storm, the shoreline became littered with makeshift graves, and the beaches became cluttered with all manner of wreckage and debris. In Cadiz itself, it took over ten days to bring all the wounded from the ships in the harbour, partly because of the weather and partly because the hospitals rapidly became choked. Churches and convents were turned into temporary hospitals, and those churches not being used to accommodate the wounded were packed with the relatives of missing Spanish sailors, constantly praying for their safe return. The streets were filled with mourning women, and sailors who had survived wandered around aimlessly in a state of shock.

An English traveller in Cadiz made a graphic record of the days following the battle:

> Ten days after the battle, they were still employed in bringing ashore the wounded; and spectacles were hourly displayed at the wharfs, and through the streets, sufficient to shock every heart not yet hardened to scenes of blood and human suffering. When, by the carelessness of the boatmen, and the surging of the sea, the boats struck against the stone piers, a horrid cry, which pierced the soul, arose from the mangled wretches on board. Many of the Spanish gentry assisted in bringing them ashore, with symptoms of much compassion; yet as they were

finely dressed, it had something of the appearance of ostentation, if there could be ostentation at such a moment. It need not be doubted that an Englishman [the writer of this report] lent a willing hand to bear them up the steps to their litters; yet the slightest false step made them shriek out, and I even yet shudder at the remembrance of the sound. On the top of the pier the scene was affecting. The wounded were carried away to the hospitals in every shape of human misery, whilst crowds of Spaniards either assisted or looked on with signs of horror. Meanwhile, their companions, who had escaped unhurt, walked up and down with folded arms and downcast eyes, whilst women sat upon heaps of arms, broken furniture, and baggage, with their heads bent between their knees. I had no inclination to follow the litters of the wounded; yet I learned that every hospital in Cadiz was already full, and that convents and churches were forced to be appropriated to the reception of the remainder. If, leaving the harbour, I passed through the town to the Point, I still beheld the terrible effects of the battle. As far as the eye could reach, the sandy side of the isthmus bordering on the Atlantic was covered with masts and yards, the wrecks of ships, and here and there bodies of the dead.[43]

The traveller was still unsure about the losses sustained by the English, particularly on hearing unconfirmed reports of the death of Nelson:

Among others I noticed a topmast marked with the name of the *Swiftsure*, and the broad arrow* of England, which only increased my anxiety to know how far the English had suffered, the Spaniards still continuing to affirm that they (the English) had lost their chief admiral, and half their fleet. While surrounded by these wrecks, I mounted on the cross-trees of a mast which had been thrown ashore, and casting my eyes over the ocean, beheld, at a great distance, several

*British Government property was identified by being marked with three lines forming a broad arrowhead.

masts and portions of wreck still floating about. As the sea was now almost calm, with a slight swell, the effect produced by these objects had in it something of a sublime melancholy, and touched the soul with a remembrance of the sad vicissitudes of human affairs. The portions of floating wreck were visible from the ramparts; yet not a boat dared to venture out to examine or endeavour to tow them in, such were the apprehensions which still filled their minds, of the enemy.[44]

As the storm at last died down towards the end of October, Collingwood opened negotiations with the Spanish authorities at Cadiz to arrange for an exchange of Spanish prisoners for British ones and to ensure that the wounded were properly cared for. There was not the same enmity between the British and Spanish as existed between the British and French, who were regarded by the British as dangerous revolutionaries, atheists and regicides. In southern Spain in particular many people felt that they had been forced into the war by Napoleon's threats, and they held similar views of the French to those of the British. Even so, the reaction of the Spanish to Collingwood's overtures was more like that of British allies (which they had been before and would soon be again) than friends of the detested French. Writing home twelve days after the battle, Collingwood recorded the Spanish response:

To alleviate the miseries of the wounded, as much as in my power, I sent a flag [of truce] to the Marquis Solana [Governor of Cadiz], to offer him his wounded. Nothing can exceed the gratitude expressed by him for this act of humanity. All this part of Spain is in an uproar of praise and thankfulness to the English. Solana sent me a present of wine, and we have free intercourse with the shore. Judge of the footing we are on, when I tell you he offered me his hospitals, and pledged the Spanish honor for the care and cure of our wounded men. Our officers and Men who were wrecked in some prize ships were received like divinities, all the country on the beach to receive them; the Priests and Women distributing wine and bread and fruit amongst them. – The soldiers turned out of their barracks to make room for them; whilst their allies the French were left to shift for themselves, with a guard over them to prevent their doing mischief . . . All the Spaniards speak of us in terms of adoration.[45]

The death of Nelson even touched the hearts of people in Cadiz, as was reported after an exchange of prisoners: 'The English Officers, who have returned from Cadiz, state, that the account of Lord Nelson's death was received there with extreme sorrow and regret by the Spaniards, and that some of them were even observed to shed tears on the occasion. – They said, "that, though he had been the ruin of their navy, yet they could not help lamenting his fall, as being the most generous Enemy, and the *greatest Commander* of the age!" '[46]

With the winds becoming more favourable, the British ships towed all the remaining prizes and those British ships needing major repairs to Gibraltar. Collingwood meanwhile began once again to organise the blockade of Cadiz because the port still contained a number of powerful warships that could cause trouble for British shipping. As the sailors began to relax for the first time, they agreed that the experience of the storm had been far worse than the battle and that never had a sailing fleet been caught in such a dangerous situation and escaped.

The storm that had reached hurricane strength on the Spanish coast reached similar proportions along the south coast of England. While unusual, such autumnal storms are not unknown. At the time only those people in England who had relatives at sea were particularly concerned by the atrocious weather, for the news from Trafalgar had not yet reached them. It was only afterwards that people along the south coast made the connection between the great storm of October 1805 and the hurricane after the battle. Years later the novelist and poet Thomas Hardy, drawing on memories of the people of Dorset, summed it up in four lines of verse:

In the wild October night-time, when the wind raved round the land,
And the Back-sea met the Front-sea, and our doors were blocked
with sand,
And we heard the drub of Dead-man's Bay, where bones of
thousands are,
We knew not what the day had done for us at Trafalgar.[47]

TWELVE

THE MESSENGERS

> Yesterday about Noon, two officers of the navy came through this Town, following each other, at about an hour's Space of Time, in two Post-Chaises and four Horses to each, from the Westward; the first reported that he brought good News of great Importance, and the second, that his Dispatches contained the best and most capital News that the Nation ever experienced.
>
> Letter dated 6 November 1805, from Captain Robert Tomlinson at Dorchester to Captain Nicholas Tomlinson at the Admiralty in London[1]

On Saturday 26 October 1805, with the storm still raging, Collingwood began to think beyond the survival of his fleet off Cadiz and ordered the lieutenant in command of the *Pickle*, John Lapenotiere, to come on board the *Euryalus*. In the five days since the battle, despite the constant violent motion of the ship, Collingwood had managed to write his report, as well as letters to relations and friends at home. Some of the captains and crew in other ships had been doing likewise, and now Collingwood proposed to entrust the schooner *Pickle* (at less than 80 feet long, the second-smallest ship in the fleet) with taking the first despatches and news of the battle back to England. With the fleet dispersed over a wide area, not everyone managed to send their letters home in the *Pickle*. A few days later Edward Codrington, captain of the *Orion*, was complaining that 'we are all in distress about our poor wives hearing of the action and not knowing if we are dead or alive'.[2]

The *Pickle* was not the obvious choice for the task, as it was more usual to send a frigate on such missions, and Captain Blackwood of the *Euryalus* had been hoping to have the honour of taking the news to England himself. He was to be disappointed. A tradition in the Lapenotiere family explained Collingwood's choice as the payment of a debt of honour; Lapenotiere and Collingwood had once both been passengers in a ship when an order was given that was likely to send it on to nearby rocks. Although only a passenger, Lapenotiere countermanded the order and saved the ship, and in gratitude Collingwood promised to do him a service if ever the opportunity arose. A thirty-five-year-old officer from Ilfracombe in Devon, who had first gone to sea at the age of ten, Lapenotiere was now entrusted with the responsibility of taking the news of the battle back to the Admiralty in London as fast as possible.

Whatever the reason for Collingwood's decision, an elated Lapenotiere immediately put all the prisoners that were aboard the *Pickle* into a boat and sent them to the *Revenge*. The *Pickle*'s log recorded simply, 'At noon, the boat returned. In boat and made sail for England.'[3] There was not a moment to lose if Lapenotiere was to gain the honour and probable reward for being the first one to inform the Admiralty of the battle. It was a dangerous voyage of over 1000 miles, and although enemy warships were still in the area that he was to cross, particularly the four that had been led away from the battle by Dumanoir, Lapenotiere knew that his greatest enemy was the weather. The *Pickle* had been on the sidelines of the battle and had not been damaged, but it had been battered by over four days of severe storms, with every prospect of running into more bad weather before reaching England.

At first the *Pickle* made good progress, but by midnight the wind changed direction, forcing the ship away from England rather than towards it. By dawn the wind swung round again, and once more the *Pickle* set a course directly for home. The next day, the 28th, another ship was sighted to the west-north-west. Recognised as a sloop, this vessel was sailing on a course to intercept, but as yet could not be identified as friend or foe. Lapenotiere prudently kept the *Pickle* moving as fast as possible. Having locked on to the *Pickle*'s course, the sloop slowly began to gain ground, and so Lapenotiere had the coded identification signal hoisted. Anxiety vanished when it was answered correctly; the sloop proved to be the *Nautilus*, commanded by Captain John Sykes who was very soon on board the *Pickle*, exchanging news with Lapenotiere. When he heard about the battle and the death of Nelson, Sykes decided he should inform the British Ambassador in Portugal and so set sail immediately, arriving at the mouth of the Tagus River at Lisbon early the next day. After two hours, a pilot still had not been found to guide the *Nautilus* into port, and so a fishing vessel was boarded and its captain was paid to deliver a despatch to the ambassador. By half past nine on the morning of the 29th, with despatches for London from the ambassador, the *Nautilus* headed to England. It was now a race between the two messengers to see who would reach the Admiralty first, for even if Lapenotiere had not been told of Captain Sykes's intention to make for England after Lisbon, it would not have been hard to guess.

By the 30th the *Pickle* was north-west of Lisbon, still on course for England, when the *Nautilus* was again sighted; despite the detour, Captain Sykes had caught up. The *Nautilus* continued in sight the next morning when both ships were struck by strong gales, but as the *Pickle* rounded Cape Finisterre at about half past nine, heavy seas swept over the bow, carrying away spars and rigging. The drain holes that allowed water from the bow to drain to the pump became blocked, and the bow started to flood. Immediately the crew began baling with buckets, but the storm was gathering strength, and they could do little more than check the rising level of water in the ship. It became obvious that there must also be a leak below the water-line, and as the ship took on more water, the pump was working at full stretch. For the rest of the day and all through the night, the men struggled to keep the *Pickle* afloat, but if anything the storm was worse the next day. Lapenotiere decided to lighten the ship: four carronades on the deck were heaved overboard, reducing the weight by over a ton and lowering the ship's centre of gravity to make the *Pickle* more stable. Having already endured the hurricane off the Spanish coast, and having baled and pumped continuously for over twenty-four hours, the crew were now exhausted, but they persisted with their efforts through the morning, and at noon came the first signs that the weather was clearing. By evening the wind had dropped to a breeze, the leak had stopped, and the *Pickle* finally managed to set sail on course for England once more. Everyone was thoroughly soaked, with hardly a dry place in the ship, but at least some of the crew could now get some rest.

The next day, 2 November, the *Pickle* entered the English Channel, and with a good following wind was sailing fast for the Lizard, about 150 miles to the north-north-east. Just as everything was at last going well and the *Pickle* was making good time, the wind dropped, leaving the ship becalmed and gradually enveloped by a thick sea mist. Lapenotiere ordered the sweeps to be used – large oars that each took three or four men to operate – and for more than four hours the crew strained at the sweeps until the first thin breaths of a breeze showed that the wind was rising again. Soon, with a strong following wind once more, the *Pickle* was making good speed up the English Channel, with an increasing number of sightings of other ships heading to and from the Channel ports. In the late afternoon of the following day, the *Pickle* met the warship *Superb*; both ships stopped, and Lapenotiere went on board.

The *Superb* was commanded by Captain Richard Keats, a good friend of Nelson, who had once written of Keats, 'I esteem his *person* alone as equal to *one* French 74[-gun ship].'[4] Keats was now taking his ship to join the blockade of Cadiz, hoping to be in time for the expected battle. Ever conscious of the need for haste, Lapenotiere related the news to Keats, observed by Edward Trelawny, then a twelve-year-old boy serving in the *Superb*:

Young as I was, I shall never forget our falling in with the *Pickle* schooner after Trafalgar, carrying the first despatches of the battle and death of its hero. Her commander, burning with impatience to be the first to convey the news to England, was compelled to heave to and come on board us. Captain Keats received him on deck. Silence reigned throughout the ship; some great event was anticipated. The officers stood in groups, watching with intense anxiety the two commanders, who walked apart. 'Battle', 'Nelson', 'ships', were the only audible words which could be gathered from their conversation. I saw the blood rush into Keats's face; he stamped the deck, walked hurriedly, and spoke with passion. I marvelled, for I had never before seen him much moved; he had appeared cool, firm, and collected on all occasions, and it struck me that some awful event had taken place, or was at hand. The Admiral [Duckworth] was still in his cabin, eager for news from the Nelson fleet. He was an irritable and violent man, and after a few minutes, swelling with wrath, he sent an order to Keats, who possibly heard it not, but staggered along the deck, struck to the heart by the news, and, for the first time in his life, forgot his respect to his superior in rank; muttering, as it seemed, curses on his fate that, by the Admiral's delay [staying three days at Plymouth to load extra mutton and potatoes], he had not participated in the most glorious battle in naval history. Another messenger enforced him to descend in haste to the Admiral, who was high in rage and impatience. Keats, for I followed him, on entering the Admiral's cabin, said in a subdued voice, as if he were choking, 'A great battle has been fought, two days ago, off Trafalgar. The combined fleets of France and Spain are annihilated, and Nelson is no more!' He then murmured, 'Had we not been detained we should have been there.' Duckworth answered not, conscience-struck, but stalked the deck. He seemed ever to avoid the look of his captain, and turned to converse with the commander of the schooner, who replied in sulky brevity, 'Yes' or 'No'. Then, dismissing him, he ordered all sail to be set, and walked the quarter-deck alone. A death-like stillness pervaded the ship, broken at intervals by the low murmurs of the crew and officers, when 'battle' and 'Nelson' could alone be distinguished. Sorrow and discontent were painted on every face.[5]

Lapenotiere in the *Pickle*, now less than 60 miles from the Lizard, carried on up the Channel and was off Falmouth in Cornwall by nine-thirty the next morning. The tide was against him, and rather than lose precious time, he went on shore by boat, leaving his second-in-command to take the *Pickle* on into Plymouth. On the morning of Monday 4 November, Lapenotiere set foot in England, nine days after he had left the British fleet off Cadiz. He still had to reach the Admiralty in London, over 260 miles away, and immediately began to arrange for transport to take him there. According to a Cornish tradition, the news was already known in Penzance; some fishing boats from that town had hailed the *Pickle*, still travelling up the Channel, and then took the news back to their home port. The mayor, Thomas Giddy, interrupted a ball at the Union Hotel in Penzance to announce the victory at Trafalgar and the death of Nelson. An annual Trafalgar Ball is held there to commemorate the first announcement of this news on British soil.

Nowadays it is difficult to imagine a world where there was no faster method of sending the news from Falmouth to London than the speed at which a relay of horses could run the distance. A telegraph system was being built between London and Plymouth that would be capable of transmitting simple messages very rapidly, but in November 1805 it was only operational between London and Portsmouth. For Lapenotiere, much further west in Falmouth, in order to inform the Lords of the Admiralty about the Battle of Trafalgar there was no alternative but to travel to London and tell them himself. He chose a post-chaise, which was the fastest method of travel other than riding a relay of horses. Its light carriage was pulled by two or four horses at a gallop and was capable of carrying two or three passengers. It was also the most expensive way to travel (modern air travel is by comparison cheaper), but this was government business, and in any case the government paid a special lower fare. Although they were the fastest carriages available, post-chaises were hardly rapid – 5 miles an hour was a normal average speed. For urgent messages, runners were often employed to take them on foot, proving quicker for long journeys, even with an overnight stop on the way. At the time, many people in rural areas never ventured beyond the hinterland of the village where they were born, and the longest journey they made was to the nearest market town. For a Cornishman needing to go to London, the cheapest transport was by wagon, but even this was expensive and the journey usually took about three weeks. Prudent travellers were known to make their last will and testament before setting out.

Lapenotiere left Falmouth at noon on 4 November, travelling up to Penryn and taking the right-hand fork to Truro, Cornwall's only city. Here the four horses were changed, and he next sped on towards Liskeard. Fortunately the roads were dry, for although the *Pickle* had struggled through so much bad weather to reach Falmouth, inland it had not rained for five days. Roads in Britain at this time were in a very poor condition and were often badly maintained. Just a small amount of rain could turn some stretches of road into wide quagmires, as successive vehicles drove on the edges, where the going was more firm, and thus broadened the boggy patches. Even when dry, the rutted mud slowed the carriages' progress and increased the discomfort of the passengers, but when the roads were saturated it was often quicker to take a detour.

From Liskeard, the post-chaise hurried on to Tavistock in Devon, and then in the darkness of the winter evening picked its way across Dartmoor. While Lapenotiere tried to snatch what sleep he could in the jolting carriage, or at least relax for the first time in several weeks, his route took him close to Princetown – close enough for him to have seen it, had it been daylight. As yet it was only a rural village, one of the bleakest on Dartmoor, but four months later the first stone would be laid for the building of Dartmoor Prison, established to cope with the growing population of French prisoners of war. The prison hulks, the hulls of obsolete battleships that held prisoners of war at Plymouth, were already seriously overcrowded, but Dartmoor would not receive its first prisoners until May 1809. At over 1400 feet above sea-level, isolated and exposed to bitter winds and unforgiving weather, Dartmoor came to be regarded as the worst of all the prisons and hulks that were used to accommodate prisoners of war. These prisons and hulks were only for the lower ranks and those officers who refused to give their parole. Officers who gave their word of honour (parole) to abide by the rules and not try to escape were allowed to lodge in one of the parole towns. There they had relative freedom within the parole boundaries of the town, the perimeter of which was marked by special boundary stones. Tavistock, the town through which Lapenotiere had just passed, was one such parole town, accommodating over a hundred French officers.

Between 1803 and 1813, fifty towns in Britain were used for parole, and they were to have a significant impact on the population of the country. Often selected for being in relatively remote rural areas, these were towns where people had rarely, if ever, seen a foreigner. Into these inward-looking communities were dropped men whose speech, manners, dress and even food preferences seemed strange or even bizarre to the local population. It was, in a way, a small-scale French invasion, but it was not just of men alone; some officers had their wives join them in captivity. The officers on parole were absorbed into the community fairly rapidly, and since they could afford to pay for their lodging, food and other necessities, they proved a boost to the local economy. To pass the time they engaged in all sorts of activities, such as the teaching of languages, music, drawing and fencing to the offspring of the local gentry, or they began to learn English or other subjects themselves; a few even opened shops. Many never returned to France, for some of the officers died before they could be exchanged for British prisoners. Others married British women, despite such marriages being declared invalid by the French Government.

Within a few weeks Lieutenant des Touches, who had been lucky to escape from the *Intrépide* before the ship was destroyed, would be lodged on parole at Tiverton in Devon – a town a few miles north of the route Lapenotiere was taking on his way to London. Des Touches thought Tiverton

quite a pleasant town, but which seemed to me remarkably monotonous after the restless life to which I was accustomed. My pay, reduced to half, amounted to fifty francs a month, which had to suffice for all my needs, at a time when the Continental blockade had made the price of all commodities rise appreciably . . . I made the most of my leisure time to refresh and complete my education. Some of my more well-read friends gave me lessons in literature and history; I repaid them by teaching them fencing, in which I always remained well practised. The population of Tiverton, moreover, made us very welcome; some of the inhabitants were even kind enough to suggest they should help me to escape, and among them one young and pretty girl who only put one condition on her offer, that I should take her with me in my flight, and that I should marry her on arrival on the Continent. I

The battle at an early stage, showing (left to right) the French *Fougueux*, the British *Belleisle*, the French *Indomptable*, the Spanish *Santa Ana* and the British *Royal Sovereign*. Despite successive broadsides that had already taken place, the artist has only portrayed serious damage to the ships' sails

Captain Thomas Masterman Hardy of the *Victory*

Captain Henry Blackwood of the frigate *Euryalus*

George Duff, from Banff in Scotland, who was captain of the British battleship *Mars*. He was killed during the battle by a broadside from the French ship *Pluton*

The shooting of Nelson on board the *Victory*. This dramatic moment during the battle was a favourite subject for Victorian artists, who invariably put a romantic gloss on the scenes of carnage on the decks of the *Victory*

The battle at about two o'clock, with the French *Redoutable* (centre) trapped between the *Temeraire* (to the left) and the *Victory* (to the right, with sunshine on the bows). Painting by W. Clarkson Stanfield

The battle late in the afternoon showing the British ship *Belleisle*, with all the masts shot away, drifting helplessly on the edge of the battle

The *Achille* on fire at the end of the battle. Aquatint engraving by Thomas Sutherland after an original by Thomas Whitcombe

The scene towards the end of the battle, at about five o'clock, showing the wrecked state of many of the ships and (far left) the *Achille* on fire. Painting by Nicholas Pocock

Jeannette being rescued from the sea after escaping the burning *Achille*, which is now sinking (left)

A near-contemporary print of a woman with her child tending a wounded seaman on the gun deck during a battle. Apart from demonstrating the frequent presence of women and children on board navy ships, it also gives a good impression of the clouds of smoke that filled the gun decks

A near-contemporary print of a woman searching for her husband among the dead and wounded seamen on the gun-deck of a battleship. As in nearly all such pictures, the artist has exaggerated the amount of space, and especially the amount of headroom, below deck

The morning after the battle outside Cadiz showing (left to right) the British ship *Defence* and the Spanish prize ship *San Ildefonso*, which had been completely dismasted and was now little more than a hulk

Captain John Richard Lapenotiere of the *Pickle*, who took the news of the victory at Trafalgar to London

Spanish sailors on the rocky shore after their ship had been wrecked in the storm

The gravestone in Gibraltar's Trafalgar Cemetery of Captain Thomas Norman of the marines, who was wounded on board the *Mars* and died in the Naval Hospital on 6 December 1805

The scene on 28 October as the *Victory* is towed by the *Neptune*. The ships are approaching Gibraltar where the *Victory*, with Nelson's body on board, underwent temporary repairs before the return to England. Painting by W. Clarkson Stanfield

did not have much trouble in resisting these temptations, but it grieved me more to tear myself away from the obsessions of some of my friends, who, not having the same ideas as me about the sacredness of one's oath, simply wanted to persuade me to escape with them.[6]

Des Touches was to live in Tiverton for six years before he was exchanged for a British prisoner of war held in France.

Having crossed Dartmoor, Lapenotiere reached the city of Exeter around midnight. At about this time the *Nautilus* arrived at Plymouth, where Captain Sykes immediately hired a post-chaise and headed for Exeter in order to join the road to London. Sykes had set foot in England about twelve hours after Lapenotiere, yet having landed in Plymouth, so much further east than Falmouth, he was now less than five hours behind. Through the morning of 5 November, Lapenotiere hurried eastwards through Honiton and Axminster and then on towards Bridport in Dorset, with no idea that Sykes was on the road behind him and gaining fast. Already some people were looking forward to the evening's celebrations, when bonfires would be lit to commemorate the failure of Guy Fawkes's plot to blow up Parliament exactly two hundred years earlier in 1605. Any opportunity was seized for merrymaking to lessen the oppression of the coming winter: without electricity or gas, the best lighting available was from candles, but the poor made do with reeds and rushes dipped in fat, or just the light from their hearth fire, so the dark days of winter could be very dark indeed. That evening, some people would hear of an extra reason to celebrate, but also to mourn. Although there was little opportunity for Lapenotiere and Sykes to spread the news except when changing their horses, Lapenotiere nevertheless had to change horses nineteen times, and Sykes nearly as many, so they left a trail of rumour across southern England.

The victory of Trafalgar, and more especially the death of Nelson, was one of those rare occasions that remained a landmark in people's memories. Years afterwards, everyone could remember where they were and what they were doing when they first heard the news that Nelson had been shot, and it was common to date events as happening so many years before or after the year of Trafalgar. Two days after the messengers passed through Bridport, a friend wrote to Midshipman Richard Roberts who was serving aboard the *Victory*, and addressed his letter to 'H.M.S. *Victory*, Portsmouth, or Elsewhere.' The letter recorded:

> We first heard of the engagement on the morning of the 5th Nov. The account was sent . . . to Burton [Burton Bradstock in Dorset, about 3 miles from Bridport] soon after Lieutenant Lapinoture [Lapenotiere] passed Bridport. It informed us of the death of Lord Nelson; and that 19 ships were taken and one blown up. Our feelings were extremely racked; all deploring the loss of the Hero; all measureably pleased the victory was so decisively in our favour. But at the same time our minds were much distressed on your account. For my own part I never experienced such incoherent emotions in my life; one minute hoping you were safe; the next doubting it from the dreadful carnage that was inevitable in such a situation. From this dilemma nothing could relieve me but hearing immediately from you. Every post was looked for, with indescribable anxiety . . . and this was not dispelled till the receipt of your very acceptable letter dated Oct. 22nd. (to your father) which he received in Bridport and immediately sent . . . to Burton. The bells rang again till several of the ropes broke! [They were rung when the news first reached the village.] They were repaired again next morning . . . I was really astonished to find you were so collected the day after the action as to be able to write such a letter.[7]

The reaction in Burton Bradstock was to be repeated in many rural towns and villages in the coming weeks.

From Bridport, Lapenotiere continued along the coast road to Dorchester, passing through the town around midday, and then turned inland and headed north-east across Salisbury

Plain. By now Sykes, who was following the same route, was only about an hour behind. As they approached London, the isolated pools of mist that had been visible in the wayside hollows grew to become a classic London fog. In the glow from the carriage lamps, it had a yellow tinge and there was a smell of smoke in the air – no longer the pleasant aroma of wood and peat smoke from rural hearths, but the sulphurous aftertaste of urban coal fires. As the fog thickened, the post-chaises slowed to a crawl. Lady Bessborough, the sister of Georgiana, Duchess of Devonshire, was also caught in the fog that night and described the experience in a letter to a friend:

I drove to town intending to go . . . to Queen Street and to Duncannon's house [Duncannon was Lady Bessborough's son], where I had appointed people to meet me. The fog, which was bad when I set out, grew thicker and thicker, but when I got into the park was so complete it was impossible to find the way out. My footman got down to *feel* for the road, and the holloing of the drivers and screams of people on foot were dreadful. I was one hour driving thro' the park; Queen St. it was impossible to find, and as I was obliged to come here, and it was as dangerous to try to go home, I set out with two men walking before the horses with flambeaux, of which we could with difficulty perceive the flame – the men not at all. Every ten or twenty yards they *felt* for the door of a house to ask where we were – it was frightful beyond measure; in three hours' time I reached Chelsea, when it began to clear a little. I find Lady Villiers, who rode to see me, was overtaken by it on her return, and nearly drown'd by riding into the Thames. How many accidents she has![8]

Lady Bessborough's friend Lady Villiers, the daughter of George Villiers, the Earl of Jersey, had been thrown from a carriage and had injured her head only a few months previously.

After a painfully slow journey through the fog across London, Lieutenant Lapenotiere arrived at the Admiralty in

Whitehall sometime after midnight, still ahead of Captain Sykes. For being first to bring the news, Lapenotiere was later rewarded with £500 and promotion to commander. The First Secretary to the Board of Admiralty, William Marsden, had only just finished work, but was called back to receive the despatches. Like so many others, Marsden was to have an indelible memory of the first time he heard the news:

In accosting me, the officer used these impressive words, 'Sir, we have gained a great victory; but we have lost Lord Nelson!' The effect this produced, it is not to my purpose to describe, nor had I time to indulge in reflections, who was at that moment the only person informed of one of the greatest events recorded in our history, and which it was my duty to make known with the utmost promptitude. The First Lord had retired to rest, as had his domestics, and it was not till after some research that I could discover the room in which he slept. Drawing aside his curtain, with a candle in my hand, I awoke the old peer [Lord Barham] from a sound slumber; and to the credit of his nerves be it mentioned, that he showed no symptom of alarm or surprise, but calmly asked: 'What news, Mr. M.?' We then discussed in few words, what was immediately to be done, and I sat up the remainder of the night, with such of the clerks as I could collect, in order to make the necessary communications.[9]

As there were many people to inform, several copies of Collingwood's despatches were made and sent out by messenger – one of the first reaching the Prime Minister, William Pitt, in the early hours of 6 November. Lord Fitzharris described Pitt's reaction:

On the receipt of the news of the memorable battle of Trafalgar . . . I happened to dine with Pitt, and it was naturally the engrossing subject of our conversation. I shall *never forget* the eloquent manner in which he described his conflicting feelings, when roused in the night to read Collingwood's despatches. Pitt observed, that he had been called up at various hours in his eventful life by the arrival of news of various hues; but that whether good or bad he could always lay his head on his pillow and sink into sound sleep again. On *this occasion*, however, the great event announced brought with it so much to weep over, as well as to rejoice at, that he could not calm his thoughts, but at length got up, though it was three in the morning.[10]

The messenger to King George III reached Windsor Castle at half past six that morning, where the royal family were seen to be deeply moved by the news, and before dawn rumours were also already beginning to spread throughout London. Captain Whitby was sent as a messenger from the Admiralty carrying letters to Lady Hamilton, including an official one from Sir Andrew Snape Hammond, Comptroller of the Navy, informing her of Nelson's death. When Whitby reached her home at Merton, Emma was still in bed, and he was ushered into her room. The look on his face and the tears in his eyes told her everything; she screamed, fell back on the pillow, and for ten hours could not speak or even shed a tear. Her first words were, 'What shall I do? How can I exist?'[11] Prostrate with grief for weeks, she was stunned by the enormity of her loss.

During the morning crowds gathered outside newspaper offices, clamouring for news, and at the Admiralty there were similar crowds, as Lady Bessborough witnessed: 'The scene at the Admiralty was quite affecting – crowds of people, chiefly women, enquiring for husbands, brothers, and children.'[12] Printers were hurrying to finish a *Gazette Extraordinary*, an unscheduled edition of *The London Gazette* (an official government journal, published twice a week), with copies of despatches and letters from Collingwood and his officers, but it came out too late for the 6 November edition of the London newspapers. The next day, *The Times* reprinted on its front page, along with other details, Collingwood's summary of the battle:

Euryalus, off Cape Trafalgar, Oct 22. 1805

Sir,

The ever-to-be-lamented death of Vice-Admiral Lord Viscount Nelson, who, in the late conflict with the enemy, fell in the hour of victory, leaves to me the duty of informing my Lords Commissioners of the Admiralty, that on the 19th instant, it was communicated to the Commander in Chief, from the ships watching the motions of the enemy in Cadiz, that the Combined Fleet had put to sea; as they sailed with light winds westerly, his Lordship concluded their destination was the Mediterranean, and immediately made all sail for the 'Streights' [Straits of Gibraltar] entrance, with the British Squadron, consisting of twenty-seven ships, three of them sixty-fours, where his Lordship was informed, by Captain Blackwood (whose vigilance in watching, and giving notice of the enemy's movements, has been highly meritorious), that they had not yet passed the Streights.

On Monday the 21st instant, at day-light, when Cape Trafalgar bore E. by S. about seven leagues, the enemy was discovered six or seven miles to the Eastward, the wind about West, and very light; the Commander in Chief immediately made the signal for the fleet to bear up in two columns, as they are formed in order of sailing; a mode of attack his Lordship had previously directed, to avoid the inconvenience and delay in forming a line of battle in the usual manner. The enemy's line consisted of thirty-three ships (of which eighteen were French, and fifteen Spanish), commanded in Chief by Admiral Villeneuve: the Spaniards, under the direction of Gravina, wore, with their heads to the Northward, and formed their line of battle with great closeness and correctness; but as the mode of attack was unusual, so the structure of their line was new; it formed a crescent, convexing to the leeward, so that, in leading down to their centre, I had both their van and rear abaft the beam; before the fire opened, every alternate ship was about a cable's length to windward of her second a-head and a-stern, forming a kind of double line, and appeared, when on their beam, to leave a very little interval between them; and this without crowding their ships. Admiral Villeneuve was in the *Bucentaure*, in the centre, and the *Prince of Asturias* bore Gravina's flag in the rear, but the French and Spanish ships were mixed without any apparent regard to order of national squadron.

As the mode of our attack had been previously determined on, and communicated to the Flag Officers, and Captains, few signals were necessary, and none were made, except to direct close order as the lines bore down.

The Commander in Chief, in the *Victory*, led the weather column, and the *Royal Sovereign*, which bore my flag, the lee.

The action began at twelve o'clock, by the leading ships of the columns breaking through the enemy's line, the Commander in Chief [Villeneuve] about the tenth ship from the van, the Second in Command [Gravina] about the twelfth from the rear, leaving the van of the enemy unoccupied; the succeeding ships breaking through, in all parts, astern of their leaders, and engaging the enemy at the muzzles of their guns; the conflict was severe; the enemy's ships were fought with a gallantry highly honourable to their Officers; but the attack on them was irresistible, and it pleased the Almighty Disposer of all events to grant his Majesty's arms a complete and glorious victory. About three P.M. many of the enemy's ships having struck their colours, their line gave way; Admiral Gravina, with ten ships joining their frigates to leeward, stood towards Cadiz. The five headmost ships in their van tacked, and standing to the Southward, to windward of the British line, were engaged, and the sternmost of them taken; the others went off, leaving to his Majesty's squadron nineteen ships of the line (of which two are first rates, the *Santissima Trinidad* and the *Santa Ana*.) with three Flag Officers, viz. Admiral Villeneuve, the Commander in Chief; Don Ignatio Maria D'Aliva, Vice Admiral; and the Spanish Rear-Admiral, Don Baltazar Hidalgo Cisneros.

After such a victory, it may appear unnecessary to enter into encomiums on the particular parts taken by the several Commanders; the conclusion says more on the subject than I have language to express; the spirit which animated all was the same: when all exert themselves zealously in their country's service, all deserve that their high merits should stand recorded; and never was high merit more conspicuous than in the battle I have described.

The *Achille* (a French 74), after having surrendered, by some mismanagement of the Frenchmen, took fire and blew up; two hundred of her men were saved by the Tenders.

A circumstance occurred during the action, which so strongly marks the invincible spirit of British seamen, when engaging the enemies of their country, that I cannot resist the pleasure I have in making it known to their Lordships; the *Temeraire* was boarded by accident, or design, by a French ship on one side, and a Spaniard on the other; the contest was vigorous, but, in the end, the Combined Ensigns were torn from the poop, and the British hoisted in their places.

Such a battle could not be fought without sustaining a great loss of men. I have not only to lament, in common with the British Navy, and the British Nation, in the Fall of the Commander in Chief, the loss of a Hero, whose name will be immortal, and his memory ever dear to his country; but my heart is rent with the most poignant grief for the death of a friend, to whom, by many years intimacy, and a perfect knowledge of the virtues of his mind, which inspired ideas superior to the common race of men, I was bound by the strongest ties of affection; a grief to which even the glorious occasion in which he fell, does not bring the consolation which, perhaps, it ought; his Lordship received a musket ball in his left breast, about the middle of the action, and sent an Officer to me immediately with his last farewell; and soon after expired.

I have also to lament the loss of those excellent Officers, Captains Duff, of the *Mars*, and Cooke of the *Bellerophon*; I have yet heard of none others.

I fear the numbers that have fallen will be found very great, when the returns come to me; but it having blown a gale of wind ever since the action, I have not yet had it in my power to collect any reports from the ships.

The *Royal Sovereign* having lost her masts, except the tottering foremast, I called the *Euryalus* to me, while the action continued, which ship lying within hail, made my signals – a service Captain Blackwood performed with great attention: after the action, I shifted my flag to her, that I might more easily communicate any orders to, and collect the ships, and towed the *Royal Sovereign* out to Seaward. The whole fleet were now in a very perilous situation, many dismasted, all shattered, in thirteen fathom water, off the shoals of Trafalgar; and when I made the signal to prepare to anchor, few of the ships had an anchor to let go, their cables being shot; but the same good Providence which aided us through such a day preserved us in the night, by the wind shifting a few points, and drifting the ships off the land, except four of the captured dismasted ships, which are now at anchor off Trafalgar, and I hope will ride safe until those gales are over.

Having thus detailed the proceedings of the fleet on this occasion, I beg to congratulate their Lordships on a victory which, I hope, will add a ray to the glory of his Majesty's crown, and be attended with public benefit to our country. I am, &c.

(signed) C. Collingwood

In this summary, Collingwood called Nelson 'a Hero, whose name will be immortal, and his memory ever dear to his country'. As millions of people across the country read these words, or had the words read out to them, Nelson's Immortal Memory and the cult of the Hero were born.

Copies of the *Gazette Extraordinary* were despatched to towns throughout Britain, and the wider propaganda value of the victory was not lost on the government, which sent three thousand copies for distribution on the Continent. In the days that followed, local newspapers carried accounts of the victory and Nelson's death, usually including full copies of the despatches published in the *Gazette*. At Great Massingham in Norfolk, where he was on holiday, the landscape painter Joseph Farington recorded in his diary how he first heard the news:

November 7.– At one o' Clock the Postmaster at Rougham sent His Post Boy [to Great Massingham] with orders to stop while an extraordinary Gazette was read. It announced an engagement off Cadiz between the English fleet under Lord Nelson & the combined fleets of France & Spain under Admiral Villeneuve &c. in which 19 French & Spanish Ships were taken & one burnt. – Admiral Villeneuve taken. – This agreeable news was attended with the painful information of the death of Lord Nelson who was killed by a musket-ball. In the evening we got a paper containing a Bulletin from the Admiralty with the substance of the above.[13]

Five days later, Farington went to Burnham Thorpe, 'and called upon Daniel Everitt the present minister there, – He having succeeded the Revd. Mr. Nelson, father of Lord Nelson. I was sorry to find that the Rectory House in which Lord Nelson was born was pulled down by the present Rector who has built a new House a little higher up than where the late house stood. – Not a stone remains of the Old House, but Everitt showed us a tree which touched the Kitchen Chimney. – I expressed a wish that an Obelisk, or something of the kind should be placed there by subscription, but Everitt did not seem to encourage it, observing that it wd. bring people to see it.'[14]

To the west of London, where people already had some idea of the news, local editors used what material they were given well before they received copies of the *Gazette Extraordinary* and *Trewman's Exeter Flying Post* for Thursday 7 November carried the following report, which is a mixture of fact, hearsay and errors:

Exeter, Wednesday, Nov. 6.

GLORIOUS and DECISIVE VICTORY over the Combined Fleets of France and Spain, On the 21st of October. Enemy 34 sail of the line – Lord Nelson's fleet 26 sail.

It is with pride and exultation we again lay before our readers the first intelligence of another glorious Victory obtained by our naval heroes over the Combined Fleet of France and Spain! A victory, unequalled in the annals of any country! – But whilst we rejoice in this further proof of the superior prowess of British seamen – our joy is checked at the consideration, that we have lost in the conflict many brave fellows, and, most particularly, a man adored by those under his command, idolized by his grateful country, and whose very name struck terror on his enemies – in a word, we have lost – NELSON; than whom a braver, never inhabited this terraqueous globe – and whose whole life has been dedicated to the service of his country. But, he fell in the arms of victory – for whilst life yet quivered on his lip, his gallant companions were decking his brow with never-fading laurels! – Yet, he will live forever in the hearts of his countrymen; and the details of his naval exploits off Cape St. Vincent – at the Nile – at Copenhagen – and off Cadiz, will adorn the annals of his native country, Great Britain, till time shall be no more. Altho' we cannot suppress the tear which the loss of this hero has drawn from us, we feel confident that in our navy will be found many, very very many, who will convince our enemies that tho' NELSON is dead, the same invincible courage he possessed still lives in the breast of every True British Tar!

To this account the Exeter newspaper also added letters with detailed information that had been written in Plymouth just after the *Nautilus* and the *Pickle* had docked the previous day – before word had even reached the Admiralty.

The news may only have reached England on 5 November, but by that time it was already spreading across Europe. The *Flying Fish* schooner sailing with supplies from Guernsey met up with the British fleet off Cadiz very soon after the battle and then carried despatches from Collingwood to Gibraltar, arriving there on 23 October. Because of this, three days after the battle, on Thursday 24 October, the *Gibraltar Chronicle* had one of the biggest scoops in the history of journalism when it published in

English and French the first report of Trafalgar, which included a letter from Collingwood to the Governor of Gibraltar, General Henry Fox:

EURYALUS, AT SEA, OCTOBER 22, 1805.

Sir,

Yesterday a Battle was fought by His Majesty's Fleet, with the Combined Fleets of Spain and France, and a Victory gained, which will stand recorded as one of the most brilliant and decisive, that ever distinguished the BRITISH NAVY.

The Enemy's Fleet sailed from Cadiz, on the 19th, in the Morning, Thirty Three sail of the Line in number, for the purpose of giving Battle to the British Squadron of Twenty Seven, and yesterday at Eleven A. M. the contest began, close in with the Shoals of Trafalgar.

At Five P. M. Seventeen of the Enemy had surrendered, and one (*L'Achille*) burnt, amongst which is the *Sta. Ana*, the Spanish Admiral DON D'ALEVA mortally wounded, and the *Santissima Trinidad*. The French Admiral VILLENEUVE is now a Prisoner on board the *Mars*; I believe THREE ADMIRALS are captured.

Our loss has been great in Men; but, what is irreparable, and the cause of Universal Lamentation, is the Death of the NOBLE COMMANDER IN CHIEF, who died in the Arms of Victory; I have not yet any reports from the Ships, but have heard that Captains DUFF and COOK fell in the Action.

I have to congratulate you upon the Great Event, and have the Honor to be, &c. &c.

(Signed) C. COLLINGWOOD.[15]

Beneath this letter was printed a less accurate summary of the battle:

In addition to the above particulars of the late Glorious Victory, we are assured that 18 Sail of the Line were counted in our possession, before the Vessel, which brought the above dispatches, left the Fleet;

and that three more of the Enemy's Vessels were seen driving about, perfect Wrecks, at the mercy of the waves, on the Barbary Shore, and which will probably also fall into our hands.

Admiral COLLINGWOOD in the *Dreadnought* led the Van of the British Fleet most gallantly into action, without firing a shot, till his yard-arms were locked with those of the *Santisima Trinidad*; when he opened so tremendous a fire, that, in fifteen minutes, she was completely dismasted, and obliged to surrender.

Lord NELSON, in the *Victory*, engaged the French Admiral most closely; during the heat of the action, his Lordship was severely wounded with a grape shot, in the side, and was obliged to be carried below. Immediately on his wound being dressed, he insisted upon being again brought upon deck, when, shortly afterwards, he received a shot through his body; he survived, however, till the Evening, long enough to be informed of the capture of the French Admiral, and of the extent of the Glorious Victory he had gained. – His last words were, '*Thank God I have outlived this day, and now I die content!!!*'[16]

Much of the news reaching England was also far from accurate, because the first reports of the battle were written before the officers had had a chance to confer and compare notes, and these early eyewitness accounts from different points within the chaos of battle often conflicted with each other. When more despatches and letters reached England, the Admiralty began to form a more precise view of what had taken place at Trafalgar, but few of these later accounts were published in the press. Most people's knowledge of the battle was dependent on those newspapers to which they had access and sometimes on letters from friends aboard the ships that had taken part; no other sources of information were widely available. In reality, the British were not concerned too much about the details, but only the three main facts: Nelson had been killed, the navy had won a great victory over the French, and there was no longer a threat of invasion.

Those men whose task it was to analyse the events were more cautious. In theory, the threat of invasion had not been removed, since neither the invasion flotilla nor the army of invasion itself had been destroyed, and Napoleon still had more than enough warships to take control of the English Channel. In practice, the moment for invasion had passed with the Combined French and Spanish Fleet in the wrong place and unable to do their part. The remaining ships of the French and Spanish fleets were dispersed in various ports, continuously blockaded by the British Navy – trapped, demoralised and lacking effective leadership.

In Cadiz, the outcome was known on the evening of the battle, and the news spread rapidly across Spain. The next day the French Ambassador in Madrid was able to send a despatch to the Ministry of Marine in Paris reporting an inconclusive battle, followed by a second despatch on 25 October with details of the French defeat. This second despatch reached Paris on 7 November, the day after the news reached London. In France, it was virtually ignored in the newspapers, but the *Journal du Commerce* briefly noted:

> It has been rumoured, on the authority of private letters, for some days, that there has been an action off the coast of Spain, between the combined fleets of France and Spain, and the English squadron. According to these accounts, the French squadron commanded by admiral Villeneuve, and the Spanish by admiral Gravina, came out of Cadiz, on the 18th or 19th of last month, when they were fallen in with by the English fleet, under the command of admiral Nelson. A most bloody action took place, in which both fleets fought with the greatest determination, and each of them suffered most severely. Towards the end of the engagement a violent storm came on, which dispersed the ships. It is reported, that one Spanish and one English ship were blown up. It is also reported that some of the commanders were killed or dangerously wounded. But these private letters, coming

from no authentic source, it would be imprudent to spread an alarm, for which, perhaps, there is no foundation: and it would be proper to suspend opinions until the official intelligence shall give some positive information respecting this important event.[17]

In stark contrast to Britain, the news was deliberately suppressed in France, so that morale was not dented, and the majority of people continued to support their emperor. As late as 1813, when his army fought its way into France from Spain, Wellington found it 'truly astonishing in what degree of ignorance as to all that was passing he [Napoleon] contrived to keep all France. We found people who had never heard of the battle of Trafalgar, and the south of France could hardly believe their eyes when they saw us come down the Pyrenees!'[18]

Members of the French Government, however, had an undistorted report of the battle and realised that Napoleon's efforts at sea could not match his exploits on land. News of Trafalgar was successfully silenced in France for over a month, and when the newspapers finally carried the story, it was announced as a tremendous victory for the Combined French and Spanish Fleet. Such claims were ridiculed in the British press, and the more cynical elements of the French population may well have wondered why such a stunning victory was not celebrated with the pomp and ceremony that Napoleon usually decreed for such occasions. By the middle of December an account of the battle reached Egypt; a few weeks later word had crossed the Atlantic to America, but it was nearly six months before the news reached India – in the form of a letter from the British Consul General in Egypt, which was published in the Calcutta newspapers in March 1806. The American ship *Laura*, having encountered both the *Pickle* and the *Nautilus* on their way to England, carried the story to Australia, where it was published in the *Sydney Gazette and New South Wales Advertiser* on 13 April 1806.

Just before Trafalgar, Napoleon had led his troops into

Germany in order to meet the threat from the Austrian Army. The advance of *La Grande Armée* was so rapid that it managed to cross the Rhine and then the Danube unopposed. After a few sharp engagements it trapped General Mack and his 50,000 Austrian troops, who were forced to surrender at Ulm on 20 October, the day before Trafalgar. On the eve of the Ulm surrender, Napoleon declared to his army: 'Soldiers, but for the army now in front of you, *we should this day have been in London; we should have avenged ourselves for six centuries of insults, and restored the freedom of the seas.*'[19] After his decisive victory and just days after occupying Vienna, the news of the French and Spanish defeat at Trafalgar reached Napoleon on 16 November, upon which 'he flew into one of those fits of passion which always disgrace a *Hero* more than an individual. Several couriers were immediately dispatched with orders, which . . . [were later] altered or changed. It is said that he sent commands to Ganteaume, instantly to revenge with the Brest Fleet the disasters of the Toulon [Villeneuve's] fleet.'[20] Napoleon eventually took notice of his aides and countermanded these orders to the Brest fleet.

Less than a month later, on 7 December, the allies of Britain suffered an even greater disaster than Ulm, when Napoleon crushed the Austro-Russian armies at Austerlitz – a defeat so decisive that it caused the British Prime Minister, William Pitt, to say of a map of Europe, 'Roll up that map; it will not be wanted these ten years.'[21] At the end of 1805, it was obvious that there was an uneasy stalemate; Britain had command of the sea, but Napoleon would shortly have control of Europe. It would be ten years before he was defeated at the Battle of Waterloo. For Britain's allies on the Continent, the immediate outlook was bleak, and from the French point of view,

He [Napoleon] desired that little should be said about Trafalgar in the French newspapers . . . [and] Europe itself was willing enough to observe that silence which he desired. The mighty resonance of his steps on the continent drowned the echoes of the cannon of Trafalgar. The powers who had the sword of Napoleon at their breast were but little cheered by a naval victory, profitable to England alone, without any other result than a new extension of her commercial domination, a domination which they disliked and tolerated only from jealousy of France. Besides, British glory did not console them for their own humiliation.[22]

THIRTEEN

AFTERMATH

We do not know whether we should mourn or rejoicc. The country has gained the most splendid and decisive Victory that has ever graced the naval annals of England; but it has been dearly purchased. The great and gallant NELSON is no more.

The Times, 6 November 1805

The announcement of the victory at Trafalgar met with a mixed reaction from the people of Britain, overshadowed as it was with sadness at the death of Nelson. On the day that the news arrived in London, cannons were fired in Hyde Park and from the Tower, and during the evening there were 'illuminations'. It is now difficult to appreciate just how dark the city was at night in the absence of effective street lighting and with no electric lights from houses and shops to shed their brilliance into the streets. Some places in London were regularly lit by oil or candle lanterns hung on the outside of buildings. These did little to dispel the gloom, but on the night of 6 November there was a full moon that even through the clouds would have diminished the black backdrop against which houses and shops set out displays lit by lanterns. The name 'Nelson' was spelled out in coloured lamps; and pictures of battleships, the figure of Britannia and other relevant scenes were painted or printed on transparent material and lit from behind. Portraits of Nelson were festooned with lamps, and everywhere various renditions of his initials were displayed. It was obviously difficult to make a triumphant illustration of the battle itself, and very few people had much idea where Cape Trafalgar was, but they knew Nelson, and he became the focus of attention. In the Strand, one display consisted of an altar with an urn surrounded by laurel sprays and oak branches; on the urn was the inscription, 'Sacred to the memory of the immortal Nelson!'[1]

Yet, for all the celebration, the capital was tinged with mourning. As the monthly journal *The Naval Chronicle* expressed it:

> The feeling with which this intelligence of the triumph and death of Lord Nelson was received by the British people . . . did honour to their character. It was a sensation at once of patriotism, of pride, and of gratitude. Not a man who would not have given up his life to achieve such a victory. Not a man who would not have surrendered every part of the victory (except the honour of Britain) to save the life of Lord Nelson . . . never was a conquest made at a moment so necessary, and so essential to the well-being of the country – but never was a battle so dearly won . . . The metropolis was very generally and brilliantly illuminated on the occasion; yet there was a damp upon the public spirit, which it was impossible to overcome.[2]

Lord Malmesbury recorded the atmosphere in London in his diary: 'I never saw so little public joy. The illumination seemed dim, and, as it were, half clouded, by the desire of expressing the mixture of contending feelings. Every common person in the streets speaking *first* of their sorrow for *him* and *then* of the victory.'[3]

In Portsmouth, where a Russian squadron was taking on supplies, Admiral Seniavin witnessed how the news was received there:

Only someone who had seen the delight of the English in similar circumstances could describe it on this occasion. From early morning the broadsheets were carried along the streets, describing the battle and the death of Nelson. Sadness and joy mingled on the face of every one, and everywhere could be heard the exclamation: Immortal Nelson! The ships and the fortress were firing their guns all day, and at night the town was wonderfully illuminated. The better houses were decorated with transparent pictures. One showed Nelson at the moment when the shot penetrated his chest and he had fallen into the arms of those surrounding him. Another portrayed Britannia with sorrowful face accepting the crown of victory. At night the streets were crowded. The garrison stood to arms and the regimental bandsmen played the National Anthem: *Britannia, Rule the Waves!*[4]

In the theatres, performances were rapidly adapted to include some sort of reference to Trafalgar, and once again it was found easier to concentrate on Nelson: his achievement and his death. The words of 'Rule Britannia', a 'national air' that was a national anthem in all but name, were rewritten for the occasion, such as at Covent Garden where an added verse proclaimed:

Again the loud ton'd trump of fame
Proclaims Britannia rules the main;
Whilst sorrow whispers Nelson's name,
And mourns the gallant Victor slain.
Rule, brave Britons, rule the main,
Avenge the god-like Hero slain.[5]

This verse was sung against a backdrop of

> a coup d'oeil at once grand and affecting. The stage represented an area, supported by two pillars, from which were suspended medallions of Nelson, St. Vincent, Duncan, Bridport, Mitchell, and Sir W. Sidney Smith. The English fleet was riding triumphantly in the perspective, and in the front of the stage a group of Naval Officers and Sailors were seen in attitudes of admiration. Suddenly a medallion descended, representing a half-length of the Hero of the Nile, surrounded with rays of glory, and with these words at the bottom:- 'HORATIO NELSON'. The effect was electrical, and the house resounded with the loudest plaudits and acclamations.[6]

Following the arrival of the news of Trafalgar, celebrations continued up and down the country for at least a week, partly because it took several days to reach the more remote places. At ports and army garrisons, gun salutes and *feux de joie* (a running fire of pistols and muskets as an expression of joy) could be heard, and everywhere the church bells rang. At Sherborne in Dorset, 'a peal was rung to the memory of the great, gallant, and ever to be lamented Nelson; and they have since been ringing merrily in honour of the brilliant and important victory.'[7] At Ipswich in Suffolk, 'the different regiments in the garrison were drawn up in their respective exercising grounds, and fired two *feu de joys*; and after presenting a third time, dropped their muskets without discharging them, as a tribute of respect to the memory of the departed Hero'.[8] Further north at Boston in Lincolnshire, 'the church bells of that loyal place proclaimed welcome tidings to the town and country around; the Volunteers assembled in a large number, at a short notice, and fired three vollies in honour of the event; the ships in the river added the thunder of their guns; and in the evening a solemn and most affecting peal was rung as a testimony of regret for the loss which our country has sustained in the death of its illustrious benefactor and chieftain, Lord Nelson.'[9]

There was a hesitancy in the rejoicing and the poet Southey recalled the public reaction:

The death of Nelson was felt in England as something more than a public calamity; men started at the intelligence and turned pale, as if they had heard of the loss of a dear friend. An object of our admiration and affection, of our pride and of our hopes, was suddenly taken from us . . . So perfectly had he performed his part that the maritime war, after the battle of Trafalgar, was considered at an end . . . The victory of Trafalgar was celebrated indeed with the usual forms of rejoicing, but they were without joy; for such already was the glory of the British Navy, through Nelson's surpassing genius, that it scarcely seemed to receive an addition from the most signal victory that ever was achieved upon the seas.[10]

Southey's friend, the poet Samuel Taylor Coleridge, was at Naples when he heard about Trafalgar, and in that city where Nelson was well known from his visits, the mourning eclipsed the victory:

when he died, it seemed as if no man was a stranger to another; for all were made acquaintances by the rights of a common anguish . . . The tidings arrived at Naples on the day that I returned to that city from Calabria; and never can I forget the sorrow and consternation that lay on every countenance. Even to this day there are times when I seem to see, as in a vision, separate groups and individual faces of the picture. Numbers stopped and shook hands with me because they had seen the tears on my cheek, and conjectured that I was an Englishman; and several, as they held my hand, burst, themselves, into tears. And though it may awake a smile, yet it pleased and affected me, as a proof of the goodness of the human heart struggling to exercise its kindness in spite of prejudices the most obstinate, and eager to carry on its love and honour into the life beyond life, that it was whispered about Naples, that Lord Nelson had become a good Catholic before his death. The absurdity of the fiction is a sort of measurement of the fond and affectionate esteem which had ripened the pious wish of some kind individual, through all the gradations of possibility and probability, into a confident assertion, believed and affirmed by hundreds.[11]

Already myths and apocryphal tales were beginning to adhere to the Nelson legend. Even the fashions were affected, and at the beginning of December it was reported that the 'Trafalgar turban is much worn and is extremely elegant; the crown of royal purple, with a Turkish roll of muslin, caught up in front with the word *Trafalgar* beautifully embroidered on purple velvet; it encircles an ostrich feather, or a sprig of laurel'.[12]

In France the news of the battle gradually filtered through to British prisoners of war. Lieutenant William Dillon, on parole at Verdun with a group of army officers, all waiting to be exchanged for French prisoners of war, recorded how he first heard the news:

I happened to enter the Caron Club about 11 o'clock one day [in December 1805] when one of the committee came in with the English newspapers containing the account of Nelson's victory over the combined fleets of France and Spain. Lord Yarmouth, Col. Abercromby and several others of my friends seized hold of me as if by one accord, and, lifting me on the table, desired me to read in a loud voice, the official report of that splendid victory. The most perfect silence having been secured, I communicated the details of Collingwood's letter to the Admiralty. When I had finished it, three hearty spontaneous cheers were given by at least one hundred members present, and those who were not near the table closed up and requested me to read the account a second time, which I readily agreed to do. I was then requested by Lord Yarmouth to explain the manner in which that battle was fought, as they did not understand the nautical description of the disposal of the two fleets. I did so by placing a parcel of books that were lying on the table in the position of the adverse fleets. We separated then, but, going out to the street, we met a crowd of French gentlemen who were anxious to know the reason of all that cheering.

I told them of our splendid victory, and they were sadly cast down on the occasion. My French friends overloaded me with questions. They allowed they could not contend with us upon the ocean. 'We do not doubt,' they said, 'that you have triumphed. But that you should have taken and destroyed so many ships without your losing any is a case we cannot admit. Our seamen can fight as well as yours, and surely you do not mean to maintain that our shot has not sunk *some* of your ships?' My only reply was that they might see Lord Collingwood's official report for themselves.[13]

Nelson had gone into the battle with hopes of a victory that would bring peace and allow him to retire and enjoy life with Emma and Horatia at Merton. History was to prove this a mere dream. The Battle of Trafalgar removed the immediate threat of an invasion of Britain, but it did not win the war. It was, however, the final part of the process that made Nelson a national figurehead, as Lady Londonderry summed up in a letter to her son-in-law:

The sentiment of lamenting the individual more than rejoicing in the victory, shows the humanity and affection of the people of England: but their good sense upon reflection will dwell only on the conquest, because no death, at a future moment, could have been more glorious. The public would never have sent him on another expedition; his health was not equal to another effort, and so might have yielded to the natural but less imposing effects of more worldly honours: whereas he now begins his immortal career, having nothing left to achieve upon earth, and bequeathing to the English fleet a legacy which they alone are able to improve. Had I been his wife, or his mother, I would [rather] have wept him dead, than seen him languish on a less splendid day. In such a death there is no sting, and in such a grave, everlasting victory.[14]

Apart from their joy at hearing about the victory and sorrow on learning of Nelson's death, a period of anxiety inevitably began for the relatives of those men involved, until they had definite news of their loved ones. Betsey Fremantle, wife of Thomas Fremantle, the captain of the *Neptune*, wrote in her diary: 'Thursday, 7th Nov. I was much alarmed by *Nelly's ghastly* appearance immediately after breakfast, who came in to say Dudley had brought from Winslow the account that a most dreadful action had been fought off Cadiz, Nelson & several Captains killed, & twenty ships were taken. I really felt undescribable misery.'[15] In London, William Marsden, First Secretary of the Admiralty, was astonished on overhearing the reaction of one mother to her loss: 'Walking in St. James's Park for the sake of a little fresh air, there were two women before me, one of whom was recounting to her companion the circumstances of the glorious victory. "It is true," she said, "that I have had the misfortune to lose two sons killed; but then, you know my dear, that it is *a feather in my cap*."'[16] For relations of officers, like Betsey Fremantle, the waiting was relatively short, because even if letters revealing the fate of their loved ones did not accompany the first despatches, lists of officers and petty officers who had been killed or wounded were published a few days later.

For relatives of seamen, however, official letters were rarely sent to inform them of the fate of their sons, brothers or fathers, and the published lists of casualties seldom provided names, only numbers, as the list for the *Tonnant* demonstrates:

Killed. – 1 Petty Officer, 16 Seamen, and 9 Marines – Total, 26.
Wounded. – 2 Officers, 2 Petty Officers, 30 Seamen, and 16 Marines – Total, 50.
Officer killed. – William Brown, Midshipman.
Officers Wounded. – Charles Tyler, Captain; Richard Little, Boatswain; William Allen, Clerk; Henry Ready, Master's-Mate; the three last slightly.[17]

Even these lists were not universally available, as local newspapers varied greatly in their coverage. For some people, it was possible to get information directly from ships just returned from the battle, but the majority received the news from letters sent by the sailors who had taken part in the battle – either survivors, or men writing on behalf of friends. It is likely that a few people never found out the fate of fallen relatives – if they had volunteered or been taken by a press-gang, they may never have been heard of again.

The final British casualty figures have been calculated as 449 dead and 1241 wounded out of some 17,000 men – about 1 in every 38 men was killed, and 1 in every 14 wounded. While these figures are relatively accurate, casualty figures for the Combined Fleet are more difficult to estimate, as many men were lost in ships that sank during the storm, and casualty lists could not be completed. From around 30,000 men in the Combined French and Spanish fleet, it is thought that approximately 1022 Spanish sailors were killed in the battle and subsequent hurricane, and about 1386 were wounded, while there were something like 3373 French dead and 1155 wounded. Approximations as they are, these figures would indicate that the total number of casualties for the Combined French and Spanish Fleet came to nearly 7000. Out of a total of over 47,000 British, French and Spanish men who took part in the battle, more than 4800 (approximately 10 per cent) were killed and over 3700 (approximately 8 per cent) were wounded.

The Combined Fleet had so far lost nineteen ships, with several others severely damaged, and Collingwood estimated that 'of men, their loss is many thousands, for I reckon, in the captured ships, we took twenty thousand prisoners'.[18] In monetary value, he thought 'the loss of the enemy may be estimated at near four millions [approximately £200 million at today's values]',[19] but unfortunately he had to report that 'most of it [has] gone to the bottom'.[20] Around 3000–4000 Spanish seamen were actually taken prisoner and over 4000 of the

French. Both the French and Spanish navies had lost many of their best officers and seamen, killed or captured, and the defeat was so complete that they were badly demoralised.

When the *Pickle* schooner was just starting out for England with despatches concerning the Battle of Trafalgar, several other ships gradually made their way to Gibraltar for repair and for supplies, carrying the wounded as well as some prisoners. Here, the Spanish prisoners were landed and sent back to Spain, but not the French prisoners, who would be taken to England. The *Revenge* was one of the first ships to reach Gibraltar after the storm, and still on board was Jeannette, the French woman who had escaped the burning *Achille*. Having endured the subsequent ordeal of the storm, Jeannette was very unhappy as they headed for Gibraltar, because her husband was lost, presumed dead, as reported by a lieutenant in the *Revenge*:

> Although placed in a position of unlooked-for comfort, Jeannette was scarcely less miserable; the fate of her husband was unknown to her. She had not seen him since the commencement of the battle, and he was perhaps killed, or had perished in the conflagration. Still, the worst was unknown to her, and a possibility existed that he was yet alive. All her enquiries were, however, unattended with success, for several days, during which I was so much busied in securing the ship's masts, and in looking after the ship in the gales which we had to encounter, that I had no time to attend to my protégée. It was on about the fourth day of her sojourn that she came to me in the greatest possible ecstacy and told me that she had found her husband, who was on board among the prisoners, and unhurt. She soon afterwards brought him to me, and in the most grateful terms and manner returned her thanks for the attentions she had received. After this, Jeannette declined coming to the ward-room, from the very proper feeling that her husband could not be admitted to the same privileges. On our arrival at Gibraltar, all our prisoners were landed by order of

the Port-Admiral, Sir John Knight, at the Neutral Ground, but under a mistake, as the Spanish prisoners only should have been landed there. Her dress, though rather odd, was not unbecoming, and we all considered her a fine woman. On leaving the ship, most, if not all of us, gave her a dollar, and she expressed her thanks as well as she was able, and assured us that the name of our ship would always be remembered by her with the warmest gratitude.[21]

At seven in the evening of 28 October, the *Victory* anchored in Gibraltar's Rosia Bay, having been towed most of the way by the *Neptune*. As the ships struggled in day by day, the wounded men were taken to the Naval Hospital, built sixty years earlier on the hillside overlooking Rosia Bay, in the south-west part of the Gibraltar promontory, and some of the surgeons from the fleet went with the wounded to help in the hospital. The arrival of these ships was watched by the crew of the *Belleisle*, one of the two vessels that had successfully made it to Gibraltar shortly after the battle. Lieutenant Paul Nicolas described the scene:

Disabled ships continued to arrive for several days, bringing with them the only four prizes rescued from the fury of the late gale. The anchorage became covered with ships. In the mole lay six dismasted hulls, whose battered sides, dismounted guns, and shattered ports, presented unequivocal evidence of the brilliant part they had taken in the gloriously contested battle: a little beyond, the more recently arrived lay at their anchors. At this proud moment no shout of exultation was heard, no joyous felicitations were exchanged, for the lowered flag which waved on the *Victory*'s mast, marked where the mourned hero lay, and cast a deepened shade over the triumphant scene. The exertion which was necessary to refit the ships did not, however, permit the mind to dwell on this melancholy subject.[22]

Ever since the battle, the crew of the *Victory* had been rigging temporary masts and sails and carrying out other repairs. This work continued for the next four days at Gibraltar, and at the same time, twenty-six wounded men were transferred to the hospital. The surgeon Dr Beatty also took the opportunity to draw off the brandy from the cask containing Nelson's body and replaced it with spirits of wine, a better preservative, ready for the journey back to England. A few days earlier during the storm there had been problems with the cask, as Beatty explained:

> The cask was placed on its end, having a closed aperture at its top and another below; the object of which was, that as a frequent renewal of spirit was thought necessary, the old could thus be drawn off below and a fresh quantity introduced above, without moving the cask, or occasioning the least agitation of the Body. On the 24th there was a disengagement of air from the Body to such a degree, that the sentinel became alarmed on seeing the head of the cask raised: he therefore applied to the Officers, who were under the necessity of having the cask spiled [vented] to give the air a discharge. After this, no considerable collection of air took place.[23]

It was rumoured that the sentries had used the opportunity to draw off and drink the brandy, but despite the air in the cask, there is no evidence that they had tampered with it. The fate of the brandy drawn off by Beatty at Gibraltar is not recorded.

The state of the *Victory* was such that Collingwood proposed to transfer Nelson's body to the *Euryalus* to transport it to England, but the crew of the *Victory* objected so strongly that they came close to mutiny, and Collingwood bowed to their wish. With Nelson's flag flying halfway up a jury-rigged mast as a sign of mourning, and with the pumps constantly manned because the ship was still leaking, the *Victory* left Gibraltar on 2 November to obtain fresh water at Tetuan in Morocco, leaving behind those of the crew who were wounded. Because the winds changed, Captain Hardy was able to return to Gibraltar to pick up these men, and finally set sail on the 4th, accompanied by the *Belleisle* and the *Bellerophon*.

In the morning of the next day, these three vessels joined the remaining fleet off Cadiz, and Collingwood ordered the *Victory* and *Belleisle* to England. That very day, 5 November, Lapenotiere and Sykes were racing across southern England to take the news of the battle to London, while out at sea the French were about to suffer another defeat. Hundreds of miles to the south-west of Britain off Ferrol, a port on the north-west coast of Spain, British ships had finally caught up with Rear-Admiral Dumanoir and the four French ships that had retreated from Trafalgar two weeks before. They had been sighted on 2 November, and a chase had ensued lasting nearly three days. The British ships were now too close to be evaded, so Dumanoir formed his small force into a battle line, and a short, vicious battle was fought between his ships and those of the British Rear-Admiral, Sir Richard Strachan. All the French ships surrendered, so that the Combined French and Spanish Fleet had now lost twenty-three vessels out of the original total of thirty-three. The British losses in this action were 24 dead and 111 wounded, but the French had a total of 750 casualties, including Dumanoir himself, who was injured in the fighting. Strachan initially thought that he had discovered ships from the French fleet at Rochefort, and in a letter published in London six days later, he described the battle:

A little before noon, the French finding an action unavoidable, began to take in their small sails, and form in a line, bearing on the starboard tack; we did the same; and I communicated my intentions, by hailing to the [British] Captains, 'that I should attack the centre and rear,' and at noon began the battle: in a short time the van Ship of the enemy tacked, which almost directly made the action close and general; the [British ship] *Namur* joined soon after we tacked, which we did as soon as we could get the Ships round, and I directed her by signal to engage the van; at half past three the action ceased, the enemy having fought to admiration, and not surrendering till their Ships were unmanageable. I have returned thanks to the Captains of the Ships of the line and the Frigates, and they speak in high terms of approbation of their Officers and Ships' companies. If any thing could add to the good opinion I had already formed of the Officers and crew of the *Caesar* [the ship that Strachan was in] it is their gallant conduct in this day's battle. The enemy have suffered much, but our ships not more than is to be expected on these occasions. You may judge of my surprise, Sir, when I found the Ships we had taken were not the Rochefort Squadron, but from Cadiz.[24]

The letter was marked as being sent from the '*Caesar*, west of Rochefort, 264 miles'.

A letter from Midshipman Francis Romney in the *Aeolus*, writing to a young woman, gave a less formal account of Dumanoir's capture:

Aeolus, Plymouth sound, Nov. 10, 1805

My Dear Mary,

I was in hopes of seeing you last time we were in; but the consequence of our being dispatched immediately with the flying squadron, under the command of Sir Richard Strachan, put a stop to all those hopes: but never mind – fortune always favours the brave . . . Nothing occurred until the 2nd Nov., when retiring to our cots, who should join us but the little *Phoenix*, with three cheers; which was returned with high glee from the whole of the squadron. She gave us information of four Sail of the line of the enemy having chased her the whole day. Not a moment was lost in making sail – we continued in chase until that happy and glorious day . . . when we came up with the *Monsieurs* – Every thing favourable – the weather mild and serene: the first gun was fired by the *St. Margaret*: a running fight was kept up for four hours; when the enemy, finding they could not escape, hove to for us – a general action then commenced – in truth we were in the warmest of it during the whole of their tacking; which they did with the intent of cutting off our Frigates. This placed us in a critical position, and obliged us to run the gauntlet with the whole of them – Thank God! we had only three men badly wounded: our rigging was cut up very much – there we continued at it, hot and warm, pelting away for three hours and twenty-five minutes, before we made them haul their haughty flag down – a happy sight – they proved to be *le Formidable*, the Admiral's Ship, *le Scipion*, *le Duguay Trouin*, and *le Mont Blanc*; two 80 guns and two 74's, which had made their escape from Nelson, fifteen days from Cadiz, all fine Ships; they are dreadfully cut up. I am not certain, but I think they had between six and seven hundred killed and wounded. The old Admiral is one of the wounded.

Our little squadron consisted of only four Sail of the line, and four Frigates – our killed and wounded is so small as not to be worth mentioning; but I have met with a sad accident: in the hurry of clearing for action they hove my sea chest overboard, with all my clothes in it, except eight dirty shirts which I had in my birth [berth]: not I alone, but three of my messmates shared the same fate: therefore I shall require assistance to new rig me, until I receive my prize-money. This will be a grand spoke in my favour when I pass my examination,* which will be the first Wednesday in next month, if we are in harbour . . . A friend on board has just informed me, if I ask leave to pass my examination, the Captain cannot with propriety refuse me; if he should, by applying to the Admiralty they will grant me leave of absence for a short time – then we shall spend some happy hours! I think I deserve to be on shore now, for during six years I have not been six weeks on shore. God bless you!

F. D. Romney.[25]

Now about nineteen years old, Romney had barely been on land since joining the navy at the age of twelve.

The four captured ships, the *Scipion*, the *Formidable*, the

*For promotion to lieutenant.

Mont-Blanc and the *Duguay-Trouin*, were sent to Plymouth, where they were all repaired and taken into service as part of the British fleet. The *Duguay-Trouin* was renamed the *Implacable*, and after serving as a battleship was used successively as a naval training vessel, a training ship for Sea Scouts, a holiday ship for children and, during World War Two, a floating storage vessel. In 1949 the ship was regarded as of no further use and so was towed out to sea from Portsmouth harbour. The hulk was loaded with 400 tons of ballast, but in an attempt to ensure that the ship sank, the navy had doubled the quantity of explosives that had been calculated to be necessary. With both the British and French ensigns flying from flagpoles on the deck because the masts had been removed, the charges were set off. They blew the bottom out of the ship, the ballast dropped to the sea bed, and the *Implacable* settled in the water, with the upper deck just awash and the flags still proudly flying. Eventually a powerful dockyard tug, the *Alligator*, was brought out from Portsmouth, and after the tug had rammed the *Implacable* several times, the hulk finally capsized and sank – a practical demonstration of just how difficult it was to sink a wooden battleship and a hint at how badly holed vessels could be kept afloat by pumping and patching. Several days later, wreckage was washed up on the French coast near Rochefort, the port from which the *Duguay-Trouin* had first set sail. The figurehead and stern façade, which had been removed beforehand, are now on display in the National Maritime Museum at Greenwich.

The four ships that were captured during the Battle of Trafalgar and had survived the storm – the *San Juan Nepomuceno*, the *Swiftsure*, the *San Ildefonso* and the *Bahama* – were also taken into service in the British Navy. The *Bahama* was broken up in 1814, and both the *Swiftsure* and the *San Ildefonso* were scrapped in 1816. The *San Juan Nepomuceno*'s name was shortened to the *San Juan*, and this ship remained at Gibraltar after being converted to a sheer hulk – a floating crane for repairing and replacing masts on damaged ships. The cabin where Captain

Churruca died was always kept locked, and one historian recorded how this gesture was appreciated by the Spanish:

> The English honoured the memory of Churruca with an exceptional demonstration of respect. The hull of the ship *San Juan* was kept for many years in the bay of Gibraltar with its wardroom locked and a memorial tablet over the door with the name of CHURRUCA in letters of gold. If any occasion arose that the room was unlocked in order to satisfy the curiosity of a distinguished visitor, they were warned to enter bareheaded, as if the very commander who had defended the ship with so much glory was present. This was an astonishing distinction that clearly showed the extraordinary merit that the English recognised in our hero.[26]

As the *Victory* and the *Belleisle* sailed to England at the beginning of November, the weather remained stormy, and a journey that should have taken just over a week lasted a month. By now, with the battle a talking point throughout the country, each newly arrived ship was greeted by anxious relatives searching for seamen who might be aboard, as Marine Lieutenant Nicolas of the *Belleisle* described: 'At length we reached our destination, and arrived in Plymouth Sound on the 4th December. Boats unnumerable floated round us with faces expressive of the torturing anxiety which was felt, and a moment ensued of such boundless joy to many, and bitter agony to others, that no pen can describe it: it would have wrung the most callous heart. I could not bear to hear the effusions of grief which burst from the childless parent, or witness the sorrow of brotherly tenderness, and I hastened to the affectionate embraces of my own family.'[27]

During the following weeks in Britain, more ships straggled in, bearing their wounded, their quota of French prisoners and letters from the seamen. Writing from the *Euryalus* was a thirteen-year-old boy with the unusual Christian name of Norwich. He had only just joined the navy and was serving as a midshipman in the

Mars, although, as was common practice for a young boy officer, he was only rated as an able seaman. He wrote home to his mother about the death of the captain of the *Mars*, George Duff:

My Dear Mamma,

You cannot possibly imagine how unwilling I am to begin this melancholy letter . . . He died like a Hero, having gallantly led his ship into action, and his memory will ever be dear to his King, his Country, and his Friends. It was about fifteen minutes past twelve in the afternoon of the 21st of October, when the engagement began, and it was not finished 'til five. Many a brave Hero sacrificed his life upon that occasion to his King and his Country. You will hear that Lord Viscount Nelson was wounded in the commencement of the engagement, and only survived long enough to learn that the victory was ours. – 'Then,' said that brave Hero, 'I die happy, since I die victorious,' and in a few minutes expired. We are now all on board the *Euryalus*, with the Hon. Captain Blackwood, and, in compliance with the wish of Admiral Collingwood [on 6 November], are now on our way to England, that we may have an opportunity of more readily knowing your wishes respecting our future conduct. Captain Blackwood has indeed been very polite and kind to me . . .

My dear Mamma, I have again to request you to endeavour to make yourself as happy and as easy as possible. It has been the will of Heaven, and it is our duty to submit.

Believe me your obedient and affectionate Son, N. Duff.[28]

Captain George Duff was his father.

It fell to William Hennah, First Lieutenant of the *Mars*, who had taken command after Captain Duff's death, to write to his widow:

Madam,

I believe that a more unpleasant task, than what is now imposed upon me, can scarcely fall to the lot of a person, whose feelings are not more immediately connected by the nearer ties of kindred: but from a sense of duty, (as first Lieutenant of the *Mars*,) as being myself the husband of a beloved partner, and the father of children; out of the pure respect and esteem to the memory of our late gallant Captain, I should consider myself guilty of a base neglect, should you only be informed of the melancholy circumstances attending the late glorious, though unfortunate victory to many, by a public gazette. The consequences of such an event, while it may occasion the rejoicings of the nation, will in every instance be attended with the deepest regrets of a few. Alas! Madam, how unfortunate shall I think myself, should this be the first intimation you may have of the irreparable loss you have met with! what apology can I make for entering on a subject so tender and so fraught with sorrow, but to recommend an humble reliance on this great truth, that the ways of Providence, although sometimes inscrutable, are always for the best.

By this, Madam, you are in all probability acquainted with the purport of my letter. Amongst the number of heroes who fell on the ever-memorable 21st inst. in defence of their King and Country; after gloriously discharging his duty to both; our meritorious and much respected Commander, Captain George Duff, is honourably classed: his fate was instantaneous; and he resigned his soul into the hands of the Almighty, without a moment's pain.

Poor Norwich is very well. Captain Blackwood has taken him on board the *Euryalus*, with the other young gentlemen that came with him, and their schoolmaster. The whole of the Captain's papers and effects are sealed up, and will be kept in a place of security until proper persons are appointed to examine them. Meanwhile, Madam, I beg leave to assure you of my readiness to give you any information, or render you any service in my power.

And am, Madam, with the greatest respect,
Your most obedient and most humble servant,
William Hennah.[29]

Among Captain Duff's effects was his last, unfinished, letter to his wife: 'Monday morning, Oct. 21, 1805. My Dearest Sophia, I have just time to tell you we are going into action with the combined fleet. I hope and trust in God that we shall all behave as becomes us, and that I may yet have the happiness of taking my beloved wife and children in my arms. Norwich is quite well, and happy. I have however ordered him off the quarter-deck.'[30]

More letters arrived as more ships returned, and from the *Defence* a midshipman, like Norwich Duff just thirteen years old, had written home to his sister immediately after the storm:

H.M.S. Defence,
At anchor off Cadiz, 28 Oct. 1805

My Dear Betty,

I have now the pleasure of writing you, after a noble victory over the French and Spanish fleets, on the 21st October, off Cape Spartel [actually Trafalgar]. We have taken, burnt and sunk, gone on shore etc., twenty one sail of the line. The names I will let [you] know after . . . We were the last station'd ship; so when we went down we had two Frenchmen and one Spaniard on us at one time. We engag'd them forty six minutes, when the *Achilles* and *Polyphemus* came up to our assistance. The Spaniard ran away; we gave him chase, and fought him one hour and forty six minutes, when he struck, and we boarded him, and have him safe at anchor, as we have not had a good wind . . . The ship we took, her name is the *San Ildifonzo*, eighty two guns, and a very fine ship, new. I don't think we will save more than twelve sail of them; but we have sunk, burnt, drove on shore, twenty one sail of the line in all; and if we had not had a gale of wind next day we would have taken every one of them. We were riding close in shore with two anchors a-head, three cables on each bower [anchor], and all our sails were shot to pieces, ditto our rudder and stern, and mainmast, and everything; but thank God I am here safe, though there was more shot at my quarters than any other part of the ship. We are now at anchor, but expect to go to Gibraltar every day. I hope in God you are all in health; I was never better in all my life. My compts. to all friends . . . and my dear father and mother.

I am,

Your affectionate brother,

Charles Reid.[31]

He then added a note on the bottom of the letter: 'You must excuse this letter, as half our hands are on board our prize, and [I] have had no time. I have been two days writing this; five minutes one time and ten minutes another time, and so on. We are just getting under way for Gibraltar.'[32]

Others had to wait until their ships were back in port before they could write letters home. On 3 December, Colin Campbell, an eighteen-year-old midshipman from Argyllshire in Scotland, wrote from his ship, the *Defiance*:

My Dearest Father,

I take first opportunity of a boat going ashore to write and inform you of our safe arrival at Spithead [an anchorage near Portsmouth], and that I am alive and hearty after the glorious action of Trafalgar. I was very sorry I had not an opportunity of writing to you from Gibraltar, but I did not join the *Defiance* there till the frigate that went to England was under weigh [he had been on board the captured Spanish ship *Argonauta*] . . . I was not a little glad when I got on board of her [the *Defiance*] again and shipped a clean shirt, a luxury I had not enjoyed for some time. We were at Gibraltar a few days and then sailed for England. Captain Durham gave me an order to act as lieutenant and I did the duty most of the way home. I suppose we shall go into dock directly as our masts and bowsprits are very badly wounded. Captain Durham left us yesterday on three week's leave for London . . . We have to-day landed 300 prisoners . . . I am afraid you will find much difficulty in reading [this], but I hope you will excuse all blunders as I can hardly stir for French buffers [prisoners] in the berth. I hope it will not be very long before I have the pleasure of seeing you . . . I hope you will have the kindness just to write me a line that I may know you are well.[33]

The difficulties of communication affected those at sea just as much as their friends and relatives on land, and mail sent to seamen serving in the navy was frequently delayed or lost altogether.

Letters also arrived in England from another midshipman, Thomas Aikenhead, who was in the *Royal Sovereign* at the very start of the fighting. In a letter to one of his sisters, dated four hours before the battle, he wrote, 'Accept perhaps for the last time your brother's love; be assured, I feel for my friends, should I die in this glorious action – glorious, no doubt, it will be. Every British heart pants for glory. Our old Admiral [Collingwood] is quite young with the thoughts of it. If I survive, nothing will give me greater pleasure than embracing my dearest relations. Do not, in case I fall, grieve – it will be to no purpose. Many brave fellows will, no doubt, fall with me, on both sides. Oh! Betsey, with what ardour I shall, if permitted by God's providence, come to England to embrace you all.'[34] To his father, he wrote, 'We have just piped to breakfast – thirty-five sail, beside smaller vessels, are now on our beam, about three miles off. Should I, my dear parents, fall in defence of my king, let that thought console you. I feel not the least dread on my spirits. Oh! my parents, sisters, brothers, dear grandfather, grandmother, and aunt, believe me, ever yours.'[35] With this letter came a list of the property in his sea chest, his will and the news that he had been killed during the battle.

A seaman who survived on board the *Royal Sovereign* also wrote home to his father:

Honoured Father,

This comes to tell you I am alive and hearty except three fingers; but that's not much, it might have been my head. I told brother Tom

I should like to see a gradely battle, and I have seen one, and we have peppered the Combined [Fleet] rarely; and for the matter of that, they fought us pretty tightish for French and Spanish. Three of our mess are killed, and four more of us winged. But to tell the truth of it, when the game began, I wished myself at Warnborough [North Warnborough in Hampshire] with my plough again; but when they had given us one duster [broadside], and I found myself snug and tight, I . . . set to in good earnest, and thought no more about being killed than if I were at Murrell Green Fair [near North Warnborough], and I was presently as busy and as black as a collier. How my fingers got knocked overboard I don't know, but off they are, and I never missed them till I wanted them. You see, by my writing, it was my left hand, so I can write to you and fight for my King yet. We have taken a rare parcel of ships, but the wind is so rough we cannot bring them home, else I should roll in money, so we are busy sinking 'em and blowing 'em up wholesale.

Our dear Admiral Nelson is killed! so we have paid pretty sharply for licking 'em. I never set eyes on him, for which I am both sorry and glad; for, to be sure, I should like to have seen him – but then, all the men in our ship who have seen him are such soft toads they have done nothing but blast their eyes, and cry, ever since he was killed. God bless you! chaps that fought like the devil sit down and cry like a wench. I am still in the *Royal Sovereign*, but the Admiral has left her, for she is like a horse without a bridle; so he is in a frigate that may be here and there and everywhere, for he's as 'cute as here and there one, and as bold as a lion, for all he can cry. I saw his tears with my own eyes, when the boat hailed and said my lord was dead. So no more at present from your dutiful son, Sam.[36]

Some of the letters from seamen were published in local newspapers and in magazines, which were largely submitted by people proud that their relatives had taken part in a famous battle. This led one publication, *The European Magazine and London Review*, to produce a parody of such letters in December 1805:

ACCOUNT *of the* BATTLE *of* TRAFALGAR: *In a* LETTER *from* JACK HANDSPECK, *on board the* TEMERAIRE, *to his* LANDLORD, BOB SPUNYARN, *at the* COMMON HARD, PORTSMOUTH.

To Mr. Bob Spunyarn, at the Sign of the Jolly Boat Boys, Public House, Common Hard, Portsmouth. Temerary, Dec. 2, 1805

Old Shipmate,

I write these presents, because as how I know that you and Sal will like to hear sum'at of the great fight that we've had, off Trafalgar, as they call it; and a noble affair it was to be sure. If our brave Commander hadn't fallen, we sho'd have liked it better; but so it pleased the High Admiral of All, and so you know we sho'dn't complain: but had it been my messmate honest Bob Binnacle, or even Sal, I cou'd not have grieved more. Lord Nelson was a brave Officer, and a seaman's friend, and never gave a lubber the best birth, nor made a Quarter-Master of a hand who was only fit to pick oakum or sweep the decks. If it had been the Purser, or the Captain's Clerk, or the Surgeon's Mate, though for my part I like them all well enough, it wo'dn't have mattered the strapping of a topsail-sheet block: but the gallant Nelson to broach to, to start about, to be let go by the run; By the mizen-mast!! I would have given my allowance of grog for six months to come, and have had nothing but banyan days, to have saved his precious life. However, clap the jigger-tackle on your spirits, honest Bob; for our chaplain says, that the brave Nelson is not dead, but that he liveth; and he must know more about it than we do. Well! fair weather, light breezes, and a smooth sea to him, wherever he may be stationed.

But to tell you all about the action . . . we bore up, going in two columns, at the rate of about six knots an hour through the water; and then we made what they call an *edge-along* movement; though for my part, not knowing naval *tictacs*, I can't say that I altogether understand what they mean by it . . . Well, there were the Frenchmen and the Dons, and so we clear'd ship for action. Up all hammocks and down with the chests. I was assisting to secure the yards, when, as the devil would have it, I jamm'd two of the fingers of my left fin all to smash in the main tackle fall: but that was nothing, you know: so I run down to the cockpit to ax the Doctor's Mate to have the kindness to clear away: and he brought out a fine cushion, and ever so many rattle-traps; but I soon call'd out avast to that. 'Come, Doctor,' said I, 'there's no time for Ottamising: you're not going to be a dog-watch about it.' So I rummaged for my own knife that I kept for cutting away the top-gallant haulyards in a squall, and away went the ticklers. But tell Sal not to grieve, for I let Mr. Splinter put on some of his fother, which looked for all the world like chopp'd rope-yarns mixed up with grease and oakum, to stop the leaks, because you know I wou'dn't appear uncivil to any man. So no more of that: I was upon deck again in a *jiffy* . . .

Well: so now we bore down, you see, in close order, hauled up the courses, and got the bull-dogs ready. I was Captain of one of the guns on the main-deck. So you see, I kept cracking my jokes as we cast off the muzzle-lashings, to show that I was just in humour for the fun. So now, having broke the enemy's line, and being muzzle to muzzle, we set to. 'Bounce away, my boys!' says I: 'handle your crows: and d——e but we'll crow over the enemy! Point well; take time, and bear a hand!' . . . So you see, when the order was given to fire, d——e but I put the lighted match which I held all ready in my hand, to the Gunner's daughter's ear, and d——e but she spoke to the Frenchman as loud as she could. So now, you see, we got at it in arnest. Fire away Flannagan – Bow wow – More cartridges and plenty of shot – Batter the hulls, and splinter the decks – Zounds! what a spattering: load, fire, spunge, and load and fire again, till the Dons have a belly-full . . . So now, you see, the fight was all over, and, of course, we had got the *Victory*: nineteen sail of the line, my boy. I don't remember the names of all the ships that we fought with; but I know there was one called Mount Blank, commanded by Capatain Fillagree [Lavillegris], since taken by Sir Richard Strachan; and one of their Admirals was called Admiral Do-no-more [Dumanoir].[37]

This 'letter' was actually written by journalist George Brewer, who had served as a lieutenant in the Swedish navy. Having left the sea, he trained as a lawyer and in 1805 was trying to make a living writing novels, plays, pamphlets and articles for magazines. It is hard to imagine such a satirical parody being published today, at least so soon after a battle when newspapers and journals still carried news of the dead and wounded, as well as charitable appeals for the widows and orphans.

FOURTEEN

Fruits of Victory

Nobly, nobly Cape Saint Vincent to the North-west died away;
Sunset ran, one glorious blood-red, reeking into Cadiz Bay;
Bluish 'mid the burning water, full in face Trafalgar lay;
In the dimmest North-east distance dawn'd Gibraltar grand and gray;
'Here and here did England help me: how can I help England?'—say,
Whoso turns as I, this evening, turn to God to praise and pray,
While Jove's planet rises yonder, silent over Africa.[1]

On 4 December 1805, the same day that the *Belleisle* arrived at Plymouth, the *Victory* anchored at Spithead, off Portsmouth. As Nelson's body was to lie in state and then be buried in London, the *Victory* sailed from Spithead six days later and had reached as far as Dover when adverse weather delayed progress, and the ship was forced to anchor for a few days. During this time, some boatloads of sightseers managed to visit the ship, and one described the scene in a letter to *The Naval Chronicle*:

Dover, December 16, 1805
Mr. Editor,
I am just come from on board the *Victory*: she is very much mauled,

both in her hull and rigging; has upwards of 80 shot between wind and water: the foremast is very badly wounded indeed, and though strongly fished, has sunk about six inches: the mainmast also is badly wounded, and very full of musket shots; she has a jury mizzenmast, and fore and main-top-masts, and has a great many shot in her bowsprit and bows; one of the figures which support the arms [the figurehead] has both the legs shot off. I clearly ascertained that Lord Nelson was killed by a shot from the maintop of the *Redoubtable*: he was standing on the starboard side of the quarter-deck, with his face to the stern, when the shot struck him, and was carried down into one of the wings: he lived about one hour, and was perfectly sensible until within five minutes of his death. When carrying down below, although in great pain, he observed the tiller ropes were not sufficiently tight, and ordered tackles to be got on them, which now remain; the ship he engaged was so close, that they did not fire their great guns on board the enemy, but only musketry, and manned the rigging to board, but nearly the whole [of the enemy] that left the deck [to board the *Victory*] were killed; the ship had 25 guns dismounted with the *Victory*'s fire; a shot carried away four spokes from the wheel of the *Victory*, and never killed or wounded any of the men steering; temporary places have been fitted up between decks for the wounded men, which are warmed by stoves. [signed] R. J.[2]

A few days later the *Victory* managed to reach the Nore anchorage at the confluence of the rivers Thames and Medway. Nelson's body was removed from the cask containing spirits of wine, and, as Dr Beatty recorded,

the remains were wrapped in cotton vestments, and rolled from head to foot with bandages of the same material, in the ancient mode of embalming. The Body was then put into a leaden coffin, filled with brandy holding in solution camphor and myrrh (the stock of spirit of wine on board was exhausted, and from the sound state of the Body, brandy was judged sufficient for its preservation). This coffin was inclosed in a wooden one, and placed in the after-part of His Lordship's cabin, where it remained till the 21st December, when an order was received from the Admiralty for the removal of the Body.'[3]

By this time the coffin that had been made from the timber of the mainmast of the French flagship *L'Orient*, which blew up during the Battle of the Nile, had been brought on board the *Victory*. Nelson's body was now removed from the lead coffin, dressed in his uniform and transferred to this wooden coffin, which was placed in a lead coffin, and that in turn was placed inside another wooden one, before being transported up the Thames to Greenwich. There it would lie in state for three days in the Painted Hall, which was effectively besieged by people; the Governor of the Royal Hospital, Admiral Lord Hood, estimated the crowds at over thirty thousand. It was calculated that, during the three days of lying in state, around sixty thousand people viewed the coffin, and it became obvious that the funeral itself was going to be a popular spectacle. Four days before the funeral, Lady Bessborough described the rising tension: 'Nothing ever equal'd the consternation this wretched news [of Nelson's death] has given – I never remember any thing to equal it. All sides, all parties, unite in one general lamentation; amongst quite the lowest class the discontent is so great that it was fear'd there would be a riot, and troops were sent for three days ago all round London.'[4]

People were travelling into London from across the country to line the route to St Paul's Cathedral, and in the days leading up to the event a flurry of advertisements appeared in the newspapers offering facilities in houses along the way:

LORD NELSON'S FUNERAL – Two or three respectable families, wishing to be accommodated, together, with a view of the procession, may, by an early application, engage one of the largest houses on the north side of Ludgate Hill, commanding a view from St. Paul's to the top of Fleet Street; offers have already been made for it, but as it is one of the best houses in the neighbourhood, none need apply who will not offer a handsome sum. Letters, post paid, addressed to W.Y. at No. 27, Fleet Street, and at No. 6 Bennett Street, St. James, will be attended to immediately.[5]

Other people, not content with the procession, were trying to find a place at the funeral itself: 'ST. PAUL'S CATHEDRAL – Wanted. One or two tickets, for the cupola or body of the cathedral, on the 9th instant. Any persons having tickets, who, from illness, or any other cause, may be prevented from attending on the occasion, and may be willing, in consequence, to dispose of the same, may hear of a purchaser, by addressing a line to A.Z. No. 26, Bread Street Hill. Secrecy may be relied on.'[6]

Nelson was buried in St Paul's Cathedral in accordance with his own wishes, which he had made known to some of his officers, as Dr Beatty recorded:

His Lordship had on several occasions told Captain Hardy, that if he should fall in battle in a foreign climate, he wished his body to be conveyed to England, and that if his Country should think proper to inter him at the public expense, he wished to be buried in Saint Paul's, as well as that his monument should be erected there. He explained his reasons for preferring Saint Paul's to Westminster Abbey, which were rather curious: he said that he remembered hearing it stated as an old tradition when he was a boy, that Westminster Abbey was built on a spot where once existed a deep morass, and he thought it likely that the lapse of time would reduce the ground on which it now stands to its primitive state of a swamp, without leaving a trace of the Abbey. He added, that his actual observations confirmed the probability of this event. He also repeated to Captain Hardy several times during the last two years of his life: 'Should I be killed, Hardy, and my Country not bury me, you know what to do with me,' meaning that his body was in that case to be laid by the side of his father's, in his native village of Burnham Thorpe in Norfolk.[7]

The funeral itself, on 9 January 1806, was said to be the most splendid in living memory, with a procession of royalty, nobility, politicians, admirals, generals, sailors and soldiers stretching all the way from Whitehall to the cathedral. Nelson's coffin had been carried from Greenwich up the River Thames to Whitehall the previous day, and now it was transferred to an elaborate

funeral car, or open hearse, decorated with a carved imitation of the head and stern of his Majesty's ship the *Victory*, surrounded with Escutcheons of the Arms of the Deceased, and adorned with appropriate mottos and emblematical devices; under an elevated Canopy, in the form of the upper part of an antient Sarcophagus, with six sable Plumes, and the coronet of a Viscount in the centre, supported by four Columns, representing Palm Trees, with wreaths of natural laurel and cypress entwining the shafts; the whole upon a four-wheeled carriage drawn by six led horses, the Caparisons adorned with Armorial Escutcheons. The head of the Car, towards the horses, was ornamented with a figure of Fame. The stern, carved and painted in the naval style, with the word '*Victory*,' in yellow raised letters on the lanthorn over the poop. Between the Escutcheons were inscribed the words '*Trinidad*' and '*Bucentaur*.' The coffin, placed on the quarter-deck, with its head towards the stern, with an English Jack pendant over the poop, and lowered half staff. The corners and sides of the Canopy were decorated with black velvet, richly fringed, immediately above which, in the front, was inscribed in gold the word 'Nile,' at one end. On one side the following motto – 'Hoste devicto, requievit [Having defeated the enemy, may he rest in peace];' behind, the word 'Trafalgar;' and on the other side the motto – 'Palmam qui meruit ferat.' [Let him who has deserved it bear the palm of victory][8]

Lady Bessborough, who witnessed the funeral procession led by the Royal Scots Greys as it made its way from Whitehall to St Paul's Cathedral, had never seen

> anything so magnificent or so affecting, and very well manag'd except now and then that fault which pervades every thing that is done, high or low, Military and civil, in our Govt. – I mean delays and not being ready. Amongst many touching things the silence of that immense Mob was not the least striking; they had been very noisy. I was in a house in Charing Cross, which look'd over a mass of heads. The moment the Car appear'd which bore the body, you might have heard a pin fall, and without any order to do so, they all took off their hats. I cannot tell you the effect this simple action produc'd; it seem'd one general impulse of respect beyond any thing that could have been said or contriv'd.[9]

Admiral Villeneuve and Captain Magendie, who were living on parole as prisoners of war near Reading in Berkshire, both attended the funeral. The mourners at the ceremony were all men, for it was not customary for women to take part in funerals, and none had been invited to the ceremony at St Paul's, although a few ladies did manage to find places within the cathedral. Both Nelson's wife, Frances, and Emma Hamilton stayed away from the pageant.

The scene inside St Paul's was described as 'sublime, appearing almost visionary, something like what is described in the "Arabian nights entertainments"',[10] and the theatrical ceremony ran smoothly until almost the end. Forty-eight sailors from the *Victory* had carried Nelson's colours in the procession, but when it came to the moment when they were supposed to fold these battle-torn flags and place them on top of the coffin, they ripped pieces from the ensign, the largest of the flags, to keep as souvenirs. Captain Codrington's wife, one of the few ladies who managed to witness the funeral, commented that the only thing that was true to Nelson himself was this group of sailors from the *Victory* – 'the rest was so much the Herald's Office'.[11] The coffin was then lowered into the crypt and set inside a stone sarcophagus that had originally been made for Cardinal Wolsey and had languished in St George's Chapel, Windsor Castle, ever since the Cardinal lost the favour of Henry VIII and had been stripped of his property.

Over a month before the funeral, a day of national thanksgiving had taken place at the instigation of King George III. On 6 November, the day the king first heard the news about the battle, he and his family had given thanks in St George's Chapel at Windsor. Later, the king decided that the battle would be known as the 'Battle of Trafalgar', and a day of national thanksgiving for the victory was set for 5 December. *The Annual Register* recorded this day of thanksgiving as being

> observed with the utmost solemnity in every part of the empire [journalistic licence, since much of the empire still had not heard the news]. All the churches and chapels were crowded; all distinctions of sects were done away; and Christian and Jew, catholic and protestant, all united in the expression of one feeling of piety and gratitude to the Almighty. In most of the churches and chapels, collections were made for the wounded, and for the widows and orphans of the gallant men who died in the service of their country, and they exceeded even the most sanguine expectation. All ranks, from the highest to the lowest, vied with each other in their patriotic gifts; remembering the last signal of our departed hero, 'that England expects every man to do his duty'.[12]

Two days before the thanksgiving, the Committee of the Patriotic Fund met at Edward Lloyd's Coffee House in London. This was the place where shipping insurance underwriters used to meet, and eventually it would become the association of underwriters now known simply as Lloyd's. The

Patriotic Fund had been set up in 1803 to provide aid to wounded soldiers and sailors and support for widows and orphans of those killed in battle, as well as to provide rewards to mark military successes. Now they began to prepare for the casualties from Trafalgar: 'The glorious victory obtained off Trafalgar, by our ever-to-be-lamented hero, Lord Nelson, and that by Sir Richard Strachan, will, as appears by the public dispatches, present about 1800 cases more to the notice of the Committee, and it cannot be doubted will require a provision from the Fund to the extent of about £80,000. If therefore every class of our fellow subjects do not immediately step forward in aid of such a cause, it must be evident to all, that the future exertions of our brave defenders must go unrewarded and unnoticed.'[13] Over the coming months the fund was boosted by various private contributions, public collections and fund-raising schemes such as concert performances 'for the benefit of the widows and orphans, and for the relief of the wounded, of those brave heroes, who . . . gained the unparalleled victory off Trafalgar'.[14]

The concept of 'retirement' did not then exist, and the only recourse left to seamen who could not make a living and were not supported by relatives was to apply to Greenwich Hospital. This had been set up over a hundred years before, and by 1805 2410 pensioners were living there. They were provided with board and lodging, and received medical care from nurses who were recruited from seamen's widows under the age of forty-five. Those unfit for work did not just include men who had lost limbs; some had wood splinters so deep in their bodies that surgeons were unable to remove them, and these invalids carried a painful reminder of the battle to the end of their days. Greenwich Hospital also supported over three thousand other ex-seamen who were provided with a pension, but lived in their own homes. A seaman who wanted to become a pensioner was thoroughly examined by a surgeon to ensure he was unfit for work, and his story was carefully checked against the records. There were various technical reasons why a seaman could be refused by Greenwich Hospital, and only a proportion of those eligible actually applied, either because they felt the pension was insufficient or because they were too proud or independent to make a claim. Many others were reduced to menial jobs, such as shining shoes on the street or outright begging. For those sailors without any claim on the Hospital, life could be harsh, as the 1861 newspaper account of William Sandilands illustrates:

A TRAFALGAR HERO

In a very poor room in a back street by Avonside, Tewkesbury, is living a man named Sandilands, eighty-three years of age (on the *Victory*'s books miscalled Sanders), one of the seamen who helped to carry Nelson down below after he had received his death-wound at the Battle of Trafalgar. At the Peace, Sandilands left the navy without claim to pension; went knocking about the world as sailors do; at last returned to his native place, Tewkesbury, and worked on the roads until old age and infirmity threw him on the parish. Some friends acquainted with his sad story made the facts known to the Nelson family, and they, after proper inquiry, forthwith agreed to allow him for life 2s. 6d. per week for extra comforts. But the parochial authorities treated the Nelson allowance as part of his weekly income, and reduced their grant to 1s. per week, thus leaving this poor old man to exist upon 3s. 6d. per week, occasionally increased by donations from kind friends in Tewkesbury. And now in his old age this poor old man, who stood by Nelson in his last moments, is slowly wearing away in a state next door to want.[15]

At the meeting on 3 December 1805, the Patriotic Fund not only discussed how to help the sailors, but also voted various rewards for the officers involved. Nelson's widow, Nelson's brother and Vice-Admiral Collingwood were each to receive a commemorative silver vase to the value of £500. Rear-Admiral the Earl of Northesk (who was present in the *Britannia*, but did not have command of any particular group of ships) and Rear-Admiral Richard Strachan would receive silver vases worth £300 each, and captains were to be given swords worth £100 each. Other officers would have sums of money according to their rank, with additional payments if they had been wounded. For seamen or marines whose wounds resulted in disability or loss of a limb, there was to be a payment of £40, with £20 for a severe wound and £10 for a slight wound. In addition, 'relief' was to be 'afforded to the widows, orphans, parents, and relatives, depending for support on the captains, officers, petty officers, seamen, and marines, who fell in these glorious engagements, as soon as their respective situations shall be made known to the committee'.[16] For a seaman who had lost a limb, the payment of £40 represented about two years' pay – very approximately, £2000 at today's value. A sailor would normally expect at least that much in prize money from such a victory and would hope for a great deal more. In fact, Parliament voted for the sum of £300,000 to be distributed as compensation for the prizes that had been lost or destroyed after the battle, but each seaman's share was small in comparison with how the officers were rewarded. Captain Hardy in the *Victory* received £973 prize money and £2389 7s 6d compensation from the government, whereas an ordinary seaman received £1 17s 6d prize money and £4 12s 6d from the government. Captain Hardy was created a baronet, and many of the other officers were promoted, automatically giving them a raise in pay and in many cases making them eligible for half-pay when not employed at sea. Collingwood was created a baron and given a pension of £2000 a year (very roughly £100,000 at today's value), while Lord Northesk was given the Order of the Bath and Sir Richard Strachan received an annual pension of £1000.

Despite the importance of the victory, official medals were

only issued to admirals and captains, as had been done after the Battle of the Nile, and junior officers were once again resentful of this lack of recognition. After the Nile, Alexander Davison, who had amassed a fortune as a government contractor and was Nelson's prize-agent, had presented the officers with an unofficial medal struck by Matthew Boulton at the Soho Mint in Birmingham. Boulton himself now paid for a commemorative medal for Trafalgar, but as before the Admiralty refused to allow it to be worn as part of naval uniform. The medal was struck in a silver version for officers and in pewter for ratings. Another medal was issued privately by Davison, but was limited to the ratings of the *Victory*.

It would be another forty-two years before Parliament allowed the award of a Naval General Service Medal to survivors of Trafalgar and various other actions. The award was limited to those who had been present at an action and were still alive on 1 June 1847 when the medal was officially announced. The wording of the announcement led several women who had been on board the ships during the battles to apply, although for Trafalgar only one woman, Jane Townshend (who had been in the *Defiance*), put her name forward. At first those in charge of vetting applications approved those from women, but later on changed their minds, possibly taking into account the view of Queen Victoria about the propriety of the women being unofficially aboard the ships. The official reason given for the refusal sheds light on the real situation: 'Upon further consideration this cannot be allowed. There were many women in the fleet equally useful [as those who had applied for the medal], and it will leave the Army exposed to innumerable applications of the same nature.'[17] Since a similar medal was being awarded to soldiers for some past battles, what probably swayed the committee's decision was the fact that there were far more eligible women who had travelled as camp followers with the British Army than were ever aboard navy ships.

Parliament decreed that Nelson's brother William should be created an earl (a higher honour than Nelson himself ever received). A sum of up to £90,000 (roughly £4.5 million at today's value) of public money was also granted to him to buy an estate, with a further £5000 per year for him and his successors. The contrast in the scale of rewards offered to officers and seamen at Trafalgar was insignificant when compared to the windfall that William, now Earl Nelson of Trafalgar, received – largely because the king (who commanded the rewards) and Parliament both wanted to make a public show of appreciating the victory, without regard either to fair dealing or observance of the wishes of those who had won the battle. Nelson's sisters were allowed £10,000 each, which was later raised to £15,000; his widow Frances was granted an annual pension of £2000.

The two people who Nelson particularly wanted to be supported after his death, Emma Hamilton and their daughter Horatia, received nothing. On the morning of the battle, Nelson had drafted a document that came to be known as the last codicil to his will:

> October the twenty-first, one thousand eight hundred and five, then in sight of the Combined Fleets of France and Spain, distant about ten miles.
>
> Whereas the eminent services of Emma Hamilton, widow of the Right Honourable Sir William Hamilton, have been of the very greatest service to our King and Country to my knowledge, without her receiving any reward from either our King or Country. First, that she obtained the King of Spain's letter, in 1796, to his brother the King of Naples acquainting him of his intention to declare war against England, from which letter the Ministry sent out orders to then Sir John Jervis to strike a stroke, if opportunity offered, against either the Arsenals of Spain or her fleets; that neither of these was done is not the fault of Lady Hamilton, the opportunity might have been offered. Secondly, the British Fleet under my command could never have

returned the second time to Egypt, had not Lady Hamilton's influence with the Queen of Naples caused letters to be wrote to the Governor of Syracuse, that he was to encourage the Fleet being supplied with everything, should they put into any Port in Sicily; we put into Syracuse and received every supply, went to Egypt, and destroyed the French Fleet. Could I have rewarded these services, I would not now call upon my Country, but as that has not been in my power, I leave Emma Hamilton therefore a legacy to my King and Country, that they will give her an ample provision to maintain her rank in life. I also leave to the beneficence of my Country my adopted daughter Horatia Nelson Thompson, and I desire she will use in future the name of Nelson only. These are the only favours I ask of my King and Country at this moment, when I am going to fight their Battle. May God bless my King and Country, and all those who I hold dear. My relations it is needless to mention; they will of course be amply provided for.[18]

Since Nelson himself had been short-changed during his lifetime in regard to honours and monetary rewards, and was all too familiar with how the king and his court, Parliament and the Admiralty operated, the last sentence of the codicil sounds prophetically ironic in the light of subsequent events.

Nelson's last wishes concerning Emma were not so much special pleading as a cry for justice. His implication that his success at the Battle of the Nile was dependent upon help arranged by Emma is arguably an overstatement, but equally her diplomatic services were so often undervalued. As wife of Sir William Hamilton, she had indeed performed a vital diplomatic role for Britain, being trusted by Queen Maria Carolina, the real power behind the throne at Naples, and she greatly helped the formation of an alliance between Britain and the Italian kingdom. When the French overran Italy in 1798, the Hamiltons were evacuated along with the royal family, but as a consequence Sir William lost a great deal of his fortune. When he finally arrived back in Britain, he received no compensation and was eventually forced to petition the king himself before being granted a pension. In order to clear his debts he had to sell much of his remaining property, and from then on lived relatively modestly. The Hamiltons' financial situation was not helped by Emma's extravagant lifestyle. When Sir William died his pension did not pass to her, and her inheritance was not enough to maintain the standard of living she had adopted, which itself was far below what she would have maintained if Sir William had not lost so much money. She was then dependent on Nelson, and after Trafalgar she rapidly fell into debt through bad financial management. In July 1814, she fled to France to avoid her creditors but, already ill, she died in Calais six months later.

Nelson's fate was in stark contrast to that of his opponent, Villeneuve. When the French admiral led the Combined French and Spanish Fleet out of Cadiz, he already knew that Vice-Admiral Rosily was on his way with orders to replace him. Villeneuve hoped for something that could be claimed as a victory or else an honourable death in battle. He must have envied Nelson, being himself cheated even of an honourable death and forced to suffer the disgrace of being captured and taken to England. The English naval officers who came into contact with Villeneuve found him not quite what they expected. He was described as 'a tallish, thin man, a very tranquil, placid English-looking-Frenchman; he wore a long-tailed uniform coat, high and flat collar, corduroy pantaloons of a greenish colour, with stripes two inches wide, half-boots with sharp toes and a watch-chain with long gold links'.[19] Captain Francis Austen, brother of the novelist Jane Austen, thought he was 'about forty-five years of age, of dark complexion, with rather an unmeaning countenance, and has not much the appearance of a gentleman. He is, however, so much of a Frenchman as to bear his misfortune with cheerfulness.'[20] Captain Fremantle summed him up as 'a very pleasant and Gentlemanlike man',[21] but, understandably, 'the poor man was very low'.[22]

Villeneuve had travelled to England in the *Euryalus*, the ship that brought the final casualty list from Trafalgar, and was landed at Gosport in early December 1805 along with his servants and Captain Magendie. He spent the night at Portsmouth, where his depression was such that he became physically ill and a doctor was called. The next day he was moved to a house at Bishops Waltham, rented by the government for his use, but Villeneuve immediately asked to be sent to London. Although not granted this request, he was offered the choice of any town at least 30 miles to the north or west of London. He chose Reading in Berkshire and within a few days moved to a house called The Grove at nearby Sonning. Here he lived as the guest of Viscount Sidmouth who, as Henry Addington (before being made a viscount), had been head of the government that had concluded the short-lived peace with France in 1802. On parole, Villeneuve had a great deal of freedom, entertaining a variety of visitors including the Prime Minister, William Pitt, but he was not to be a prisoner of war for long. In April 1806 he was exchanged for four British captains and returned to his native country. He first set foot in France again at Morlaix in Brittany, travelled on to Rennes and from 17 April stayed at the Hôtel de la Patrie in the rue des Foulons where, five days later, he was found dead, with a letter addressed to his wife on the table beside him:

Rennes, April 21, 1806.
To Madame Villeneuve, née Dantoine, at Velensole (Basse-Alpes)

My dearest love, how will you receive this blow? Alas, I am crying more about you than about myself. It is a fact, I have reached the point where life is a source of shame and death a duty. Alone here, excommunicated by the Emperor, rejected by his minister, who was my friend, troubled by the huge liability for a disaster which is attributed to me, and to which fate dragged me, I must die! I know that you might not appreciate any apology for my action. I ask for your forgiveness, a thousand times over, but it is necessary and I am carried along by the most intense despair. Don't worry, take consolation from the sweet feelings of faith that sustain you; my hope is that you will find in it a peace of mind that has been denied me. Farewell! Farewell! Dry the tears of my family, and all those to whom I am most dear. I wanted to finish, but I cannot. What good fortune that I have no child to inherit my dreadful legacy and to be burdened with the weight of my name! Ah! I was not made for such a fate; I did not seek it, I have been dragged there in spite of myself. Farewell! Farewell!

Villeneuve[23]

The official investigation found that Villeneuve was discovered lying on his back on his bed with five knife wounds to the chest and a sixth with a table knife driven in up to the hilt. His room had been locked and the key was on the inside; it was concluded that he had taken his own life. Villeneuve's body was buried at night, without the usual military honours, and the letter to his wife was withheld by the French Government when his other effects were returned to his family. His death was published as suicide, but few details were given, and there was immediate speculation about it. In the absence of reliable facts, the most inaccurate reports were circulated, and in Britain the painter Farington recorded in his diary for 12 May 1806: 'In the public papers it is stated, "That Admiral Villeneuve, who commanded the French fleet in the battle of Trafalgar, died suddenly at the Hotel in which He lodged at Rennes, on his route to Paris, on the night of the 16th. of April. – It is said He shot himself; but there is much reason to suppose that He, like Pichegru and Wright, fell by the order of Buonaparte. He was, however, buried with military honours."'[24] Pichegru was a French general who had been arrested for conspiracy and was found dead in his cell in suspicious circumstances; Wright was a British naval officer who was captured off the French coast and also died in prison. Both men were reported to have committed suicide, but murder was widely suspected, and many others met a similar fate.

With Villeneuve's death, people across Europe once again sarcastically commented on Napoleon's good fortune that so many of those who displeased him killed themselves and saved him the trouble. Rumours proliferated to such an extent that eventually even Captain Magendie was accused of the murder of Villeneuve. In 1814 he felt the need to publish a statement of his close friendship with Villeneuve that also contained an account of the admiral's death based on the inquest held at Rennes. The facts were further obscured in 1825 with the publication of the *Mémoires de Robert Guillemard*, in which Guillemard maintained that not only had he witnessed the scene just after Villeneuve's death, which he claimed was certainly murder, but that he was the man who had shot Nelson. The book caused a sensation in France, and the publication of the facts and Villeneuve's letter to his wife a few years later did nothing to dent its impact. Even the confession by Lardier in 1830, that he had written the *Mémoires* as a hoax and that Guillemard was a fictional character, did not entirely quash the story.

Two years after Villeneuve's death, in stark contrast to the way Emma Hamilton was treated, Madame Villeneuve was awarded a pension of 4000 francs a year. Cynics regarded this as an attempt by the authorities to end the controversy – if so, it failed. As soon as it was announced, Villeneuve's death became a political issue – to those favouring Napoleon, it was suicide; to those against him, it was murder – and it has been debated ever since. The weight of the evidence, however, points one way only. The authenticity of Villeneuve's letter has been questioned, but even if genuine, it is not fully convincing as a suicide note; the phrases used could be taken to imply that Villeneuve was being forced to write it. People close to Villeneuve attested that he was not a coward in battle, nor was he likely to take his own life, but perhaps most telling of all is the evidence of his wounds. He was stabbed six times in the left lung and once in the heart, although whether the wound to the heart was last is unclear. Even if it was possible for Villeneuve to stab himself six times in this way, it is difficult to imagine a military man, trained in the use of arms, being so inept. There seems little doubt that Villeneuve was murdered.

There are no clues as to who might have murdered Villeneuve, nor is it known whether or not Napoleon ordered it or even knew about it. It is more likely, though, that he was happy to be rid of an admiral who he blamed for the collapse of his invasion plans. Napoleon's attitude is demonstrated by the newspaper report of how he reacted to other naval officers who were repatriated at the time:

At the audience which took place yesterday [6 May 1806] at St. Cloud, Captains Lucas and l'Infernet, who have lately arrived from England, were presented to His Majesty. Captain Lucas commanded the *Redoubtable*, in the battle of Trafalgar, and conducted himself in the most gallant manner; he attempted to board the *Victory*, Lord Nelson's ship. Captain l'Infernet also behaved in the bravest manner. After an unfortunate affair, it is gratifying to acknowledge such conduct. His Majesty said to the Captains, Lucas and l'Infernet, 'If all my vessels had conducted themselves as well as those which you commanded, the victory would have been ours. I know that there are several who have not imitated your example, but I have ordered their conduct to be investigated. I have appointed you Commanders of the Legion of Honour. The Captains of the vessels who, instead of boarding the enemy, kept out of cannon-shot, shall be prosecuted, and, if convicted, made a dreadful example of.'[25]

FIFTEEN

Heroes and Villains

> The memory of Trafalgar can never fade so long as England remains a nation, nor even so long as the English tongue is spoken or the history of England is remembered in any part of the world. It was so transcendent an event, so far-reaching in its consequences, so heroic in its proportions, so dramatic in its incidents, so tragic in its catastrophe, that it is difficult to name any single event in all history which quite equals it . . . It changed the face of Europe, and set the world's stage for the successive acts of that tremendous drama which ended ten years later at Waterloo. It was, moreover, the last great fight of the sailing-ship period of naval warfare.
>
> Comment in *The Times*, Saturday 21 October 1905, on the centenary of the battle

The Battle of Trafalgar may have temporarily removed any possibility of a French invasion, but it had not won the war. Nor had the battle given automatic naval superiority to the British. A fortnight before the battle, Nelson had summed up the situation: 'It is . . . annihilation that the Country wants, and not merely a splendid Victory of twenty-three to thirty-six [ships], – honourable to the parties concerned, but absolutely useless in the extended scale to bring Buonaparte to his marrow-bones: numbers can only annihilate.'[1] The battle had not completely annihilated the combined French and Spanish naval forces, but it had broken their power and given Britain the advantage.

The British fleet did not lose any ships, although several needed drastic repairs, and so victory gave Britain naval superiority for as long as the small groups of French and Spanish ships sheltering in various ports were prevented by the continuing blockade from building another large fleet. Despite the overwhelming nature of the victory at Trafalgar, these French and Spanish vessels could still pose a significant threat; the blockade was essential to maintaining Britain's hard-won naval supremacy. Because the blockade was successful, Trafalgar was in fact the last major fleet action of the Napoleonic Wars. With the developments in technology during the peace that followed Napoleon's final defeat, battleships came to be powered by steam rather than wind, and so Trafalgar also proved to be the last major battle fought by sailing ships.

After Trafalgar, Collingwood was continuously on board ship for nearly five years as he commanded a fleet involved in the blockade. While this dragged on, the stress of the responsibility and the hardships of being constantly at sea in all weathers gradually undermined his spirit and his health. He longed to be on shore with his family, and almost his only consolation was the companionship of his pet dog Bounce, which by 1807 was nearly eighteen years old and, like his master, was also ailing. Collingwood wrote:

> Tell the children that Bounce is very well and very fat, yet he seems not to be content, and sighs so piteously these long evenings, that I am obliged to sing him to sleep, and have sent them the song:

Sigh no more, Bouncey, sigh no more,
Dogs were deceivers never;
Though ne'er you put one foot on shore,
True to your master ever.
Then sigh not so, but let us go,
Where dinner's daily ready,
Converting all the sounds of woe
To heigh phiddy diddy.[2]

Even the comfort of this faithful friend was taken from him when Bounce fell overboard and drowned in August 1809, by which time Collingwood's health was in serious decline. His letters show him becoming increasingly ill until he was forced to request the Admiralty to allow him to return home. He set sail for England, but it was too late: he died at sea in March 1810 at the age of sixty-two, having never seen his wife and children since before Trafalgar.

For those like Captain Bolton, who had not been at Trafalgar to share the glory, the years of sailing up and down the same stretch of water to maintain the blockade soon took their toll, and he wrote to Emma Hamilton: 'It was formerly a pleasure to serve – it is now become a toil.'[3] Even Captain Codrington, who had commanded the *Orion* during the battle, admitted he was now 'hipped [depressed], dissatisfied and indifferent to the service'.[4] While thoughts of imminent invasion no longer occupied people's thoughts on land, for the men at sea the prospect of wearying years of patrolling was as gloomy as the expectation of an end to the war bringing an end to their employment. With no sea battles in prospect, officers were denied promotion and the opportunity of reaching a sufficiently high rank to provide financial security. Their crews also had no chance of sharing prize money. For many, the reward for success at Trafalgar was numbing tedium and an uncertain future.

If the situation was bad for the officers, it was obviously

worse for the lower ranks, many of whom were 'turned over' (transferred from ship to ship) without being allowed on shore for fear they would desert. This policy was self-fulfilling, since the more the seamen were denied a break from constantly being at sea, the more inclined they were to desert at the first opportunity. After the battle, many sailors were aggrieved that they had to return immediately to the dull routine of the blockade when they felt that they had earned a rest. These grievances were compounded by the captain of each ship having absolute command over the crew, leading to anomalies between ships. Less than two months after the battle, the crew of the *Royal Sovereign* were sufficiently embittered to present a petition to the Admiralty. Their complaints included not receiving their rightful provisions and alcohol allowance after the battle, only six men each day being allowed on shore, no letters received on board, not being permitted to send out their clothes to be washed, and receiving no rewards or encouragement following their bravery in the battle, despite the crews of other ships being given better treatment.

Such petitions rarely achieved anything. Parliament cared little about the welfare of seamen, and the Admiralty's concern seldom went further than the bare minimum necessary to maintain an efficient fighting force. For many more years to come, the fortunes of the seamen depended almost totally on the attitude of their officers, and continued to vary tremendously from ship to ship. Nevertheless, the Admiralty did take notice of the terrible toll that continuous blockading took on the men and, more particularly, on the ships. Immediately after Trafalgar it was thought safe to relax one part of the blockade, allowing the Channel Fleet to take refuge from the winter weather in the shelter of Torbay rather than suffer the constant battering of the storms in the Channel. This proved to be a mistake. On 13 December, less than two months after Trafalgar, the blockading British fleet withdrew from its station outside Brest because of the foul weather, and the French in Brest harbour seized their chance. The French ships were divided into two fleets. One, led by Vice-Admiral Leissègues, was to take one thousand soldiers to the West Indies to reinforce the French garrison at San Domingo and then cruise off Jamaica to disrupt British trade. The other, commanded by Rear-Admiral Willaumez, was to head for Cayenne on the coast of South America, via Martinique or Guadeloupe in the West Indies, on a similar mission to raid British merchant shipping, taking whatever prizes they could find, before returning to Europe.

The French almost succeeded in slipping away unnoticed, but two days out from Brest they were spotted by a convoy of British merchant ships, whose naval escort sent the news back to Britain. On the way the messenger, Captain Brisbane in the *Wasp*, met Admiral Sir John Duckworth, who set off with his squadron in pursuit of the French. He arrived in Barbados, having sighted the fleet led by Willaumez, but mistakenly let it go without attacking before joining up with Admiral Alexander Cochrane. They found the fleet commanded by Leissègues just too late to prevent the French reinforcements being landed at San Domingo, but in time to stop the fleet preying on British shipping and disrupting trade with the West Indies. In the ensuing battle, two large French battleships were destroyed and three captured. Only two French frigates and a corvette escaped, and the British ships were relatively undamaged.

Meanwhile, news of the French breakout reached Britain, and two squadrons led by Vice-Admiral Warren and Rear-Admiral Sir Richard Strachan were sent out to find and intercept the French. By sheer chance, Warren found a small French force of one battleship, two troop carriers and several frigates, led by Rear-Admiral Linois. Having left Brest in March 1803 on an unsuccessful mission to capture Pondicherry in India, this fleet had since then been harassing British shipping in the Indian Ocean and subsequently on the Atlantic route between St

Helena and the Canaries. Initially mistaking Warren's fleet for a merchant convoy, Linois gave chase and only realised his mistake when he was too close to avoid a battle. Just one of Linois's frigates escaped, and once again British damage and casualties were much lighter than those of the French.

The French fleet under Willaumez was more fortunate, cruising in the South Atlantic and around the West Indies for several months, raiding the convoys of merchant ships. In August 1806, the fleet was dispersed by a hurricane, and Strachan's squadron caught up with them off the coast of America. One French ship was driven ashore and wrecked, three others managed to escape into the estuaries of the Chesapeake and Delaware rivers (although only one vessel made it back to France afterwards); the other two sailed straight back to Europe. This breakout of the French had been neutralised relatively quickly, but not before reinforcements had been delivered to the French at San Domingo. It was a practical demonstration of how much harder it was to find and destroy French fleets once they were at sea than to keep them cooped up in their ports.

Over the next two years a few small ships slipped through the blockade, but everyone's attention was focused on events on the Continent, as Napoleon gradually expanded his empire. In November 1806 he had sufficient control of western Europe to declare a blockade of Britain. Since France did not have control of the sea, this meant closing European ports to British ships, thus denying Britain supplies from Europe and outlets for British manufactured goods. This became known as the 'Continental System' and was designed to destroy Britain's power by cutting the source of its wealth – trade, manufacturing and commerce. Napoleon still had not given up the idea of invading Britain, but he needed a stronger navy, which, to him, with the attitude of a soldier, did not mean more well-trained sailors, but simply more ships. In 1807, at a meeting with Tsar

Alexander I at Tilsit, a small town on the Polish-Lithuanian border, Napoleon agreed a peace treaty after the French had decisively beaten the Russian Army at the Battle of Friedland. With Russia under the sway of Napoleon, the Continental System soon began to have a serious effect on Britain. Of more immediate concern was another part of the treaty that was meant to remain secret, which covered how France and Russia would divide up Europe between them with an aggressive application of the Continental System, amalgamate the French and Russian fleets, which were to be increased by more shipbuilding, and seize the fleets of Portugal and Denmark – both still neutral states.

The secret treaty was known almost instantly in Britain, the information being carried by an English smuggler turned spy, and the government realised that it must act quickly to preempt Napoleon's plan. The Portuguese royal family and the Portuguese fleet were escorted to the safety of the colony of Brazil on the other side of the Atlantic. Meanwhile, a Russian fleet in the Tagus River in Portugal was blockaded by British ships, leaving a few Russian vessels isolated and relatively powerless in the Adriatic. A plan was then set in motion to deal with the Danish fleet at Copenhagen, which was important not so much for the ships there as the seamen, since the Danish Government required every seafarer to serve six years in the navy, if they were needed, with four thousand men always available and a reserve of over twenty thousand. These were all skilled and experienced seamen – the essential element that the French Navy lacked.

On 25 July 1807, the British Admiral Lord Gambier set sail with a strong force of battleships and transport ships to Copenhagen, on the correct assumption that the Crown Prince of Denmark would refuse to surrender his navy. After several days of bombardment, partially from ships, but mainly from artillery batteries that had been established ashore, the city surrendered on 7 September. British losses were minimal, but about 250 Danish soldiers were killed, and because General Peyman who commanded the Danish defence had earlier refused to take advantage of the British offer to evacuate the city, over two thousand civilians also died. Those Danish ships that were not considered worth taking to Britain were destroyed, and the operation effectively stopped Napoleon's revised plans for invasion.

From now on Napoleon relied on the Continental System to bring Britain to its knees, and there appeared to be every possibility of doing so. Bad harvests in 1808, 1809 and 1810, as well as the continuing mechanisation of both agriculture and industry in Britain, caused widespread unrest and often violent opposition. Luddites smashed factory machines; turnpike cottages were burned in anger against road tolls; and serious rioting occurred in several places. If strictly enforced, the Continental System would have succeeded, since by 1811 English factories were being forced to close down because there was no market for their products and because warehouses were already choked with unsold goods. The problem for Napoleon was that the cutting of trade between the Continent and Britain hurt the Continental countries almost as much. The Continental System was everywhere subverted or only half-heartedly applied. Corruption and smuggling were rife, and even Napoleon himself sanctioned the relaxation or circumvention of the rules when it suited him. In France, the bourgeoisie – Napoleon's most faithful supporters – were alienated by goods being unobtainable or else scarce and overpriced. The end result was an even greater strain on his imperial economy that had already been suffering under the burden of financing his military campaigns. The final straw was his invasion of Russia in 1812. Not merely a military disaster, the campaign made an implacable enemy of the Tsar. One by one the allies of France switched their allegiance to Britain and Russia, until Napoleon was forced to abdicate two years later and was finally defeated at the Battle of Waterloo in 1815.

After the assault on Copenhagen in 1807, only minor confrontations took place between the navies of Britain and France, the most serious being the breakout of a fleet from Brest in 1809 with orders to destroy British trade in the West Indies. Pursued by the British, the French ships fled along the coast and sought shelter in the outer anchorage off Aix, known as Basque Roads. Here they were again blockaded, but the British were concerned that they might slip past and so considered ways of attacking the French within the anchorage. The Admiralty agreed that this was necessary, but as the commanders controlling the blockade could not agree a plan and were afraid of failure, the Admiralty finally ordered Captain Thomas Cochrane, an officer not involved with the blockade, to plan and lead an assault. An attack with fire ships, some packed with explosives, led to the destruction of most of the French ships as they collided with each other in the confusion, most of them running aground. Cochrane himself was nearly killed by falling wreckage. Having lit the fuse on a vessel full of explosives, he was being rowed away when he remembered that the ship's pet dog was still aboard. His boat returned, the dog was rescued, and when the ship blew up, the debris flew clear over them. If Cochrane had not been delayed by the rescue, his boat would have been underneath the deadly shower of timber fragments.

For the rest of the war, the ceaseless blockade of French ports ensured British naval superiority, since many French ships never went to sea again. Immobilised, the French fleet was steadily robbed of sailors who were conscripted into Napoleon's army, which was so desperate for troops. The British fleet, though, was still at liberty to assist military campaigns on the Continent, delivering armies and equipment as well as supporting the supply chain. The most notable success was the ferrying of supplies to the armies in Spain during the Duke of Wellington's campaigns through the Spanish peninsula. As Wellington himself commented, 'If anyone wishes to know the history of this war, I will tell them that it is our maritime superiority which gives me the power of maintaining my army while the enemy are unable to do so.'[5]

Away from the war in Europe, the British Navy was heavily involved in protecting trade and, wherever possible, taking over former colonies of France and its allies. The colony of the Cape of Good Hope had been returned to the Dutch in the peace treaty of 1802, but on 12 January 1806, just a few days after Nelson's funeral, a British expedition defeated the Dutch garrison and took control. This not only prevented the French from trading with the colony, which largely produced fruit, wool and wine, but it also protected British merchant shipping to India and China. After the people of Spain rebelled against French rule in 1808, the British Navy had an increasing role in protecting commerce with the Spanish colonies in South America, particularly the beef, hides and wheat that were traded through the port of Buenos Aires. In the West Indies there was an ongoing struggle to protect the shipping that carried sugar, rum and other goods to Britain. This area was regarded as a key target by Napoleon, who, unable to send a large fleet, authorised a host of privateers to carry on a guerilla war. These ships were considered pirates by the British Navy, which concentrated on denying them safe havens within the Caribbean islands. In a war of attrition that was designed to destroy British trade, it was actually French control and influence that were gradually eroded instead.

In the East Indies the situation was very complex. Various countries supplied essential goods to Britain (opium, sugar and cotton from India; tea from India, Ceylon and China – which was also the source of silk; and hardwoods from Malaya and Burma), but the Dutch and French were strong and sometimes ruthless competitors. In India, the British East India Company, with its own private army and a small navy, had already gained the upper hand against the French by the time of Trafalgar. Elsewhere in the region, British trading links were more tenuous although growing in strength. As in the West Indies, the main naval involvement was in dealing with French privateers and a few French naval vessels that were raiding British shipping. The war in this area was effectively over by 1812, but a fleet remained to protect British interests, eventually coming to control all the major trade routes of the region.

By 1815, all the main competitors to British trade had effectively been swept from the sea. In the war against privateers, many local traders had also been eliminated, further reducing competition. Now Britain's navy dominated the world's shipping lanes while the merchant fleet dominated trade, enjoying a monopoly of colonial markets for British goods. The small British Empire that had been struggling for survival before the Napoleonic Wars was on a much firmer footing and was set to expand rapidly. British seaborne trade increased, bringing timber, flax and turpentine from the Baltic in exchange for coal; sugar, rum and molasses from the West Indies, which had in turn been traded for slaves; and spices, silks and saltpetre from the East Indies in exchange for wool and tin. The American colonies might have been lost in 1783, but both Canada and Australia were now producing exports of raw materials as well as providing markets for Britain's manufactured goods. Armies raised to protect trade in foreign lands came to control the areas where they were deployed, and the trading stations became colonies that grew to dominate their host countries. One by one they were added to the British Empire, and through the nineteenth century Britain grew ever more prosperous.

A final, but most important, export from Britain was people. The story of one man is graphically illustrative of this. In early April 1815, a small boy's earliest memory was watching the Royal Scots Greys in their magnificent dress uniforms, marching down the steep hill of Park Street in Bristol, with the same impressive display as when they had led Nelson's funeral procession through London ten years earlier. Acclaimed as the finest cavalry in Europe, they were on their way from winter quarters to fame and glory at the Battle of Waterloo, where Napoleon was finally defeated on 18 June 1815. The boy in the crowd watching the parade was Henry Creswicke Rawlinson. Born in 1810 and dying in 1895, his life spanned the nineteenth century and also the rise of the British Empire. He spent nearly a third of his long life abroad, initially in India as a soldier with the East India Company, and then as a key officer during the First Afghan War. In his years as a successful political agent and British Consul at Baghdad, he became fascinated by the ancient empires of the plain of Mesopotamia and was the first to copy many archaic inscriptions, eventually deciphering the cuneiform script, the earliest form of writing in the world. He was also an explorer, mapping unknown territory in what is now Iran. Returning to Britain, he became a Member of Parliament and a director of the East India Company, while continuing his studies of cuneiform at the British Museum. As an accomplished linguist, scholar, soldier, explorer and diplomat, Rawlinson was exceptional but far from unique. It was not just emigrants and transported convicts who left Britain for the colonies, but a whole array of such talented people, seeking fame and fortune or just careers that they were not free to follow at home. Among them were many whose skills were at a premium in the developing colonies. And with these people went the English language.

One of the most important elements of the victory at Trafalgar was that the subsequent development of British naval supremacy allowed the growth of the empire. Even if Napoleon had not invaded Britain, a defeat at Trafalgar might just have led to naval supremacy for France. It was British sea-power that transported Wellington's army to invade Spain and also helped keep that army supplied. Without the Battle of Trafalgar in 1805 there might not have been a Battle of Waterloo ten years later. Perhaps more importantly, one of Napoleon's aims was to expand France's trade by increasing the number of its colonies, and with French naval supremacy he would undoubtedly have tried to extend his empire beyond Europe. If it had grown as large as the British Empire, French would probably be the dominant world language by now. Instead, the British Empire expanded to encompass a quarter of the world's population and to cover a quarter of the world's land surface, becoming the biggest empire ever seen – with English as the most widespread language in the world.

Parallel to the rise of the British Empire was the establishment of Nelson as the archetypal national hero. The possibility of such celebrity status for senior naval officers was almost an inevitable consequence of the conditions of warfare at the time. Now that instant communications are available, it is difficult to appreciate just how haphazard were the available methods of sending long-distance messages. Because there was no reliable way of transmitting messages to ships at sea, officers commanding ships or fleets of ships had to be given specific tasks and a great deal of latitude, so that success or failure rested largely with individual men. Success was met with public praise, but failure led to a court martial. In 1757, Admiral Byng was tried by court martial and shot for failing to relieve the French siege of Port Mahon on Minorca, with the result that the island was lost to the French. This caused a public controversy, since Byng had been made a political scapegoat for the failings of the British Government. His fate inspired the remark by Voltaire in *Candide* that in England it was sometimes necessary to shoot an admiral 'pour encourager les autres' (to encourage the others).[6] After Byng's execution, naval officers did their utmost to present their own actions in the best possible light, as much to protect themselves as to enhance their careers. Other admirals besides Nelson created what would now be labelled 'cults of the personality' – but Nelson had a natural flair for it.

In public, Nelson maintained a persona calculated to enhance his celebrity status, but behind this façade the real man was very different, as Sir Arthur Wellesley (later to become the Duke of Wellington) was amazed to find on the only occasion the two men met. Waiting in the anteroom of the Colonial Office in Downing Street on the day before Nelson set sail from England to his destiny at Trafalgar, Wellesley found

> a gentleman, whom from his likeness to his pictures and the loss of an arm, I immediately recognised as Lord Nelson. He could not know who I was, but he entered at once into conversation with me, if I can call it conversation, for it was almost all on his side and all about himself, and in, really, a style so vain and so silly as to surprise and almost disgust me. I suppose something that I happened to say may have made him guess that I was *somebody*, and he went out of the room for a moment, I have no doubt to ask the office-keeper who I was, for when he came back he was altogether a different man, both in manner and matter. All that I had thought a charlatan style had vanished, and he talked of the state of this country and of the aspect and probabilities of affairs on the Continent with a good sense, and a knowledge of subjects both at home and abroad that surprised me equally and more agreeably than the first part of our interview had done; in fact, he talked like an officer and a statesman. The Secretary of State kept us long waiting, and certainly, for the last half or three-quarters of an hour, I don't know that I ever had a conversation that interested me more. Now, if the Secretary of State had been punctual, and admitted Lord Nelson in the first quarter of an hour, I should have had the same impression of a light and trivial character that other people have had, but luckily I saw enough to be satisfied that he was really a very superior man; but certainly a more sudden or complete metamorphosis I never saw.[7]

Nelson was also a realist, taking the view that 'it is much better [for an officer] to serve an ungrateful Country, than to give up his own fame. Posterity will do him justice.'[8]

Within the navy itself, Nelson and officers such as Collingwood and Sir James Saumarez won popularity because of their fairness, kindness and humanity. Nelson could be a ruthless disciplinarian, but he always struggled to be even-handed and just, because he was aware of the harshness of the lives of the seamen and did what he could to alleviate their hardships. The result was a fierce personal loyalty to Nelson from the men who served under him. In battle, they fought harder and were generally less prone to rebellion and mutiny, because he left them their pride and self-respect, where other more autocratic, aristocratic officers sought to break the will of their crews. In return, the men respected Nelson and even loved him. It did not, however, stop many of them deserting – something Nelson never really understood, because he was driven by a religious belief in his God, King and Country, while they had more mundane reasons for being in the navy.

During Nelson's lifetime, stories about his kindness circulated by word of mouth, but immediately after Trafalgar, similar stories were published that almost took the form of parables or moral exemplars. Less than a month after news of the battle reached Britain, an account was published concerning Colonel Tyrwhitt, Vice-Warden of the Stannaries in Cornwall and Devon, who came across a young boy claiming Nelson was his godfather. The colonel 'found the father, who had lost a limb in the *Minotaur*, in the battle of the Nile, and his wife and four children, clean, though poorly dressed'.[9] The mother 'was a washerwoman on board the *Minotaur* of 74 guns, Captain Louis: when the child was born in the bay of Leghorn, his Lordship, Sir Wm. and Lady Hamilton said they would stand sponsors. He [Nelson] had promised when the boy grew up to put him to sea, and give him a nautical education. But after the

Peace of Amiens, these poor people, through ignorance, forgot (though desired by his Lordship when he sailed for England) to write him where they were settled.'[10] The boy's mother produced a certificate of his baptism 'at the British Factory Chapel, Leghorn, July 1800, attested by the Clergyman, Rev. Mr. Cummins – and signed Emma Hamilton, William Hamilton, Nelson and Bronte'.[11]

Colonel Tyrwhitt investigated further, and

> after talking over the circumstance of the intended kindness of Lord Nelson to this poor little boy, if he had known their situation and place of abode [described as a 'cottage' or 'hut'], Colonel Tyrwhitt, determined to follow up his Lordship's good wishes, has taken the boy as his *protegé*, and with his usual humanity had him directly clothed, and has put him to school, meaning to give him a regular nautical education to fit him for the naval service of his country. A little purse [appeal for donations], by way of subscription for present purposes, has been opened under the patronage of Mrs. Admiral Sutton, which will no doubt be soon filled, out of respect to the memory of a Hero, beloved, admired, and almost adored, and whose memory will be cherished and entwined round the heart-strings of every lover of British naval virtue and heroism.[12]

The child had been christened Horatio Nelson – his parents' surname was not published.

Factors other than kindness, humanity and a string of victories also helped turn Nelson into a national icon. Men missing one or more limbs had become a common sight in Britain, since amputation was then the only treatment for many wounds, and some seamen had the bravado to consider it a badge of honour, as one man aboard the *Victory* was reported as saying: 'This, by some, would be considered a misfortune, but I shall be proud of it as I shall resemble the more our brave Commander in Chief.'[13] Nelson's loss of an arm was a visible reminder of his bravery and a tenuous connection with the common people. Above all, his death in the hour of his greatest triumph ensured his status as a saviour of his country, and his name and legend immediately became inseparable from the victory at Trafalgar. It had been achieved by the efforts of the thousands of men and women aboard the British ships, but now came to be regarded as the achievement of one man – Nelson. In a simplistic echo of Christian theology, Nelson was seen as the saviour of Britain, a saviour who had died in his hour of triumph and whose name at least would be immortal. On the day that the news of Trafalgar and Admiral Nelson's death was published in Britain, the development of the cult of the Hero Nelson, a prominent aspect of the final years of his life, was finally complete.

At that time, there was relatively little to tarnish Nelson's name, since the extent of his involvement with Emma Hamilton was not known. For the masses, the niceties of 'Our Nel's' personal relationships might provide a joke now and then, but did not seriously detract from his status. There had been controversy over the harsh way that he had dealt with the Jacobin rebels when he reoccupied Naples after it had been overrun by the French in 1798, but again this made little impression on most people, to whom foreigners were of little or no account. For most purposes, Nelson could be held up as an example of what every British man should be: God-fearing, patriotic, courageous, kind, humane, just and, above all, victorious. These were the qualities needed by empire-builders – men who could believe they were superior to other races and who could conquer, colonise and administer territories across the globe. Indeed, Nelson believed 'that one Englishman was equal to three Frenchmen',[14] and as a parting gift he had even provided a slogan – 'England expects that every man will do his duty' – which rapidly became a patriotic rallying call. Missing the point, Napoleon grasped at the symbolism like a magic formula and ordered the phrase 'France expects everyone will do his duty'[15] to be prominently displayed on all the surviving ships of the French Navy.

Nelson became the best-loved hero of the nation, eclipsing the legendary King Arthur and Sir Francis Drake, and he was a model for all subsequent heroes of Victorian Britain. He provided an image of selfless service and sacrifice for the sake of the mother country, which was propagated as an ideal of British manhood throughout the Victorian era. Deliberately fostered in schools, this model of patriotism was emulated by military men, explorers and missionaries. Whole towns were named after him in Lancashire, South Wales, New Zealand and Canada – where the Nelson River also flows into Hudson Bay. There is a Cape Nelson on the coast of Victoria in Australia, and across the empire numerous Trafalgar Squares and Nelson Roads sprang up, with over fifty in the Greater London area alone.

The principal monument by which the hero is remembered is Nelson's Column in Trafalgar Square at the very heart of London, the protracted outcome of a committee set up in 1838 to erect a memorial. The column was built in 1842, and the monument was finally completed with the addition of the lions at its base in 1867. At 165 feet tall, it is shorter than the column in Boulogne. This monument, begun in 1803 and finally completed in 1841, was originally planned to commemorate Napoleon's invasion of England. With the exile of Napoleon and the restoration of the Bourbon dynasty in France, it became the Colonne des Bourbons, but is now a monument to the soldiers of France known as the Colonne de la Grande Armée. From the top there are extensive views across the Channel into England, a tantalising panorama of the land Napoleon failed to invade.

In 1905, one hundred years after the Battle of Trafalgar, centenary celebrations were held all over the world and the emphasis, once again, was on Nelson. In New York a banquet was held 'in honour of the Nelson centenary. Speeches were delivered in praise of the hero and toasts drunk to King Edward and President Roosevelt',[16] while in Tokyo the newspapers carried 'cordially-worded articles on the occasion of the Nelson centenary, and . . . portraits of the great Admiral [Nelson] and Admiral Togo side by side'.[17] In London, Nelson's Column was the focus for commemorative wreaths to Nelson and to all who lost their lives at Trafalgar. An enormous floral anchor was inscribed: 'To the immortal memory of Nelson, from the surviving sons and daughters of officers who fought at Trafalgar.'[18] The long list of contributors that followed included the daughter of Jack Spratt, wounded in the attack on the *Aigle*, and the two daughters of John Pollard, who had become known as the 'Avenger of Nelson' after shooting all the sharpshooters in the mizzentop of the *Redoutable*. There were also many smaller wreaths with individual inscriptions such as 'from the 12 surviving grandchildren of Admiral Sir Henry Digby, who commanded the *Africa* at Trafalgar'[19] and 'In memory of Captain George Duff, killed at Trafalgar in command of H.M.S. *Mars*, and of his son, Admiral Norwich Duff, present at the battle as a midshipman in his father's ship.'[20]

The victory at Trafalgar, which put the finishing touch to Nelson's status as a national hero, gave Britain a dominance of the world's sea-borne trading routes that would not be seriously challenged until the Battle of Jutland in 1916. Out of that dominance arose an empire on which literally the sun never set. Nelson might have provided the inspiration and example, but it was the thousands of ordinary men and women aboard the ships who made the difference, as Nelson himself said: 'It must strike forcibly every British seaman, how superior their conduct is, when in discipline and good order.'[21] The sailors themselves felt deeply that 'a British seaman has a right to be proud, for he is incomparable when placed alongside those of any other nation. Great Britain can truly boast of her hearts of oak.'[22]

Nearly seventeen thousand men from Britain took part in the Battle of Trafalgar, at a time when the total population of England, Scotland and Wales is estimated to have been approximately eleven million people (the current population of Greater London alone is over seven million). These men were drawn from nearly every town and county in the land, and most areas had their local heroes who eventually returned home with tales to tell about the battle. Where the victory had provoked a rash of (mainly bad) poetry among the middle and upper classes, songs and ballads about the battle were sung by the working classes throughout the country, with the better ones being handed down from generation to generation to become part of the country's folk heritage. As late as the 1950s these songs were still being collected and written down, sometimes for the first time since they were composed.

In the latter part of the nineteenth century, the deaths of these local heroes often merited a paragraph in the local newspaper, such as occurred in 1863 when John Pringle died:

DEATH OF LORD NELSON'S COXWAIN

Lord Nelson's coxwain on board the *Victory*, Mr. John Pringle, died at his residence, Newton Bushel, Devon, on the 5th instant, having attained the extraordinary age of 103 on the 19th of May last. The deceased veteran had only been ill about a month. Prior to his illness, although he was rather infirm, still his mental faculties were unimpaired, and he was accustomed to display those social qualities which so distinguished him in early life. On his birthday for several years past he was in the habit of driving round the town in company with his wife, and the old respected couple were the observed of all observers on the occasion. He was by birth a Scotchman, having been born in the county of Fife, and on attaining the age of twenty-one he joined the Royal navy. Whilst in the service he took an active part in many of our celebrated naval battles, and among others those of the Nile, Trafalgar and Alexandria. He was in receipt of a pension, and at the ripe age of ninety-two he married, and his wife survives him.[23]

In France the Battle of Trafalgar produced no acclaimed heroes; when the facts became known, the battle was regarded as a disgraceful disaster. Its survivors mingled with the other demobilised, demoralised seamen, who were in turn swamped by the influx of returning soldiers after the war. Writing forty years after the battle, the French historian Louis Adolphe Thiers summed up the situation:

Our sailors . . . had mingled with the Spanish seamen in the port of Cadiz, when they were informed that the king of Spain gave a step in rank to every Spaniard who had been present at the battle of Trafalgar, besides particular distinctions to those who had behaved best. The Spaniards . . . said to the latter that probably they would soon receive the recompense of their courage. This was not the case: the brave and the cowards among the French also shared the same treatment, and that treatment was oblivion.[24]

It would be decades before the French came to terms with Trafalgar and paid due honour to their countrymen who had fought in the battle, but by 1892 it was possible for Queen Victoria to include in her itinerary a meeting with the very last French survivor of the battle during a visit to France. He had served under Captain Lucas in the *Redoutable*, but sadly died at the age of 101, at Hyères, just before she met him: 'Her Majesty . . . received from the family of the late M. Cartigny, the centenarian French naval veteran of Trafalgar, a bouquet of flowers, which he would himself have offered to her, as a tribute of esteem, if he had lived a few days longer. His grandson, M. Bodinier, keeper of the Hyères town archives, is invited to see the Queen.'[25]

In stark contrast to the French, from the moment news reached Cadiz the Spanish regarded Trafalgar as a respectable defeat, and it was proclaimed as an occasion when the Spanish Navy had done its duty with courage and honour, irrespective of the outcome. Every Spanish officer who had taken part in the battle was promoted, and every sailor and soldier who was there received treble pay for that day. The battle was celebrated in Spanish poems, and later on relics of the battle were displayed in museums. In 1859 the Spanish Government granted the remaining survivors of the battle a pension for life.

The Spanish may have felt no disgrace in losing the battle, but the defeat that many Spanish captains had predicted was a bitter one, because they believed that it had been imposed on them by the French, who had bullied them into an unwelcome alliance. Trafalgar was to be the last time that Spain and Britain fought each other, and within three years the Spanish found that their French ally had turned enemy as Napoleon's troops invaded their country. It was the French occupation and rule, following the destruction of the cream of the Spanish Navy at Trafalgar, that caused lasting damage to Spain, since its American colonies seized their freedom; the loss of the bulk of its overseas empire was a death-blow to the Spanish economy.

For the French, blockaded closely and unable to concentrate ships in a sufficiently large fleet to challenge the British, the war at sea changed from grand strategies to small-scale actions. Often desperately fought between a handful of ships, or even in what were effectively duels between one ship and another, these naval battles added up to a war of attrition between, on the one side, the French Navy and pirates from various nations, both intent on destroying Britain's trade and, on the other, the British Navy, which was defending it. Although frequently hard pressed, the British built on the advantage afforded by Trafalgar and gradually gained the upper hand, with Britain becoming richer and more able to sustain its navy as trade became more secure – a trend that continued after the defeat of Napoleon.

With the ending of the war in 1815, many European countries had an influx of returning soldiers who were no longer needed, while in Britain in particular there were great numbers of returning sailors as well. Most of them were at first overjoyed, as the seaman John Nicol recalled: 'I was once more my own master, and felt so happy, I was like one bewildered. Did those on shore only experience half the sensations of a sailor at perfect liberty, after being seven years on board ship without a will of his own, they would not blame his eccentricities, but wonder he was not more foolish.'[26] The seamen were usually released with their back-pay and sometimes with prize money; in their euphoric state they were often easy prey. The song of the dock-side girls at Gosport in Hampshire in 1780 was still relevant nearly forty years later, and was probably still being sung then:

Sailors they get all the money,
Soldiers they get none but brass;
I do love a jolly sailor,
Soldiers they may kiss my arse.[27]

Many sailors lost all their money in the first few days ashore, and the results were all too obvious, as a commentator at the time of Waterloo complained:

At the conclusion of a war, or rather series of wars, which for twenty-three years have agitated and overwhelmed Europe with desolation, misery, and I had almost said despair, from which England, happy England, has alone been exempted, it is no doubt necessary and proper to pay off and reduce our Naval establishments, and to allow our brave seamen who have served so long, and fought their country's battles so manfully, to return to their homes; yet it is truly pitiable and lamentable to see how very few of these honest tars have brought either pay or prize-money with them – all, all is gone – spent, in a few days, what had required months and years to acquire, and now these poor fellows are wandering about London and all the out-ports, without money and without employment.[28]

At the peak of the war, the navy had been employing up to 145,000 men, but by 1817 the estimate of manpower required had dropped to around nineteen thousand – barely two thousand more than had fought at Trafalgar. The sad situation of returning sailors became a recurring theme of letters to newspapers and journals, and most often the government was rightly blamed for their distress, as in one letter to *The Naval Chronicle* in 1817:

> The government, my good Sir, have much to answer for: in these times of sad distress, the multitude of wandering sailors, begging *every day* at my door for bread, is truly lamentable; on beholding them, it fills me with the most poignant grief – half naked, without a shoe on their feet, and starving for hunger, declaring they can neither get work on shore nor on board: what a shame to the government of a nation, of the first rank in civilised Europe, to turn her brave defenders adrift, to taste the bitters of misery, and all for the sake of saving a few thousand pounds.[29]

Some of the paid-off seamen found other employment at sea, filling the gaps where crews of merchant ships and fishing vessels had lost sailors pressed into service with the navy, but there were far more sailors than were needed. Many had no chance of other employment in the continuing upheaval of agriculture and manufacturing that would become known as the Industrial Revolution, competing as they were against unemployed agricultural workers and returning soldiers. They were frequently reduced to begging or turned to crime to survive. As is often the case, the people who fought and won the war were regarded as a nuisance and a burden once the first wave of relief at the return of peace had ebbed away. Nelson himself had experienced it after the end of the American War of Independence in 1783, and in speaking about the navy as a whole, he had denounced the situation in a letter written in 1797: 'We are a neglected set, and, when peace comes, are shamefully treated.'[30]

In the years following the defeat of Napoleon, the seamen laid off from the navy were indeed shamefully treated. The king and Parliament found it far more convenient (and cheaper) to regard the Battle of Trafalgar as having been won by Nelson than by the thousands of men and the handful of women who had fought on that day. The triumph of 21 October 1805 was followed by many personal tragedies among the people who had made it possible. Just over a decade after the battle, the fate of many of them was summed up in a few poignant lines of verse:

Who is it knocks so gently at my door?
That looks so way-worn, desolate, and poor;
A paid-off Sailor, once his Country's pride
But now a wanderer on the highway's side;
Whose haggard looks real misery bespeak
Famine, and care, o'rspread his sun-burnt cheek;
'Help a poor Seaman,' is his suppliant cry,
'Grant me a pittance, lest for want I die –
'At Trafalgar, I play'd a Briton's part;
'Strength in my limbs, and courage in my heart:
'But now a-drift, distress has brought me low,
'As this poor wasted form will plainly shew.
'I little thought, the day great Nelson fell,
'That I should live so sad a tale to tell:
'Far better I had died that glorious morn,
'Than lived a wretch so miserably forlorn.'
Come in, my friend, and share a poor man's meal,
Curse on the caitiff [villain], with a heart of steel,
That cannot for your fate some pity feel.[31]

SHIPS AND THEIR CAPTAINS

The following is an alphabetical list of the ships that took part in the Battle of Trafalgar, giving their nationality, the nominal number of guns they carried (many carried extra ones) and the name of the ship's commander. **English** ship names are in **bold**, *French* ship names in *italics* and <u>Spanish</u> ship names are <u>underlined</u>.

Ship	Nationality	Rate	Commander
Achilles	English	74 guns	Captain Sir Richard King
Achille	French	74 guns	Captain Gabriel Denieport
Africa	English	64 guns	Captain Henry Digby
Agamemnon	English	64 guns	Captain Sir Edward Berry
Aigle	French	74 guns	Captain Pierre-Paul Gourrège
Ajax	English	74 guns	Lieutenant John Pilford
Algésiras	French	74 guns	Captain Laurent Le Tourneur
Argonauta	Spanish	80 guns	Captain Don Antonio Pareja
Argonaute	French	74 guns	Captain Jacques Epron
Argus	French	16 guns	Lieutenant Yves François Taillard
Bahama	Spanish	74 guns	Commodore Don Donisio Alcalá Galiano
Belleisle	English	74 guns	Captain William Hargood
Bellerophon	English	74 guns	Captain John Cooke
Berwick	French	74 guns	Captain Jean-Gilles Filhol-Camas
Britannia	English	100 guns	Captain Charles Bullen
Bucentaure	French	80 guns	Captain Jean-Jacques Magendie
Colossus	English	74 guns	Captain James Nicoll Morris
Conqueror	English	74 guns	Captain Israel Pellew
Cornélie	French	40 guns	Captain Jules François Martinencq

Ship	Nationality	Rate	Commander
Defence	English	74 guns	Captain George Johnstone Hope
Defiance	English	74 guns	Captain Philip Charles Durham
Dreadnought	English	98 guns	Captain John Conn
Duguay-Trouin	French	74 guns	Captain Claude Touffet
Entreprenante	English	8 guns	Lieutenant Robert Benjamin Young
Euryalus	English	36 guns	Captain Hon. Henry Blackwood
Formidable	French	80 guns	Captain Jean-Marie Letellier
Fougueux	French	74 guns	Captain Louis-Alexis Beaudouin
Furet	French	18 guns	Lieutenant Pierre Antoine Toussaint Demay
Hermione	French	40 guns	Captain Jean Michel Mahe
Héros	French	74 guns	Captain Jean-Baptiste-Joseph-René Poulain
Hortense	French	40 guns	Captain La Marre La Meillerie
Indomptable	French	80 guns	Captain Jean-Joseph Hubert
Intrépide	French	74 guns	Captain Louis-Antoine-Cyprien Infernet
Leviathan	English	74 guns	Captain Henry William Bayntun
Mars	English	74 guns	Captain George Duff
Minotaur	English	74 guns	Captain Charles John Moore Mansfield
Monarca	Spanish	74 guns	Captain Don Teodoro de Argumosa
Montañes	Spanish	74 guns	Captain Don Francisco Alcedo

Ship	Nationality	Rate	Commander
Mont-Blanc	French	74 guns	Captain Guillaume-Jean-Noël La Villegris
Naiad	English	38 guns	Captain Thomas Dundas
Neptune	English	98 guns	Captain Thomas Francis Fremantle
Neptune	French	80 guns	Commodore Esprit-Tranquille Maistral
Neptuno	Spanish	80 guns	Commodore Don Cayetano Valdés
Orion	English	74 guns	Captain Edward Codrington
Phoebe	English	36 guns	Captain Hon. Thomas Bladen Capel
Pickle	English	10 guns	Lieutenant John Richard Lapenotiere
Pluton	French	74 guns	Commodore Julien-Marie Cosmao Kerjulien
Polyphemus	English	64 guns	Captain Robert Redmill
Prince	English	98 guns	Captain Richard Grindall
Principe de Asturias	Spanish	112 guns	Captain Rafael de Hore
Rayo	Spanish	100 guns	Captain Don Enrique MacDonnell
Redoutable	French	74 guns	Captain Jean-Jacques-Etienne Lucas
Revenge	English	74 guns	Captain Robert Moorsom
Rhin	French	40 guns	Captain Michel Chesneau
Royal Sovereign	English	100 guns	Captain Edward Rotheram
San Agustín	Spanish	74 guns	Captain Don Felipe Jado Cagigal
San Francisco de Asís	Spanish	74 guns	Captain Don Luis de Flores

Ship	Nationality	Rate	Commander
<u>San Ildefonso</u>	Spanish	74 guns	Captain Don José de Vargas
<u>San Juan Nepomuceno</u>	Spanish	74 guns	Captain Don Cosmé Churruca
<u>San Justo</u>	Spanish	74 guns	Captain Don Miguel Gastón
<u>San Leandro</u>	Spanish	64 guns	Captain Don José Quevedo y Cheza
<u>Santa Ana</u>	Spanish	112 guns	Captain Don José Gardoqui
<u>Santísima Trinidad</u>	Spanish	130 guns	Commodore Don Francisco de Uriarte y Borja
Scipion	French	74 guns	Captain Charles Bérenger
Sirius	English	36 guns	Captain William Prowse
Spartiate	English	74 guns	Captain Sir Francis Laforey
Swiftsure	English	74 guns	Captain William George Rutherford
Swiftsure	French	74 guns	Captain C. E. L'Hospitalier-Villemadrin
Temeraire	English	98 guns	Captain Eliab Harvey
Thémis	French	32 guns	Captain Nicolas Jugan
Thunderer	English	74 guns	Lieutenant John Stockham
Tonnant	English	80 guns	Captain Charles Tyler
Victory	English	100 guns	Captain Thomas Masterman Hardy

NOTES

PROLOGUE: OPENING FIRE, pp. xix–xxiii

1 Fraser 1906, pp. 213–14.
2 Fraser 1906, p. 214.
3 Fraser 1906, pp. 214–15.
4 Fraser 1906, pp. 215–17.
5 Fraser 1906, p. 217.

ONE: INVASION, pp. 1–12

1 Thiers 1845, p. 103.
3 Wheeler and Broadley 1908, vol. 2, p. 213.
4 Broadley and Bartelot 1909, p. 148.
5 Fremantle (ed.) 1935, p. 348.
6 Wheeler and Broadley 1908, vol. 1, p. 185.
7 Wheeler and Broadley 1908, vol. 2, p. 223.

TWO: BEFORE THE BATTLE, pp. 13–28

1 Nicolas 1846, p. 5.
2 Pemberton 1929, pp. 191–3.
3 *The Naval Chronicle* 1805, vol. 14, pp. 170–1.
4 *The Naval Chronicle* 1805, vol. 14, pp. 169–70.
5 *The Times* 10 August 1805, p. 2.
6 Desbrière 1907, p. 114.
7 Desbrière 1907, p. 117.
8 Hughes (ed.) 1957, p. 161.
9 *Bell's Weekly Messenger* 3 November 1805, p. 347.
10 Harrison 1806, p. 108.

THREE: THE STAGE IS SET, pp. 29–66

1 Moorhouse (ed.) 1910, p. 281.
2 Moorhouse (ed.) 1910, p. 254.
3 Moorhouse (ed.) 1910, p. 258.
4 Desbrière 1907, appendix, p. 122.

5 Lovell 1879, pp. 20–1 (Badcock later changed his surname to Lovell).
6 Burney 1815, p. 40.
7 Raigersfeld 1929, p. 24.
8 Nicolas 1845b, p. 43.
9 Raigersfeld 1929, pp. 20–1.
10 Ashton 1886, pp. 295–6.
11 Ashton 1886, p. 452.
12 Nicolas 1846, p. 60.
13 Nicolas 1846, pp. 90–1.
14 *The Times* 11 October 1805, p. 3.
15 Jackson (ed.) 1900, pp. 322–3.
16 Fraser 1906, p. 82, fn.
17 Jackson (ed.) 1900, p. 160.
18 Jackson (ed.) 1900, p. 160.
19 Fraser 1906, p. 82, fn.
20 Cumby 1899, p. 719.
21 Cumby 1899, p. 719.
22 Lovell 1879, p. 44 (Badcock later changed his surname to Lovell).
23 Nicolas 1846, p. 132.
24 Nicolas 1846, pp. 132–3.
25 Nicolas 1846, p. 132.
26 Beresford and Wilson, 1897, pp. 210–11.
27 Desbrière 1907, appendix, p. 122.
28 Desbrière 1907, appendix, p. 122.

FOUR: INTO ACTION, pp. 67–92

1 Des Touches 1905, p. 417.
2 Robinson 1858, pp. 205–6.
3 Robinson 1858, pp. 205–6.
4 Lovell 1879, p. 44 (Badcock later changed his surname to Lovell).
5 Lovell 1879, p. 45 (Badcock later changed his surname to Lovell).
6 Taylor 1950, p. 290.
7 Nicolas 1846, pp. 139–40.
8 Taylor 1950, p. 291.
9 Lovell 1879, p. 45 (Badcock later changed his name to Lovell).
10 Account published under the pseudonym 'Calcuttensis', in *Notes and Queries*, 6th series, vol. 4, quoted in Wyndham-Quin 1912, p. 145.
11 Account published under the pseudonym 'Calcuttensis', in *Notes and Queries*, 6th series, vol. 4, quoted in Wyndham-Quin 1912, p. 145.
12 Tucker 1844, p. 193.
13 Tucker 1844, p. 414.
14 Tucker 1844, p. 414.
15 *The Times* 13 May 1863, p. 9.
16 Robinson 1836, pp. 14–16.
17 Letter from John Brown on board the *Victory* to his friend Thomas Windever, dated 28 December 1805, in Thursfield (ed.) 1951, p. 364.

18 Letter from John Brown on board the *Victory* to his friend Thomas Windever, dated 28 December 1805, in Thursfield (ed.) 1951, p. 364.
19 Ellis 1866, p. 4.
20 Galdós 1884, pp. 129–30.
21 Report of Bazin, second-in-command of the *Fougueux*, in Desbrière 1907 appendix, p. 217.
22 Taylor 1950, p. 294.
23 Taylor 1950, p. 294.
24 Nicolas 1846, p. 150.

FIVE: FIRST SHOT, pp. 93–108
1 Nicolas 1846, p. 241, fn. 9.
2 Pemberton 1929, pp. 183–5.
3 Fraser 1913, p. 227.
4 Ellis 1866, p. 5.
5 Desbrière 1907, appendix, p. 179.
6 Lovell 1879, p. 46 (Badcock later changed his surname to Lovell).
7 Robinson 1836, p. 20
8 Lovell 1879, p. 46 (Badcock later changed his surname to Lovell).
9 Pemberton 1929, pp. 183–5.
10 Collingwood 1829, p. 124.
11 Nicolas 1846, p. 151.
12 Fraser 1913, p. 247.
13 Fraser 1913, p. 249.
14 Fraser 1913, p. 249.

SIX: SECOND STRIKE, pp. 109–137
1 Robinson 1836, pp. 27–8.
2 Fraser 1913, p. 249.
3 Collingwood 1829, pp. 127–8.
4 *The Times* 21 October 1912, p. 7.
5 Collingwood 1829, pp. 128–9.
6 Letter of Colonel (previously Lieutenant) Owen cited in Allen (ed.) 1841, pp. 140–2.
7 Account of Marine Lieutenant Paul Harris Nicolas, originally published in the *Bijou* periodical for 1829, and reprinted in Allen (ed.) 1841, pp. 281–2.
8 Account of Marine Lieutenant Paul Harris Nicolas, originally published in the *Bijou* periodical for 1829, and reprinted in Allen (ed.) 1841, p. 282.
9 Cumby 1899, pp. 721–3.
10 Cumby 1899, p. 723.
11 Desbrière 1907, appendix, p. 248.
12 Mackenzie 1913, p. 167.
13 Robinson 1836, pp. 18–19.
14 Beatty 1807, pp. 26–7.
15 Beatty 1807, pp. 27–9.
16 Nicolas 1845a, p. 332.

17 Lovell 1879, p. 50 (Badcock later changed his surname to Lovell).
18 Mahan 1897, p. 383.
19 Beatty 1807, p. 30.
20 Desbrière 1907, appendix, p. 199, fn. 1.
21 Desbrière 1907, appendix, pp. 199–200.
22 The French naval historian, Admiral Jurien de la Gravière, as quoted in Fraser 1906, p. 116.
23 Page 21 of 'In the days of Trafalgar, extracts from the journal of Second Lieut. L. B. Halloran, Royal Marines, on board H.M.S. "Britannia"', an account published by his granddaughter in *English Illustrated Magazine* 34, 1905–6, pp. 18–23.
24 *The Times* 19 October 1905, p. 5.
25 Anonymous officer quoted in Fraser, 1906, p. 270.

SEVEN: SLAUGHTER, pp. 138–155
1 Letter by Richard Francis Roberts to his parents, dated 22 October 1805, from the *Victory* at sea, quoted in Moorhouse (ed.) 1910, p. 293.
2 Robinson 1836, p. 36.
3 Witnessed by Lieutenant John Pasco, in Nicolas 1846, p. 150; confirmed by Blackwood himself in Blackwood 1833, pp. 11 and 12.
4 Beatty 1807, p. 34.
5 Beatty 1807, p. 36.
6 Gatty and Gatty 1842, pp. 185–6.
7 Gatty and Gatty 1842, p. 186.
8 Beatty 1807, pp. 37–9.
9 Fraser 1906, pp. 182–3.
10 Beatty 1807, p. 31.
11 Desbrière 1907, appendix, pp. 200–1.
12 Jackson (ed.) 1900, p. 225.
13 Beatty 1807, pp. 32–3.
14 Desbrière 1907, appendix, p. 201.
15 Desbrière 1907, appendix, pp. 201–2.
16 Desbrière 1907, appendix, p. 181.
17 Desbrière 1907, appendix, p. 202.
18 Desbrière 1907, appendix, p. 215.
19 Desbrière 1907, appendix, p. 215.

EIGHT: VISIONS OF HELL, pp. 158–179
1 *The Naval Chronicle* 1806, vol. 15, pp. 16–17.
2 Anonymous seaman quoted in Fraser 1913, pp. 271–2.
3 Des Touches 1905, p. 424.
4 Nicolas 1846, p. 241, fn. 9.
5 Desbrière 1907, appendix, p. 234.
6 Story supposedly related by Mr Chevers, surgeon of the *Tonnant*, in *The Naval Chronicle* 1805, vol. 14, pp. 494–5.
7 Hoffman 1901, p. 218.
8 Jackson (ed.) 1900, p. 257.

9 Fraser 1913, p. 323.
10 Account published under the pseudonym 'Calcuttensis', in *Notes and Queries*, 6th series, vol. 4, quoted in Wyndham-Quin 1912, pp. 144–5.
11 Account of Marine Lieutenant Paul Harris Nicolas, originally published in the *Bijou* periodical for 1829 and reprinted in Allen (ed.) 1841, p. 285.
12 Cumby 1899, pp. 723–4.
13 Cumby 1899, p. 724.
14 Cumby 1899, pp. 724–5.
15 Cumby 1899, p. 725.
16 Smith 1923, p. 118.
17 Robinson 1836, pp. 19–20.
18 Robinson 1836, p. 25.
19 Robinson 1836, p. 26.
20 Letter from Pernot, in Dillon 1956, appendix 1, pp. 57–8.

NINE: SURRENDER, pp. 180–195

1 Smith 1923, pp. 118–19.
2 Desbrière 1907, appendix, pp. 202–3.
3 Beatty 1807, p. 56.
4 Collingwood 1829, p. 130.
5 Fraser 1906, p. 259.
6 Desbrière 1907, appendix, pp. 234–5.
7 Page 329 of 'Le Contre-Amiral Magon', *Revue Maritime* 134 (1897), pp. 66–100 and 287–335.
8 Desbrière 1907, appendix, p. 235.
9 Hoffman 1901, pp. 213–14.
10 Hoffman 1901, p. 214.
11 Hoffman 1901, p. 214.
12 Fraser 1913, p. 321.
13 Hoffman 1901, p. 214.
14 Desbrière 1907, appendix, p. 248.
15 Letter from Marine Colonel (previously Lieutenant) Owen in Allen (ed.) 1841, pp. 143–4.
16 Letter from Marine Colonel (previously Lieutenant) Owen in Allen (ed.) 1841, p. 144.
17 Allen (ed.) 1841, p. 130.
18 Murray 1846, p. 61.
19 Murray 1846, pp. 61–2.
20 *Gibraltar Chronicle*, 11 January 1806.
21 Murray 1846, p. 62.
22 Murray 1846, p. 63.
23 Beatty 1807, pp. 39–40.
24 Beatty 1807, pp. 40–1.
25 Beatty 1807, pp. 41–2.

TEN: LOST AND WON, pp. 196–216

1 Nicolas 1846, p. 314.
2 Beatty 1807, p. 42.
3 Beatty 1807, pp. 42–6.
4 Des Touches 1905, p. 419.
5 Des Touches 1905, pp. 419–20.
6 By permission of the National Maritime Museum, Greenwich, manuscript reference LBK/38.
7 Beatty 1807, pp. 56–8.
8 *Gibraltar Chronicle* 2 November 1805.
9 Beatty 1807, pp. 46–7.
10 Beatty 1807, pp. 47–50.
11 Beatty 1807, pp. 50–1.
12 Beatty 1807, pp. 51–2.
13 Southey 1813, p. 346.
14 Desbrière 1907, appendix, p. 235.
15 Des Touches 1905, p. 420.
16 Des Touches 1905, p. 419.
17 Desbrière 1907, appendix, pp. 360–1.
18 Letter from Marine Colonel (previously Lieutenant) Owen in Allen (ed.) 1841, pp. 144–5.
19 Account of Marine Lieutenant Paul Harris Nicolas, originally published in the *Bijou* periodical for 1829 and reprinted in Allen (ed.) 1841, p. 287.
20 Fraser 1906, pp. 220–1.
21 Pages 22–3 of 'In the days of Trafalgar, extracts from the journal of Second Lieut. L. B. Halloran, Royal Marines, on board H.M.S. "Britannia"', an account published by his granddaughter in *English Illustrated Magazine* 34, 1905–6, pp. 18–23.
22 Fraser 1906, pp. 221–2.
23 Fraser 1906, pp. 222–3.
24 Fraser 1906, pp. 223–5.
25 Ekins 1824, p. 279.

ELEVEN: HURRICANE, pp. 217–255

1 *Bell's Weekly Messenger* 3 November 1805, p. 351.
2 *The Naval Chronicle* 1816, vol. 36, p. 372.
3 Jackson (ed.) 1900, p. 143.
4 Account of Marine Lieutenant Paul Harris Nicolas, originally published in the *Bijou* periodical for 1829 and reprinted in Allen (ed.) 1841, p. 285.
5 Account of Marine Lieutenant Paul Harris Nicolas, originally published in the *Bijou* periodical for 1829 and reprinted in Allen (ed.) 1841, pp. 285–6.
6 Robinson 1836, pp. 21–2.
7 Dillon 1956, p. 52.
8 Account of Marine Lieutenant Paul Harris Nicolas, originally published in the *Bijou* periodical for 1829 and reprinted in Allen (ed.) 1841, p. 289.
9 Account of Marine Lieutenant Paul Harris Nicolas, originally published in the *Bijou* periodical for 1829 and reprinted in Allen (ed.) 1841, pp. 289–90.

10 Jackson (ed.) 1900, p. 326.
11 Fraser 1906, p. 298.
12 Beatty 1807, pp. 62–3.
13 *The Western Gazette* 10 December 1864, p. 3.
14 Jackson (ed.) 1900, p. 283.
15 Fraser 1906, pp. 299–301.
16 Desbrière 1907, appendix, pp. 237–9.
17 By permission of the National Maritime Museum, Greenwich, manuscript reference JOD/41.
18 Fraser 1906, p. 301.
19 Blackwood 1833, p. 13.
20 Cumby 1899, p. 726.
21 Cumby 1899, p. 727.
22 By permission of the National Maritime Museum, Greenwich, manuscript reference JOD/41.
23 Desbrière 1907, appendix, pp. 239–40.
24 Desbrière 1907, appendix, p. 241.
25 By permission of the National Maritime Museum, Greenwich, manuscript reference JOD/41.
26 By permission of the National Maritime Museum, Greenwich, manuscript reference JOD/41.
27 Jackson (ed.) 1900, p. 193.
28 Gardiner (ed.) 1997a, p. 166.
29 Jackson (ed.) 1900, p. 173.
30 Fraser 1906, p. 314.
31 Prothero 1890, p. 769.
32 Fraser 1906, pp. 316–17.
33 Fraser 1906, pp. 317–18.
34 *The Naval Chronicle* 1806, vol. 15, pp. 207–8.
35 Des Touches 1905, pp. 421–3.
36 Jackson (ed.) 1900, p. 281.
37 Desbrière 1907, appendix, p. 226.
38 By permission of the National Maritime Museum, Greenwich, manuscript reference LBK/38.
39 Nicolas 1846, p. 251.
40 Gardiner (ed.) 1997a, p. 166.
41 Dillon 1956, p. 59.
42 *The Naval Chronicle* 1816, vol. 36, pp. 372–3.
43 *The Naval Chronicle* 1807, vol. 18, pp. 466–7.
44 *The Naval Chronicle* 1807, vol. 18, p. 467.
45 *Gibraltar Chronicle* 28 December 1805.
46 *Gibraltar Chronicle* 9 November 1805.
47 Fraser 1906, p. 346. The quotation is part of a longer poem in Hardy's epic drama, *The Dynasts*. Thomas Hardy was a distant relation of Thomas Masterman Hardy, captain of the *Victory*.

TWELVE: THE MESSENGERS, pp. 256–281

1 Bullocke (ed.) 1935, p. 321.
2 Bourchier 1873, p. 70.
3 Jackson (ed.) 1900, p. 319.
4 Kennedy 1951, p. 284.
5 Baring-Gould 1908, pp. 443–4.
6 Des Touches 1905, pp. 425–6.
7 Broadley and Bartelot 1909, pp. 270–1.
8 Granville 1916, p. 131.
9 Marsden 1838, pp. 116–17.
10 Lord Fitzharris's notebook, quoted in Malmesbury (ed.) 1844, p. 341, fn.
11 Fraser 1986, p. 330.
12 Granville 1916, p. 133.
13 Farington 1924, p. 123.
14 Farington 1924, p. 124.
15 *Gibraltar Chronicle Extraordinary* 24 October 1805.
16 *Gibraltar Chronicle Extraordinary* 24 October 1805.
17 Quoted on the front page of *Trewman's Exeter Flying Post* 21 November 1805.
18 Jennings (ed.) 1884a, pp. 340–1.
19 *Bell's Weekly Messenger* 10 November 1805, p. 354.
20 From a private letter written in Paris on 21 November and published in *Bell's Weekly Messenger* 8 December 1805, p. 385.
21 Rose 1923, pp. 548–9.
22 Thiers 1845, pp. 95–6.

THIRTEEN: AFTERMATH, pp. 282–307

1 Fraser 1906, p. 359.
2 *The Naval Chronicle* 1805, vol. 14, pp. 497–8.
3 Malmesbury (ed.) 1844, p. 342.
4 Quoted in Terraine 1976, p. 203, translated from the Russian by J. N. Westwood from the original in V. Bronevskii (1836) *Zapiski morskogo ofitsera*, Russian Imperial Academy, St Petersburg, Part I, p. 60.
5 *The Naval Chronicle* 1805, vol. 14, p. 499.
6 *The Naval Chronicle* 1805, vol. 14, p. 499.
7 *Bell's Weekly Messenger* 10 November 1805, p. 355.
8 *Bell's Weekly Messenger* 10 November 1805, p. 355.
9 *The Lincoln, Rutland and Stamford Mercury* 15 November 1805.
10 Southey 1813, pp. 344–5.
11 Coleridge 1866, pp. 380–1.
12 *Bell's Weekly Messenger* 1 December 1805, p. 382.
13 Dillon 1956, pp. 50–1.
14 Lady Londonderry, quoted in Ekins 1824, p. 288.
15 Fremantle (ed.) 1935, pp. 414–15.
16 Letter to Admiral Young, dated November 1805, published in Marsden 1838, p. 119, fn.
17 *The Naval Chronicle* 1805, vol. 14, p. 507.

18 Nicolas 1846, p. 235.
19 Nicolas 1846, p. 236.
20 Nicolas 1846, p. 236.
21 Fraser 1906, pp. 225–6.
22 Account of Marine Lieutenant Paul Harris Nicolas, originally published in the *Bijou* periodical for 1829, and reprinted in Allen (ed.) 1841, pp. 291–2.
23 Beatty 1807, p. 63.
24 *The Naval Chronicle* 1805, vol. 14, p. 427.
25 *The Naval Chronicle* 1805, vol. 14, pp. 491–3.
26 Ferrer de Couto 1851, pp. 144–5.
27 Account of Marine Lieutenant Paul Harris Nicolas, originally published in the *Bijou* periodical for 1829 and reprinted in Allen (ed.) 1841, p. 292.
28 *The Naval Chronicle* 1806, vol. 15, p. 293.
29 *The Naval Chronicle* 1806, vol. 15, pp. 274–5.
30 *The Naval Chronicle* 1806, vol. 15, pp. 292–3.
31 *The Mariner's Mirror* 1923, vol. 9, p. 60.
32 *The Mariner's Mirror* 1923, vol. 9, p. 60.
33 Smith 1923, p. 116.
34 *The Naval Chronicle* 1806, vol. 15, p. 119.
35 *The Naval Chronicle* 1806, vol. 15, p. 119.
36 Fraser 1913, pp. 258–9.
37 Brewer 1805, pp. 433–5.

FOURTEEN: FRUITS OF VICTORY, pp. 308–325

1 'Home-Thoughts from the Sea' by Robert Browning (1812–89): Browning, 1888, vol. 6, p. 97.
2 *The Naval Chronicle* 1806, vol. 15, pp. 34–5.
3 Beatty 1807, p. 72.
4 Granville (ed.) 1916, p. 154.
5 *The Times* 2 January 1806.
6 *The Times* 2 January 1806.
7 Beatty 1807, pp. 76–7.
8 *The Gentleman's Magazine* 1806, vol. 76, pp. 68–9.
9 Granville (ed.) 1916, p. 155.
10 Farington 1924, p. 138.
11 Oman 1947, p. 648.
12 *The Annual Register* 1807, p. 433.
13 *The Naval Chronicle* 1805, vol. 14, p. 464.
14 Advert in *Trewman's Exeter Flying Post* 26 December 1805, p. 4.
15 *Illustrated London News* 28 September 1861, p. 317.
16 *The Naval Chronicle* 1805, vol. 14, p. 466.
17 Rowbotham 1937, p. 366.
18 Nicolas 1846, pp. ccxxxix–ccxl.
19 Harvey 1909, p. 42.
20 Moorhouse (ed.) 1910, p. 280.
21 Fremantle (ed.) 1935, p. 418.

22 Fremantle (ed.) 1935, p. 418.
23 Fraser 1906, p. 399.
24 Farington 1924, p. 227.
25 *The Naval Chronicle* 1806, vol. 15, p. 456.

FIFTEEN: HEROES AND VILLAINS, pp. 326–350

1 Nicolas 1846, p. 80.
2 Collingwood 1829, p. 262.
3 Kennedy 1951, p. 333.
4 Kennedy 1951, p. 333.
5 Woodman 2001, p. 10.
6 Kemp (ed.) 1976, p. 124.
7 Jennings (ed.) 1884b, pp. 233–4.
8 Nicolas 1844, pp. 273–4.
9 *The Naval Chronicle* 1805, vol. 14, p. 478.
10 *The Naval Chronicle* 1805, vol. 14, p. 478.
11 *The Naval Chronicle* 1805, vol. 14, p. 478.
12 *The Naval Chronicle* 1805, vol. 14, p. 479.
13 *The Naval Chronicle* 1805, vol. 14, p. 479.
14 Nicolas 1844, p. 397.
15 Howarth and Howarth 1988, p. 371.
16 *The Times* 23 October 1905, p. 5.
17 *The Times* 23 October 1905, p. 5.
18 *The Times* 21 October 1905, p. 14.
19 *The Times* 21 October 1905, p. 14.
20 *The Times* 21 October 1905, p. 14.
21 *The Naval Review* 1925, vol. 13, p. 35.
22 Robinson 1836, p. 105.
23 *The Bridgwater Standard, Burnham Times, and West of England Gazette* 16 December 1863, p. 6.
24 Thiers 1845, p. 95.
25 *Illustrated London News* 2 April 1892, vol. 100, p. 419.
26 Nicol 1822, p. 196.
27 A bowdlerised version is quoted in Gardner 1906, p. 16.
28 *The Naval Chronicle* 1815, vol. 34, p. 395.
29 *The Naval Chronicle* 1817, vol. 37, p. 376.
30 Letter to Dixon Hoste 30 June 1797, in Nicolas 1845a, p. 402.
31 *The Naval Chronicle* 1817, vol. 38, pp. 71–2.

ACKNOWLEDGEMENTS

It is a pleasure to acknowledge the help of many people and organisations during the writing of this book. The staff of numerous libraries and archives gave me invaluable assistance, most notably the Caird Library at the National Maritime Museum, Greenwich; the British Library; the Public Record Office; University of Bristol Arts and Social Sciences Library; Exeter University Library; Exmouth Branch of the Devon Library and Information Services; the Library of the Devon and Exeter Institution; Devon Record Office; Somerset Record Office; the Admiralty Library of the Ministry of Defence; the Wellcome Institute for the History of Medicine Library; the Centre for Oxfordshire Studies; the Naval Studies Section of Plymouth Central Library; and the Service Historique de la Marine, Château de Vincennes, Paris. I am also grateful to all the staff of the St Thomas Branch of the Devon Library and Information Services, especially Jill Hughes, Lisa Podbury, Sarah O'Neill and Judith Prescott; the staff of the London Library, especially Lisa Seager; and the staff of the Somerset Studies Library, particularly David Bromwich and Wilf Deckner.

Dr Ralph Jackson of the British Museum, Glynis Robertson and Alex Leith of 3BMTV, Peter J. Milford of Newnet plc, Sir Ludovic Kennedy, Stuart Davison, Mike Dash, Julian Stockwin, Clare Gillett, and Gill and Alfred Sims all provided help with various aspects of research, for which I am most grateful. Gillian Rickard of *Kent Genealogical, Historical and Biographical Research* and Dan and Helen Adam of *Your Scottish Kin* undertook valuable genealogical research. I also owe a debt of thanks to Lord de Saumarez and to Mr W. R. Serjeant, Archivist to Lord de Saumarez, for information about Ann Hopping/Nancy Perriam. Further information about Nancy Perriam was provided by the staff of Exmouth Museum. Thanks also to Sue and Tony Hall for their practical help.

In Gibraltar I must acknowledge Mrs B. Soiza of the Gibraltar Heritage Trust; Moira Dalmedo and Stephen Davenport of the Rock Hotel; Claire Valarino, Geraldine Finlayson and Dr Darren Fa of Gibraltar Museum; and Ann and Tito Benady. I am particularly indebted to Lorna Swift of the Garrison Library and Dennis Beiso of the Gibraltar Archives. Special thanks must also go to Charles Rosado and Pepe Rosado for ensuring that my time in Gibraltar and the forays along the Spanish coast were enjoyable, as well as rewarding.

I am grateful to the National Maritime Museum Greenwich for permission to publish extracts from manuscripts held there, and to the Navy Records Society for permission to use quotations from their publications. Dr John N. Westwood also kindly gave permission to quote from his translation of the words of Admiral Seniavin. Celia Levett had the responsibility for copy-editing, David Atkinson undertook the index while Catherine Hill was the desk editor. Thanks are also due to Roger Cazalet, Cecilia Duraes, Alison Menzies, Viv Redman, John Turnbull and the rest of the wonderful team at Time Warner.

My greatest thanks must be to Bill Hamilton, Sara Fisher, Ben Mason and everyone at A. M. Heath in London; to Emma Parry of Carlisle and Co. in the US; to Richard Beswick at Time Warner UK; to Rick Kot at Penguin US; and to Lesley Adkins for much editing, translation, taking on numerous chores, criticism and constant support.

SELECTED READING

'The past is a foreign country: they do things differently there.' These opening words of *The Go-Between* by L. P. Hartley are as true of the cusp of the eighteenth and nineteenth centuries as they are of the time of the ancient Britons or the Anglo-Saxons. The people of the period of the wars with the French thought, acted and spoke in ways that we would now regard as alien. Women of all classes wore no knickers beneath their skirts because they were not regarded as respectable items of clothing; only later in the nineteenth century would they become fashionable, being adopted first by young girls and prostitutes. There was no public healthcare, no concept of 'social welfare', and with the exception of those countries in the throes of revolution, all European societies had rigid class structures that were usually based on breeding rather than wealth. The lowest classes were slaves in all but name; sometimes they were worse off than the actual slaves owned by some of the upper classes. Oysters, now an expensive delicacy, were then so common that only the lower classes ate them. Steam power and the use of gas were in their infancy; electricity was still misunderstood; oil, nuclear and solar energy were unknown; but the most common, most flexible and most reliable source of power was muscle-power, provided by men, women, children and animals.

It was a time of social upheaval, with secular governments being formed for the very first time, and major conflicts between the *citizens* of France, led by an Emperor of the French (not 'Emperor of France'), and the *subjects* of the Catholic and Protestant kings of the European monarchies. Intellectuals were discussing everything, trying to make sense of a planet about which, in comparison with modern knowledge, they knew virtually nothing. At the same time they also looked for a morality and a philosophy to replace the failing superstitious piety that had maintained this state of ignorance for so long. From the intimately personal to the public and political, it was a very different world, yet because the written languages of the time are still easily read today and because modern costume dramas, using modern speech and accents, greatly reduce the feeling of strangeness in portrayals of the period, it is easy to form a false impression that life two hundred years ago was closer to life today than it actually was. When reading anything about naval warfare at the beginning of the nineteenth century, whether it is a modern synthesis or a two-hundred-year-old record that has survived from that time, it is useful to pause occasionally and remember how the world has changed in the last five or ten years and how much more it has changed in the last two centuries.

Accessible books that cover events immediately before the Battle of Trafalgar include *The Terror before Trafalgar* by Tom Pocock, and *Trafalgar, Countdown to Battle 1803–1805* by Alan Schom. The wider context is presented in *Maritime Power and the Struggle for Freedom: Naval Campaigns that Shaped the Modern World 1788–1851* by Peter Padfield.

Stephen Biesty's Cross-Sections: Man-of-War by Stephen Biesty and Richard Platt is an excellent visual primer of life in the navy during the Napoleonic period, while *Life in Nelson's Navy* by Dudley Pope and *Sea Life in Nelson's Time* by John Masefield give vivid accounts of the frequent privations and infrequent pleasures of a sailor's life. *Heart of Oak: A Sailor's Life in Nelson's Navy* by James McGuane is an excellent photographic essay based on objects surviving from that period, and *Medicine Under Sail* by Zachary Friedenberg gives a good overview of naval surgeons and the problems they faced. A handy and readable reference is *The Illustrated Companion to Nelson's Navy* by Nicholas Blake and Richard Lawrence. More academic but nevertheless accessible accounts are to be found in *Nelson's Navy: The Ships, Men and Organisation 1793–1815* by Brian Lavery, and *The Wooden World: An Anatomy of the Georgian Navy* by N. A. M. Rodger.

The accounts of men who actually served in the navy around the time of Trafalgar often provide surprising details about life on board ship. These include *Jack Nastyface: Memoirs of an English Seaman* by William Robinson (which is a modern reprint of the earlier title, *Nautical Economy*); *Nelsonian Reminiscences: Leaves from Memory's Log, A Dramatic Eye-Witness Account of the War at Sea 1795–1810* by G. S. Parsons, *The Life and Adventures of John Nicol, Mariner*, edited by Tim Flannery; *A Sailor of King George* by Frederick Hoffman and *Above and Under Hatches: The Recollections of James Anthony Gardner*, edited by R. V. Hamilton and J. K. Laughton.

Research into the experiences of women aboard navy ships has only been done systematically in recent years. Some information about such women around the time of Trafalgar can be found in *Female Tars: Women Aboard Ship in the Age of Sail* by Suzanne Stark, *Heroines and Harlots: Women at Sea in the Great Age of Sail* by David Cordingly; and *She Captains: Heroines and Hellions of the Sea* by Joan Druett.

Several of the ships at Trafalgar have had books devoted to them, including *H.M.S. Victory* by Kenneth Fenwick; *Nelson's Favourite: HMS Agamemnon at War 1781–1809* by Anthony Deane; *The First Bellerophon* by C. A. Pengelly; and *Billy Ruffian* by David Cordingly. *The Construction and Fitting of the Sailing Man of War 1650–1850* by Peter Goodwin gives detailed and well-illustrated coverage of the type of ships that fought at

Trafalgar. *Trafalgar and the Spanish Navy* by John Harbron deals specifically with the Spanish ships.

There are many books that examine the naval strategy and tactics of the period, including *Nelson's War* by Peter Padfield, *Nelson against Napoleon: From the Nile to Copenhagen, 1798–1801*, edited by Robert Gardiner; *The Campaign of Trafalgar 1803-1805*, also edited by Robert Gardiner; and *Nelson's Battles: The Art of Victory in the Age of Sail* by Nicholas Tracy. *Seamanship in the Age of Sail* by John Harland with Mark Myers is a well-illustrated account of its subject, which provides an understanding of the possibilities and limitations of ship-to-ship warfare at the time of Trafalgar.

The classic work on the invasion threat to Britain is *Napoleon and the Invasion of England: The Story of the Great Terror* by H. F. B. Wheeler and A. M. Broadley. The subject is also dealt with in *The French Are Coming! The Invasion Scare of 1803–5* by Peter Lloyd, and in *Britain at Bay: Defence against Bonaparte, 1803–14* by Richard Glover. *Secret Service: British Agents in France 1792–1815* by Elizabeth Sparrow is a good account of the espionage of the period, which is also covered by *Most Secret and Confidential: Intelligence in the Age of Nelson* by Steven Maffeo.

There have been many biographies of Nelson. No single volume that has been collected and cherished over the years can do him complete justice, simply because of the sheer quantity of material, including not only what he wrote himself but what others wrote about him. For an in-depth study of the man, a good place to start is the classic *Nelson* by Carola Oman. This could be followed by more modern biographies such as *Horatio Nelson* by Tom Pocock, and *Nelson: The Man and the Legend* by Terry Coleman, who takes a different viewpoint from most other biographers. For a rounded view, it is also necessary to read *Nelson's Women* by Tom Pocock; *Fields of Fire: A Life of Sir William Hamilton* by David Constantine; and *Beloved Emma: The Life of Emma, Lady Hamilton* by Flora Fraser. *The*

Nelson Encyclopedia by Colin White is an essential reference work and is also very readable. If only one biography of Nelson is to be read, it has to be *Nelson: Love and Fame* by Edgar Vincent.

Napoleon has also had many biographers. *Napoleon Bonaparte* by Alan Schom and *Napoleon: A Biography* by Frank McLynn are particularly readable, as is *Napoleon and Josephine: An Improbable Marriage* by Evangeline Bruce.

Great Storms by Carr Laughton and V. Heddon, which has a chapter on the storm after Trafalgar, is the only book to cover this subject in any detail. More recent analysis of the storm is contained in three journal articles by D. A. Wheeler: 'The Trafalgar storm 22–29 October 1805' in *The Meteorological Magazine*; 'The weather at the Battle of Trafalgar' in *Weather*; and 'The Weather of the European Atlantic seaboard during October 1805' in *Climatic Change*.

Apart from the non-fiction books about naval warfare during the Napoleonic period, the number of novels on the subject is growing. The Jack Aubrey series by Patrick O'Brian, of which the first is *Master and Commander*, gives an accurate portrayal of naval warfare and conveys a flavour of how different late eighteenth- and early nineteenth-century society was from that of today. Also to be recommended is the Thomas Kydd series of novels by Julian Stockwin (the first one is simply called *Kydd*), which chronicles the lives and adventures of ordinary seamen rather than concentrating on the officers.

BIBLIOGRAPHY

Although this is not a comprehensive list of all the books, articles and manuscripts that were consulted during the preparation of this book, this bibliography includes the sources cited in the notes and those named in the selected reading.

Allen, J. (ed.), 1841, *Memoir of the Life and Services of Admiral Sir William Hargood, G.C.B., G.C.H., Compiled From Authentic Documents Under the Direction of Lady Hargood by Joseph Allen Esq.*, Greenwich

Ashton, J., 1886, *The Dawn of the XIXth Century in England: A Social Sketch of the Times*, London

Baring-Gould, S., 1908, *Cornish Characters and Strange Events*, London

Beatty, W., 1807, *Authentic Narrative of the Death of Lord Nelson: with the circumstances preceding, attending, and subsequent to, that event; the Professional Report on His Lordship's Wound; and several interesting anecdotes*, London

Beresford, C. W. D. and Wilson, H. W., 1897, *Nelson and his Times*, London

Biesty, S. and Platt, R., 1993, *Stephen Biesty's Cross-Sections: Man-of-War*, London

Blackwood, H., 1833, 'Memoir of Vice-Admiral the Honourable Sir Henry Blackwood, Bart. K. C. B., K. G. H., *Blackwood's Edinburgh Magazine*, 34, pp. 1–24

Blake, N. and Lawrence, R., 1999, *The Illustrated Companion to Nelson's Navy*, London

Bourchier, J. B. (ed.), 1873, *Memoir of the Life of Admiral Sir Edward Codrington, with selections from his public and private correspondence*, vol. 1, London

Brewer, G., 1805, 'Account of the Battle of Trafalgar: In a Letter from Jack Handspeck, on board the Temeraire, to his landlord, Bob Spunyarn, at the Common Hard, Portsmouth, *European Magazine and London Review*, 48, pp. 433–5

Broadley, A. M. and Bartelot, R. G., 1909, *Nelson's Hardy: His Life, Letters and Friends*, London

Browning, R. 1888, *The Poetical Works of Robert Browning*: vol. VI, *Dramatic Lyrics: Luria*, London

Bruce, E., 1995, *Napoleon and Josephine: An Improbable Marriage*, London

Bullocke, J. G. (ed.), 1935, *The Tomlinson Papers: Selected from the Correspondence and Pamphlets of Captain Robert Tomlinson, R.N., and Vice-Admiral Nicholas Tomlinson*, Navy Records Society, 74, London

Burney, W., 1815, *A New Universal Dictionary of the Marine (originally compiled by William Falconer)*, London

Coleman, T., 2002 (revised edn), *Nelson: The Man and the Legend*, London

Coleridge, S. T., 1866, *The Friend: A Series of Essays to aid in the formation of fixed principles in politics, morals and religion with literary amusements interspersed*, London

Collingwood, G. L. N., 1829, *A Selection from the Public and Private Correspondence of Vice-Admiral Lord Collingwood: Interspersed with Memoirs of his Life*, London

Constantine, D., 2001, *Fields of Fire: A Life of Sir William Hamilton*, London

Cordingly, D., 2001, *Heroines and Harlots: Women at Sea in the Great Age of Sail*, London

Cordingly, D., 2003, *Billy Ruffian: The* Bellerophon *and the Downfall of Napoleon, the Biography of a Ship of the Line, 1782–1836*, London

Craik, G. L. and Macfarlane, C., 1844, *The Pictorial History of England during the Reign of George the Third*, vol. 4, London

Cumby, W. P., 1899, 'The Battle of Trafalgar (an unpublished narrative)', *The Nineteenth Century, A Monthly Review*, 46, pp. 717–28

Deane, A., 1996, *Nelson's Favourite: HMS Agamemnon at War 1781–1809*, London

Desbrière, E., 1907, *La Campagne Maritime de 1805: Trafalgar*, Paris

Des Touches, G., 1905, 'Souvenirs d'un marin de la République', *Revue des Deux Mondes*,28, pp. 177–201 and 407–36

Dillon, W. H., 1956 (ed. M. A. Lewis), *A Narrative of My Professional Adventures (1790-1839: vol. II, 1802–1839*, Navy Records Society, 97, London

Druett, J., 2000, *She Captains: Heroines and Hellions of the Sea*, New York and London

Ekins, C., 1824, *Naval Battles from 1744 to the Peace in 1814*, London

Ellis, S. B., 1866 (ed. Lady Ellis), *Memoirs and Services of the Late Lieutenant-General Sir S. B. Ellis, K.C.B., Royal Marines, from his own memoranda*, London

Farington, J., 1924 (ed. J. Greig), *The Farington Diary (September 14, 1804, to September 19, 1806)*, London

Fenwick, K., 1959, *H.M.S. Victory*, London

Ferrer de Couto, J., 1851, *Historia del Combate Naval de Trafalgar precedida de la del renacimiento de la marina española durante el siglo XVIII*, Madrid

Fraser, E., 1906, *The Enemy at Trafalgar: An Account of the Battle from*

Eye-Witnesses' Narratives and Letters and Despatches from the French and Spanish Fleets, London

Fraser, E., 1913, *The Sailors Whom Nelson Led: Their Doings Described by Themselves*, London

Fraser, F., 1986, *Beloved Emma: The Life of Emma Lady Hamilton*, London

Fremantle, A. (ed.), 1935, *The Wynne Diaries 1789–1820*, Oxford

Friedenberg, Z. B., 2002, *Medicine Under Sail*, Annapolis

Galdós, B. P., 1884, *Trafalgar: A Tale* (translated by C. Bell), London

Gardiner, R. (ed.), 1997a, *The Campaign of Trafalgar 1803–1805*, London

Gardiner, R. (ed.), 1997b, *Nelson against Napoleon: From the Nile to Copenhagen, 1798–1801*, London

Gardner, J. A., 1906 (eds R. V. Hamilton and J. K. Laughton), *Recollections of James Anthony Gardner Commander R.N. (1775–1814)*, Navy Records Society, 31, London

Gardner, J. A., 2000 (eds R. V. Hamilton and J. K. Laughton), *Above and Under Hatches: The Recollections of James Anthony Gardner Commander R.N. (1775–1814)* (reprint of Gardner, 1906), London

Gatty, A. and Gatty, Mrs A., 1842, *Recollections of the Life of Rev. A. J. Scott, D.D. Lord Nelson's Chaplain*, London

Glascock, W. N., 1835, *Naval Sketch Book*, vol. 1, London

Glover, R., 1973 *Britain at Bay: Defence against Bonaparte, 1803–14*, New York and London

Goodwin, P., 1987, *The Construction and Fitting of the Sailing Man of War 1650–1850*, London

Granville, C. (ed.), 1916, *Lord Granville Leveson Gower (First Earl Granville), Private Correspondence 1781 to 1821*, vol. 2, London

Harbron, J. D., 1988, *Trafalgar and the Spanish Navy*, London

Harland, J. (with M. Myers), 1985 (revised edn), *Seamanship in the Age of Sail: An Account of the Shiphandling of the Sailing Man-of-War 1600–1860, Based on Contemporary Sources*, London

Harrison, J., 1806, *The Life of the Right Honourable Horatio Lord Viscount Nelson*, vol. 1, London

Harvey, C., 1909, *The Naval History of the Patey Family*, Witney

Hibbert, C., 1994, *Nelson: A Personal History*, London

Hoffman, F., 1901 (eds A. Beckford Bevan and H. B. Wolryche-Whitmore), *A Sailor of King George: The Journals of Captain Frederick Hoffman, R.N. 1793–1814*, London

Hoffman, F., 1999 (eds A. Beckford Bevan and H. B. Wolryche-Whitmore), *A Sailor of King George: The Journals of Captain Frederick Hoffman, R.N. 1793–1814* (reprint of Hoffman, 1901), London

Howarth, D. and Howarth, S., 1988, *Nelson: The Immortal Memory*, London

Hughes, E. (ed.), 1957, *The Private Correspondence of Admiral Lord Collingwood*, Navy Records Society, 98, London

Jackson, T. S. (ed.), 1900, *Logs of the Great Sea Fights 1794–1805*, vol. 2, Navy Records Society, 18, London

Jennings, L. J. (ed.), 1884a, *The Croker Papers. The Correspondence and Diaries of the Late Right Honourable John Wilson Croker, LL.D., F.R.S.*, vol. 1, London

Jennings, L. J. (ed.), 1884b, *The Croker Papers: The Correspondence and Diaries of the Late Right Honourable John Wilson Croker, LL.D., F.R.S.*, vol. 2, London

Kemp, P. (ed.), 1976, *The Oxford Companion to Ships and the Sea*, Oxford

Kennedy, L., 1951, *Nelson's Band of Brothers*, London

King, D. (with J. B. Hattendorf and J. W. Estes), 2000, *A Sea of Words: A Lexicon and Companion to the Complete Seafaring Tales of Patrick O'Brian*, New York

Laughton, C. and Heddon, V., 1927, *Great Storms*, London

Lavery, B., 1989, *Nelson's Navy: The Ships, Men and Organisation 1793–1815*, London

Lloyd, P., 1991, *The French are Coming! The Invasion Scare of 1803–5*, Tunbridge Wells

The Log Book; or, National Miscellany, 1830, London

Lovell, W. S., 1879 (2nd ed), *Personal Narrative of Events from 1799 to 1815 with Anecdotes*, London

McGuane, J. P., 2002, *Heart of Oak: A Sailor's Life in Nelson's Navy*, New York and London

Mackenzie, R. H., 1913, *The Trafalgar Roll: Containing the Names and Services of all Officers of the Royal Navy and the Royal Marines who participated in the Glorious Victory of the 21st October 1805, together with a History of the Ships engaged in the Battle*, London

McLynn, F., 1997, *Napoleon: A Biography*, London

Maffeo, S. E., 2000, *Most Secret and Confidential: Intelligence in the Age of Nelson*, London

Mahan, A. T., 1897, *The Life of Nelson: The Embodiment of the Sea Power of Great Britain*, vol. 2, London

Malmesbury, 3rd Earl of (ed.), 1844, *Diaries and Correspondence of James Harris, First Earl of Malmesbury*, vol. 6, London

Marsden, W., 1838, *A Brief Memoir of the Life and Writings of the Late William Marsden D.C.L., F.R.S. &c. &c.*, London

Masefield, J., 1905, *Sea Life in Nelson's Time*, London

Moorhouse, E. H. (ed.), 1910, *Letters of the English Seamen: 1587–1808*, London

Murray, A., 1846, *Memoir of the Naval Life and Services of Admiral Sir Philip C.H.C. Durham, G.C.B.*, London

Nicol, J., 1822, *The Life and Adventures of John Nicol, Mariner*, Edinburgh and London

Nicol, J., 1997 (ed. T. Flannery), *The Life and Adventures of John Nicol, Mariner* (reprint of Nicol, 1822), New York

Nicolas, N. H., 1844, *The Dispatches and Letters of Vice Admiral Lord Viscount Nelson,* vol. 1, London

Nicolas, N. H., 1845a, *The Dispatches and Letters of Vice Admiral Lord Viscount Nelson,* vol. 2, London

Nicolas, N. H., 1845b, *The Dispatches and Letters of Vice Admiral Lord Viscount Nelson,* vol. 3, London

Nicolas, N. H., 1846, *The Dispatches and Letters of Vice Admiral Lord Viscount Nelson,* vol. 7, London

O'Brian, P., 1970, *Master and Commander*, London

Oman, C., 1947, *Nelson*, London

Padfield, P., 1976, *Nelson's War*, London

Padfield, P., 2003, *Maritime Power and the Struggle for Freedom: Naval Campaigns that Shaped the Modern World 1788–1851*, London

Parsons, G. S., 1998 (ed. W. H. Long), *Nelsonian Reminiscences: Leaves from Memory's Log, A Dramatic Eye-Witness Account of the War at Sea 1795–1810* (first published 1843, Boston, Massachusetts), London

Pemberton, C. R., 1929, *The Autobiography of Pel Verjuice by Charles Reece Pemberton, with an introduction on his life and work*, London

Pengelly, C. A., 1966, *The First Bellerophon*, London

Pocock, T., 1987, *Horatio Nelson*, London

Pocock, T., 1999, *Nelson's Women*, London

Pocock, T., 2002, *The Terror before Trafalgar: Nelson, Napoleon and the Secret War*, London

Pope, D., 1997, *Life in Nelson's Navy*, Rochester

Prothero, G. W., 1890, 'The Battle of Trafalgar', *English Historical Review*, 5, pp. 767–9

Raigersfeld, J. Baron de, 1929, *The Life of a Sea Officer* (reprint of the edition privately published c. 1830), London

Robinson, H., 1858, *Sea Drift*, Portsea

Robinson, W., 1836, *Nautical Economy or Recollections of Events During the Last War Dedicated to the Brave Tars of Old England by a Sailor politely called by the officers of the navy Jack Nasty-face*, London

Robinson, W., 1973, *Jack Nastyface: Memoirs of an English Seaman* (reprint of Robinson 1836), Rochester

Rodger, N. A. M., 1986, *The Wooden World: An Anatomy of the Georgian Navy*, London

Rose, J. H., 1923, *Life of William Pitt*, London

Rowbotham, W. B., 1937, 'The naval general service medal 1793–1840', *Mariner's Mirror*, 23, pp. 351–70

Schom, A., 1990, *Trafalgar, Countdown to Battle 1803–1805*, New York

Schom, A., 1997, *Napoleon Bonaparte*, New York

Smith, D. B., 1923, 'The *Defiance* at Trafalgar', *Scottish Historical Review*, 20, pp. 116–21

Southey, R., 1813, *The Life of Horatio Lord Nelson* (1900 reprint of the 1896 edition), London

Sparrow, E., 1999, *Secret Service: British Agents in France 1792–1815*, Woodbridge

Stark, S. J., 1996, *Female Tars: Women Aboard Ship in the Age of Sail*, London

Stockwin, J., 2001, *Kydd*, London

Taylor, A. H., 1950, 'The Battle of Trafalgar', *Mariner's Mirror*, 36, pp. 281–321

Terraine, J., 1976, *Trafalgar*, London

Thiers, L. A., 1845, *The History of the Consulate and Empire of Napoleon*, vol. 5, London

Thursfield, H. G. (ed.), 1951, *Five Naval Journals 1789–1817*, Navy Records Society, 91, London

Tracy, N., 1996, *Nelson's Battles: The Art of Victory in the Age of Sail*, London

Tucker, J. S., 1844, *Memoirs of Admiral the Right Hon^e^ the Earl of St. Vincent, G.C.B. &c.*, vol. 1, London

Vincent, E., 2003, *Nelson: Love and Fame*, New Haven, London

Wheeler, D. A., 1985, 'The weather at the Battle of Trafalgar', *Weather*, 40, pp. 338–46

Wheeler, D. A., 1987, 'The Trafalgar storm 22–29 October 1805', *The Meteorological Magazine*, 116, pp. 197–205

Wheeler, D. A., 2001, 'The weather of the European Atlantic seaboard during October 1805: an exercise in historical climatology', *Climatic Change*, 48, pp. 361–85

Wheeler, H. F. B. and Broadley, A. M., 1908, *Napoleon and the Invasion of England: The Story of the Great Terror*, vols 1 and 2, London and New York

White, C., 2002, *The Nelson Encyclopaedia*, Rochester

Woodman, R., 2001, *The Victory of Seapower: Winning the Napoleonic War 1806–1814*, London

Wyndham-Quin, W. H., 1912, *Sir Charles Tyler, G. C. B. Admiral of the White*, London

INDEX

Achille, 112, 120, 173–4; catches fire and explodes, 131, 190, 211–12, 217–18, 249, 272, 276; survivors, 213, 215–16, 291
Achilles, 23, 301
Adair, Captain Charles William, 124, 145, 147
admirals (terminology), 15n
Admiralty, 18, 23, 29, 81, 296, 320, 328–9, 334; telegraph links, 7–8; warrants, 77; receives news of battle and Nelson's death, 256–8, 261–2, 267–9, 275; forms precise view of events, 277; refuses to recognise Trafalgar medal, 318
Aeolus, 295
Africa, 94, 98, 344; in battle, 122, 135, 137, 199
African ancestry, seamen of, 50
Agamemnon, 62, 151, 180, 207
Aigle, 117–18, 120, 171–3, 344; surrenders, 180, 190, 192–3, 246; run aground, 246–7
Aikenhead, Midshipman Thomas, 303
Ajax, 74, 85, 95, 180, 207, 241
Álava y Navarrete, Vice-Admiral Ignacio María de, 68, 110, 271, 276; surrenders, 182, 184
Alexander I, Tsar, 331–2, 333
Algésiras, 107, 116, 118, 120, 162–3; surrenders, 185–6, 206, 229; casualties, 187; damage, 229; reaches Cadiz, 230, 238
Allen, William, 289
Alligator, 297
America, *see* United States of America
American War of Independence, 147, 349
Americans, 50, 218
Amiens, Peace of, 4, 341
ammunition: see cannon-balls; canister shot; chain-shot; grape-shot; musket-balls
amputations, 82, 130, 156, 164, 166–71, 193, 202, 213, 221; lack of anaesthetics, 166–8; as badge of honour, 341
Andalusia, Spain, 217
animals, 37, 75; *see also* cats; cockerel; dogs
Ardent, 227
Ardpatrick, Scotland, 173
Argonauta, xiv, 193, 211, 302; offers to fight for British, 202; scuttled, 249
Argonaute, xiv, 120, 207
Argus, 189, 232
army, *see* British Army
arrow, identifying mark, 253n
Arthur, King, 343
artillery batteries, 332
Atcherley, Captain James, 152–3
Atkinson, Master Thomas, 123–4
Atlantic Ocean, 3, 66, 91, 179, 213, 252
Austen, Captain Francis, 321
Austerlitz, Battle of, 280
Australia, 279, 336, 343
Austria, 23–4; Army, 280
Axminster, Devon, 265

Badcock, Midshipman William, 33, 63, 68, 73, 97; describes food at sea, 33; describes battle, 98, 126, 241
Bahama, 117, 120; surrenders, 189–90, 249; in service with British fleet, 297
ballast, 179, 238
Baltic Sea, 4, 336
Barbados, 18, 330
Barham, 216
Barham, Lord, 268
Barker, Midshipman George, 228, 231
Basque Roads, 334
Bastia, siege of, 26
Bath, Somerset, 122
Battersea Bridge, 11
battleships (terminology), 56
Bayntun, Captain Henry William, 156
bayonets, 128, 130, 181, 192
Bazin, Commander François Marie, 154
beacon fires, 8
beakhead, 43
Beatty, Dr William, 123–4, 145, 148, 181, 293, 311; attends Nelson, 141–2, 193–4, 196–7, 203, 205; horrified at Dumanoir's treachery, 201; prepares Nelson's body for return to England, 227, 309–10

Beaudouin, Captain Louis-Alexis, 90, 154
beer, 32–3, 46
Belleisle, 55, 98, 216; joins battle, 107, 113–16, 153, 170; original name, 113; damage, 190–1; casualties, 191, 220–1; takes prize, 211; in danger of wreck, 223–4; reaches Gibraltar, 292; returns to England, 294, 298, 308
Bellerophon, 60, 62, 95, 225, 243, 294; joins battle, 116–18, 120, 153–4, 171–2, 190, 201; nickname, 116; captain killed, 118, 272; action against Kerjulien's force, 233
Bennett, Lieutenant Charles, 229
Berwick, xiv, 173, 193, 248
Bessborough, Lady, 267, 269, 310, 313
biscuits, *see* ship's biscuits
Bishop's Waltham, Hampshire, 322
Blackheath, Kent, 11
Blackwall, London, 11
Blackwood, Captain Hon. Henry, 61–2, 141, 184, 257, 270, 273, 299–300; letter to wife, 29, 233
Bligh, Lieutenant George Miller, 198
blockades, 4, 12, 21, 89, 264, 278, 327, 330–1, 347; of Basque Roads, 334; of Brest, 18, 30, 329–30; of Cadiz, xxiii, 13–15, 17, 29–30, 54, 58–9, 66–7, 78, 254, 257, 260; Continental System, 331–3; of Russian fleet, 332; toll on crews, 32, 57, 63, 328–9
boarding/boarding parties, 90, 131–3, 162–3, 171, 186, 192; from *Redoutable*, 128, 132–3, 146–7, 309; on *Redoutable*, 181, 201
Bolton, Captain, 328
Booth, George, 169
Boston, Lincolnshire, 285
Boulogne, France, 5, 22, 24, 343
Boulton, Matthew, 318
Bounce (dog), 327–8
bounties, 48, 50; *see also* prizes
boys, 77, 88; *see also* children
brandy, 166, 227, 245, 293, 309
Brazil, 332
Brazilians, 50
bread, 33–4, 46, 254; *see also* ship's biscuits
Brest, France, 16–18, 21, 30, 280, 329–30, 334
Brewer, George, 307
Bridport, Dorset, 265–6
brigs, 189
Brisbane, Captain, 330
Britain: alliance with Italy, 320; blockaded under Continental System, 331–3; emigration, 336–7; government, 2, 4; naval supremacy, 3, 280, 326–7, 334–7, 347; invasion threat, 4–12, 23–4, 277–8, 288, 326, 328, 331, 333, 337; popularity of navy, 51; population, 345; response to Nelson's death, 282–8, 342–3; Victorian, 343; *see also* trade
Britannia, 135, 317; in battle, 151, 180, 200, 207, 213, 245; age, 122
British Army, 51, 318; *see also* marines; militias
British East India Company, 335, 337
British Empire, 336–8, 344; building of, 2–3
British Navy: assistance to armies, 334–5; gunnery, 57, 89–90, 128, 160, 161, 207; manpower, 349; popularity, 51; superiority, 51, 161, 207
'Britons strike home', 97
Brontë, Patrick, 64n
Brown, John, 85
Brown, Lieutenant George, 92, 148
Brown, Midshipman William, 289
Brueys, Admiral François-Paul, 107
Bucentaure, 96, 271; joins battle, 122, 126–8, 133–5, 151–3, 205, 210; derivation of name, 96n; surrenders, 152, 198–9, 207; casualties, 152; abandoned by British, 233–4; wrecked, 235–6, 236; commemorated on Nelson's funeral car, 312
Buenos Aires, Argentina, 335
Buick, Mary, 227
Bulkeley, Richard (Hardy's aide-de-camp), 194
bulkheads, 74, 76
burial at sea, 178–80, 220, 221, 226, 240; in ballast, 179; on land, 251; *see also* funerals
Burke, Walter (*Victory* purser), 143, 194, 196–8, 204–5
Burma, 335
Burnham-on-Sea, Somerset, 228
Burnham Thorpe, Norfolk, 274, 312
Burton Bradstock, Dorset, 266
butter, 36
Byng, Admiral John, 338

Cadiz, Spain, 63, 93, 207, 223, 225, 238, 261, 275; British blockade, xxiii, 13–15, 17, 29–30, 54, 58–9, 61, 66–7, 78, 254, 257, 260; city and history, 13–14; lighthouse, 14, 23, 65, 230–1, 235, 246; Villeneuve in harbour, 29–30; animosities within, 58; French and Spanish ships leave, 60, 64, 69, 72, 91, 278, 321; bodies washed up, 179, 250, 252; theatre, 213; response to battle, 217–18, 250–2, 278, 346; Kerjulien threatens from, 232, 234–5, 245; French and Spanish ships, 234–6, 236–8, 271, 294–6; map of port, 237; wounded come ashore, 248, 250, 252; makeshift graves, 250; English traveller's description, 251–3; Spanish sailors rewarded, 346
Cadiz Bay, 14, 235
Cadiz Point, 235
Caesar, 294
Calais, France, 5, 321
Calcutta, India, 279
Calder, Vice-Admiral Sir Robert, 13, 19–21, 22, 58
Calvi, siege of, 26
Campbell, Midshipman Colin, 173, 180, 302
Camperdown, Battle of, 3
Canada, 336, 343
Canadians, 50
Candide (Voltaire), 338
canister shot, 105, 121, 136, 162, 173

cannon-balls, xx, 26, 76, 83, 101–2, 107, 109, 134, 176, 177, 186, 219; loading, 158, 160; noise, 106; sizes and types, 76, 105–6; *see also* canister shot; chain-shot; grape-shot
cannons, 38, 55, 77, 87–8, 104–6, 157–60, 223, 281; aiming, 104, 157; firing mechanisms, 104–5, 159–60; firing into rigging xix–xx, 104–5, 122–3, 125, 153, 173; firing routine, 158–60; heard in Cadiz, 217; holes made by, 176; improving design, 84; in Martello Towers, 9; noise, 85, 94, 105, 205; types of shot, 76, 105–6; rates of fire, 89, 101–2, 158; relative numbers, 89; secured, 230; to weight corpses, 178; *see also* carronades; flintlocks; gunpowder; matches; priming iron; tompions; touch-holes; 'worm'
Cape Finisterre, 19, 258
Cape Nelson, 343
Cape of Good Hope, 335
Cape Spartel, 301
Cape Trafalgar, 14, 66, 69, 93, 179, 218, 223, 270, 283; derivation of name, 69n; shoals, 65, 229, 273
capstan bars, 245n
carbines, 128
Caribbean, 187, 335
carpenters, 77, 174, 176
carronades, xx, 113, 117, 121, 134, 151, 154, 163; description, 76; thrown overboard, 259
Carter, John, 249
Cartigny, M. (French veteran), 346
cartridges, 76, 86–8, 102, 104, 158, 160
casks, *see* leaguer
Castle, Midshipman George, 111
casualty lists/numbers, 219, 289–90, 294, 322
catheads, 43n
Catholicism, 90, 179, 286
cat-o'-nine-tails, 45
cats, 241
Cawsand, Cornwall, 144
Cawsand Bay, 30
Cayenne, French Guiana, 330
Cayetano Valdés, Captain Don, 210, 240
Cellardyke, Scotland, 227
Ceylon, 335
chain-shot, 105
chains, xxiin, 43
Channel Fleet, 79, 329
Channel Islands, 9
Chatham, Kent, 8, 10
cheese, 36
Chelsea, London, 11, 267
Chesapeake, River, 331
Chevalier, Henry Lewis (Nelson's steward), 204–5
Chevers, Forbes, 75, 169–70
Chigwell, Essex, 147
children, 6–7, 77–8; *see also* boys; girls; Nelson, Horatia; Nelson, Horatio
China, 335
Churruca, Captain Don Cosmé, 71, 187–8, 298
Cisneros, Don Baltazar Hidalgo, 271
Clarence, Duke of, 51
Classen, Lieutenant Asmus, 247
Clavell, Lieutenant John, 100
Clement, Lieutenant Benjamin, 188
clothes, 40–2, 78, 81, 99–100, 106, 287, 296, 302, 329; removed from Nelson's corpse, 227; of Jeannette, 214–16; stripped off for swimming, 213–14; *see also* uniforms
coalitions, 1, 23–4
cobbler, 176–7
Cochrane, Admiral Alexander, 330
Cochrane, Captain Thomas, 334
cockerel, 120
cock-fighting, 47
cockpit, 85, 164, 168–9, 221–2, 233; midshipmen's living quarters, 81, 221; of *Victory*, 106, 141–2, 161, 193, 202, 204–5
Codrington, Captain Edward, 257, 313, 328
coffins, 178; Nelson's, 178, 309–10, 313; *see also* leaguer
Coleridge, Samuel Taylor, 286
Collingwood, Midshipman Edward, 144, 182
Collingwood, Vice-Admiral Cuthbert: stationed off Cadiz, 22–4, 29–30, 54; letters quoted, 23, 30; discipline, 45; leads south column, 94, 97, 108; clothing, 100; congratulated by Rotheram, 110; demeanour, 112; response to Nelson's signal, 126–7; orders *Royal Sovereign* taken in tow, 184; in *Dreadnought* prior to battle, 187; informed of Nelson's injury, 202–3; learns of Nelson's death and assumes command, 218–19, 223, 233; injuries, 219; transfers to *Euryalus*, 219; reliance on crews, 222; describes situation of fleet, 241; describes period after battle, 249; negotiation with Spanish authorities, 253–4; reports of battle, 256–7, 268–73, 275–7, 287–8; estimate of casualties, 290; and *Victory*'s return to England, 293–4; elated after battle, 303; rewarded, 316–17; created baron, 317; career after Trafalgar and death, 327–8; relationship with crews, 340
Colossus, 23, 62, 120, 189–90
communications, 16, 63, 66, 338; *see also* semaphore; signal posts; signals; telegraphs
Conelly (marine), 164, 169
Connor, Ann, 64
Conqueror, 136–7, 151–2, 164, 180, 207; dog rescued, 216; abandons *Bucentaure*, 234
conscription, 49, 52, 334; *see also* press-gangs
constipation, 42, 45, 165
Continental System, 331–3
Cooke, Captain John, 62, 116–18; reports of death, 272, 276
Copenhagen, Battle of, 227, 275, 332–4
Cornélie, 189, 232
Cornwallis, Lord, 21
Coron, Greece, 33

Spain, 22
, 330
223
Wexford, Ireland, 142
ng, James, 48
nt, 80, 81
nals, 49
can, Aaron (first casualty), 164
mby, First Lieutenant William Pryce, 62, 116–17, 171–2, 233
Cummins, Rev., 341
cutlasses, 86, 128, 132, 192, 243
cutters, 56, 68, 189

Danes, 50
Danube, River, 280
Dartmoor, 263
Davison, Alexander, 318
Dawlish, Devon, 193
deafness, 86, 94
Deal, Kent, 7
Defence, 61–2, 120, 122, 212, 301
defences (on land), 9–10, 11, 13
Defiance, 173–4, 180, 192, 246, 302, 318
Delaware, River, 331
Denmark, 4, 332; *see also* Danes
Deptford, London, 11
des Touches, Lieutenant Pierre-Guillaume Gicquel, 67, 160, 198–9, 207–8, 245; paroled in Tiverton, 264–5
desertion, 83, 100, 329, 340
Despard, Colonel Edward, 47
Diamond shoals, 238, 247
Digby, Captain (later Admiral) Henry, 122, 135, 137, 344
Dillon, Lieutenant William, 287
dirks, 132
discipline, *see* naval discipline
disease, *see* sickness, illness and disease
doctors, 46, 85, 165; *see also* surgeons
dogs, 216, 327–8, 334
dollars, 123n, 292
Donegal, 245, 248
Dorchester, Dorset, 256, 266
Dover, Kent, 5, 10, 308
Drake, Sir Francis, 343
Dreadnought, 23, 187–8; rate of fire, 187
drink, 32–3, 46, 329; *see also* beer; brandy; grog; lemonade; lime juice; rum; wine
Drudésit, Lieutenant, 154
Dublin, Ireland, 67
Duckworth, Admiral Sir John, 260–1, 330
Duff, Captain George, 153, 344; reports of death, 272, 276, 299–301
Duff, Midshipman (later Admiral) Norwich, 298–301, 344
Duguay-Trouin, 162, 198, 296; as the *Implacable*, 297
Dumanoir Le Pelley, Rear-Admiral Pierre-Etienne-René-Marie, 68–9, 122; ignores Villeneuve's order and sails away, 126–8, 139, 151; turns back join action, 162, 180, 195, 198–200; fires on Spanish ships, 201–2; ceases fire and leaves battle, 207, 257; defeated off Ferrol, 294–6
Duncan, Admiral Viscount Adam, 285
Dungeness, Kent, 10
Dupetit-Thouars, Admiral Aristide Aubert, 107
Durham, Captain Philip Charles, 192–3, 302
Durham, Co. Durham, 111
Dutch, 3, 50, 335; Navy, 9

Eagle, Imperial, 96, 134, 152
earrings, 100
East Indies, 335–6
Edwards, John, 242
Egypt, 3, 27, 279, 320
Ellis, Lieutenant Samuel, 85, 95
empires, 2–3; *see also* British Empire
English Channel, 259, 261, 343; Napoleon's invasion threat, 1, 5, 12, 15, 17, 278
English language, 337–8
Entreprenante, xiv, 189, 212
Euryalus, 29, 61, 67, 141, 233, 293, 298–300, 322; takes *Royal Sovereign* in tow, 184, 189; becomes Collingwood's flagship, 219, 256–7, 270, 273, 276
Everitt, Daniel, 274
Exeter, Devon, 265, 275
Exmouth, Devon, 80

Falmouth, Cornwall, 261–2, 265
Farington, Joseph, 273–4, 323
fearnought, 86, 95
Ferdinand, King of the Two Sicilies, 64n
Ferrol, Spain, 20, 22, 294
Feuillet, Pierre François (Magon's secretary), 230
fevers, *see* malaria, sickness, typhus
Fife, Scotland, 227
fire (conflagration), xxi–xxii, 86, 131, 150, 172, 185, 211–12, 245, 246, 272
Firma, 20
Fitzharris, Lord, 268
flags, 96–7, 297, 313; see also signals
fleas, 40–1
fleet (terminology), 19n
flintlocks, 104–5, 129, 159, 161
Flying Fish, 275
fog, 19, 20, 267
food, 22, 33–8, 46, 74, 329; *see also* bread; butter; cheese; lobscouse; meat; rats; ship's biscuits; skillagree
forecastle, 151n, 156, 171
Formidable, 162, 198, 200, 296
Fort Amherst, Kent, 10
Fort Santa Catalina, Spain, 235
fortifications, *see* defences (on land)
Fougueux, xix–xxiii, 90, 101–2, 107–8, 111, 115,

153–5; surrenders, 154–5, xxiii; casualties, 155, 226; wrecked, 226, 247
Fox, General Henry, 276
France: alienation of bourgeoisie, 333; alliance with Russia, 332; European jealousy of, 281; invasion threat, 24; naval power, 3–4, 337–8; Queen Victoria visits, 346; reactions to battle, 279, 287–8, 346; Revolution and Napoleonic wars, 1–5
Fremantle, Betsey, 8, 289
Fremantle, Captain Thomas Francis, 8, 13, 73, 289; description of Villeneuve, 322–3
French: casualties, 290, 294; enmity with British, 90, 253–4; on board *Victory*, 50; prisoners, 291, 298, 302; relations with Spanish, 58, 90–1, 347; sailors overlooked, 346; trade competition, 335
French Army, conscription into, 52, 334
French language, 338
French Navy: breakout from Brest, 330–1, 334; burial habits, 179; command structure, 51–2, 126; conscription, 52; in disarray, 3; 'France expects', 343; gunnery, xix–xx, 52, 89, 102, 160; inexperience, 332; morale, 52; sailors drafted into army, 334
French Revolution, 1, 4, 51
French Revolutionary and Napoleonic Wars, 1–2, 79, 81, 327
Friedland, Battle of, 332
friendly fire, 98
frigates, 55, 57, 61, 68, 189, 232, 236, 295–6, 330
funerals, 178, 310–14
Furet, 189, 232

Galdós, Benito Pérez, 88–9
Galera bank, 236
galley fires, 74, 85, 95
Gambier, Admiral Lord, 332
gangrene, 170
Ganteaume, Vice-Admiral Honoré-Joseph-Antoine, 16–18, 280
Gazette Extraordinary, 269, 273–4
George III, King, 2, 47; dislike of capital punishment, 48; hears of battle and Nelson's death, 269; instigates day of thanksgiving, 314
Germans, 50
Germany, 24, 280
Gibraltar, 14, 18, 21, 23, 29, 79, 125, 156n, 193, 243, 244; destination after battle, 216, 223, 225, 254, 291–2, 302; prisoners exchanged, 243; receives news of battle and Nelson's death, 275–5; *San Juan* in service at, 297–8; *see also* Straits of Gibraltar
Gibraltar Chronicle, 275
Giddy, Thomas, 261
girls, 77; *see also* children; Nelson, Horatia
'God save the King', 97
Gordon, Joseph, 240
Gosport, Hampshire, 322, 348
grape-shot, 105, 109, 136, 154, 164, 173, 186, 277
grapnels, 128, 133
Gravina, Admiral Frederico Carlos, 16–19, 22, 58, 270–1, 278; commands reserve squadron, 69; joins line of battle, 72; signals general recall, 206; wounded, 207
Great Massingham, Norfolk, 273–4
Greenwich, London, 11, 310, 312; National Maritime Museum, 297; Royal Hospital, 126, 310, 315 16
grenades, 128, 131–2, 139, 146, 171–2
grog, 32–3, 45, 46, 85
grogram, 32n
Guadeloupe, 330
Guernsey, 275
Guillemard, Robert, 143, 324
gun crews, 52, 88–90, 99, 101, 132, 157–8
gun decks, 75–7, 81, 83, 94, 148, 156, 176
gunners, 77, 86–7, 94, 104–5, 158–60, 172–3, 176, 230; *see also* gun crews; powder monkeys
gunpowder, 76, 87, 89, 104, 106, 129, 148, 151, 159; fumes, 83, 156–7; quality of, 84; tools for handling, 87; *see also* cartridges
guns, *see* cannons; carbines; carronades; musketoons; muskets; pistols; rifles; swivel guns

halliards, 110n
Halloran, Lieutenant Lawrence, 135–6, 213
Hallowell, Benjamin, 178
Halstead, Essex, 137
Hamilton, Emma, 54, 140, 196, 198, 203, 288, 324, 328; relationship with Nelson, 25–8, 342; Nelson's last letter, 63–4, 65; bequeathed to nation, 143, 204, 320, 319–20; learns of Nelson's death, 269; absent from Nelson's funeral, 313; extravagant lifestyle, 321; death, 321; and Nelson's godson, 340–1
Hamilton, Sir William, 25–8, 35, 319–21, 340–1
hammocks, 41, 74, 77, 178, 305; nettings, 223
Hammond, Sir Andrew Snape, 269
Hampstead, London, 11
hanging, 45, 47–8
Hardy, Captain Thomas Masterman: in battle, 124, 127–8, 145; delivers Nelson's last letter, 63; background and career, 125–6; and death of Nelson, 141, 143, 144, 311; rallies British fleet, 180; with Nelson, 194–5, 196, 202–4, 226, 249; informs Collingwood of Nelson's death, 218; return to England, 293; prize money, 317; created baronet, 317
Hardy, Thomas, 255
Hargood, Captain William, 113–14, 211
Harrel's Cross, Ireland, 192
Harvey, Captain Eliab, 147
heads, *see* toilets
helm, 189n
Hennah, William, 299–300
Hermione, 189, 232
hernias, 158, 165
Hero, 20

Héros, 122, 134–5, 198, 200, 207
Hicks, Midshipman William, 136
Highgate, London, 11
Hills, Lieutenant Alexander, 202
Hoffman, Lieutenant Frederick, 164, 169, 186–8
Honiton, Devon, 265
Hood, Admiral Lord, 310
hoops, 98n
Hopping, Ann ('Nancy') (also Ann Perriam), 79–81
Hopping, Edward, 80
Hore, Captain Rafael de, 207
Hortense, 189, 232, 235–6
hospitals, 252, 254, 292; *see also* Greenwich, Royal Hospital
Howe, Admiral Lord, 91
hulks, 137, 206, 263, 297
hurricanes, *see* storms
Hyères, France, 346
hygiene, 40–2, 82

Ilfracombe, Devon, 257
illness, *see* sickness
Implacable, see *Duguay-Trouin*
India, 50, 279, 335, 337
Indian Ocean, 330
Indomptable, 111, 115, 207, 232; runs aground, 235; casualties, 235
Infernet, Captain Louis-Antoine-Cyprien, 198–200; commended by Napoleon, 325
Intrépide, 67, 160, 162, 198–200, 207, 210; damage, 208; surrenders, 208; evacuation, 245–6, 264; set alight and blown up, 246
invasions: 264; of Italy, 27; Napoleon's plans, 4–7, 12, 15–17, 22, 23–4, 278, 280, 325, 331, 333, 343, 347; of Russia, 333; threat to Britain, 4–12, 23–4, 277–8, 288, 326, 328, 331, 333, 337; threat to France, 24
Ipswich, Suffolk, 285
Ireland, 9, 97
Isle of Wight, 8
Italians, 50
Italy, 24, 27, 320

Jackson, Lieutenant William, 213
Jacobins, 342
Jamaica, 330
Jeannette (French survivor), 215–16; reunited with husband, 291–2
Jervis, Rear-Admiral Sir John, 78–9, 319
John Bull, 13
Jolley, John, 136
jury masts, 144n, 293, 309
Jutland, Battle of, 344

Keats, Captain Richard, 93n, 260
Kerjulien, Captain Julien-Marie Cosmao, 232–5, 244, 250
King, John, 144
King, Lieutenant Andrew, 148
Kingdom of the Two Sicilies, 25, 27
Knight, Sir John, 292

lady's hole, 79
lanterns, 82–3, 87, 169, 246, 283
Lapenotiere, Lieutenant John Richard, 256–68, 294; rewarded and promoted, 268
larboard (terminology), 109n
Lardier (hoaxer), 143, 324
Larrey, Dominique-Jean, 168
Laura, 279
lavatories, *see* toilets
Lea, River, 11
leaguer (cask), 227, 293, 309
leeches, 165
leeward (terminology), 19n
Leghorn, Italy, 340–1
Leissègues, Vice-Admiral, 330
lemonade, 194
Le Tourneur, Captain Laurent, 162, 185–6
Leviathan, 135, 156, 180, 198, 200, 244
L'Hospitalier-Villemadrin, Captain C. E., 118, 189
lice, 40–1
lime juice, 39–40
Linois, Rear-Admiral Charles Alexandre Leon Durand, 330–1
linstocks, 159–61
Lisbon, Portugal, 258
Liskeard, Cornwall, 262–3
Liston, Professor Robert, 167–8
literacy, 44
Little, Richard, 289
Littleham, Devon, 80
livestock, *see* animals
Livorno, Italy, 26
Lizard, the, Cornwall, 259, 261
Lloyd, Lieutenant Robert, 136
loblolly boys, 82, 85
London, 280, 294; fog, 267; news of battle arrives, 261–2, 278; preparations for Nelson's funeral, 310; protective measures against invasion, 9–11; Charing Cross, 313; Colonial Office, 339; Covent Garden Theatre, 284; Fleet Street, 311; Hyde Park, 282; Lloyd's Coffee House, 314; Ludgate Hill, 310; St James's Park, 289; St Paul's Cathedral, 310–11, 313; Strand, 283; Tower, 282; Trafalgar Square, 343; Westminster Abbey, 311; Whitehall, 268, 312–13; *see also* Nelson's Column
Londonderry, Lady, 288
Looe, Cornwall, 114
L'Orient, 178, 310
L'Orient, Battle of, 80
Louis, Captain Thomas, 340
Louis XVI, King, 4
Lucas, Captain Jean-Jacques-Etienne, 122, 128, 132–4, 139, 145–7, 150–1, 153, 228, 232, 346;

name, xv; refuses to surrender, 150; surrenders, 181; commended by Napoleon, 325

Mack, General Karl, 280
Maclay, John (quartermaster), 188
Macnamara, Charles (black seaman), 188
Madeira, 95, 99
Madrid, Spain, 53, 59, 278
magazines, 77, 86–8, 95, 117, 172, 215, 236; explosion risk, 86–7
Magendie, Captain Jean-Jacques, 96, 152; prisoner in England, 313, 322; attends Nelson's funeral, 313; accused of Villeneuve's murder, 324
maggots, 33–5
Magon, Rear-Admiral Charles-René, 163; death, 185–7
Main, Thomas, 156
Maistral, Commodore Esprit-Tranquille, 127
malaria, 26, 165
Malaya, 335
Malcolm, Captain Pulteney, 248
Malmesbury, Lord, 283
Maltese, 50
Marengo, Battle of, 200
Maria Carolina, Queen of the Two Sicilies, 320
marines, 53, 74, 83, 88, 131; uniform, 100
marksmen, *see* sharpshooters
Mars, 62, 276, 299; joins battle, 115–16, 152–3, 163, 198, 201; captain killed, 153, 272, 299–300, 344
Marsden, William, 268, 289
Martello Towers, 9, 55
Martinique, 16–17, 18, 35, 330
mast-heads (terminology), 83n
Matcham, Catherine, 141
matches, 104, 159–60
meat, 33, 35–7, 85
medals, 6, 317–18
medical treatment, 39, 46, 130, 164–71; *see also* amputations; injuries; sickness and disease
Mediterranean, 15, 18, 21, 60, 63, 66, 78, 270; French supremacy, 3, 54, 59; wine, 32–3
Mediterranean Fleet, 78
Medway, River, 9, 309
merchant shipping, 48–9
Merton, Surrey, 24, 28, 64, 269, 288
messes, 38
midshipmen, 132, 201–2, 223, 229, 246; boys, 77; living quarters, 81, 221; toilets, 43; weapons, 132
militias, 7, 52
Minerve, 125
Minotaur, 189, 198, 200, 208, 210, 340; takes *Neptuno* in tow, 230–1
Monarca, 107, 116, 118, 153–4, 162; evacuation, 244–5; wrecked, 247
Montague, 33
Montañes, 117, 207
Mont-Blanc, 162, 198, 296; in service with British fleet, 297
Moorsom, Captain Robert, 120
Morel, Lieutenant Luc, 185
Morlaix, France, 322
Motrico, Spain, 187
Munich, Germany, 24
Murrell Green, Hampshire, 304
musical instruments, 90, 97
musket-balls, xx, xxiii, 26, 82, 101, 125, 129–31, 134; Nelson killed by, 206, 272; noise, 106
musketoons, 132, 181
muskets, 94, 101, 129–31, 144, 146, 150, 163, 192, 217; see also flintlocks; ramrods; touch-holes
mutiny, 49, 147, 293

Naiad, 189, 223, 225
Namur, 294
Naples, Italy, 25–7, 54, 59, 64n, 286, 320, 342
Napoleon Bonaparte: quoted, 1; ignorance of naval warfare, 3–4, 16, 23, 331; invasion plans, 4–7, 12, 15–17, 22, 23–4, 278, 325, 331, 333, 343; crowned emperor, 4, 15; as ogre, 6; control over admirals, 16–17, 22; orders to Villeneuve, 54, 59–60, 66; grief at Magon's death, 186; Churruca's dislike for, 188; promotes ignorance of battle, 279–81; invades Germany, 279–80; learns of defeat, 280; control of Europe, 280–1, 331; involvement in Villeneuve's death, 323–5; commends naval officers, 325; necessity of annihilation, 327; introduces Continental System, 331, 333; authorises privateers, 335; aims to expand French trade, 338; adopts Nelson's symbolism, 342–3; defeat and exile, 1, 343, 347, 350
nationalities, of seamen, 50
Nautilus, 258, 265, 275, 279
naval discipline, 45–6, 49, 52, 340; *see also* punishments
navies, *see* British Navy; French Navy; Spanish Navy
Nelson, Admiral Lord Horatio: Battle of the Nile, 3, 26, 80, 85; birth, 274; letter to Fremantle quoted, 13; blockade of Cadiz, 15; pursuit of Villeneuve, 18, 21; returns to England, 24–5; relationship with Emma Hamilton, 25–8, 342; marriage, 25, 27; injuries, 26, 82, 140, 167, 341; background, 27, 51; illnesses, 26, 35, 39–40; relationship with crews, 35, 79, 92, 222, 340; character witness for Despard, 47; assumes command, 54, 59; strategy, 54, 56–8, 69, 100–1, 108, 126, 127, 161, 207; gives chase to Villeneuve, 62–3; last letter to Emma Hamilton, 63–4, 65; made Duke of Brontë, 64n; last diary entry, 71–2; encourages crew, 85; final signals, 91–2, 100–1; 'England expects' signal, 92, 95–6, 126–7, 314, 342; explanation of tactics quoted, 93; attention to detail, 98; admiration for Collingwood, 108; cuts enemy line, 121, 133–4; demeanour, 124; fate sealed, 128; dress, 140;

Nelson, Admiral Lord Horatio – *continued*
premonitions of death, 140–1; injury during Battle of Trafalgar and death, 141–3, 146, 193–5, 196–8, 202–6, 249, 284, 309; coffin, 178, 309–10, 313; visited by Hardy, 194–5, 202–4; gives order to anchor, 203, 218; 'Kiss me, Hardy', 203; fatal wound caused by stray bullet, 206; Collingwood learns of death, 218–19; body prepared and returned to England, 226–8, 293, 309–10; reports of death, 252, 261, 265–6, 268–70, 272–7, 342; commendation of Keats, 260; cult of hero, 273, 338–9, 341–4; impact of death, 282–8, 310; supposed conversion, 286; funeral, 310–14; wishes concerning burial, 311–12; codicil to will, 319–20; on need for total victory, 326–7; Wellington meets, 339; realism, 340; godson, 340–1; centenary, 344; denounces neglect of navy, 349–50
Nelson, Frances, 25, 27, 81, 316; absent from Nelson's funeral, 313; awarded pension, 319
Nelson, Horatia, 28, 64, 140, 203, 288, 319; bequeathed to nation, 143, 204, 320
Nelson, Horatio (godson of Nelson), 340–1
Nelson, Rev. Edmund, 274
Nelson, River, 343
Nelson, William, 316, 319
'Nelson chequer', 97–9
'Nelson's Blood', 227
Nelson's Column, 343–4
'Nelson Touch', 54, 66
Neptune (British), xiv, 8, 63, 68, 97–8, 242, 289; tries to take lead from *Victory*, 73; joins battle, 126, 135, 180, 207; tows *Victory* to Gibraltar, 292
Neptune (French), xiv, 127, 134–5, 207, 232
Neptuno, xiv, 162, 208, 210; taken in tow by British, 230–1; recovered by French, 234–6; wrecked, 240
netting, 74, 223
Newcastle-upon-Tyne, Northumberland, 107
Newton Bushel, Devon, 345
New York, United States, 343–4
New Zealand, 343
Nicol, John, 348
Nicolas, Lieutenant Paul Harris, 170, 211, 292, 298; describes battle, 114–15; describes casualties, 220–1; describes storm, 223–5
Niger, 23
Nile, Battle of the, 3, 26, 59, 80, 85, 107, 178, 275, 310, 340, 345; commemorated on Nelson's funeral car, 312; medals, 318; Emma Hamilton's supposed role, 320
Nore anchorage, 309
Northesk, Rear-Admiral the Earl of, 317
North Warnborough, Hampshire, 304
Norwegians, 50
Norwood, London, 11

officers: boys, 77; coffins, 178; conditions, 37, 40, 43; effect of Byng's execution, 338–9; French, 51–2, 223; lack of recognition, 318; paternalism, 107; possessions, 75; promotion, 63, 328; recruitment, 51; Spanish, 53; uniform, 100; weapons, 132; *see also* midshipmen; pursers; warrant officers
Ogilvie, Midshipman David, 182
opium, 167, 335
Ordnance Survey maps, 7
Orion, 80–1, 246, 257, 328; in battle, 189–90, 199–200
orlop deck, 81–2, 151, 166, 176–7, 190
Overton, Master Edward, 117
Owen, Lieutenant John, 113–14, 190–1, 211

Paddington, London, 11
Palermo, Sicily, 27
Paris, France, 185, 278
parole, 263–4, 313, 322
parole towns, 263–4
Pasco, Lieutenant John, 92, 193
Patriotic Fund, 314–16
Patton, Midshipman Robert, 172
pay, 46–8, 348
Peake, Lieutenant James Godwin, 197
Pearson, Midshipman George, 233–4
Pellew, Captain Israel, 136, 152
Peltier, Lieutenant François Marie, 154
Pemberton, Charles, 14, 95, 99
Peninsular War, 335
Penryn, Cornwall, 262
Penzance, Cornwall, 261
Pernot, Captain, 177, 250
Perriam, Ann (Nancy), *see* Hopping, Ann
Peyman, General, 333
Philibert, Lieutenant Pierre Henri, 185–6, 206; describes boarding party, 162–3; describes experiences in storm, 229–30, 238
Phoebe, 61–2, 189, 226
Phoenix, 295
Pichegru, General Jean Charles, 323–4
Pickle, 189, 212–13, 216; carries despatches to Britain, 256–62, 275, 279, 291
pigtails, 99
pikes, 132
Pilgrim (wounded Italian), 136
pinnace, 211n
pirates, 105, 132, 335, 347
pistols, 128, 130–2, 163
Pitt, William, 268–9, 280, 322
Plassan, Lieutenant Pierre Joseph Leblond, 185
Pluton, 107, 116, 153, 162, 177, 207, 249; damage, 232
Plymouth, Devon, 217, 260–3, 265, 275, 297, 308
Plymouth Sound, 298
poetry, 347
Pollard, Midshipman John, 144–5, 344
Polyphemus, 174, 191, 211, 301
Pondicherry, India, 330
poop, 114, 121, 124, 133, 171, 200, 231; terminology,

111n; on *Victory*, 144
Pontypool, Wales, 14
Popham, Sir Home, 91
Port Mahon, Minorca, 338
Portsmouth, Hampshire, 21, 54, 243, 284, 297, 305, 322; telegraph connection, 8, 262
Portugal, 332
Portuguese, 50
post-chaises, 256, 262–3
Poullain, Lieutenant, 245–6
powder monkeys, 77, 79, 81, 88, 158, 169
press-gangs, 49–51, 290
Preston, Lancashire, 60, 225
Prigny, Captain Jean-Baptiste, 222
priming iron, 159
Prince, 207, 210–12, 241
Princetown, Devon, 263
Principe de Asturias 120–1, 173–4, 192, 206–7, 271
Pringle, John, 345
prisoners, 155, 187, 202, 214, 216, 220, 245, 276, 290–2; in Britain, 263–5; British, 235–6, 240, 253, 287–8, 298, 302; exchange of, 243, 253, 265, 287; in France, 287–8; numbers 290–1; in storm, 229, 248; *see also* Jeannette; parole
prisons, 48, 263
privateers, 335–6
prize money, 48, 63, 123, 135, 296, 328, 348; amounts, 317
prizes (prize ships), 50, 214, 225, 229, 233, 254, 292, 296–8, 302, 317, 330; lost in storm, 226, 228–32, 233, 243, 249, 253, 317; taking possession of, 210, 211; terminology, 48
Puerta Santa Maria, Spain, 58
punishments, 45–6, 47–8; *see also* cat-o'-nine-tails; hanging; prisons; transportation; whipping
pursers, 38, 46, 82, 85

quarterdeck, 107, 118, 155, 163, 171, 191, 220, 231, 233–4; terminology, 111n; on *Victory*, 124, 133, 142, 309
Queen Camel, Somerset, 233
Quilliam, Lieutenant John, 123–4

Raigersfeld, Jeffrey, 34, 38
Ram, Lieutenant William, 142, 251
ramrods, 129–30
rats, 38, 40–1
Rawlinson, Henry Creswicke, 337
Rayo, 162, 200, 207, 232, 235, 244; wrecked, 247–8
Reading, Berkshire, 313, 322
Ready, Henry, 289
rear-admirals (terminology), 15
Redoutable, 309, 325, 346; in battle, 122, 127–8, 132–4, 138–42, 144–8, 150–1, 153–5, 199; marksmen, 141, 144–5, 205, 344; casualties, 151, 155, 232; surrenders, 180–2, 201, 228; sinks, 228–9, 233; survivors rescued, 231–2
Reeves, Lieutenant Lewis Buckle, 197
Reid, Midshipman Charles, 301–2
religion, 77, 90; and burial at sea, 179
Rennes, France 322–4
Revenge, 84, 98, 243, 257; report of midshipman's death quoted, 109; joins battle, 120–1, 173–4, 176, 211; receives survivors, 213–14, 216; decks cleared, 221–2; reaches Gibraltar, 291
Rhin, 189, 232
Rhine, River, 280
rickets, 40
rifles, 129
rigging, 36, 53, 74, 110n, 137, 152, 182, 190; on *Aeolus*, 296; climbing, 99; dog lodged in, 216; falling, 240; firing from, 131, 211; firing into, xix–xx, 104–5, 122–3, 125, 153, 173; men working in, 164; swept away from *Pickle*, 258–9; on *Victory*, 309
Rivers, Midshipman William, 197
roads, 262–3
Roberts, Midshipman Richard, 138, 266
Robespierre, Maximilien de, 201
Robinson, Midshipman Hercules, 61, 67
Robinson, William, 98, 120; describes preparations for battle, 84–5; describes battle, 120–1, 174, 176–7; describes aftermath of battle, 221–2
Rochefort, France, 294–5, 297
Romans, 14, 39
Romney, Midshipman Francis D., 295–6
Romney Marsh, Kent, 10
Rosia Bay, Gibraltar, 21, 292
Rosily, Vice-Admiral François-Etienne, 59–60, 321
Roskruge, Lieutenant Francis, 136
Rota, Spain, 235
Rotheram, Captain Edward, 110, 160, 201, 248; cocked hat, 107–8
Rougham, Norfolk, 274
Royal Military Canal, 10
Royal Scots Greys, 313, 336
Royal Sovereign, 94, 100, 160, 187, 218, 248, 271, 304; joins battle, xix–xx, 101–2, 106–15, 117, 120–2, 127, 182, 184, 201; damage, 182, 184, 219, 272; taken in tow, 184, 189, 273; casualties, 184; crew complain to Admiralty, 329
'Rule Britannia', 97, 156, 284
rum, 32, 33, 166, 222, 227, 335–6
Russia, 4, 332; Napoleonic invasion, 333

St Cloud, France, 325
St Columb, Cornwall, 136
St George, Lieutenant William, 136
St Helena, 330–1
St Margaret, 295
St Vincent, Battle of, 3, 4, 80, 275
St Vincent, Lord, 12, 35, 285
Salisbury Plain, Wiltshire, 266–7
Sam (seaman), 304
San Agustín, xiv, 135, 198, 200; set on fire, 249
sand, 81, 83, 89, 157
sand-glasses, 112

Sandilands, William, 316
San Domingo, 330–1
San Francisco de Asís, xiv, 162, 200, 207, 232; wrecked, 235
San Ildefonso, 174; surrenders, 193, 249, 301; in service with British fleet, 297
San Juan Nepomuceno, 71; surrenders, 185, 187–9, 249; casualties, 187; in service with British fleet, 297–8
San Justo, 107, 111, 115, 127, 134, 207, 247
San Leandro, 107, 111, 127, 134, 207
San Lucar shoals, 235, 247
San Raphael, 20
Santa Ana, xx–xxi, 101–2, 107–8, 109–12, 114–15, 182, 184–5; casualties, 184; recovered by French, 234–6; captured, 233, 271, 276
Santa Brigada, 123
Santa Cruz, Tenerife, 26
Santísima Trinidad, 88, 98, 271; joins battle, 122, 126–7, 134–7, 147; size, 135; refuses to surrender, 137; crippled, 137, 152, 210; fired on by French, 201; surrenders, 210, 276–7; sinks, 241–3; casualties, 241–2; evacuation, 242–3; commemorated on Nelson's funeral car, 312
Saumarez, Captain Sir James, 80, 81, 340
Saunders, Lieutenant Lawrence, 116, 172
schooners, 56, 68; *see also Pickle*
Scipion, 162, 198, 296
Scott, Dr Alexander John (Nelson's chaplain), 141–3, 194, 197–8, 204–5, 251
Scott, John (Nelson's secretary), 124, 141
scurvy, 32, 33, 38–40
scuttle-butts, 78
sea chests, 74, 81, 296
seamen: conditions, 32–46, 340; discipline in aftermath of battle, 222–3; possessions, 75; provision for, 315–17, 348–50; 'turned over', 329; welfare, 329; *see also* boys; midshipmen; officers
seamen's letters, 298–307
Secker, Sergeant James, 141
semaphore, 8
Seniavin, Admiral, 284
Servaux, Pierre, xix–xxii, 226
Seven Years War, 39
Seville, Spain, 14, 58, 184
sharpshooters, 128, 140–1, 144–5, 205, 344
Sheerness, Kent, 10
Sherborne, Dorset, 285
ships: in aftermath of battle, 222; basic plan, 55; construction, 31–2; design, 31, 83–4; deterioration, 30, 32; identification of, 96–8; manoeuvrability, 70; preparations for battle, 74–6, 81–5; ratings, 56–7; tactics, 55–6; technology, 83–4, 327; *see also* ballast; beakhead; bower anchor; bulkheads; capstan bars; catheads; chains; cockpit; forecastle; gun decks; halliards; helm; hoops; jury masts; lady's hole; magazines; mast-heads; orlop deck; poop; quarterdeck; rigging; strakes; studding-sails; taffrail
ship's biscuits, 34–5, 38
shot, *see* cannon-balls
shot plugs, 174, 176
shrapnel, 89, 101
Sicily, 25; *see also* Kingdom of the Two Sicilies
sickness, illness and disease, 32, 35–6, 40, 53, 164–5, 171; *see also* gangrene; injuries; malaria; medical treatment; rickets; scurvy; tetanus; typhus; venereal disease
Sidmouth, Viscount (Henry Addington), 322
signal codes, 91–2
signal posts, 8
signals, 58, 61–2, 63–4, 65–6, 68, 91–2, 100–1, 152; distress, 238; Dumanoir's, 162; 'England expects', 92, 95–6, 126–7, 314, 342; hand, 98; Hardy's, 180; identification, 258; spurious, 29; Villeneuve's, 69, 71, 126–7, 134, 151; *see also* flags
Sirius, 61, 189
skillagree, 36
slippers, felt, 86
'smashers', 76; *see also* carronades
Smith, Henry (amputee), 164
Smith, Assistant Surgeon Neil, 143
Smith, Lieutenant John, 137
Smith, Midshipman Robert, 198
Smith, Sir William Sidney, 285
smugglers, 49, 332
smuggling, 3, 333
Solana, Marquis, 253
soldiers, 53, 90, 131, 134, 168
songs and ballads, 97, 156, 284, 345
Soto, Don Diego de, 231
South Africa, 9
South America, 187, 330, 335
Southey, Robert, 205, 285
Spain, 278–9, 291, 334–5, 337; allied with France, 3, 4, 15; sympathy with Britain, 252–3, 347
Spanish: attitude towards battle, 346–7; casualties, 290; prisoners, 290–2; relations with British, 240, 253–4; relations with French, 58, 90–1, 253
Spanish Armada, 5
Spanish Navy, 4, 52–3, 346–7; burial habits, 179; command structure, 126; gunnery, 89, 102, 160
Spanish Supreme Council of Admiralty, 184
Spartiate, 189, 198, 200, 208, 210
Sperring, Mary, 227–8
Spithead, Hampshire, 302, 308
splinters, 75–6, 89, 101, 106, 142, 173, 177, 220; Collingwood injured by, 100; Hardy hit by, 124; Magon hit by, 185
Spratt, James, 192–3, 344
squadron (terminology), 19n
storms, 22, 91, 329–30, 331; following battle, 66, 203, 217–18, 222–6, 228–51, 253–9, 262, 272–3, 278, 292, 298, 301; meteorological description, 225n
Strachan, Rear-Admiral Sir Richard, 294–5, 315,

317, 330–1
Straits of Gibraltar, 17, 23, 63, 65, 69, 270
strakes, 110n
Streatham, London, 11
studding-sails, 73n, 125
suicide, 48, 323
Sullivan, Margaret, 47
sulphur, 185, 222
Superb, 260
surgeons, 77, 81–2, 156, 164–71, 177, 190, 220–1, 233, 292; French, 202; at Greenwich Hospital, 315; instruments, 82; knowledge of disease, 40, 41–2, 82, 165–6; *see also* Beatty, Dr William; doctors; loblolly boys; medical treatment
survivors, 213–16, 220, 241; from *Bucentaure*, 234–5; from *Redoutable*, 231–2; from *Santísima Trinidad*, 243–4; Spanish rewarded, 347
Sutton, Mrs Admiral, 341
Sweden, 4
Swedes, 50
swimming, 164, 188, 193, 213
Swiftsure (British), 174, 191, 211, 228, 231, 252
Swiftsure (French), 118, 120, 189; surrenders, 190, 249; casualties, 190; in service with British fleet, 297
Swiss, 50
swivel guns, 133
Sydenham, London, 11
Sykes, Captain John, 258, 265, 267–8, 294
Syracuse, Sicily, 320

tacking, 70–1
taffrail, 189n
Tagus, River, 258, 332
Tamar, River, 217
tattoos, 100
Tavistock, Devon, 263
taxation, 1–2
Teignmouth, Devon, 193
telegraphs, 7–8, 261–2
Temeraire, 73, 97, 226, 229; guns, 56; joins battle, xxii, 133–5, 146–8, 150–1, 153–4, 181–2, 200–2, 272; name, 147
Tenerife, 82
tetanus, 170
Tetuan, Morocco, 293
Tewkesbury, Gloucestershire, 316
Thames, River, 11, 267, 309–10, 312; Estuary, 9
Thémis, 189, 207, 232
Thiers, Louis Adolphe, 346
Thompson, John, 249
Thorpe, William (seaman), 230, 235, 239–40
Tilsit, Treaty of, 332
Times, The, 21, 58, 79, 202, 269, 282, 326
Tiverton, Devon, 264–5
tobacco, 32, 33–4, 45, 46, 130
toilet paper, 44
toilets, 42–5, 165
Tokyo, Japan 344
tomahawks, 132, 186
Tomkins, Midshipman Bowham, 136
Tomlinson, Captain Nicholas, 256
Tomlinson, Captain Robert, 256
tompions, 95
Tonnant, 75; joins battle, 116, 118, 153, 162–4, 169, 185–8, 201; accepts surrender of *Algésiras*, 206, 229; casualty list, 289
Tooting, London, 11
Torbay, Devon, 329
touch-holes, 104, 129, 131, 159
Toulon, France, 16–17, 280
tourniquets, 166–7
Townshend, Jane, 81, 318
trade, 1–4, 281, 330–1, 333–6, 338, 344, 347
Trafalgar, *see* Cape Trafalgar
Trafalgar, Battle of: fleets sight each other, 61–2, 68, 71, 91; weather conditions, 66, 69, 73, 85, 91, 161–2, 203; lines of battle form, 68–73, 93–4; last battle fought by sailing ships, 84, 327; relative strengths of fleets, 89; relative manpower, 90; first shot, 101; plan of approaching fleets, 102–3; enemy line cut, 108, 121, 133–4, 138–9; plan of opening phase, 118–19; turning point, 127; plan at 1.15 p.m., 148–9; fortune favours British, 161, 198; plan at 2 p.m., 174–5; plan at 2.45 p.m., 182–3; closing stages, 206–7; plan at 4.30 p.m., 208–9; taking of prizes, 211; storm following battle, 217–18, 222–6, 228–51, 253–9, 262, 272, 278, 298; Kerjulien's raid, 232–5, 245; numbers of ships wrecked or sunk, 249; as landmark memory, 265–6; press reports, 269–80; accuracy of reports, 277, 278–9; Napoleon's reaction, 279–81; international reaction, 281; casualty figures, 290; casualties return home, 315–17; commemorative medal struck, 318; centenary celebrations, 343–4
'Trafalgar turban', 287
transportation, 47
Trelawny, Edward, 260
Trewman's Exeter Flying Post, 274
Tribuno (newspaper), 184
Truro, Cornwall, 262
trusses, 165
Turks, 213
Turner, J. M. W., 147
Tyler, Captain Charles, 289
typhus, 41
Tyrwhitt, Colonel Thomas, 340–1

Ulm, Battle of, 280
uniforms, 99, 100, 321; Nelson's, 140; *see also* clothes
Union Jack, 97, 244
United States of America, 50, 279, 331, 336
urine, 42, 44

Vallack, Captain Joseph, 112
Vasquez, Gaspar Costela, 184

venereal disease, 46
Verdreau, Lieutenant Guillaume Joseph, 163
Verdun, France, 287
Vernon, Admiral Edward, 32
vice-admirals (terminology), 15
Victoria, Queen, 318, 346
Victory, 54, 62, 73, 85, 94, 97, 106, 108, 251, 266, 271, 341, 345; joins battle, 121–8, 133–5, 138–48, 150, 152–3, 161, 180–2, 195, 201, 277; guns, 56, 76; crew, 50; cuts enemy line, 121; age, 122; steering damaged, 123–4; collides with *Redoutable*, 134, 205–6; Nelson wounded and dies on board, 141–3, 146, 193–5, 196–8, 202–6, 219, 226; ceases firing, 145, 147; French attempt to board, 146–7, 325; Nelson's body prepared for return to England, 226–8, 293; casualties, 240–1; reaches Gibraltar, 292–3; returns to England, 294, 298, 308–10; description of damage, 308–9; commemorated on Nelson's funeral car, 312; sailors at Nelson's funeral, 313–14; prize money, 317; commemorative medal issued to crew, 318
Vienna, Austria, 280
Vigo, Spain, 22
Villeneuve, Madame, 324
Villeneuve, Vice-Admiral Pierre-Charles-Jean-Baptiste-Silvestre de: appearance, 321–2; escapes blockade, 15–18; engagement with Calder's squadron, 19–22, 58; returns to Cadiz, 22–3, 29, 53; remarks on state of British fleet, 30–1; renunciation of aristocratic origins, 52; preparations, 53–4; tactics, 58–9, 65–6; success at Battle of Nile, 59; recognises inevitability of battle, 66; forms line of battle, 68–9, 71–2; order to open fire, 96; order to Dumanoir ignored, 126–8, 151; rallies crew, 134; obliged to surrender, 152; predicts Nelson's strategy, 161; comment on Nelson quoted, 196; in reports of battle, 270–1, 276, 278; prisoner, 274, 313, 321–2; attends Nelson's funeral, 313; death, 143, 322–5
Villiers, Lady, 267
vinegar, 222
Vitoria, Spain, 184
Voltaire, 338
volunteers, 7, 50, 290

Walker, Midshipman Henry, 60, 95, 225
Wandsworth, London, 11
warping, 192n
warrant officers, 43, 77
Warren, Vice-Admiral Sir John Borlase, 330–1
Wasp, 330
watches, 112
water, 22, 29, 32, 33, 42, 78, 83, 194, 292
Waterloo, Battle of, 280, 326, 334, 337–8, 348
water tiers, 151n
Watson, Thomas, 227
weapons: *see* bayonets; cannons; carbines; carronades; cutlasses; dirks; grenades; musketoons; muskets; pikes; pistols; rifles; swivel guns; tomahawks
wearing, 70–1
Weedon Bec, Northamptonshire, 12
weevils, 33, 34–5, 46
Wellington, Duke of, 279, 334, 337; describes Nelson, 339
Westemburg, Assistant Surgeon, 143
West Indies, 330–1, 334–6; seamen from, 50; Villeneuve's sortie to, 16–18, 21–2, 31, 35–6, 53, 59
Westphal, Midshipman George, 106, 198
whipping, 48
Whipple, Thomas, 106
Whitby, Captain, 269
Whitby, Yorkshire, 120
White Ensign, 97
Willaumez, Rear-Admiral, 330–1
William IV, King, 51
Williams, Lieutenant Edward, 148
Windsor Castle, Berkshire, 269; St George's Chapel, 314
wine, 32–3, 46, 85, 194, 253; spirits of, 293, 309
Wolsey, Cardinal, 314
women (on board ships), 77–81, 88, 169–70, 318, 340; involved in preparing Nelson's body, 227–8; survivors, 213–16; *see also* Jeannette
World War Two, 297
'worm', 158
Wright (murdered naval officer), 323–4

Yon, Midshipman Jacques, 146
Yule, Lieutenant John, 148